# The Active Reader
*Composing in Reading and Writing*

# The Active Reader
## Composing in Reading and Writing

**Anne Ruggles Gere**
*University of Michigan*

**Jeffrey Carroll**
*University of Hawaii*

Holt, Rinehart and Winston, Inc.
Fort Worth   Chicago   San Francisco   Philadelphia
Montreal   Toronto   London   Sydney   Tokyo

*Publisher*   Charlyce Jones Owen
*Acquisitions Editor*   Michael Rosenberg
*Design and Production*   Publications Development Co. of Texas
*Production Manager*   Kathleen Ferguson
*Design Supervisor/Cover*   Vicki McAlindon Horton
*Cover Design*   Rhonda Campbell
*Cover Photograph*   Henderson/Muir Photography, A Division of Henderson, Collins, and Muir, Inc.

**Text and photo credits appear on page 400.**

Copyright © 1990 by Holt, Rinehart and Winston, Inc.

All rights reserved. No part of this publication may be reproduced or transmitted in any form or by any means, electronic or mechanical, including photocopy, recording or any information storage and retrieval system, without permission in writing from the publisher.

Requests for permission to make copies of any part of the work should be mailed to: Copyrights and Permissions Department, Holt, Rinehart and Winston, Inc., Orlando, FL 32887.

*Address Orders to:*   6277 Sea Harbor Drive, Orlando, FL 32887
   1-800-782-4479, or 1-800-433-0001 (in Florida)

*Address Editorial Correspondence to:*   301 Commerce Street, Suite 3700, Fort Worth, TX 76102

Printed in the United States of America

Library of Congress Cataloging-in-Publication Data

Gere, Anne Ruggles. 1944–
    The active reader : composing in reading and writing / Anne
  Ruggles Gere. Jeffrey Carroll.
        p.     cm.
      ISBN 0-03-014132-X
        College readers.   2. English language—Rhetoric.     I. Carroll,
  Jeffrey, 1949–  . II. Title.
    PE1417.G46   1990                                                89-48696
    808'.0427—dc20                                                       CIP

0  1  2  3    090    9  8  7  6  5  4  3  2  1

Holt, Rinehart and Winston, Inc.
The Dryden Press
Saunders College Publishing

For Cynthia Margaret Gere
and Samuel Yong-Woon Gere,
You give me great hope for the future
                    ARG


For my mother Doris Carroll
and in memory of my father Glenn Carroll
You opened many books for me
                    JGC

# Contents

**Rhetorical Contents**     x
**Instructor's Preface**     xi
**Introduction**     1

**Chapter 1   Worlds of Experience**     7

    Cave Painting, Spain     10
    Herodotus, "The Egyptians"     13
    Kalporu Cirunuraivar, "What She Said"     21
    William Shakespeare, Sonnet #116     23
    Brule Sioux Indians, "The Vision Quest"     25
    Margaret Fuller, "Letter to Her Brother"     29
    Sergei Eisenstein, Film Stills from
        *Battleship Potemkin*     32
    Beryl Markham, *West With the Night*     35
    Bruce Springsteen, "Used Cars"     47
    Russell Baker, *Growing Up*     49

**Chapter 2   Profiling and Portraying People**     57

    John Earle, "An Antiquary"     60
    Alexander Hesler, Photograph of Abraham Lincoln     63
    Abraham Lincoln, "Address at the Dedication of the
        Gettysburg National Cemetery"     66
    Emily Collins, "Reminiscences of Emily Collins"     69
    Charles Darwin, "Struggle for Existence"     75
    Mary Cassatt, "Girl Arranging Her Hair"     82
    Meridel LeSueur, "Women on the Breadlines"     84
    Oliver Sacks, "Hands"     92

## Chapter 3 Journeys 99

Homer, "New Coasts and Poseidon's Son," Book Nine, *The Odyssey* 101
Anonymous, "The Seafarer" 105
Gerardus Mercator, Map of the World 108
Marco Polo, "The Imperial Palace of Kanbalu," *The Travels of Marco Polo* 112
Virginia Reed, Letter on the Donner Party 117
H. G. Wells, "The Country of the Blind" 124
George Orwell, "Shooting an Elephant" 146
Maxine Hong Kingston, *The Woman Warrior* 154
Tom Wolfe, "The Angels," *The Right Stuff* 164

## Chapter 4 Work and Play 179

Jost Amman, "The Carpenter" 182
Francis Bacon, "Of Studies" 184
Izaak Walton, *The Complete Angler* 188
Mary Wollstonecraft Shelley, Journal 192
Edgar Degas, "Dancers Practicing at the Bar," "The Rehearsal," "The Dancing Class" 197
Mark Twain, "The Boy's Ambition" 202
Rube Goldberg, "Professor Butts' Moth Exterminator" 207
Camara Laye, *The Dark Child* 210
Dorothea Lange, Bindle Stiff 215
John McPhee, *A Sense of Where You Are: A Profile of Bill Bradley at Princeton* 218
*Foxfire*, "Shoemaking" 223
Carol Mont Parker, "The Anatomy of a New York City Debut: A Chronicle" 230
Box Score, Baseball 235

## Chapter 5 Power and Justice 237

The Prophet Amos, *The Bible* 239
Niccolo Machiavelli, *The Prince* 246
Thomas Jefferson, Declaration of Independence 251
Francisco Jose de Goya, *The 3rd of May, 1808* 257
Sojourner Truth, "Ain't I a Woman?" 259
John Stuart Mill, "The Subjection of Women" 262

Africa Map  267
Virginia Woolf, *A Room of One's Own*  270
Eddie Adams, Vietnam Photograph  287

## Chapter 6  Humor and Irony  291

Aesop, "The Fox and the Hedgehog"  294
Jonathan Swift, "A Modest Proposal"  296
The Igbo People, "The Tortoise's Friendship
   with the Birds"  305
Fanny Fern, "Tom Pax's Conjugal Soliloquy"  308
Apollinaire, "It's Raining"  313
René Magritte, "The Key of Dreams"  315
Dorman Smith, Cartoon  318
Fred Dickenson, "How to Iron a Telephone Book"  320
Gore Vidal, "Drugs"  326
Judy Syfers, "I Want A Wife"  330
Mal Inc., Cartoon  334

## Chapter 7  Worlds of Language  337

Trajan Inscription  339
Gold Buckle, Sutton Hoo Excavation  341
Chartres Cathedral, Nave  344
Benjamin Franklin, Cartoon  347
Wolfgang Amadeus Mozart, 12 *Variationen*  349
John Ruskin, *The Stones of Venice*  352
Advertisement, Hires Rootbeer  357
Laban, Dance Notation  360
Group, The Lincoln House Plan  363
Steuben, Advertisement  365
Alfa Romeo, Wiring Diagram  368
Bob Wallace, PC Write  372
Konica, Advertisement  374
John Updike, "The Illustrative Itch"  377

## Glossary  383
## Subject Index  387
## Credits and Permissions  400

# Rhetorical Contents

**Cause and Effect**

Fuller, 29
Eisenstein, 32
Springsteen, 47
Darwin, 75
Sacks, 92
Orwell, 146
Goldberg, 207
Laye, 210
Parker, 230
Woolf, 270
Swift, 296
Aesop, 294
Igbo People, 305
Vidal, 326

**Argumentation**

Shakespeare, 23
Darwin, 75
LeSueur, 84
Earle, 60
Bacon, 184
Twain, 202
Amos, 239
Machiavelli, 246
Jefferson, 251
Truth, 259
Mill, 262
Swift, 296
Fern, 308
Apollinaire, 313
Smith, 318
Syfers, 330
MAL, 334
Franklin, 347
Hires Advertisement, 357
Stuben Advertisement, 365
Konica Advertisement, 374
Updike, 377

**Description**

Herodotus, 13
Markham, 35
Hesler, 63
Cassatt, 82
Mercatur, 108
Polo, 112
Amman, 182
Walton, 188
Foxfire, 223
Goya, 257
Africa Map, 267
Adams, 287
Magritte, 315
Trajan, 339
Gold Buckle, 341
Chartres, 344
Ruskin, 352
Alfa Romeo, 368
Group House Plan, 363
Dickenson, 320

**Narration**

Mesolithic Era, 10
Cirunuraivar, 21
Byule Sioux Indians, 25
Baker, 49
Lincoln, 66
Collins, 69
Sacks, 92
Homer, 101
Anglo-Saxons, 105
Reed, 117
Wells, 124
Orwell, 146
Kingston, 154
Wolfe, 164
Degas, 197
Lange, 215
McPhee, 218
Laban, 360

# Instructor's Preface

Designed for courses that unite reading and writing, *The Active Reader* uses the term composing to describe both writing and reading. This term has been used as a synonym for writing and has been described as including processes such as prewriting, drafting, and revising. However, composing involves more than a series of procedures. Composing describes the creation of meaning in both reading and writing. We see reading and writing as two parts of the same whole.

To compose in writing is to borrow from or respond to texts we read. Composing enables writers to represent their views on some aspect of the world, thereby bridging text and world. We might, for example, read a story, see a film based on the story, read a review of the film, talk with friends about the film, and write a new version of the original story's events and ideas. In writing the new version, we would probably borrow from the texts of the story, the film, the review, and our conversations, but the new version would represent our own views because we would not copy any of these texts directly. Rather, we would have internalized each and composed or put elements together to create our own meaning. In borrowing from various texts to create our own texts and writings, we link our compositions with other texts in the world around us.

Reading is also an act of composing because it, too, involves the making of meaning. Texts have meaning only when we read, understand, and interpret them. They require our active participation with them in order to make them *work* for us. Just as musical notation cannot make music without a musician to interpret and respond to it with voice or instrument, so texts cannot have meaning by themselves. Readers give meaning to texts by composing or making sense of them.

The composing of reading aids the composing of writing because our reading energies resemble our writing energies—we interpret, question, imagine, and analyze as we read. These energies enable us to create our own texts, the interior texts that enable us to follow the narrative of a novel or trace the images of a poem. This exercise of reading energies resembles writing in everything but one aspect—reading produces no visible text.

The word "text" has often been reserved exclusively for writing, and in schools the definition has frequently been restricted to written works assigned by experts to the "canon" or list of texts that are reputed to meet certain standards of critical judgment. We extend the meaning of "text" in three directions. First, we assume that "text" describes what readers create in their minds as they read. The growing representation of meaning that has no tangible form but which enables a reader to distinguish one reading experience from another can be described as a text. Second, our definition of texts moves well beyond the traditional literary canon. While *The Active Reader* includes texts usually described as canonical—a sonnet by Shakespeare, essays by Bacon, Swift, Woolf, and Ruskin—it also includes journal entries, song lyrics, and letters written by people whose names are less familiar. While some selections will be very familiar, other selections such as a poem by Cirunuraivar, a tale popular among the Igbo people, and an account of an Indian vision quest, will probably be entirely unfamiliar. We include this variety to develop a creative tension between the familiar and the unfamiliar. As students encounter distinctly different kinds of texts, they will begin to recognize the need to bring the full measure of their composing skill to the task of reading.

Third, we extend "text" to include graphic as well as verbal representation—a photograph of a migrant worker is as much a text as is an essay by George Orwell. Advertisements, wiring diagrams, maps, and house plans draw upon the same energies of interpreting, questioning, imagining and analyzing as do essays, poems, novels, and plays. Students who frequently bifurcate their "life" and "school" experiences take pleasure in and draw confidence from the realization that ability to compose meaning with a familiar comic strip translates into ability to compose meaning with a poem or essay. Students who become conscious of their own expertise at composing meaning from cartoons where humor turns on distinctions between fantasy and reality, bring that awareness to their reading of a satirical essay which suggests that young children become the food supply for a starving nation.

Students can bring that same consciousness to composing in writing. As they become more aware of patterns operating in the texts they compose in reading, they bring that awareness to writing. They will learn to imitate a turn of phrase or modify a borrowed image just as they borrow spoken phrases from previous conversations. They will also use a text as a point of departure, developing ideas that extend beyond its boundaries. Just as the texts of eyewitness accounts led Goya to paint "The Third of May," and newspaper accounts of drug use led Gore Vidal to write his "Drugs," so students will compose their own meanings in writing when they understand the connections between reading and writing, between their own lives and the life of the classroom.

Thematic units provide a way of drawing "school" and "life" closer together. Reading texts about journeys or power and justice allows students to draw connections between what they read and what they have lived. Even as we note the inherent potential of themes, we also acknowledge their weaknesses. Themes leak. Markham's account of flying across the Atlantic could as easily be listed under "journeys" as under "worlds of experience," and Lincoln's Gettysburg Address could be included with selections on "power and justice" rather than "profiling and portraying people." But, having acknowledged this limitation, we point to another advantage of thematic units: They enable us to address aspects of writing such as voice, audience, and revision.

*The Active Reader* is organized around several thematic patterns, and each of these themes reflects an aspect of composing in writing. The first chapter, "Worlds of Experience," includes a wide variety of texts that explore how people have experienced life-shaping events across time and space. These texts encourage attention to the parts of writing usually called *prewriting* and *drafting*, the early stages when accounts of experience flow freely.

"Profiling and Portraying People," the second chapter, incorporates texts that look closely at individuals. Some of these individuals are, like Abraham Lincoln, famous people known from history while others are anonymous or ordinary people selected for careful scrutiny. The selections in this chapter can enliven understandings of *focus* in writing, demonstrating how composers can foreground some aspects while leaving others in the background.

The third chapter focuses on journeys of various types and invites composing that considers travel across space as well as internal journeys. Selections in this chapter stretch across time offering perspectives from those who sailed uncharted seas thousands of years ago to contemporary immigrants faced with a new culture. Appropriately, this chapter focuses on the *discovery* inherent in writing.

"Work and Play," the fourth chapter, also includes texts from a variety of historical periods, but it focuses on the more narrow theme suggested by the title. The selections included in this chapter explore the various meanings we assign to the words *work* and *play,* and offer opportunities to examine relationships between the two. Simultaneously, these selections offer perspective on the alternations of work and play that comprise composing in writing. In particular, it considers the work of *revision.*

Selections in "Power and Justice," the fifth chapter, explore the dimensions of power and politics, touching on issues such as the nature of justice, independence, exploitation, and privilege. Familiar texts such as the Declaration of Independence and a Vietnam photograph are juxtaposed with prophetic literature from the Bible, a map, and a variety of other texts. Taken together, these texts offer opportunities to consider the importance of *audience* in writing.

"Humor and Irony," the sixth chapter, includes selections that demonstrate the pleasure language provides, particularly when composers allow themselves to take a playful attitude and push beyond the limits of the ordinary. Although texts come from many historical periods and geographical locations, they all share a comic perspective. This chapter brings *voice* and *register* under consideration.

The final chapter, "Worlds of Language," explores the variety of languages available for human communication. These languages, including musical scores, computer programs, architectural drawings, and advertisements, invite readers to consider ways of conveying and acting upon information. The emphasis upon precision in many of these languages leads to considerations of *diction* and *conventions* in writing.

The selections in all seven chapters are grouped in chronological order according to the time when they were originally produced. Most selections are relatively brief so that students can "see the whole piece" as they might see a poem on a page. The brevity of selections also enables students to follow the impulse of "connecting" questions and move comfortably from one selection to another. Even if they have not previously read a selection mentioned in a question, students will be able to give it a quick first reading. This process of moving between relatively familiar and unfamiliar texts fosters active reading at the same time that it prepares the way for subsequent readings.

In keeping with its emphasis upon encouraging responses to and with existing texts, *The Active Reader* avoids introductory remarks at the beginning of each selection. Readers are invited to compose their own meanings without the mediation of descriptors such as "a noted nineteenth century . . ." "one of the best . . ." and "famous for . . ." Background information appears in the questions that follow each selection. Additional information about each selection appears in the Instructor's Manual, the Glossary at the back of the book provides definitions for terms that may be unfamiliar. And the Rhetorical Index categorizes selections according to familiar modes.

Questions following each selection are designed to help students understand and think about the text, to consider the conditions under which the text was composed, and to explore the values the text may have for today. Background information about the text's composer and received critical judgments about it are kept to a minimum because the weight of history and critical traditions adds little to the composing students do with texts and may actually impede their construction of meaning. Questions take a deliberately uneven form. Some are open-ended while others direct students to specific places in the text. We have found that this kind of variety enables people of various backgrounds and abilities to engage with the texts.

Questions for rereading direct students back to the text while questions for discussing invite them to consider alternate meanings, to probe the *possibilities* of meaning. Questions for connecting suggest ways of drawing different cultures and times together in interesting or stimulating ways in order to consider how alike or universal some texts are and, conversely, how various composers in different cultures view themselves and their world. Frequently connecting questions refer to selections students may not yet have studied, thereby inviting an early preview of texts that will be read in more detail later. Questions for writing encourage students to get their responses and new ideas and observations on paper so they can produce their own views and meanings about texts. To participate in a dialogue of author and world is one way to look at human history. *The Active Reader* offers an invitation to join this dialogue through composing in reading and writing.

# *Introduction*

*A* musician reads a series of notes and plays sounds you recognize as music, and a carpenter reads a two-dimensional line drawing and builds a three-dimensional structure you call a house. Similarly, this book shows you how to approach a text as an active reader, so that you can perform it in your mind, creating it, recreating it, composing it.

Composing encompasses but is not limited to both reading and writing. Seeing is itself a form of composing. Young children compose individual features to create familiar faces and the meanings that yield food, comfort, and play. You compose as you interact with various symbols, making sense of and participating with them. The daily newspaper and the television news shows, for example, usually contain a weather map (Figure 1). Each person has various reasons for composing this map—to schedule outdoor activities, to make decisions about clothing, to compare your own weather with that in another region where you have family or friends. You also have multiple ways of composing weather maps. You may survey the whole, noting coldest and warmest places along with general weather patterns, or you may begin with your own area and work out from there. Regardless of how you proceed, you make meaning of the words, numbers, and symbols, thereby constructing statements about the weather. More than a passive absorption of information, this composing can involve further action such as deciding what to wear, determining whether or not to attend an outdoor sports event, or imagining the results of unusual weather patterns such as tornadoes or freezing temperatures in the South.

The words "weather patterns" may remind you that this text came from a group of meteorologists and lead you to think about complex networks of satellite photographs, processes of recording official temperatures, movement of air masses, wind and cloud patterns, and the tools and techniques of predicting the weather. As you compose

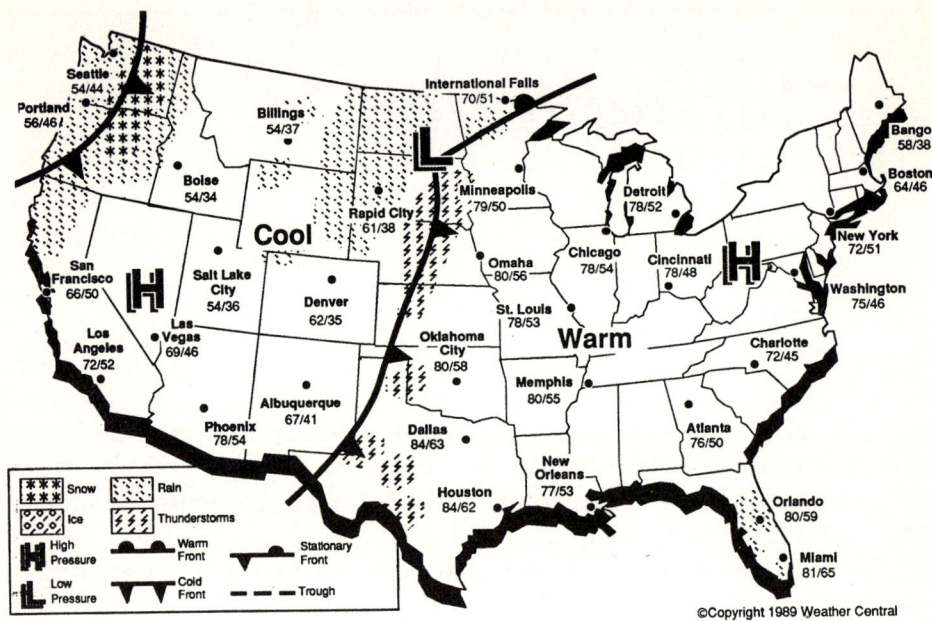

Figure 1

today's weather map, you recognize that this text will be replaced by another tomorrow, and you look at it for signs of what the next text will show—moving storm patterns, shifting high and low pressure areas, and changing temperatures.

These processes of thinking about why and how one reads the map, about where these maps originate and what effects they have are the same for any act of composing, whether the text is a weather map or a sonnet by William Shakespeare. Many of us—students and instructors alike—often think that school texts are different, that skills common to the "real world" have no relevance in school. But this book assumes that what you know about forming meaning by putting symbols together will be useful in school tasks, that composing meaning from a weather map resembles composing meaning from texts such as the Gettysburg Address or a Degas painting or an advertisement.

## You Already Know a Great Deal about Composing

You may be accustomed to drawing careful distinctions between the classroom and "the real world," and you may assume that what goes on in one bears no relation to the other. You may assume that the skills you have developed in "the real world" have no place in school. We assume the reverse, taking for granted the fact that you already know a great deal about composing. Although you may not have called it composing, you have spent many years interacting with the network of signs and symbols that constitute your environment. In composing your wardrobe, for example, you created and transformed it each time you made a purchase or discarded something. Similarly you have composed with the wardrobes of others, making meanings of their clothing. On the basis of what people wear, you have made decisions about their status and personal appeal. You have developed skills that you may overlook because they are so familiar, but these skills, like those for composing meaning with a weather map, can be used with a wide variety of texts.

You know about many kinds of texts, especially those associated with popular culture such as song lyrics and advertisements. In *The Active Reader* you will find a variety of texts including woodcuts, maps, advertisements, computer programs, photographs, inscriptions, and cartoons as well as essays, poems, and narratives. Some of these texts will be familiar, and others may be unlike any you have seen before. Your ability to compose meanings with familiar texts will enable you to move comfortably to unfamiliar ones.

## You Need to Know More about Composing

Even though you already know a great deal about composing, there is still more to learn. Your college work will require you to read and write with a variety of unfamiliar texts, and you will need to extend your abilities in composing to meet these challenges. Specifically, you will need to develop your own critical capacity to decide what is good or convincing and what is weak or silly. As you compose meaning with others' texts, you will need to interpret the language of the text, raise questions about parts that are controversial or unclear, imagine the circumstances under which the text was composed, and analyze how the various parts contribute to the whole text. As you interpret, question, imagine, and analyze in these ways you will develop the skills of critical reading. You may be more comfortable with memorizing information or finding the "right" answer than with making decisions about texts for yourself, but effective reading depends upon your ability to make critical judgments.

Developing critical capacity will also enable you to compose more effectively in writing. Your instructor can provide valuable comments and suggestions designed to improve your writing, but eventually you will need to depend upon yourself, to critique your own writing. Your ability to interpret the language of your own writing, to raise questions about unclear parts, to imagine the audience and purpose for your writing, and to analyze how the parts contribute to the whole piece will help you assess the quality of what you write.

*The Active Reader* will aid the development of your critical skills by inviting you to consider where texts come from, to consider their structures, to look at them in relation to other texts, to respond to them by composing your own texts. In other words, it invites you to be actively engaged in composing meanings.

## Reading Is Active

Our culture describes reading in many ways that make it seem passive. Phrases such as "curling up with a good book" or "reading myself to sleep" or "sitting quietly to read" suggest passivity. But effective readers are *active* readers. To be an active reader means becoming engaged with the text by examining it closely, continually making meaning with its symbols. It is the same process whether the symbols are "50° F" and "H" or "We are now engaged in a great Civil War, testing whether that nation or any nation so conceived and so dedicated can long endure." In each case, the reader recognizes the text as a record of a transaction between a composer and the language (of letters, numbers, or graphic forms) and strives to understand the situation in which it was created as well as its purposes and effects. Active readers frequently talk back to their texts, asking questions, writing notes, and drawing analogies to other texts. In many cases, this talking back takes written form, so that composing occurs in writing. Marginal comments, proposals submitted in response to requests from funding agencies, and letters to the editor of a newspaper illustrate a few of the ways active readers talk back to texts.

Active reading extends beyond talking back to texts, however. As a result of the processes of interpreting, questioning, imagining, and analyzing the texts of others, active readers develop their own texts. These texts may draw upon or make allusion to other texts, but they stand on their own. In writing his essay about legalizing drugs, for example, Gore Vidal drew on a number of newspaper and magazine texts about the drug problem in our society, but we don't need to read all of these other texts to find meaning in the selection titled "Drugs." Similarly, your own written texts draw upon the composing you do as you read.

In *The Active Reader*, each selection is preceded by title, author, and date only. Descriptive introductions have been omitted so that your first reading of each text will be unencumbered by what you "ought" to think. Background information about each selection follows the selection. In addition, you may wish to turn to the Glossary at the back of the book to learn about unfamiliar words. The statements and questions following each selection are organized under four categories:

- Rereading
- Discussing
- Connecting
- Writing

Questions about rereading help you understand the text more fully by emphasizing features you may have overlooked during a first reading, and by suggesting different ways of making meaning with it. Questions for discussing invite you to talk about texts, raise questions, and explore answers. These questions assume that texts can lead readers to more than one meaning and discussing alternatives with other readers can enlarge your understanding. Questions for connecting enable you to look at one text in terms of another, to consider similarities and differences. Questions for writing encourage you to compose your own written texts.

Composing in writing takes many forms—reviews, essays, poems, summaries, imitations, and comparisons. The review that criticizes or praises a book or a play or a film results from active reading of the text under consideration, and at the same it contributes to the ongoing conversation about the issues raised. Goya, for example, did not witness the scene portrayed in "The 3rd of May," but he composed it after reading eyewitness accounts of the massacre. In composing "The 3rd of May," he contributed to a continuing conversation about the nature of power and justice. *The Active Reader* invites you to compose your own written texts that contribute to ongoing conversations about a variety of issues.

# One

# *Worlds of Experience*

*L*anguage helps us make sense of ourselves, the world, and ourselves in the world. It also allows us to express that sense to others. Our need to understand our lives, to speculate about what has happened, what is happening, what will happen—all of these needs find expression through language.

But *language* is not just spoken or written words. Language can be thought of as action or actions that stand for something more, something important. Thus, the cave painting that begins this chapter is language, as is the essay by Russell Baker that concludes it. Dancing is language, and making music is language, too. There are numerous languages in this world, and conversely, there are many worlds expressed through language.

As readers and writers, we turn to language to express ourselves. We may have had an interesting day, or an interesting idea—the scope or the size of the moment (or event) is not important. What matters to us is telling about it. "Telling" can be making a phone call, talking over breakfast or lunch, writing a note to ourselves, or sitting down and starting an essay or poem or story that might capture that moment or event's features—or even meanings. The cave-painting, we can imagine, was done after many days of hunting; the necessity of such a task made it central to ancient peoples. On the other hand, for Beryl Markham, "experience" was not only on a physical level, but included ideas and thought. She was expressing a faith in technology and the meaning of teamwork.

We share experience in both reading and writing. As we read, we reach into other places and times, assume different identities, different points of view—and we share experiences normally out of reach. As we write, we reach into our own place and time, and express what no one else has experienced in just that way, and thus we share experiences with others as we are read by others. One way to look at the composing process is to see our lives as *pre-writing*—the raw material for what we write, even as they apply to writing school papers about our beliefs and opinions. Shakespeare might tell us that his sonnet defines love as unchanging, and we can see from the poem's last line that Shakespeare has "liv'd" this experience first, and written about it second. We can experience the event, and re-experience it through the first listing or drafting or telling or brainstorming that we do through language. This early work in composing or *pre-writing* serves to get us started in ways other than having to write a paper. Pre-writing is generating ideas, details, maps, word-clusters—so that the pieces of the composing puzzle can be laid out in front of us. Putting the pieces in order—or into a good shape—is like finding the picture in the puzzle.

Language—whether written, visual, or graphic—is a way to preserve the precious and the memorable, the tragic and the comic. The Tamil poet Cirunuraivar looks at love a little differently from Shakespeare; the ancient world of southeastern India is worlds away from Shakespeare, and from us, yet similarities in these poets' experiences and ideas can also be discovered. As different as cultures are, and as long as centuries are, language unites us through its power to express the human condition—even one as quiet or common as the one Bruce Springsteen captures in "Used Cars."

"Moments alive in language"—we can define writing about experience this way. And we can look at the film stills of Eisenstein, and the cave painting of thousands of years earlier, and see that the film director and the painter saw and knew the experience of conflict, of death and life. Both knew, too, that language could express the meanings they saw in these experiences.

Our lives are not so exciting, perhaps, as the hunters, or the Sioux Indian youth on his vision quest. But as we begin to think about writing, as we scribble and cross out, as we gaze out the window or read a difficult book, the process of writing is the same one that Shakespeare experienced. What begins as a single stroke of a crude paintbrush, or a quill pen, eventually can be built on and modified into something complete and powerful, speaking to all places, all times, and all peoples.

This chapter offers the broadest spectrum of experience (and expressed experience) so that we as readers and writers can sample from a history of humanity's efforts to make sense of the world. The anonymous artist of the cave painting still has something to tell us, as much as a story written just 10 years ago. Experience has the capability to be "forever"—and not just a passing event. Certainly for the painter, the writer, the filmmaker, the songwriter, expressing experience through language helped that person understand the self and the world. Our goals as writers are the same: to see, feel, think, act—and think again, through the many ways we can use language to understand.

# Cave Painting, Spain
**(Mesolithic Era)**

Cave Painting, Spain 11

## Questions for Rereading, Discussing, Connecting, and Writing

REREADING

1. Reading this cave painting, for the modern reader, is a matter of "figuring out" its various elements and meanings. Imagine what the man or woman or child of the Mesolithic Era would see when he or she "read" this painting.

2. What forms of communication that we enjoy today could this ancient painting resemble? Do we read these modern forms of communication for pleasure or learning—or both?

DISCUSSING

3. Speculate on the reasons for ancient man and woman painting stories and figures upon the walls of caves.

4. Discuss the importance of hunting to prehistoric mankind. The scene depicted in the painting could be the record of a year's most important moment. Why?

CONNECTING

5. The concept of the "survival of the fittest" and the "struggle for existence" seems especially applicable to ancient man. Look at this selection along with the Darwin (p. 75), "The Seafarer" (p. 105), and Virginia Reed's Donner Party Letter (p. 117)—and try to define what "the fittest" meant to the artists and authors and cultures that gave rise to these works of art.

6. Hunting was an almost daily experience to ancient people, the gathering of food was another. Connect this daily activity to the one modern or contemporary activity that you think best defines our daily "struggle" for existence. Can you find this activity represented in the selections? If not, locate a treatment of it in another source—book, newspaper, photo, or other source.

WRITING

7. Write the story that precedes the event shown in the painting. Show what led up to the hunting of the deer. Give your hunters names, and write of a time and place suitable to the climax shown in the painting.

**8.** The buck at the upper right of the painting seems uninjured, and the hunter opposite it seems to have loosed all his arrows. Between these two adversaries, what happens next?

**9.** Write this moment of the hunt from any one of these three points of view: the hunters', the deer's, or a spectator's, who watches from a close vantage point.

## Herodotus

# The Egyptians (5th Century B.C.)

Concerning Egypt itself I shall extend my remarks to a great length, because there is no country that possesses so many wonders, nor any that has such a number of works which defy description. Not only is the climate different from that of the rest of the world, and the rivers unlike any other rivers, but the people also, in most of their manners and customs, exactly reverse the common practice of mankind. The women attend the markets and trade, while the men sit at home at the loom; and here, while the rest of the world works the woof up the warp, the Egyptians work it down; the women likewise carry burthens upon their shoulders, while the men carry them upon their heads. They eat their food out of doors in the streets, but retire for private purposes to their houses, giving as a reason that what is unseemly, but necessary, ought to be done in secret, but what has nothing unseemly about it, should be done openly. A woman cannot serve the priestly office, either for god or goddess, but men are priests to both; sons need not support their parents unless they choose, but daughters must, whether they choose or no.

In other countries the priests have long hair, in Egypt their heads are shaven; elsewhere it is customary, in mourning, for near relations to cut their hair close; the Egyptians, who wear no hair at any other time, when they lose a relative, let their beards and the hair of their heads grow long. All other men pass their lives separate from animals, the Egyptians have animals always living with them; others make barley and wheat their food; it is a disgrace to do so in Egypt, where the grain they live on is spelt, which some call *zea*. Dough they knead with their feet; but they mix mud, and even take up dirt, with their hands. They are the only people in the world—they at least, and such as have learnt the practice from them—who use circumcision. Their men wear two garments apiece, their women but one. They put on the rings and fasten the ropes to sails inside; others put them outside. When they write or calculate, instead of going, like the Greeks, from left to right, they move their hand from right to left; and they insist, notwithstanding, that it is they who go to the right, and the Greeks who go to the left. They have two quite different kinds of writing, one of which is called sacred, the other common.

They are religious to excess, far beyond any other race of men, and use the following ceremonies:—They drink out of brazen cups, which they scour every day: there is no exception to this practice. They wear linen garments, which they are specially careful to have always fresh washed. They practice circumcision for the sake of cleanliness, considering it better to be cleanly than comely. The priests shave their whole body every other day, that no lice or other impure thing may adhere to them when they are engaged in the service of the gods. Their dress is entirely of linen, and their shoes of the papyrus plant: it is not lawful for them to wear either dress or shoes of any other material. They bathe twice every day in cold water, and twice each night; besides which they observe, so to speak, thousands of ceremonies. They enjoy, however, not a few advantages. They consume none of their own property, and are at no expense for anything; but every day bread is baked for them of the sacred grain, and a plentiful supply of beef and of goose's flesh is assigned to each, and also a portion of wine made from the grape. Fish they are not allowed to eat; and beans,—which none of the Egyptians ever sow, or eat, if they come up of their own accord, either raw or boiled—the priests will not even endure to look on, since they consider it an unclean kind of pulse. Instead of a single priest, each god has the attendance of a college, at the head of which is a chief priest; when one of these dies, his son is appointed in his room.

Male kine are reckoned to belong to Epaphus, and are therefore tested in the following manner:—One of the priests appointed for the purpose searches to see if there is a single black hair on the whole body, since in that case the beast is unclean. He examines him all over, standing on his legs, and again laid upon his back; after which he takes the tongue out of his mouth, to see if it be clean in respect of the prescribed marks (what they are I will mention elsewhere); he also inspects the hairs of the tail, to observe if they grow naturally. If the animal is pronounced clean in all these various points, the priest marks him by twisting a piece of papyrus round his horns, and attaching thereto some sealing-clay, which he then stamps with his own signet-ring. After this the beast is led away; and it is forbidden, under the penalty of death, to sacrifice an animal which has not been marked in this way.

The following is their manner of sacrifice:—They lead the victim, marked with their signet, to the altar where they are about to offer it, and setting the wood alight, pour a libation of wine upon the altar in front of the victim, and at the same time invoke the god. Then they slay the animal, and cutting off his head, proceed to flay the body. Next they take the head, and heaping imprecations on it, if there is a marketplace and a body of Greek traders in the city, they carry it there and sell it instantly; if, however, there are no Greeks among them, they throw the head into the river. The imprecation is to this effect:—They pray that if any evil is impending either over those who sacrifice, or over universal Egypt, it may be made to fall upon that head. These practices, the imprecations upon the heads, and the libations of wine, prevail all over Egypt, and extend to victims of all sorts; and hence the Egyptians will never eat the head of any animal. (II, 35-39)

With respect to the Egyptians themselves, it is to be remarked that those who live in the grain country, devoting themselves, as they do, far more than any other people in the world, to the preservation of the memory of past actions, are the best skilled in history of any men that I have ever met. The following is the mode of life habitual to them:— For three successive days in each month they purge the body by means of emetics and clysters, which is done out of a regard for their health, since they have a persuasion that every disease to which men are liable is occasioned by the substances whereon they feed. Apart from any such precautions, they are, I believe, next to the Libyans, the healthiest people in the world—an effect of their climate, in my opinion, which has no sudden changes. Diseases almost always attack men when they are exposed to a change, and never more than during changes of the weather. They live on bread made of spelt, which they form into loaves called in their own tongue *cyllestis*. Their drink is a wine which they obtain from barley, as they have no vines in their country. Many kinds of fish they eat raw, either salted or dried in the sun. Quails also, and ducks and small birds, they eat uncooked, merely first salting them. All other birds and fishes, excepting those which are set apart as sacred, are eaten either roasted or boiled.

In social meetings among the rich, when the banquet is ended, a servant carries round to the several guests a coffin, in which there is a wooden image of a corpse, carved and painted to resemble nature as nearly as possible, about a cubit or two cubits in length. As he shows it to each guest in turn, the servant says, "Gaze here, and drink and be merry; for when you die, such will you be." (II, 77-78)

There is another custom in which the Egyptians resemble a particular Greek people, namely the Lacedaemonians. Their young men, when they meet their elders in the streets, give way to them and step aside; and if an elder come in where young are present, these latter rise from their seats. In a third point they differ entirely from all the nations of Greece. Instead of speaking to each other when they meet in the streets, they make an obeisance, sinking the hand to the knee.

They wear a linen tunic fringed about the legs, and called *calasiris;* over this they have a white woolen garment thrown on afterward. Nothing of woolen, however, is taken to their temples or buried with them, as their religion forbids it. Here their practice resembles the rites called Orphic and Bacchic, but which are in reality Egyptian and Pythagorean; for no one initiated in these mysteries can be buried in a woolen shroud, a religious reason being assigned for the observance.

The Egyptians likewise discovered to which of the gods each month and day is sacred; and found out from the day of a man's birth, what he will meet with in the course of his life, and how he will end his days, and what sort of man he will be—discoveries whereof the Greeks engaged in poetry have made a use. The Egyptians have also discovered more prognostics than all the rest of mankind besides. Whenever a prodigy takes place, they watch and record the result; then, if anything similar ever happens again, they expect the same consequences.

With respect to divination, they hold that it is a gift which no mortal possesses, but only certain of the gods: thus they have an oracle of Heracles, one of Apollo, of Athena, of Artemis, of Ares, and of Zeus. Besides these, there is the oracle of Latona at Buto, which is held in much higher repute than any of the rest. The mode of delivering the oracles is not uniform, but varies at the different shrines.

Medicine is practiced among them on a plan of separation; each physician treats a single disorder, and no more: thus the country swarms with medical practitioners, some undertaking to cure diseases of the eye, others of the head, others again of the teeth, others of the intestines, and some those which are not local.

The following is the way in which they conduct their mournings and their funerals:—On the death in any house of a man of consequence, forthwith the women of the family beplaster their heads, and sometimes even their faces, with mud; and then, leaving the body indoors, sally forth and wander through the city, with their dress fastened by a band, and their bosoms bare, beating themselves as they walk. All the female relations join them and do the same. The men too, similarly begirt, beat their breasts separately. When these ceremonies are over, the body is carried away to be embalmed.

There are a set of men in Egypt who practice the art of embalming, and make it their proper business. These persons, when a body is brought to them, show the bearers various models of corpses, made in wood, and painted so as to resemble nature. The most perfect is said to be after the manner of him whom I do not think it religious to name in connection with such a matter; the second sort is inferior to the first, and less costly; the third is the cheapest of all. All this the embalmers explain, and then ask in which way it is wished that the corpse should be prepared. The bearers tell them, and having concluded their bargain, take their departure, while the embalmers, left to themselves, proceed to their task. The mode of embalming, according to the most perfect process, is the following:—They take first a crooked piece of iron, and with it draw out the brain through the nostrils, thus getting rid of a portion, while the skull is cleared of the rest by rinsing with drugs; next they make a cut along the flank with a sharp Ethiopian stone, and take out the whole contents of the abdomen, which they then cleanse, washing it thoroughly with palm wine, and again frequently with an infusion of pounded aromatics. After this they fill the cavity with the purest bruised myrrh, with cassia, and every sort of spicery except frankincense, and sew up the opening. Then the body is placed in natrum for seventy days, and covered entirely over. After the expiration of that space of time, which must not be exceeded, the body is washed, and wrapped round, from head to foot, with bandages of fine linen cloth, smeared over with gum, which is used generally by the Egyptians in the place of glue, and in this state it is given back to the relations, who enclose it in a wooden case which they have had made for the purpose, shaped into the figure of a man. Then fastening the case, they place it in a sepulchral chamber, upright against the wall. Such is the most costly way of embalming the dead. (II, 80–86)

Till the death of Rhampsinitus, the priests said, Egypt was excellently governed, and flourished greatly; but after him Cheops succeeded to the throne, and plunged into all manner of wickedness. He closed the temples, and forbade the Egyptians to offer sacrifice, compelling them instead to labor, one and all, in his service. Some were required to drag blocks of stone down to the Nile from the quarries in the Arabian range of hills; others received the blocks after they had been conveyed in boats across the river, and drew them to the range of hills called the Libyan. A hundred thousand men labored constantly, and were relieved every three months by a fresh lot. It took ten years' oppression of the people to make the causeway for the conveyance of the stones, a work not much inferior, in my judgment, to the pyramid itself. This causeway is five furlongs in length, ten fathoms wide, and in height, at the highest part, eight fathoms. It is built of polished stone, and is covered with carvings of animals. To make it took ten years, as I said—or rather to make the causeway, the works on the mound where the pyramid stands, and the underground chambers, which Cheops intended as vaults for his own use: these last were built on a sort of island, surrounded by water introduced from the Nile by a canal. The pyramid itself was twenty years in building. It is a square, eight hundred feet each way, and the height the same, built entirely of polished stone, fitted together with the utmost care. The stones of which it is composed are none of them less than thirty feet in length.

The pyramid was built in steps, battlement-wise, as it is called, or, according to others, altar-wise. After laying the stones for the base, they raised the remaining stones to their places by means of machines formed of short wooden planks. The first machine raised them from the ground to the top of the first step. On this there was another machine, which received the stone upon its arrival, and conveyed it to the second step, whence a third machine advanced it still higher. Either they had as many machines as there were steps in the pyramid, or possibly they had but a single machine, which, being easily moved, was transferred from tier to tier as the stone rose—both accounts are given, and therefore I mention both. The upper portion of the pyramid was finished first, then the middle, and finally the part which was lowest and nearest the ground. There is an inscription in Egyptian characters on the pyramid which records the quantity of radishes, onions, and garlic consumed by the laborers who constructed it; and I perfectly well remember that the interpreter who read the writing to me said that the money expended in this way was 1600 talents of silver. If this then is a true record, what a vast sum must have been spent on the iron tools used in the work, and on the feeding and clothing of the laborers, considering the length of time the work lasted, which has already been stated, and the additional time—no small space, I imagine—which must have been occupied by the quarrying of the stones, their conveyance, and the formation of the underground apartments. (II, 124–125)

## Questions for Rereading, Discussing, Connecting, and Writing

### Rereading

1. One of the common patterns of organization readers encounter in texts is that of "comparison and contrast"; Herodotus, in enumerating the wonders of Egypt, uses this pattern. Point to examples of this pattern in the first paragraph.

2. In addition to comparison and contrast, Herodotus uses "process analysis" to show the reader exactly how something happens, or how something is done. Process analysis is especially effective when the reader is unfamiliar with the event being described. Point to two or three of these processes being analyzed by Herodotus.

3. "History" has probably always been a subject of reading—both required and personal reading. There are categories of history—for example, social, political, military, and cultural. What types of history can you discover in this excerpt from *The Persian Wars?* Which do you think is most vivid or interesting? Why?

Discussing

4. Discuss what history is. Sometimes it is easier to define something by saying what it isn't; for instance, what kinds of writing are not history—and why not? Try to arrive at an agreed-upon definition of history.

5. What custom or activity among the Egyptians do you find most strange or interesting? Discuss how Herodotus has captured your interest by the way he has written about this custom or activity.

6. What custom or activity of your time, or your community, do you imagine would most interest the ancient Egyptians—either for its strangeness or attractiveness? Look again at the selection by Herodotus for customs that Egyptians did not know—but that we do and enjoy.

Connecting

7. Compare Herodotus to Marco Polo (p. 112). Which account of an exotic society is more reliable—seems more factual or trustworthy? What are your reasons for choosing one over the other?

8. Herodotus' account of embalming and pyramid-building could be called "directions for doing." What other activities in this book are rendered as exactly as Herodotus describes these activities? Look, for example, at the Foxfire selection (p. 223) on shoemaking, or the Laban dance notation (p. 360). What kind of writing makes for good "directions for doing"?

9. Many of the selections in this book could be shifted to other chapters. Herodotus on the Egyptians is a good example; look at this book's chapter headings, and then find sections in Herodotus that would justify moving the selection to other chapters. This "moveability" suggests that the writing of history can have many areas of concern; list some of these areas and find them in Herodotus.

## Writing

**10.** Herodotus does not describe in detail any individual. Take one of those processes analyzed in the selection and write about it from the viewpoint of the individual. In other words, write about the process as one involved in it.

**11.** One of the most interesting passages in the selection concerns the building of Cheops' pyramid. Choose an engineering feat of your time—perhaps one you witnessed or were particularly impressed by—and write a brief history of it, much as Herodotus did with the pyramids.

**12.** Take a social custom of today and write about it in the role of historian—describe it carefully, and then suggest its importance or meaning to those who observe the custom.

## Kalporu Cirunuraivar

# *What She Said* (1st-3rd Century)

People say, "You will have to bear it."
 Don't they know what passion is like,
 or is it that they are so strong?

As for me, if I do not see my lover
 grief drowns my heart,

 and like a streak of foam in high waters
 dashed on the rocks

 little by little I ebb
 and become nothing.

*Questions for Rereading,
Discussing, Connecting, and Writing*

### REREADING

1. Lyric poetry such as this ancient example from India can often contain metaphors linking mankind and nature. What link can you find in this poem?

2. Whose voice are you hearing as you read this poem aloud to yourself? Look at the title of the poem as well as the characters involved in the poem who are referred to as "people" and "my lover."

3. As you look at the poem printed on the page, you may notice that it narrows down and becomes quite spare at the end. How does this visual appearance on the page reinforce the meaning or meanings of the poem?

4. When questions appear in a poem or prose piece, we tend to try to answer. How did you answer the questions posed in the third line of "What She Said"? Did that answer put you on the side of the "people" or the "she" of the title?

### DISCUSSING

5. This poem was written in Tamil, an ancient language of South Asia spoken by over 30 million people, but there is no trace of age or antiquity in the

translation. Discuss what the translator of a poem has to consider in making the change from an ancient foreign language to the language of the English-speaking population. In other words, how can a translator be true to a poem—and still make it readable in another language?

6. Tamil poets of early centuries used five landscapes to express states of body and mind: mountains for lovers' joy, forest or pasture for lovers' domesticity, countryside for a lover's unfaithfulness, seashore for lovers' anxiety or separation, and the wasteland for hardship in romantic or parental love. Discuss how Cirunuraivar employs one of these in "What She Said."

7. Emotional response to poetry is unpredictable—but we usually assume that the poet intends us to "feel" a certain way about his lyrics. How do you think Cirunuraivar intends us to feel about "What She Said," and how does he achieve this emotional effect?

## CONNECTING

8. Cirunuraivar's poem and Shakespeare's sonnet (p. 23) share some themes; but "What She Said" sounds more contemporary, although it is really much older. Consider how Shakespeare could be written in contemporary English, and try making it short and to the point. Is this also an act of translation?

9. Find other expressions of love in this book—not just romantic love, but other kinds as well. List some of the features of this emotion.

## WRITING

10. The poem seems to be an exposition on not only what true love is, but how love cannot be easily understood by those not experiencing it. Write an essay on this theme pointing to specific evidence in the poem to support this view.

11. Using the five landscapes noted in 6, choose one or more and try to write similar poems in the voice of "What She Said" to express other lyrics of lovers.

12. Imagine "the lover" of the poem replying to this poem using another kind of writing—an essay or journal entry, or a personal letter. Write this reply, taking into account the anxiety of the speaker and the advice of the "people."

# William Shakespeare

## Sonnet # 116 (1609)

Let me not to the marriage of true minds
Admit impediments. Love is not love
Which alters when it alteration finds,
Or bends with the remover to remove:
O, no! it is an ever-fixed mark
That looks on tempests and is never shaken;
It is the star to every wandering bark,
Whose worth's unknown, although his height be taken.
Love's not Time's fool, though rosy lips and cheeks
Within his bending sickle's compass come:
Love alters not with his brief hours and weeks,
But bears it out even to the edge of doom.
   If this be error and upon me proved,
   I never writ, nor no man ever loved.

## Questions for Rereading, Discussing, Connecting, and Writing

REREADING

1. The true subject of the first line of Shakespeare's sonnet is the reader. When the poet writes "Let me not," he could be saying, "Don't you let me . . . ." What effect can this direct address have upon you as you consider the poem? Does it make you less or more involved in understanding it? By comparison, imagine the poem if it had been written as a private entry in a journal.

2. Scholars tell us that Shakespeare's sonnets were written to a specific person. If you accept this proposition, place yourself in this person's place and consider what the poet wishes to accomplish. After reading this poem, what is your first response?

3. There are a few difficult words in this poem, even, perhaps, to the reader of the sixteenth century: impediments, tempests, bark, sickle—none are words used daily in our writing or conversation. How can you determine the meanings of these words?

## Discussing

**4.** Many of us consider poetry to be the "hardest" literature to read. Discuss why this is true—or may not be true.

**5.** Many critics and scholars—and millions of readers through the centuries—consider Shakespeare to be the greatest writer who ever lived. Discuss what the term "greatest" means when we speak about writers; and discuss whether it is possible for us to choose any writer to be the greatest writer.

## Connecting

**6.** Writing about love must be one of the most popular themes in our uses of language. What other ways of writing about love are there? Consider, for example, the valentine, sky writing, notes, and messages in the newspaper.

**7.** The Indian poet Kalporu Cirunuraivar (p. 21) writes about love in a different way, yet in the form we call poetry. Imagine this poet and Shakespeare sitting down together to talk about writing and emotions. How would they agree on certain matters, and how would they disagree on others?

## Writing

**8.** A piece of writing without a title is rare. This sonnet has only a number. Devise a title for this poem, and write an essay giving your reasons why your title fairly represents or introduces the poem.

**9.** What is the central image in the poem? Write an essay defining this central image in terms of details and words that Shakespeare gives us to "fill out" this central image.

**10.** The sense of this poem seems to be that "true love endures." By contrast, what kind of love does not endure, but "bends" or "alters"? Write a prose piece or poem concerning this other kind of love that bends or alters.

## Brule Sioux Indians

# *The Vision Quest* (19th Century)

*A* young man wanted to go on a *hanbleceya,* or vision seeking, to try for a dream that would give him the power to be a great medicine man. Having a high opinion of himself, he felt sure that he had been created to become great among his people and that the only thing lacking was a vision.

The young man was daring and brave, eager to go up to the mountaintop. He had been brought up by good, honest people who were wise in the ancient ways and who prayed for him. All through the winter they were busy getting him ready, feeding him *wasna*, corn, and plenty of good meat to make him strong. At every meal they set aside something for the spirits so that they would help him to get a great vision. His relatives thought he had the power even before he went up, but that was putting the cart before the horse, or rather the travois before the horse, as this is an Indian legend.

When at last he started on his quest, it was a beautiful morning in late spring. The grass was up, the leaves were out, nature was at its best. Two medicine men accompanied him. They put up a sweat lodge to purify him in the hot, white breath of the sacred steam. They sanctified him with the incense of sweet grass, rubbing his body with sage, fanning it with an eagle's wing. They went to the hilltop with him to prepare the vision pit and make an offering of tobacco bundles. Then they told the young man to cry, to humble himself, to ask for holiness, to cry for power, for a sign from the Great Spirit, for a gift which would make him into a medicine man. After they had done all they could, they left him there.

He spent the first night in the hole the medicine men had dug for him, trembling and crying out loudly. Fear kept him awake, yet he was cocky, ready to wrestle with the spirits for the vision, the power he wanted. But no dreams came to ease his mind. Toward morning before the sun came up, he heard a voice in the swirling white mists of dawn. Speaking from no particular direction, as if it came from different places, it said: "See here, young man, there are other spots you could have picked; there are other hills around here. Why don't you go there to cry for a dream? You disturbed us all night, all us creatures, animals and birds; you even kept the trees awake. We couldn't sleep. Why should you cry here? You're a brash young man, not yet ready or worthy to receive a vision."

But the young man clenched his teeth, determined to stick it out, resolved to force that vision to come. He spent another day in the pit, begging for enlightenment which would not come, and then another night of fear and cold and hunger.

The young man cried out in terror. He was paralyzed with fear, unable to move. The boulder dwarfed everything in view; it towered over the vision pit. But just as it was an arm's length away and about to crush him, it stopped. Then, as the young man stared openmouthed, his hair standing up, his eyes starting out of his head, the boulder ROLLED UP THE MOUNTAIN, all the way to the top. He could hardly believe what he saw. He was still cowering motionless when he heard the roar and ramble again and saw that immense boulder coming down at him once more. This time he managed to jump out of his vision pit at the last moment. The boulder crushed it, obliterated it, grinding the young man's peace pipe and gourd rattle into dust.

Again the boulder rolled up the mountain, and again it came down. "I'm leaving, I'm leaving!" hollered the young man. Regaining his power of motion, he scrambled down the hill as fast as he could. This time the boulder actually leapfrogged over him, bouncing down the slope, crushing and pulverizing everything in its way. He ran unseeingly, stumbling, falling, getting up again. He did not even notice the boulder rolling up once more and coming down for the fourth time. On this last and most fearful descent, it flew through the air in a giant leap, landing right in front of him and embedding itself so deeply in the earth that only its top was visible. The ground shook itself like a wet dog coming out of a stream and flung the young man this way and that.

Gaunt, bruised, and shaken, he stumbled back to his village. To the medicine men he said: "I have received no vision and gained no knowledge." He returned to the pit, and when dawn arrived once more, he heard the voice again: "Stop disturbing us; go away!" The same thing happened on the third morning. By this time he was faint with hunger, thirst, and anxiety. Even the air seemed to oppress him, to fight him. He was panting. His stomach felt shriveled up, shrunk tight against his backbone. But he was determined to endure one more night, the fourth and last. Surely the vision would come. But again he cried for it out of the dark and loneliness until he was hoarse, and still he had no dream.

Just before daybreak he heard the same voice again, very angry: "Why are you still here?" He knew then that he had suffered in vain; now he would have to go back to his people and confess that he had gained no knowledge and no power. The only thing he could tell them was that he got bawled out every morning. Sad and cross, he replied "I can't help myself; this is my last day, and I'm crying my eyes out. I know you told me to go home, but who are you to give me orders? I don't know you. I'm going to stay until my uncles come to fetch me, whether you like it or not."

All at once there was a rumble from a larger mountain that stood behind the hill. It became a mighty roar, and the whole hill trembled. The wind started to blow. The young man looked up and saw a boulder poised on the mountain's summit. He saw lightning hit it, saw it sway. Slowly the boulder moved. Slowly at first, then faster and faster, it came tumbling down the mountainside, churning up the earth, snapping huge trees as if they were little twigs. And the boulder WAS COMING RIGHT DOWN ON HIM! "I have made the spirits angry. It was all for nothing."

"Well, you did find out one thing," said the older of the two, who was his uncle. "You went after your vision like a hunter after buffalo, or a warrior after scalps. You were fighting the spirits. You thought they owed you a vision. Suffering alone brings no vision nor does courage, nor does sheer will power. A vision comes as a gift born of humility, of wisdom, and of patience. If from your vision quest you have learned nothing but this, then you have already learned much. Think about it."

—*Told by Lame Deer at Winner, Rosebud Indian Reservation, South Dakota, 1967, and recorded by Richard Erdoes.*

## Questions for Rereading, Discussing, Connecting, and Writing

### REREADING

1. A tale or myth will very often have certain qualities that make it quickly recognizable as "larger than life." As you read this tale, note language and incidents that place it apart from the usual story and make its proportions more mythic.

2. As you read, notice how general certain features are—names of persons, places, people, things. What effect does this level of generality have on your seeing the tale as more or less universal?

3. Several readers have remarked that this tale leaves out something important—the ending! Speculate on the reason or reasons why the teller of the tale left it out.

## DISCUSSING

4. What is a legend, and what sets it apart from story? The terms "myth" and "tale" are related to legend, and can be a part of any discussion of this special category of narratives we call *legends*.

5. Discuss what features of "The Vision Quest" make it an American Indian tale rather than, for example, a Norse legend. Or does "The Vision Quest" seem sufficiently universal for almost any culture's store of legend?

6. The meaning of the events in the tale are spelled out at the end. Is this a good strategy for "The Vision Quest"? Or should we not reveal what a tale means in such straightforward language? When should meanings be left to the reader?

## CONNECTING

7. Learning and enjoying often go hand-in-hand as we read and write about ourselves and our world. Legends can combine "lessons" and "fun" with great ease. What other selections in this book do this well? Don't disregard the visual work such as Degas (p. 197), Apollinaire (p. 313), the advertisements, and the cartoons—or the serious enjoyment of works such as Chartres Cathedral (p. 344) or the Bible (p. 239).

8. Young people learn about the limits and the possibilities of life in several selections in this chapter. The youth of "The Vision Quest" finds both of these qualities through his experience. Find other such experiences of limits *and* possibilities in the cave painting (p. 10) and the Springsteen (p. 47) selections.

## WRITING

9. Write an essay describing the main challenge presented to the young man in "The Vision Quest"—point to specific passages in the myth.

10. It has been said that only the man who admits he is a fool is truly wise. Write about the last time you did something foolish, and what you learned from this event and feeling.

11. The history of the American Indian is rich with storytelling and myth-making. Find another Indian tale and tell it in your own words, just as "The Vision Quest" has been retold countless times.

Margaret Fuller

# Letter to her Brother (1843)

*Milwaukie, July 20, 1843.*

**D**ear R.: * * * Daily I thought of you during my visit to the Rock-river territory. It is only five years since the poor Indians have been dispossessed of this region of sumptuous loveliness, such as can hardly be paralleled in the world. No wonder they poured out their blood freely before they would go. On one island, belonging to a Mr. H., with whom we stayed, are still to be found their "caches" for secreting provisions,—the wooden troughs in which they pounded their corn, the marks of their tomahawks upon felled trees. When he first came, he found the body of an Indian woman, in a canoe, elevated on high poles, with all her ornaments on. The island is a spot, where Nature seems to have exhausted her invention in crowding it with all kinds of growths, from the richest trees down to the most delicate plants. It divides the river which there sweeps along in clear and glittering current, between noble parks, richest green lawns, pictured rocks crowned with old hemlocks, or smooth bluffs, three hundred feet high, the most beautiful of all. Two of these,—the Eagle's Nest, and the Deer's Walk, still the resort of the grand and beautiful creature from which they are named,—were the scene of some of the happiest hours of my life. I had no idea, from verbal description, of the beauty of these bluffs, nor can I hope to give any to others. They lie so magnificently bathed in sunlight, they touch the heavens with so sharp and fair a line. This is one of the finest parts of the river; but it seems beautiful enough to fill any heart and eye all along its course, nowhere broken or injured by the hand of man. And there, I thought, if we two could live, and you could have a farm which would not cost a twentieth part the labor of a New England farm, and would pay twenty times as much for the labor, and have our books and our pens and a little boat on the river, how happy we might be for four or five years,—at least, *as* happy as Fate permits mortals to be. For we, I think, are congenial, and if I could hope permanent peace on the earth, I might hope it with you.

You will be glad to hear that I feel overpaid for coming here. Much is my life enriched by the images of the great Niagara, of the vast lakes, of the heavenly sweetness of the prairie scenes, and, above all, by the heavenly region where I would so gladly have lived. My health, too, is materially benefited. I hope to come back better fitted for toil and care, as well as with beauteous memories to sustain me in them.

Affectionately always, & c.

## Questions for Rereading, Discussing, Connecting, and Writing

### Rereading

1. Written in the middle of the last century, this personal letter combines personal greetings with the author's "enriched" life after a visit to "Rock-river territory." As you read, note the many nouns and adjectives that create impressions of wealth and beauty. Taken together, how do these words affect your imagining the "Rock-river territory"?

2. The Indians are gone from the territory, yet they form a real presence for Margaret Fuller. How does she depict the Indians? Point to images or detail that may indicate her *feelings* about them as well.

3. Fuller moves from experience to "dreams" or wishes in this letter to her brother. Although the letter is mostly about her experiences, what method does Fuller use to keep her reader fully engaged in what he or she is reading?

### Discussing

4. What are the purposes of personal letters? Does Fuller's letter exhibit some or all of these purposes?

5. Can a letter be "personal" and "public" at the same time? How? Point to sections of Fuller's letter as an example of how a writer may combine personal and public matters.

6. Fuller describes nature in such a way as to make it a "healer" or a tremendously beneficial environment for her. Have you had a similar experience in nature? Discuss the potential healing powers of nature—and how writing about them may be a part of their effectiveness.

## Connecting

**7.** Contrast this and other pictures of the "positive experience" or good journey—Polo, p. 112, for example, with one of hardship and hard lessons—Reed (p. 117), for example, or the Wells (p. 124) short story. Can you discover a common thread running through these accounts and stories concerning the reasons for taking the journey?

**8.** Fuller sees nature as a place of wonder. Look at the "The Vision Quest" (p. 25) and the selections by Polo (p. 112), Mercator (p. 108), and Apollinaire (p. 313) for different sorts of "wonder" associated with nature. Try to define these varying reactions to "wond'rous nature."

**9.** Fuller's view of the American landscape and its native people is wholly positive. From your own experience and reading, contrast this view with some popular conceptions we have about the dangers of life and travel in the mid-nineteenth century. Discuss whether one view is more legitimate than the other—or whether both are correct.

## Writing

**10.** For Fuller, this "heavenly region" is the best place she's ever been. Write about your own "heavenly region"—no matter where—in the form of a letter to a friend.

**11.** Rewrite the letter (in 10) in the form of an expository essay that you might imagine being published in the travel section of a Sunday newspaper.

**12.** Rewrite the essay (in 11) in the form of an argument directed at travellers looking for the perfect place to visit. Remember that these travellers are undecided about their destination—and that you would like them to visit (but not stay).

*Sergei Eisenstein*

# *Film Stills from* Battleship Potemkin *(1925)*

Eisenstein / *Film Stills from* Battleship Potemkin      33

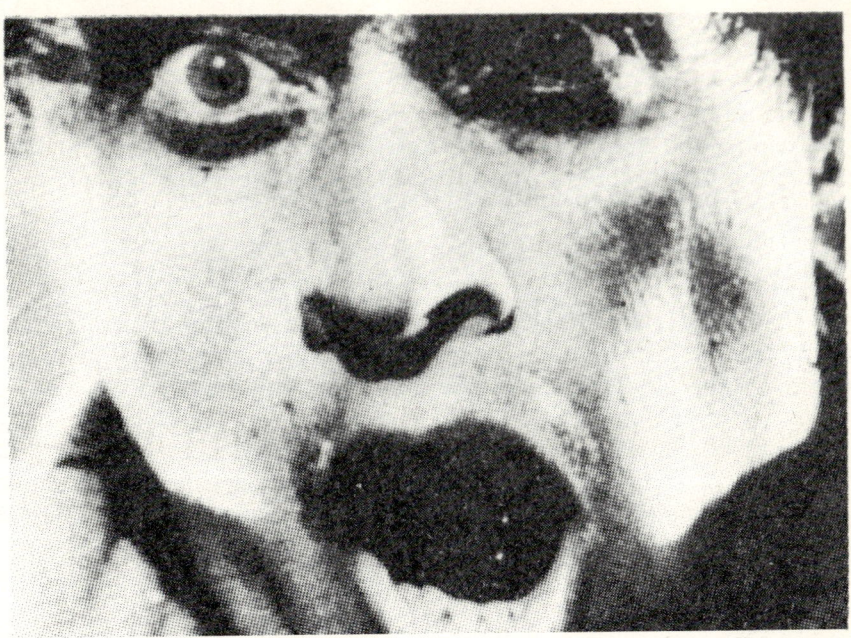

## *Questions for Rereading, Discussing, Connecting, and Writing*

### Rereading

1. What do these two pictures show? They are still photographs—or frames—taken from a silent film by the Soviet director Sergei Eisenstein. *Battleship Potemkin* is about a mutiny and subsequent crushing of popular support for the sailors. Given these two bare facts, read as much detail into these two frames as possible.

2. Your answer to 1 probably contains some thinking about the relationship between the two frames. Enlarge on your thinking, and begin to speculate on why these two frames are exactly matched (the child followed by the woman) in the finished, complete film.

### Discussing

3. There are always gaps in our writing. In other words, we could always say more. Movies, as full as they seem of sound and movement, can also be added to, filled out. In groups, work out story boards—a series of drawn or sketched frames—that could link these two frames from Eisenstein's movie.

Write captions describing the action in each frame and present these frames to the class.

4. The child has fallen on the steps. The woman stares in horror. Speculate on the connection between these two moments, and how they might contribute to the film's theme as described in the first question in the Rereading section.

CONNECTING

5. Movies are a relatively new art. Can you find another kind of communication in this book that is even newer? On the other hand, argue for one kind of text to be the oldest, and use examples from this book and elsewhere.

6. Making movies is one way to "give voice to experience," but they usually involve a whole company of artists working together. If you could make up a perfect moviemaking team from this book's artists and authors, who would they be? And what movie would you make?

WRITING

7. Write a response to the last good movie you saw. Be sure to include a discussion of two images—two pictures on the screen—that were memorable and effective. If they occurred one right after the other, discuss how they worked so well.

8. Rebellions, and the reactions they cause, are not only the stuff of movies, of course. Recent events in Asia illustrate as sharply as any art form the excitement, fear, and horror such events arouse in people—both participants and observers. Write a brief essay on the Chinese situation—its meanings and effects on future political action in China and—perhaps—elsewhere.

*Beryl Markham*

# West With the Night (1942)

*I* have seldom dreamed a dream worth dreaming again, or at least none worth recording. Mine are not enigmatic dreams; they are peopled with characters who are plausible and who do plausible things, and I am the most plausible amongst them. All the characters in my dreams have quiet voices like the voice of the man who telephoned me at Elstree one morning in September of nineteen-thirty-six and told me that there was rain and strong head winds over the west of England and over the Irish Sea, and that there were variable winds and clear skies in mid-Atlantic and fog off the coast of Newfoundland.

'If you are still determined to fly the Atlantic this late in the year,' the voice said, 'the Air Ministry suggests that the weather it is able to forecast for tonight, and for tomorrow morning, will be about the best you can expect.'

The voice had a few other things to say, but not many, and then it was gone, and I lay in bed half-suspecting that the telephone call and the man who made it were only parts of the mediocre dream I had been dreaming. I felt that if I closed my eyes the unreal quality of the message would be re-established, and that, when I opened them again, this would be another ordinary day with its usual beginning and its usual routine.

But of course I could not close my eyes, nor my mind, nor my memory. I could lie there for a few moments—remembering how it had begun, and telling myself, with senseless repetition, that by tomorrow morning I should either have flown the Atlantic to America—or I should not have flown it. In either case this was the day I would try.

I could stare up at the ceiling of my bedroom in Aldenham House, which was a ceiling undistinguished as ceilings go, and feel less resolute than anxious, much less brave than foolhardy. I could say to myself, 'You needn't do it, of course,' knowing at the same time that nothing is so inexorable as a promise to your pride.

I could ask, 'Why risk it?' as I have been asked since, and I could answer, 'Each to his element.' By his nature a sailor must sail, by his nature a flyer must fly. I could compute that I had flown a quarter of a million miles; and I could foresee that, so long as I had a plane and the sky was there, I should go on flying more miles.

There was nothing extraordinary in this. I had learned a craft and had worked hard learning it. My hands had been taught to seek the controls of a plane. Usage had taught them. They were at ease clinging to a stick, as a cobbler's fingers are in repose grasping an awl. No human pursuit achieves dignity until it can be called work, and when you can experience a physical loneliness for the tools of your trade, you see that the other things—the experiments, the irrelevant vocations, the vanities you used to hold—were false to you.

Record flights had actually never interested me very much for myself. There were people who thought that such flights were done for admiration and publicity, and worse. But of all the records—from Louis Blériot's first crossing of the English Channel in nineteen hundred and nine, through and beyond Kingsford Smith's flight from San Francisco to Sydney, Australia—none had been made by amateurs, nor by novices, nor by men or women less than hardened to failure, or less than masters of their trade. None of these was false. They were a company that simple respect and simple ambition made it worth more than an effort to follow.

The Carberrys (of Seramai) were in London and I could remember everything about their dinner party—even the menu. I could remember June Carberry and all her guests, and the man named McCarthy, who lived in Zanzibar, leaning across the table and saying, 'J. C., why don't you finance Beryl for a record flight?'

I could lie there staring lazily at the ceiling and recall J. C.'s dry answer: 'A number of pilots have flown the North Atlantic, west to east. Only Jim Mollison has done it alone the other way—from Ireland. Nobody has done it alone from England—man or woman. I'd be interested in that, but nothing else. If you want to try it, Beryl, I'll back you. I think Edgar Percival could build a plane that would do it, provided you can fly it. Want to chance it?'

'Yes.'

I could remember saying that better than I could remember anything—except J. C.'s almost ghoulish grin, and his remark that sealed the agreement: 'It's a deal, Beryl. I'll furnish the plane and you fly the Atlantic—but, gee, I wouldn't tackle it for a million. Think of all that black water! Think how cold it is!'

And I had thought of both.

I had thought of both for a while, and then there had been other things to think about. I had moved to Elstree, half-hour's flight from the Percival Aircraft Works at Gravesend, and almost daily for three months now I had flown down to the factory in a hired plane and watched the Vega Gull they were making for me. I had watched her birth and watched her growth. I had watched her wings take shape, and seen wood and fabric moulded to her ribs to form her long, sleek belly, and I had seen her engine cradled into her frame, and made fast.

The Gull had a turquoise-blue body and silver wings. Edgar Percival had made her with care, with skill, and with worry—the care of a veteran flyer, the skill of a master designer, and the worry of a friend. Actually the plane was a standard sport model with a range of only six hundred and sixty miles. But she had a special undercarriage built to carry the weight of her extra oil and petrol tanks. The tanks were fixed into the wings, into the centre section, and into the cabin itself. In the cabin they formed a wall around my seat, and each tank had a petcock of its own. The petcocks were important.

'If you open one,' said Percival, 'without shutting the other first, you may get an airlock. You know the tanks in the cabin have no gauges, so it may be best to let one run completely dry before opening the next. Your motor might go dead in the interval—but she'll start again. She's a De Havilland Gipsy—and Gipsys never stop.'

I had talked to Tom. We had spent hours going over the Atlantic chart, and I had realized that the tinker of Molo, now one of England's great pilots, had traded his dreams and had got in return a better thing. Tom had grown older too; he had jettisoned a deadweight of irrelevant hopes and wonders, and had left himself a realistic code that had no room for temporizing or easy sentiment.

'I'm glad you're going to do it, Beryl. It won't be simple. If you can get off the ground in the first place, with such an immense load of fuel, you'll be alone in that plane about a night and a day—mostly night. Doing it east to west, the wind's against you. In September, so is the weather. You won't have a radio. If you misjudge your course only a few degrees, you'll end up in Labrador or in the sea—do don't misjudge anything.'

Tom could still grin. He had grinned; he had said: 'Anyway, it ought to amuse you to think that your financial backer lives on a farm called "Place of Death" and your plane is being built at "Gravesend." If you were consistent, you'd christen the Gull "The Flying Tombstone."'

I hadn't been that consistent. I had watched the building of the plane and I had trained for the flight like an athlete. And now, as I lay in bed, fully awake, I could still hear the quiet voice of the man from the Air Ministry intoning, like the voice of a dispassionate court clerk:

'. . . the weather for tonight and tomorrow . . . will be about the best you can expect.' I should have liked to discuss the flight once more with Tom before I took off, but he was on a special job up north. I got out of bed and bathed and put on my flying clothes and took some cold chicken packed in a cardboard box and flew over to the military field at Abingdon, where the Vega Gull waited for me under the care of the R.A.F. I remember that the weather was clear and still.

Jim Mollison lent me his watch. He said: 'This is not a gift. I wouldn't part with it for anything. It got me across the North Atlantic and the South Atlantic too. Don't lose it—and, for God's sake, don't get it wet. Salt water would ruin the works.'

Brian Lewis gave me a life-saving jacket. Brain owned the plane I had been using between Elstree and Gravesend, and he had thought a long time about a farewell gift. What could be more practical than a pneumatic jacket that could be inflated through a rubber tube?

'You could float around in it for days,' said Brian. But I had to decide between the life-saver and warm clothes. I couldn't have both, because of their bulk, and I hate the cold, so I left the jacket.

And Jock Cameron, Brian's mechanic, gave me a sprig of heather. If it had been a whole bush of heather, complete with roots growing in an earthen jar, I think I should have taken it, bulky or not. The blessing of Scotland, bestowed by a Scotsman, is not to be dismissed. Nor is the well-wishing of a ground mechanic to be taken lightly, for these men are the pilot's contact with reality.

It is too much that with all those pedestrian centuries behind us we should, in a few decades, have learned to fly; it is too heady a thought, too proud a boast. Only the dirt on a mechanic's hands, the straining vise, the splintered bolt of steel underfoot on the hangar floor—only these and such anxiety as the face of a Jock Cameron can hold for a pilot and his plane before a flight, serve to remind us that, not unlike the heather, we too are earthbound. We fly, but we have not 'conquered' the air. Nature presides in all her dignity, permitting us the study and the use of such of her forces as we may understand. It is when we presume to intimacy, having been granted only tolerance, that the harsh stick falls across our impudent knuckles and we rub the pain, staring upward, startled by our ignorance.

'Here is a sprig of heather,' said Jock, and I took it and pinned it into a pocket of my flying jacket.

There were press cars parked outside the field at Abingdon, and several press planes and photographers, but the R.A.F. kept everyone away from the grounds except technicians and a few of my friends.

The Carberrys had sailed for New York a month ago to wait for me there. Tom was still out of reach with no knowledge of my decision to leave, but that didn't matter so much, I thought. It didn't matter because Tom was unchanging—neither a fairweather pilot nor a fairweather friend. If for a month, or a year, or two years we sometimes had not seen each other, it still hadn't mattered. Nor did this. Tom would never say, 'You should have let me know.' He assumed that I had learned all that he had tried to teach me, and for my part, I thought of him, even then, as the merest student must think of his mentor. I could sit in a cabin overcrowded with petrol tanks and set my course for North America, but the knowledge of my hands on the controls would be Tom's knowledge. His words of caution and words of guidance, spoken so long ago, so many times, on bright mornings over the veldt or over a forest, or with a far mountain visible at the tip of our wing, would be spoken again, if I asked.

So it didn't matter, I thought. It was silly to think about.

You can live a lifetime and, at the end of it, know more about other people than you know about yourself. You learn to watch other people, but you never watch yourself because you strive against loneliness. If you read a book, or shuffle a deck of cards, or care for a dog, you are avoiding yourself. The abhorrence of loneliness is as natural as wanting to live at all. If it were otherwise, men would never have bothered to make an alphabet, nor to have fashioned words out of what were only animal sounds, nor to have crossed continents—each man to see what the other looked like.

Being alone in an aeroplane for even so short a time as a night and a day, irrevocably alone, with nothing to observe but your instruments and your own hands in semi-darkness, nothing to contemplate but the size of your small courage, nothing to wonder about but the beliefs, the faces, and the hopes rooted in your mind—such an experience can be as startling as the first awareness of a stranger walking by your side at night. You are the stranger.

It is dark already and I am over the south of Ireland. There are the lights of Cork and the lights are wet; they are drenched in Irish rain, and I am above them and dry. I am above them and the plane roars in a sobbing world, but it imparts no sadness to me. I feel the security of solitude, the exhilaration of escape. So long as I can see the lights and imagine the people walking under them, I feel selfishly triumphant, as if I have eluded care and left even the small sorrow of rain in other hands.

It is a little over an hour now since I left Abingdon. England, Wales, and the Irish Sea are behind me like so much time used up. On a long flight distance and time are the same. But there had been a moment when Time stopped—and Distance too. It was the moment I lifted the blue-and-silver Gull from the aerodrome, the moment the photographers aimed their cameras, the moment I felt the craft refuse its burden and strain toward the earth in sullen rebellion, only to listen at last to the persuasion of stick and elevators, the dogmatic argument of blueprints that said she *had* to fly because the figures proved it.

So she had flown, and once airborne, once she had yielded to the sophistry of a draughtsman's board, she had said, 'There: I have lifted the weight. Now, where are we bound?'—and the question had frightened me.

'We are bound for a place thirty-six hundred miles from here—two thousand miles of it unbroken ocean. Most of the way it will be night. We are flying west with the night.'

So there behind me is Cork; and ahead of me is Berehaven Lighthouse. It is the last light, standing on the last land. I watch it, counting the frequency of its flashes—so many to the minute. Then I pass it and fly out to sea.

The fear is gone now—not overcome nor reasoned away. It is gone because something else has taken its place; the confidence and the trust, the inherent belief in the security of land underfoot—now this faith is transferred to my plane, because the land has vanished and there is no other tangible thing to fix faith upon. Flight is but momentary escape from the eternal custody of earth.

Rain continues to fall, and outside the cabin it is totally dark. My altimeter says that the Atlantic is two thousand feet below me, my Sperry Artificial Horizon says that I am flying level. I judge my drift at three degrees more than my weather chart suggests, and fly accordingly. I am flying blind. A beam to follow would help. So would a radio—but then, so would clear weather. The voice of the man at the Air Ministry had not promised storm.

I feel the wind rising and the rain falls hard. The smell of petrol in the cabin is so strong and the roar of the plane so loud that my senses are almost deadened. Gradually it becomes unthinkable that existence was ever otherwise.

At ten o'clock P.M. I am flying along the Great Circle Course for Harbour Grace, Newfoundland, into a forty-mile headwind at a speed of one hundred and thirty miles an hour. Because of the weather, I cannot be sure of how many more hours I have to fly, but I think it must be between sixteen and eighteen.

At ten-thirty I am still flying on the large cabin tank of petrol, hoping to use it up and put an end to the liquid swirl that has rocked the plane since my take-off. The tank has no gauge, but written on its side is the assurance: 'This tank is good for four hours.'

There is nothing ambiguous about such a guaranty. I believe it, but at twenty-five minutes to eleven, my motor coughs and dies, and the Gull is powerless above the sea.

I realize that the heavy drone of the plane has been, until this moment, complete and comforting silence. It is the actual silence following the last splutter of the engine that stuns me. I can't feel any fear; I can't feel anything. I can only observe with a kind of stupid disinterest that my hands are violently active and know that, while they move, I am being hypnotized by the needle of my altimeter.

I suppose that the denial of natural impulse is what is meant by 'keeping calm,' but impulse has reason in it. If it is night and you are sitting in an aeroplane with a stalled motor, and there are two thousand feet between you and the sea, nothing can be more reasonable than the impulse to pull back your stick in the hope of adding to that two thousand, if only by a little. The thought, the knowledge, the law that tells you that your hope lies not in this, but in a contrary act—the act of directing your impotent craft toward the water—seems a terrifying abandonment, not only of reason, but of sanity. Your mind and your heart reject it. It is your hands—your stranger's hands—that follow with unfeeling precision the letter of the law.

I sit there and watch my hands push forward on the stick and feel the Gull respond and begin its dive to the sea. Of course it is a simple thing; surely the cabin tank has run dry too soon. I need only to turn another petcock . . .

But it is dark in the cabin. It is easy to see the luminous dial of the altimeter and to note that my height is now eleven hundred feet, but it is not easy to see a petcock that is somewhere near the floor of the plane. A hand gropes and reappears with an electric torch, and fingers, moving with agonizing composure, find the petcock and turn it; and I wait.

At three hundred feet the motor is still dead, and I am conscious that the needle of my altimeter seems to whirl like the spoke of a spindle winding up the remaining distance between the plane and the water. There is some lightning, but the quick flash only serves to emphasize the darkness. How high can waves reach—twenty feet, perhaps? Thirty?

It is impossible to avoid the thought that this is the end of my flight, but my reactions are not orthodox; the various incidents of my entire life do not run through my mind like a motion-picture film gone mad. I only feel that all this has happened before—and it has. It has all happened a hundred times in my mind, in my sleep, so that now I am not really caught in terror; I recognize a familiar scene, a familiar story with its climax dulled by too much telling.

I do not know how close to the waves I am when the motor explodes to life again. But the sound is almost meaningless. I see my hand easing back on the stick, and I feel the Gull climb up into the storm, and I see the altimeter whirl like a spindle again, paying out the distance between myself and the sea.

The storm is strong. It is comforting. It is like a friend shaking me and saying, 'Wake up! You were only dreaming.'

But soon I am thinking. By simple calculation I find that my motor had been silent for perhaps an instant more than thirty seconds.

I ought to thank God—and I do, though indirectly. I thank Geoffrey De Havilland who designed the indomitable Gipsy, and who, after all, must have been designed by God in the first place.

A lighted ship—the daybreak—some steep cliffs standing in the sea. The meaning of these will never change for pilots. If one day an ocean can be flown within an hour, if men can build a plane that so masters time, the sight of land will be no less welcome to the steersman of that fantastic craft. He will have cheated laws that the cunning of science has taught him how to cheat, and he will feel his guilt and be eager for the sanctuary of the soil.

I saw the ship and the daybreak, and then I saw the cliffs of Newfoundland wound in ribbons of fog. I felt the elation I had so long imagined, and I felt the happy guilt of having circumvented the stern authority of the weather and the sea. But mine was a minor triumph; my swift Gull was not so swift as to have escaped unnoticed. The night and the storm had caught her and we had flown blind for nineteen hours.

I was tired now, and cold. Ice began to film the glass of the cabin windows and the fog played a magician's game with the land. But the land was there. I could not see it, but I had seen it. I could not afford to believe that it was any land but the land I wanted. I could not afford to believe that my navigation was at fault, because there was no time for doubt.

South to Cape Race, west to Sydney on Cape Breton Island. With my protractor, my map, and my compass, I set my new course, humming the ditty that Tom had taught me: 'Variation West—magnetic best. Variation East—magnetic least.' A silly rhyme, but it served to placate, for the moment, two warring poles—the magnetic and the true. I flew south and found the lighthouse of Cape Race protruding from the fog like a warning finger. I circled twice and went on over the Gulf of Saint Lawrence.

After a while there would be New Brunswick, and then Maine—and then New York. I could anticipate. I could almost say, 'Well, if you stay awake, you'll find it's only a matter of time now'—but there was no question of staying awake. I was tired and I had not moved an inch since that uncertain moment at Abingdon when the Gull had elected to rise with her load and fly, but I could not have closed my eyes. I could sit there in the cabin, walled in glass and petrol tanks, and be grateful for the sun and the light, and the fact that I could see the water under me. They were almost the last waves I had to pass. Four hundred miles of water, but then the land again—Cape Breton. I would stop at Sydney to re-fuel and go on. It was easy now. It would be like stopping at Kisumu and going on.

Success breeds confidence. But who has a right to confidence except the Gods? I had a following wind, my last tank of petrol was more than three-quarters full, and the world was as bright to me as if it were a new world, never touched. If I had been wiser, I might have known that such moments are, like innocence, short-lived. My engine began to shudder before I saw the land. It died, it spluttered, it started again and limped along. It coughed and spat black exhaust toward the sea.

There are words for everything. There was a word for this—airlock, I thought. This had to be an airlock because there was petrol enough. I thought I might clear it by turning on and turning off all the empty tanks, and so I did that. The handles of the petcocks were sharp little pins of metal, and when I had opened and closed them a dozen times, I saw that my hands were bleeding and that the blood was dropping on my maps and on my clothes, but the effort wasn't any good. I coasted along on a sick and halting engine. The oil pressure and the oil temperature gauges were normal, the magnetos working, and yet I lost altitude slowly while the realization of failure seeped into my heart. If I made the land, I should have been the first to fly the North Atlantic from England, but from my point of view, from a pilot's point of view, a forced landing was failure because New

York was my goal. If only I could land and then take off, I would make it still . . . if only, if only . . .

The engine cuts again, and then catches, and each time it spurts to life I climb as high as I can get, and then it splutters and stops and I glide once more toward the water, to rise again and descend again, like a hunting sea bird.

I find the land. Visibility is perfect now and I see land forty or fifty miles ahead. If I am on my course, that will be Cape Breton. Minute after minute goes by. The minutes almost materialize; they pass before my eyes like links in a long slow-moving chain, and each time the engine cuts, I see a broken link in the chain and catch my breath until it passes.

The land is under me. I snatch my map and stare at it to confirm my whereabouts. I am, even at my present crippled speed, only twelve minutes from Sydney Airport, where I can land for repairs and then go on.

The engine cuts once more and I begin to glide, but now I am not worried; she will start again, as she has done, and I will gain altitude and fly into Sydney.

But she doesn't start. This time she's dead as death; the Gull settles earthward and it isn't any earth I know. It is black earth stuck with boulders and I hang above it, on hope and on a motionless propeller. Only I cannot hang above it long. The earth hurries to meet me, I bank, turn, and sideslip to dodge the boulders, my wheels touch, and I feel them submerge. The nose of the plane is engulfed in mud, and I go forward striking my head on the glass of the cabin front, hearing it shatter, feeling blood pour over my face.

I stumble out of the plane and sink to my knees in muck and stand there foolishly staring, not at the lifeless land, but at my watch.

Twenty-one hours and twenty-five minutes.

Atlantic flight. Abingdon, England, to a nameless swamp—nonstop.

A Cape Breton Islander found me—a fisherman trudging over the bog saw the Gull with her tail in the air and her nose buried, and then he saw me floundering in the embracing soil of his native land. I had been wandering for an hour and the black mud had got up to my waist and the blood from the cut in my head had met the mud halfway.

From a distance, the fisherman directed me with his arms and with shouts toward the firm places in the bog, and for another hour I walked on them and came toward him like a citizen of Hades blinded by the sun, but it wasn't the sun; I hadn't slept for forty hours.

He took me to his hut on the edge of the coast and I found that built upon the rocks there was a little cubicle that housed an ancient telephone—put there in case of shipwrecks.

I telephoned to Sydney Airport to say that I was safe and to prevent a needless search being made. On the following morning I did step out of a plane at Floyd Bennett Field and there was a crowd of people still waiting there to greet me, but the plane I stepped from was not the Gull, and for days while I was in New York I kept thinking about that and wishing over and over again that it had been the Gull, until the wish lost its significance, and time moved on, overcoming many things it met on the way.

*Questions for Rereading,*
*Discussing, Connecting, and Writing*

## Rereading

1. Beryl Markham was the first pilot to make a solo west to east flight across the Atlantic from England. As you read, notice how the author involves you in the experience of her flight. Note places where she captures your interest and makes you want to read on.

2. The second part of this piece is written in the present tense, while the rest is in the past tense. How does the shift in tense affect your reading?

3. This selection includes a number of statements about the nature of the world in general—statements such as "There are words for everything," and "We fly, but we have not 'conquered' the air"—that indicate a world view rather than just an observation about a particular moment. Identify a few such statements and note what they contribute to your reading of the whole piece.

## Discussing

4. In one sense, Markham's flight can be described as a failure because she did not reach New York City in her Gull. Discuss ways in which Markham's flight is and is not a failure.

5. Markham mentions several individuals—her financial backer J. C., her instructor Tom, the builder Edgar Percival, the plane owner Brian Lewise, the mechanic Jock Cameron, her friends the Carberrys, and Geoffrey De Haviland—who contributed to her flight. In what ways, then, can hers be called a solo flight?

**6.** Ernest Hemingway wrote this about Beryl Markham and *West With the Night:* "I knew her fairly well in Africa and never would have suspected that she could and would put pen to paper except to write in her flyer's log book. As it is, she has written so well, and marvelously well, that I was completely ashamed of myself as a writer. I felt that I was simply a carpenter with words, picking up whatever was furnished on the job and nailing them together and sometimes making an okay pig pen." What image, analogous to Hemingway's image of himself as a carpenter, might be used to describe Markham's writing?

## CONNECTING

**7.** Throughout this selection, Markham personifies her plane in many ways. What does this strategy of giving human qualities to a mechanical object have in common with, say, the comparisons Herodotus (p. 13) draws between Egyptians and Persians? How can you compare the ways these writers convey their experiences?

**8.** This account includes a good deal of technical information about planes and flying, information that invites comparison with other selections in this book. For example, when Markham likens her pilot's hands to those of a cobbler grasping an awl, you may be reminded of the Foxfire selection (p. 223). With what other selections do you find comparisons?

**9.** Markham narrates her personal experience at the same time that she discusses the technology of flying. Compare the qualities and effects of this use of narrative with that of Baker (p. 49). What perspective does the narrative of each author give you on the subject under discussion?

## WRITING

**10.** Write an account of Markham's flight as it might have been reported by a news writer who witnessed her arrival in New York City in September of 1936.

**11.** Write about an experience of your own which could be described as both success and failure depending upon your perspective.

**12.** Markham's book was the subject of a PBS documentary titled *World without Walls.* Write an account of how you would represent her flight in a film.

Bruce Springsteen

# Used Cars (1982)

My little sister's in the front seat with an ice cream cone
My ma's in the back seat sittin' all alone
As my pa steers her slow out of the lot for a test drive
   down Michigan Avenue
Now my ma she fingers her wedding band
And watches the salesman stare at my old man's hands
He's tellin' us all 'bout the break he'd give us if he could
   but he just can't
Well if I could I swear I know just what I'd do

Now mister the day the lottery I win I ain't ever gonna ride
   in no used car again

Now the neighbors come from near and far
As we pull up in our brand new used car
I wish he'd just hit the gas and let out a cry and tell 'em all
   they can kiss our asses goodbye

My dad he sweats the same job from mornin' to morn
Me I walk home on the same dirty streets where I was born
Up the block I can hear my litter sister in the front seat
   blowin' that horn
The sounds echoin' all down Michigan Avenue

Now mister the day my number come in I ain't ever gonna
   ride in no used car again

## Questions for Rereading, Discussing, Connecting, and Writing

REREADING

1. Reading the lyrics of a song could be said to be unfair to the songwriter. Why?

2. As you read "Used Cars" imagine it being sung by the songwriter Bruce Springsteen. Note at what points you could expect Springsteen to pause—or

to give emphasis. These features can't be indicated on the page, and yet the lyrics always gain power through them. Then listen to the songwriter sing this song, and compare your "directions" with his.

3. "Diction" is a feature of language having to do with a level of formality or informality in the vocabulary we choose. How would you characterize Springsteen's diction in "Used Cars"?

## Discussing

4. Popular music like Springsteen's is sometimes overlooked when discussions of "art" or "poetry" begin. Is popular music art? Point to specific songs or singers or groups that you think are creating art through their music.

5. "Used Cars" is, on the surface, about buying a car the narrator is really not happy with. But what are the narrator's underlying reasons for hating this "brand new used car"?

6. The only solution to the narrator's predicament—according to the lyrics—is the lottery. Discuss what a lottery is, how it works, and whether you think the lottery is really the answer.

## Connecting

7. The voice of the narrator sounds youthful; it is the brother's. Compare this voice to the one in the Baker selection (p. 49) and try to discover what makes a voice "sound youthful"—word choice, slang, certain sentence structure?

8. If you could have Bruce Springsteen transform any of the selections in this book into a song, which would it be—and why? Discuss Springsteen's skills as a songwriter, and your preferences as music listener.

## Writing

9. Springsteen has chosen a common event to write and sing about. Buying a car becomes, though, a statement about poverty and dreams. Write a poem or lyric about your dreams—or a dream that really matters to you now.

10. We sense that the mother and father in this song have stories of their own to tell, yet the songwriter maintains their silence. Tell us what the parents are like, and what they are thinking as they buy their used car. What do they express about the human condition?

Russell Baker

# Growing Up *(1982)*

*F*ifty years ago parents still asked boys if they wanted to grow up to be President, and asked it not jokingly but seriously. Many parents who were hardly more than paupers still believed their sons could do it. Abraham Lincoln had done it. We were only sixty-five years from Lincoln. Many a grandfather who walked among us could remember Lincoln's time. Men of grandfatherly age were the worst for asking if you wanted to grow up to be President. A surprising number of little boys said yes and meant it.

I was asked many times myself. No, I would say, I didn't want to grow up to be President. My mother was present during one of these interrogations. An elderly uncle, having posed the usual question and exposed my lack of interest in the Presidency, asked, "Well, what *do* you want to be when you grow up?"

I loved to pick through trash piles and collect empty bottles, tin cans with pretty labels, and discarded magazines. The most desirable job on earth sprang instantly to mind. "I want to be a garbage man," I said.

My uncle smiled, but my mother had seen the first distressing evidence of a bump budding on a log. "Have a little gumption, Russell," she said. Her calling me Russell was a signal of unhappiness. When she approved of me I was always "Buddy."

When I turned eight years old she decided that the job of starting me on the road toward making something of myself could no longer be safely delayed. "Buddy," she said one day, "I want you to come home right after school this afternoon. Somebody's coming and I want you to meet him."

When I burst in that afternoon she was in conference in the parlor with an executive of the Curtis Publishing Company. She introduced me. He bent low from the waist and shook my hand. Was it true as my mother had told him, he asked, that I longed for the opportunity to conquer the world of business?

My mother replied that I was blessed with a rare determination to make something of myself.

"That's right," I whispered.

"But have you got the grit, the character, the never-say-quit spirit it takes to succeed in business?"

My mother said I certainly did.

"That's right," I said.

He eyed me silently for a long pause, as though weighing whether I could be trusted to keep his confidence, then spoke man-to-man. Before taking a crucial step, he said, he wanted to advise me that working for the Curtis Publishing Company placed enormous responsibility on a young man. It was one of the great companies of America. Perhaps the greatest publishing house in the world. I had heard, no doubt, of the *Saturday Evening Post*?

Heard of it? My mother said that everyone in our house had heard of the *Saturday Post* and that I, in fact, read it with religious devotion.

Then doubtless, he said, we were also familiar with those two monthly pillars of the magazine world, the *Ladies Home Journal* and the *Country Gentleman*.

Indeed we were familiar with them, said my mother.

Representing the *Saturday Evening Post* was one of the weightiest honors that could be bestowed in the world of business, he said. He was personally proud of being a part of that great corporation.

My mother said he had every right to be.

Again he studied me as though debating whether I was worthy of a knighthood. Finally: "Are you trustworthy?"

My mother said I was the soul of honesty.

"That's right," I said.

The caller smiled for the first time. He told me I was a lucky young man. He admired my spunk. Too many young men thought life was all play. Those young men would not go far in this world. Only a young man willing to work and save and keep his face washed and his hair neatly combed could hope to come out on top in a world such as ours. Did I truly and sincerely believe that I was such a young man?

"He certainly does," said my mother.

"That's right," I said.

He said he had been so impressed by what he had seen of me that he was going to make me a representative of the Curtis Publishing Company. On the following Tuesday, he said, thirty freshly printed copies of the *Saturday Evening Post* would be delivered at our door. I would place these magazines still damp with the ink of the presses, in a handsome canvas bag, sling it over my shoulder, and set forth through the streets to bring the best in journalism, fiction, and cartoons to the American public.

He had brought the canvas bag with him. He presented it with reverence fit for a chasuble. He showed me how to drape the sling over my left shoulder and across the chest so that the pouch lay easily accessible to my right hand, allowing the best in journalism, fiction, and cartoons to be swiftly extracted and sold to a citizenry whose happiness and security depended upon us soldiers of the free press.

The following Tuesday I raced home from school, put the canvas bag over my shoulder, dumped the magazines in, and, tilting to the left to balance their weight on my right hip, embarked on the highway of journalism.

We lived in Belleville, New Jersey, a commuter town at the northern fringe of Newark. It was 1932, the bleakest year of the Depression. My father had died two years before, leaving us with a few pieces of Sears, Roebuck furniture and not much else, and my mother had taken Doris and me to live with one of her younger brothers. This was my Uncle Allen. Uncle Allen had made something of himself by 1932. As salesman for a soft-drink bottler in Newark, he had an income of $30 a week; wore pearl-gray spats, detachable collars, and a three-piece suit; was happily married; and took in threadbare relatives.

With my load of magazines I headed toward Belleville Avenue. That's where the people were. There were two filling stations at the intersection with Union Avenue, as well as an A&P, a fruit stand, a bakery, a barber shop, Zuccarelli's drugstore, and a diner shaped like a railroad car. For several hours I made myself highly visible, shifting position now and then from corner to corner, from shop window to shop window, to make sure everyone could see the heavy black lettering on the canvas bag that said *The Saturday Evening Post*. When the angle of the light indicated it was suppertime, I walked back to the house.

"How many did you sell, Buddy?" my mother asked.

"None."

"Where did you go?"

"The corner of Belleville and Union Avenues."

"What did you do?"

"Stood on the corner waiting for somebody to buy a *Saturday Evening Post*."

"You just stood there?"

"Didn't sell a single one."

"For God's sake, Russell!"

Uncle Allen intervened. "I've been thinking about it for some time," he said, "and I've about decided to take the *Post* regularly. Put me down as a regular customer." I handed him a magazine and he paid me a nickel. It was the first nickel I earned.

Afterwards my mother instructed me in salesmanship. I would have to ring doorbells, address adults with charming self-confidence, and break down resistance with a sales talk pointing out that no one, no matter how poor, could afford to be without the *Saturday Evening Post* in the home.

I told my mother I'd changed my mind about wanting to succeed in the magazine business.

"If you think I'm going to raise a good-for-nothing," she replied, "you've got another think coming." She told me to hit the streets with the canvas bag and start ringing doorbells the instant school was out next day. When I objected that I didn't feel any aptitude for salesmanship, she asked how I'd like to lend her my leather belt so she could whack some sense into me. I bowed to superior will and entered journalism with a heavy heart.

My mother and I had fought this battle almost as long as I could remember. It probably started even before memory began, when I was a country child in northern Virginia and my mother, dissatisfied with my father's plain workman's life, determined that I would not grow up like him and his people, with calluses on their hands, overalls on their backs, and fourth-grade educations in their heads. She had fancier ideas of life's possibilities. Introducing me to the *Saturday Evening Post*, she was trying to wean me as early as possible from my father's world where men left with their lunch pails at sunup, worked with their hands until the grime ate into the pores, and died with a few sticks of mail-order furniture as their legacy. In my mother's vision of the better life there were desks and white collars, well-pressed suits, evenings of reading and lively talk, and perhaps—if a man were very, very lucky and hit the jackpot, really made something important of himself—perhaps there might be a fantastic salary of $5,000 a year to support a big house and a Buick with a rumble seat and a vacation in Atlantic City.

And so I set forth with my sack of magazines. I was afraid of the dogs that snarled behind the doors of potential buyers. I was timid about ringing the doorbells of strangers, relieved when no one came to the door, and scared when someone did. Despite my mother's instructions, I could not deliver an engaging sales pitch. When a door opened

I simply asked, "Want to buy a *Saturday Evening Post?*" In Belleville few persons did. It was a town of 30,000 people, and most weeks I rang a fair majority of its doorbells. But I rarely sold my thirty copies. Some weeks I canvassed the entire town for six days and still had four or five unsold magazines on Monday evening; then I dreaded the coming of Tuesday morning, when a batch of thirty fresh *Saturday Evening Posts* was due at the front door.

"Better get out there and sell the rest of those magazines tonight," my mother would say.

I usually posted myself then at a busy intersection where a traffic light controlled commuter flow from Newark. When the light turned red I stood on the curb and shouted my sales pitch at the motorists.

"Want to buy a *Saturday Evening Post?*"

One rainy night when car windows were sealed against me I came back soaked and with not a single sale to report. My mother beckoned to Doris.

"Go back down there with Buddy and show him how to sell these magazines," she said.

Brimming with zest, Doris, who was then seven years old, returned with me to the corner. She took a magazine from the bag, and when the light turned red she strode to the nearest car and banged her small fist against the closed window. The driver, probably startled at what he took to be a midget assaulting his car, lowered the window to stare, and Doris thrust a *Saturday Evening Post* at him.

"You need this magazine," she piped. "and it only costs a nickel."

Her salesmanship was irresistible. Before the light changed half a dozen times she disposed of the entire batch. I didn't feel humiliated. To the contrary. I was so happy I decided to give her a treat. Leading her to the vegetable store on Belleville Avenue, I bought three apples, which cost a nickel, and gave her one.

"You shouldn't waste money," she said.

"Eat your apple." I bit into mine.

"You shouldn't eat before supper," she said. "It'll spoil your appetite."

Back at the house that evening, she dutifully reported me for wasting a nickel. Instead of a scolding, I was rewarded with a pat on the back for having the good sense to buy fruit instead of candy. My mother reached into her bottomless supply of maxims and told Doris, "An apple a day keeps the doctor away."

By the time I was ten I had learned all my mother's maxims by heart. Asking to stay up past normal bedtime, I knew that a refusal would be explained with, "Early to bed and early to rise, makes a man healthy, wealthy, and wise." If I whimpered about having to get up early in the morning, I could depend on her to say, "The early bird gets the worm."

The one I most despised was, "If at first you don't succeed, try, try again." This was the battle cry with which she constantly sent me back into the hopeless struggle whenever I moaned that I had rung every doorbell in town and knew there wasn't a single potential buyer left in Belleville that week. After listening to my explanation, she handed me the canvas bag and said, "If at first you don't succeed . . . "

Three years in that job, which I would gladly have quit after the first day except for her insistence, produced at least one valuable result. My mother finally concluded that I would never make something of myself by pursuing a life in business and started considering careers that demanded less competitive zeal.

One evening when I was eleven I brought home a short "composition" on my summer vacation which the teacher had graded with an A. Reading it with her own schoolteacher's eye, my mother agreed that it was top-drawer seventh grade prose and complimented me. Nothing more was said about it immediately, but a new idea had taken life in her mind. Halfway through supper she suddenly interrupted the conversation.

"Buddy," she said, "maybe you could be a writer."

I clasped the idea to my heart. I had never met a writer, had shown no previous urge to write, and hadn't a notion how to become a writer, but I loved stories and thought that making up stories must surely be almost as much fun as reading them. Best of all, though, and what really gladdened my heart, was the ease of the writer's life. Writers did not have to trudge through the town peddling from canvas bags, defending themselves against angry dogs, being rejected by surly strangers. Writers did not have to ring doorbells. So far as I could make out, what writers did couldn't even be classified as work.

I was enchanted. Writers didn't have to have any gumption at all. I did not dare tell anybody for fear of being laughed at in the schoolyard, but secretly I decided that what I'd like to be when I grew up was a writer.

## Questions for Rereading, Discussing, Connecting, and Writing

### REREADING

1. When we read of a past time—and a place we as readers may not be familiar with—what are our expectations? What do we want the writer to show us? Does Baker fulfill some of these expectations in this excerpt from his memoir? Note passages as you read that seem to recreate another place and time.

2. Russell, in writing of a time 50 years ago, uses a word that we as readers of another time might not recognize: "gumption." What do you think Baker's intention is in using this work—and what effect does it have on you? If its meaning is not immediately apparent, can you find clues to its meaning?

3. What the young Russell Baker calls "the highway of journalism" is distant from the journalism that Baker eventually practiced with the *New York Times.* Find the moment in this excerpt that describes the turning point in Baker's young career—and note how Baker uses "the ease of the writer's life" as comic contrast to his former occupation.

### DISCUSSING

4. Making money can be hard work at any age. Share with the class your money-making experiences—were they, as Baker would say, a matter of "gumption"?

5. The title of the book from which the excerpt is taken, *Growing Up,* could indicate a thematic concern of the author. How does this excerpt help to define "growing up" in terms of "maturing"?

6. Baker's mother liked maxims—or words of wisdom. Discuss how one or more of the maxims mentioned in this excerpt have particular meaning to you and your view of "hard work."

### CONNECTING

7. Baker is concerned with telling the story of how he became what he is today—a writer. Look for other such accounts in this book—for example, the Laye (p. 210), Parker (p. 230) and Reed (p. 117) selections—and try to discover what common element of experience in these lives contributed most importantly to "growing up."

**8.** Baker's difficulties with becoming a salesman are humorously told—although his experiences were certainly not humorous at the time. Look at Twain (p. 202) and "The Vision Quest" (p. 25) and note how each author uses "ironic distance" to create a "then and now" contrast.

## WRITING

**9.** Baker never did succeed at selling magazines. Can you discover a time of frustration or failure in your life—and write about it with "ironic distance"?

**10.** Baker's A grade on a composition sets him onward to a career in writing. Look at your experiences in school and describe the achievement that yielded you the greatest positive recognition.

**11.** "Growing up" is a theme of much of our writing about ourselves. Look to the experiences of a friend or family member—and write about "growing up" as a process of doing and learning.

# Two

# Profiling and Portraying People

$A$ great deal of our writing is about people. Almost every newspaper story contains somewhere within it a person or people; short stories and novels concern humans and their lives. Men, women, and children make things happen—and it is motion, change, action, experience that make us *need* to write. This "putting into motion" is one way of defining just what fascinates us about people—and makes us write about people.

When we choose to write about people—or a person—we have already done something important. We have, as a part of the composing process, decided to *foreground* an individual or individuals. Foregrounding is a part of focusing—or choosing what will stand out. When we arrange to take a snapshot of someone, we have our subject stand in front of a scene or backdrop. This, too, is foregrounding. The camera is focused on the subject, not the background. So, too, is the reader or viewer. Focus is sometimes a difficult step to master in the composing process, but when we deal with people, we can begin to overcome this challenge. When we decide it is time to write, one decision to be made is, "Who or what will be at the center (the foreground) of my word-picture?" When this question is answered, we can emphasize this subject, giving it detail and attention—and so signal to our readers that we have moved some material forward into focus and some material back into the background.

The photograph of Abraham Lincoln in this chapter is an example of focus or foregrounding. As readers or viewers, we observe no distractions; we have only Lincoln to look at. This studio portrait was for publicity purposes before Lincoln ran for office in Illinois. He hoped to convey by his image alone what he hoped were qualities of leadership. We can compare this to modern presidential portraits, in which the President is always shown against a backdrop of the Oval Office, or the American flag, or other elements that provide context.

Lincoln, in the Gettysburg Address, gave us one of the most famous and eloquent examples of a portrait of people. The people are, of course, the American people, placed against a wide, sweeping backdrop of the founding of a nation and the maturing of its spirit despite tragedies such as the Civil War. We can say that his focus is not on a single individual, but on a whole nation of individuals. In a short text, Lincoln manages to cover almost a century of American history, the famous "four score and seven years" of this country's life. He has chosen to foreground the American people against the background of the American experience.

Writing about a single person is another challenge. It is like a close-up in a movie or the photograph of Lincoln. The reader, if he or she is shown just one individual, must be able to "see" that person; otherwise, the foreground remains out of focus, and the text's intentions or purposes might go unrealized. Oliver Sacks profiles Madeleine J., an old woman with a medical problem, and Meridel LeSueur, profiles a succession of women looking for work. Both authors were trying to capture the essence of these people. If we could not see and believe in their subjects, the rest of the "picture" wouldn't matter much. So the authors used such devices as close descriptive detail, gesture, speech, and closely narrated action to show us what really made Madeleine J. or Bernice or Mrs. Grey unique in the eyes of the authors. Composing can mean surrounding a center—or central figure—with detail that supports it.

In writing texts about people, composers usually find action matched to portrait. Cassatt shows us the simple domestic detail of getting oneself ready, while Darwin shows us the entire human race in a common struggle to survive. The particular moment of Pound's poem—and the timeless conclusions about mankind that Darwin makes—demonstrates the way focus can be narrow or broad. Humanity can be one person or all persons.

As readers, we like to learn and enjoy—to experience something we haven't experienced before, or to understand better an experience we do know. It is hard to escape being "us"—individuals in a society of other individuals. Much of our writing, then, is from this perspective (although it can be fun to write from other perspectives, say that of an animal or inanimate object). We think of ourselves speaking *as* persons *to* persons *about* persons. There are exceptions, of course, but we always have a sense of a single person speaking out, and another hearing. For this reason, we need to discover what makes us real and unique and valuable to our readers. Whether we are writing about ourselves or others, our writing should have the same life in it that our subjects do.

## John Earle

## *An Antiquary* (1628)

He is a man strangely thrifty of time past, and an enemy indeed to his maw, whence he fetches out many things when they are now all rotten and stinking. He is one that hath that unnatural disease to be enamored of old age and wrinkles, and loves all things (as Dutchmen do cheese), the better for being moldy and worm-eaten. He is of our religion, because we say it is most ancient; and yet a broken statue would almost make him an idolater. A great admirer he is of the rust of old monuments, and reads only those characters where time hath eaten out the letters. He will go you forty miles to see a saint's well or a ruined abbey; and if there be but a cross or stone foot-stool in the way, he'll be considering it so long till he forget his journey. His estate consists much in shekels, and Roman coins; and he hath more pictures of Caesar than James or Elizabeth. Beggars cozen him with musty things which they have raked from dunghills, and he preserves their rags for precious relics. He loves no library but where there are more spiders' volumes than authors', and looks with great admiration on the antique work of cobwebs. Printed books he contemns, as a novelty of this latter age, but a manuscript he pores on everlastingly, especially if the cover be all moth-eaten, and the dust make a parenthesis between every syllable. He would give all the books in his study (which are rarities all) for one of the old Roman bindings, or six lines of Tully in his own hand. His chamber is hung commonly with strange beasts' skins, and is a kind of charnel-house of bones extraordinary; and his discourse upon them, if you will hear him, shall last longer. His very attire is that which is the eldest out of fashion and you may pick a criticism out of his breeches. He never looks upon himself till he is gray-haired, and then he is pleased with his own antiquity. His grave does not fright him, for he has been used to sepulchers, and he likes death the better, because it gathers him to his fathers.

## Questions for Rereading, Discussing, Connecting, and Writing

### REREADING

1. Some profiles of individuals are positive in tone; the text is somehow appreciative of its subject. Others can be negative, and such an argument can be made for John Earle's profile of an antiquary. As you read, what words or phrases contribute to this sense of negative criticism?

2. For a text written more than three-and-a-half centuries ago, "An Antiquary" sounds relatively up-to-date—but with a few important exceptions. Pick out the words that are, like cheese to a Dutchman, a little "moldy and worm-eaten" by time.

3. Note how densely packed the metaphors and references of age or antiquity are in this text. List all the items you find—and there are many—that refer to things "old" and "musty."

### DISCUSSING

4. We could simplify the antiquary's life and say that he is a collector. Discuss what collecting means in various walks of life, including yours. Do you collect things? Why—or why not?

5. The antiquary collects old things. We could say that he doesn't just read or write about history, he collects it. How does the author show a critical view of this occupation or habit?

### CONNECTING

6. The author's point of view is critical—or, at the very least, unsympathetic. Find other selections in this book that seem to be similar. Look at Swift (p. 296), for example, or Goya (p. 257), or the "Join, or Die" cartoon (p. 347). Note strategies for establishing a critical or negative tone in either written or visual texts.

7. The antiquary does not seem to enjoy the living pleasures of the world contemporary to him—but only the relics of the past. What works in this book would you introduce the antiquary to—a baseball boxscore, or an advertisement for a soft drink—in order to get him involved in current events, current enjoyments? How would you persuade him to give up his obsession with the past for the pleasures of the present?

WRITING

**8.** Decide whether you live in the past, the present, or the future—one more than the others, all three? Write an essay describing your life in terms of your outlook—back, around you, or forward?

**9.** Describe your life or someone else's in terms of your, or their, possessions. If someone saw what you own, what would they guess about you?

**10.** Profiling people involves as much analysis of surroundings as it does the person being portrayed. Try to profile a real or imagined person only in terms of habits or daily tasks, without actually describing the person's personality or appearance or occupation.

*Alexander Hesler*

# Photograph of Abraham Lincoln (1857)

Photograph by Alexander Hesler, taken in Chicago on February 28, 1857

## Questions for Rereading, Discussing, Connecting, and Writing

### Rereading

1. This photograph was taken three years before Lincoln ran for President. What elements in the photograph surprise you? Does Lincoln *look* like a future President? Are there hints of greatness that you can discover in Lincoln's posture or face?

2. What single feature of this photograph is most interesting to you? Remember to look not only at Lincoln but his clothing, his posture, and the overall quality of the photograph itself.

3. The photographer recalled that Lincoln looked *too neat* when Lincoln appeared for the photo session. What signs of informality can you detect that the photographer may have added to the scene?

### Discussing

4. Running for President is a great undertaking. If you were advising someone running for President today, what qualities would you suggest he or she borrow from Lincoln? Can those qualities be seen in this photo, or in "The Gettysburg Address"?

5. Could Lincoln or someone like him run for President today? Some might say that a candidate must be handsome (and rich) to win. Consider whether this statement is true, and whether Lincoln could be called a "serious candidate" if he were alive today.

### Connecting

6. Abraham Lincoln is considered by most of us to be a great man. What other individuals in this book can you call great men or great women? What contributes most to their greatness—some inner qualities they possess or their being in the right place at the right time? Or is it a combination of these and other factors?

7. Compare this photograph to the other photos in the book—the Vietnam photo (p. 287), the Lange photo (p. 215), the film stills (p. 32). Argue that the photograph is more powerful than either words or paintings in conveying truth. Show how our modern society seems to value the photograph so highly.

WRITING

**8.** Write an essay that focuses on two elements of the photograph—for example, Lincoln's clothing, or his facial expression—and explain how these two features seem to capture the essence of what you know about Abraham Lincoln.

**9.** Imagine you are Lincoln's media consultant; you are preparing him for an important speech. What would be your advice on how to look, how to act? What would you change that you see in the photograph?

**10.** Imagine you are a photographer in Lincoln's day and that you wish to have a day with the President to take photos of him. Write Lincoln a letter describing your desire to see him, and try to persuade him to let you come to the White House for a day.

*Abraham Lincoln*

# Address at the Dedication of the Gettysburg National Cemetery (1863)

*F*our score and seven years ago our fathers brought forth on this continent, a new nation, conceived in Liberty, and dedicated to the proposition that all men are created equal.

Now we are engaged in a great civil war, testing whether that nation, or any nation so conceived and so dedicated, can long endure. We are met on a great battle-field of that war. We have come to dedicate a portion of that field, as a final resting place for those who here gave their lives that that nation might live. It is altogether fitting and proper that we should do this.

But, in a larger sense, we can not dedicate—we can not consecrate—we can not hallow—this ground. The brave men, living and dead, who struggled here, have consecrated it, far above our poor power to add or detract. The world will little note, nor long remember what we say here, but it can never forget what they did here. It is for us the living, rather, to be dedicated here to the unfinished work which they who fought here have thus far so nobly advanced. It is rather for us to be here dedicated to the great task remaining before us—that from these honored dead we take increased devotion to that cause for which they gave the last full measure of devotion—that we here highly resolve that these dead shall not have died in vain—that this nation, under God, shall have a new birth of freedom—and that government of the people, by the people, for the people, shall not perish from the earth.

## Questions for Rereading, Discussing, Connecting, and Writing

### Rereading

1. The writer must always indicate a sense of time in his or her writing. The reader usually finds this sense of time in verb tenses. How does Lincoln achieve a comprehensive sense of time as you read from paragraph to paragraph?

2. Why is the first paragraph so memorable, so famous? "Fame" can rest on not only what words mean and do; ease of memorization can also contribute to a text's fame.

3. Transitions like the "but" that begins paragraph 3 signal a change in point of view. Define the "switch" Lincoln makes in terms of the address's meaning.

### Discussing

4. Discuss the familiarity of the Gettysburg Address and consider if that knowledge is connected more to memorization than to understanding.

5. The "Pledge of Allegiance" is another text with which many of us are familiar. Are there other texts that many of us know—or know about? Discuss the reasons why these texts are learned or studied today.

6. If each of us could assign the world one text to memorize and understand, what would it be?

### Connecting

7. "Devotion" is a theme in Lincoln's address. Compare this devotion to the kind LeSueur (p. 84) writes of—and to the "devotion" of Darwin's (p. 75) survival of the fittest. What does each author see in the human spirit?

8. War and death can separate humans from their environment; they can also make humans value their environments more highly. Define how tragedy in LeSueur (p. 84), Goya (p. 257), and the Vietnam photograph (p. 287) can change how we view our relationship with the world.

### Writing

9. Select one sentence from Lincoln's address and enlarge it, elaborating upon it as if you were to give a second Gettysburg address in the same general spirit as Lincoln's.

**10.** Define the probable listeners of the address, and create their probable responses to Lincoln. How, for example, would a general reply? How, for example, would a soldier's widow reply?

**11.** What public event in your lifetime seems to require—or should have required—a great public speech? Write a brief essay about that subject, and perhaps write a second version in the form of a speech.

*Emily Collins*

# Reminiscences of Emily Collins *(1881)*

*I* was born and lived almost forty years in South Bristol, Ontario County—one of the most secluded spots in Western New York; but from the earliest dawn of reason I pined for that freedom of thought and action that was then denied to all womankind. I revolted in spirit against the customs of society and the laws of the State that crushed my aspirations and debarred me from the pursuit of almost every object worthy of an intelligent, rational mind. But not until that meeting at Seneca Falls in 1848, of the pioneers in the cause, gave this feeling of unrest form and voice, did I take action. Then I summoned a few women in our neighborhood together and formed an Equal Suffrage Society, and sent petitions to our Legislature; but our efforts were little known beyond our circle, as we were in communication with no person or newspaper. Yet there was enough of wrong in our narrow horizon to rouse some thought in the minds of all.

In those early days a husband's supremacy was often enforced in the rural districts by corporeal chastisement, and it was considered by most people as quite right and proper—as much so as the correction of refractory children in like manner. I remember in my own neighborhood a man who was a Methodist class-leader and exhorter, and one who was esteemed a worthy citizen, who, every few weeks, gave his wife a beating with his horsewhip. He said it was necessary, in order to keep her in subjection, and because she scolded so much. Now this wife, surrounded by six or seven little children, whom she must wash, dress, feed, and attend to day and night, was obliged to spin and weave cloth for all the garments of the family. She had to milk the cows, make butter and cheese, do all the cooking, washing, making, and mending for the family, and, with the pains of maternity forced upon her every eighteen months, was whipped by her pious husband, "because she scolded." And pray, why should he not have chastised her? The laws made it his privilege—and the Bible, as interpreted, made it his duty. It is true, women repined at their hard lot; but it was thought to be fixed by a divine decree, for "The man shall rule over thee," and "Wives, be subject to your husbands," and "Wives, submit yourselves unto your husbands as unto the Lord," caused them to consider their fate inevitable, and to feel that it would be contravening God's law to resist it. It is ever thus; where Theology enchains the soul, the Tyrant enslaves the body. But can any one, who has any knowledge of the laws that govern our being—of heredity and pre-natal influences—be astonished that our jails and prisons are filled with criminals, and our hospitals with sickly specimens of humanity? As long as the mothers of the race are subject to such unhappy conditions, it can never be materially improved. Men exhibit some common sense in breeding all animals except those of their own species.

All through the Anti-Slavery struggle, every word of denunciation of the wrongs of the Southern slave, was, I felt, equally applicable to the wrongs of my own sex. Every argument for the emancipation of the colored man, was equally one for that of woman; and I was surprised that all Abolitionists did not see the similarity in the condition of the two classes. I read, with intense interest, everything that indicated an awakening of public or private thought to the idea that woman did not occupy her rightful position in the organization of society; and, when I read the lectures of Ernestine L. Rose and the writings of Margaret Fuller, and found that other women entertained the same thoughts that had been seething in my own brain, and realized that I stood not alone, how my heart bounded with joy! The arguments of that distinguished jurist, Judge Hurlburt, encouraged me to hope that men would ultimately see the justice of our cause, and concede to women their natural rights.

I hailed with gladness any aspiration of women toward an enlargement of their sphere of action. . . .

But, it was the proceedings of the Convention, in 1848, at Seneca Falls, that first gave a direction to the efforts of the many women, who began to feel the degradation of their subject condition, and its baneful effects upon the human race. They then saw the necessity for associated action, in order to obtain the elective franchise, the only key that would unlock the doors of their prison. I wrote to Miss Sarah C. Owen, Secretary of the Women's Protective Union, at Rochester, as to the line of procedure that had been proposed there. In reply, under date of October 1, 1848, she says:

Your letter has just reached me, and with much pleasure I reply to the echo of inquiry, beyond the bounds of those personally associated with us in this enterprise. It is indeed encouraging to hear a voice from South Bristol in such perfect unison with our own.

Possibly, extracts from my next letter to Miss Owen, dated Oct. 23, 1848, will give you the best idea of the movement:

> I should have acknowledged the receipt of yours of the 1st inst. earlier, but wished to report somewhat of progress whenever I should write. Our prospects here are brightening. Every lady of any worth or intelligence adopts unhesitatingly our view, and concurs in our measures. On the 19th inst. we met and organized a Woman's Equal Rights Union. Living in the country, where the population is sparse, we are consequently few; but hope to make up in zeal and energy for our lack of numbers. We breathe a freer, if not a purer atmosphere here among the mountains, than do the dwellers in cities,—have more independence,—are less subject to the despotism of fashion, and are less absorbed with dress and amusements. . . . A press entirely devoted to our cause seems indispensable. If there is none such, can you tell me of any paper that advocates our claims more warmly than the *North Star?* A lecturer in the field would be most desirable; but how to raise funds to sustain one is the question. I never really wished for Aladdin's lamp till now. Would to Heaven that women could be persuaded to use the funds they acquire by their sewing-circles and fairs, in trying to raise their own condition above that of "infants, idiots, and lunatics," with whom our statutes class them, instead of spending the money in decorating their churches, or sustaining a clergy, the most of whom are striving to rivet the chains still closer that bind, not only our own sex, but the oppressed of every class and color.
>
> The elective franchise is now the one object for which we must labor; that once attained, all the rest will be easily acquired. Moral Reform and Temperance Societies may be multiplied *ad infinitum,* but they have about the same effect upon the evils they seek to cure, as clipping the top of a hedge would have toward extirpating it. Please forward me a copy of the petition for suffrage. We will engage to do all we can, not only in our own town, but in the adjoining ones of Richmond, East Bloomfield, Canandaigua, and Naples. I have promises of aid from people of influence in obtaining signatures. In the meantime we wish to disseminate some able work upon the enfranchisement of women. We wish to present our Assemblyman elect, whoever he may be, with some work of this kind, and solicit his candid attention to the subject. People are more willing to be convinced by the calm perusal of an argument, than in a personal discussion. . . .

Our Society was composed of some fifteen or twenty ladies, and we met once in two weeks, in each other's parlors, alternately, for discussion and interchange of ideas. I was chosen President; Mrs. Sophia Allen, Vice-President; Mrs. Horace Pennell, Treasurer; and one of several young ladies who were members was Secretary. Horace Pennell, Esq., and his wife were two of our most earnest helpers. We drafted a petition to the Legislature to grant women the right of suffrage, and obtained the names of sixty-two of the most intelligent people, male and female, in our own and adjoining towns, and sent it to our Representative in Albany. It was received by the Legislature as something absurdly ridiculous, and laid upon the table. We introduced the question into the Debating Clubs, that were in those days such popular institutions in the rural districts, and in every way sought to agitate the subject. I found a great many men, especially those of the better class, disposed to accord equal rights to our sex. And, now, as the highest tribute that I can pay to the memory of a husband, I may say that during our companionship of thirty-five years, I was most cordially sustained by mine, in my advocacy of equal rights to women. Amongst my own sex, I found too many on whom ages of repression had wrought their natural effect, and whose ideas and aspirations were narrowed down to the confines of "woman's sphere," beyond whose limits it was not only impious, but infamous to tread. "Woman's sphere" *then*, was to discharge the duties of a housekeeper, ply the needle, and teach a primary or ladies' school. From press, and pulpit, and platform, she was taught that "to be unknown was her highest praise," that "dependence was her best protection," and "her weakness her sweetest charm." She needed only sufficient intelligence to comprehend her husband's superiority, and to obey him in all things. It is not surprising, then, that I as often heard the terms "strong-minded" and "masculine" as opprobrious epithets used against progressive women, by their own sex as by the other; another example only of the stultifying effect of subjection, upon the mind, exactly paralleled by the Southern slaves, amongst many of whom the strongest term of contempt that could be used was *"Free Nigger."* Our Equal Rights Association continued to hold its meetings for somewhat over a year, and they were at last suspended on account of bad weather and the difficulty of coming together in the country districts. We, however, continued to send petitions to the Legislature for the removal of woman's disabilities.

From 1858 to 1869 my home was in Rochester, N. Y. There, by brief newspaper articles and in other ways, I sought to influence public sentiment in favor of this fundamental reform. In 1868 a Society was organized there for the reformation of abandoned women. At one of its meetings I endeavored to show how futile all their efforts would be, while women, by the laws of the land, were made a subject class; that only by enfranchising woman and permitting her a more free and lucrative range of employments, could they hope to suppress the "social evil." My remarks produced some agitation in the meeting and some newspaper criticisms. In Rochester, I found many pioneers in the cause of Woman Suffrage, and from year to year we petitioned our Legislature for it.

Since 1869 I have been a citizen of Louisiana. Here, till recently, political troubles engrossed the minds of men to the exclusion of every other consideration. They glowed with fiery indignation at being, themselves, deprived of the right of suffrage, or at having their votes annulled, and regarded it as an intolerable outrage; yet, at the same time, they denied it to all women, many of whom valued the elective franchise as highly, and felt as intensely, as did men, the injustice that withheld it from them. In 1879, when the Convention met to frame a new Constitution for the State, we strongly petitioned it for an enlargement of our civil rights and for the ballot. Mrs. Elizabeth L. Saxon was indefatigable in her efforts, and went before the Convention in person and plead our cause. But the majority of the members thought there were cogent reasons for not granting our petitions; but they made women eligible to all school offices—an indication that Louisiana will not be the last State in the Union to deny women their inalienable rights.

*Questions for Rereading,*
*Discussing, Connecting, and Writing*

### REREADING

1. A *thesis* is a text's central idea. Autobiographical writing like Collins' text displays a thesis about the writer's life and times. As you read this selection, note what thesis is developed in the first paragraph and then expanded on in the following paragraphs. Quote directly from Collins.

2. After finding Collins' thesis, note or list several images that Collins employs to illustrate it. Other forms of "evidence" to make a point are the question and the quotation. Note these, and decide which, if any, you consider especially effective in furthering Collins' argument.

3. "Autobiography" is self-portraying for the sake of showing the audience what life is—or was—for example, for an individual and a society. As you read, notice how Collins advances these two portraits—self and society—and try to decide which she handles more successfully. Do you think Collins was more concerned with the "self" or "society"? Why?

## DISCUSSING

4. "Suffrage" is a significant term in Collins' memoirs—and in the history of the American nation. What is suffrage, and can you find definitions and examples of it in this selection?

5. Whether a piece of autobiography is successful or not very often hinges on whether we believe the author's view of him- or herself. Does Collins seem like a real person? Why, or why not? Discuss what qualities you do or do not recognize in Emily Collins.

## CONNECTING

6. Collins describes the relationship between women's rights and the slavery question then under intense public debate in America. How are these issues related—and do you find, overall, greater comparisons or contrasts between the two? Look at the selections of Mill (p. 262), Lincoln, (p. 66), Sojourner Truth (p. 259), LeSueur (p. 84), and Syfers (p. 330) for supporting information.

7. How would a visual artist—a Cassatt (p. 82), or Goya (p. 257), or Eisenstein (p. 32)—portray the person, society, and issues that Emily Collins writes of? Describe some possible visual treatments of these issues.

## WRITING

8. Write an essay in response to Collins, in which you argue that some or all of her grievances have been taken care of.

9. Write an argument which supports Collins for our time—and which points out the continued injustices of society.

10. Consider yourself a subject of an autobiographical piece on your role as a man or woman in our society. Try to define this role and to point out how this role may change in the future.

Charles Darwin

# Struggle for Existence (1859)

*Its bearing on natural selection—The term used in a wide sense—Geometrical ratio of increase—Rapid increase of naturalised animals and plants—Nature of the checks in increase—Competition universal—Effects of climate—Protection from the number of individuals—Complex relations of all animals and plants throughout nature—Struggle for life most severe between individuals and varieties of the same species: often severe between species of the same genus—The relation of organism to organism the most important of all relations.*

Before entering on the subject of this chapter, I must make a few preliminary remarks, to show how the struggle for existence bears on Natural Selection. It has been seen in the last chapter that amongst organic beings in a state of nature there is some individual variability: indeed I am not aware that this has ever been disputed. It is immaterial for us whether a multitude of doubtful forms be called species or subspecies or varieties; what rank, for instance, the two or three hundred doubtful forms of British plants are entitled to hold, if the existence of any well-marked varieties be admitted. But the mere existence of individual variability and of some few well-marked varieties, though necessary as the foundation for the work, helps us but little in understanding how species arise in nature. How have all those exquisite adaptations of one part of the organisation to another part, and to the conditions of life, and of one organic being to another being, been perfected? We see these beautiful co-adaptations most plainly in the woodpecker and the mistletoe; and only a little less plainly in the humblest parasite which clings to the hairs of a quadruped or feathers of a bird; in the structure of the beetle which dives through the water; in the plumed seed which is wafted by the gentlest breeze; in short, we see beautiful adaptations everywhere and in every part of the organic world.

Again, it may be asked, how is it that varieties, which I have called incipient species, become ultimately converted into good and distinct species which in most cases obviously differ from each other far more than do the varieties of the same species? How do those groups of species, which constitute what are called distinct genera, and which differ from each other more than do the species of the same genus, arise? All these results, as we shall more fully see in the next chapter, follow from the struggle for life. Owing to this struggle, variations, however slight and from whatever cause proceeding, if they be in any degree profitable to the individuals of a species, in their infinitely complex relations to other organic beings and to their physical conditions of life, will tend to the preservation of such individuals, and will generally be inherited by the offspring. The offspring, also, will thus have a better chance of surviving, for, of the many individuals of any species which are periodically born, but a small number can survive. I have called this principle, by which each slight variation, if useful, is preserved, by the term Natural Selection, in order to mark its relation to man's power of selection. But the expression often used by Mr. Herbert Spencer of the Survival of the Fittest is more accurate, and is sometimes equally convenient. We have seen that man by selection can certainly produce great results, and can adapt organic beings to his own uses, through the accumulation of slight but useful variations, given to him by the hand of Nature. But Natural Selection, as we shall hereafter see, is a power incessantly ready for action, and is as immeasurably superior to man's feeble efforts, as the works of Nature are to those of Art.

We will now discuss in a little more detail the struggle for existence. In my future work this subject will be treated, as it well deserves, at greater length. The elder De Candolle and Lyell have largely and philosophically shown that all organic beings are exposed to severe competition. In regard to plants, no one has treated this subject with more spirit and ability than W. Herbert, Dean of Manchester, evidently the result of his great horticultural knowledge. Nothing is easier than to admit in words the truth of the universal struggle for life, or more difficult—at least I have found it so—than constantly to bear this conclusion in mind. Yet unless it be thoroughly engrained in the mind, the whole economy of nature, with every fact on distribution, rarity, abundance, extinction, and variation, will be dimly seen or quite misunderstood. We behold the face of nature bright with gladness, we often see superabundance of food; we do not see or we forget, that the birds which are idly singing round us mostly live on insects or seeds, and are thus constantly destroying life; or we forget how largely these songsters, or their eggs, or their nestlings, are destroyed by birds and beasts of prey; we do not always bear in mind, that, though food may be now superabundant, it is not so at all seasons of each recurring year.

## The Term, Struggle for Existence, Used in a Large Sense

I should premise that I use this term in a large and metaphorical sense including dependence of one being on another, and including (which is more important) not only the life of the individual, but success in leaving progeny. Two canine animals, in a time of dearth, may be truly said to struggle with each other which shall get food and live. But a plant on the edge of a desert is said to struggle for life against the drought, though more properly it should be said to be dependent on the moisture. A plant which annually produces a thousand seeds, of which only one of an average comes to maturity, may be more truly said to struggle with the plants of the same and other kinds which already clothe the ground. The mistletoe is dependent on the apple and a few other trees, but can only in a far-fetched sense be said to struggle with these trees, for, if too many of these parasites grow on the same tree, it languishes and dies. But several seedling mistletoes, growing close together on the same branch, may more truly be said to struggle with each other. As the mistletoe is disseminated by birds, its existence depends on them; and it may methodically be said to struggle with other fruit-bearing plants, in tempting the birds to devour and thus disseminate its seeds. In these several senses, which pass into each other, I use for convenience' sake the general term of Struggle for Existence.

## Geometrical Ratio of Increase

A struggle for existence inevitably follows from the high rate at which all organic beings tend to increase. Every being, which during its natural lifetime produces several eggs or seeds, must suffer destruction during some period of its life, and during some season or occasional year, otherwise, on the principle of geometrical increase, its numbers would quickly become so inordinately great that no country could support the product. Hence, as more individuals are produced than can possibly survive, there must in every case be a struggle for existence, either one individual with another of the same species, or with the individuals of distinct species, or with the physical conditions of life. It is the doctrine of Malthus applied with manifold force to the whole animal and vegetable kingdoms; for in this case there can be no artificial increase of food, and no prudential restraint from marriage.

Although some species may be now increasing, more or less rapidly, in numbers, all cannot do so, for the world would not hold them.

There is no exception to the rule that every organic being naturally increases at so high a rate, that, if not destroyed, the earth would soon be covered by the progeny of a single pair. Even slow-breeding man has doubled in twenty-five years, and at this rate, in less than a thousand years, there would literally not be standing-room for his progeny. Linnæus has calculated that if an annual plant produced only two seeds—and there is no plant so unproductive as this—and their seedlings next year produced two, and so on, then in twenty years there should be a million plants. The elephant is reckoned the slowest breeder of all known animals, and I have taken some pains to estimate its probable minimum rate of natural increase; it will be safest to assume that it begins breeding when thirty years old, and goes on breeding till ninety years old, bringing forth six young in the interval, and surviving till one hundred years old; if this be so, after a period of from 740 to 750 years there would be nearly nineteen million elephants alive, descended from the first pair.

But we have better evidence on this subject than mere theoretical calculations, namely, the numerous recorded cases of the astonishingly rapid increase of various animals in a state of nature, when circumstances have been favourable to them during two or three following seasons. Still more striking is the evidence from our domestic animals of many kinds which have run wild in several parts of the world; if the statements of the rate of increase of slow-breeding cattle and horses in South America, and latterly in Australia, had not been well authenticated, they would have been incredible. So it is with plants; cases could be given of introduced plants which have become common throughout whole islands in a period of less than ten years. Several of the plants, such as the cardoon and a tall thistle, which are now the commonest over the whole plains of La Plata, clothing square leagues of surface almost to the exclusion of every other plant, have been introduced from Europe; and there are plants which now range in India, as I hear from Dr. Falconer, from Cape Comorin to the Himalaya, which have been imported from America since its discovery. In such cases, and endless others could be given, no one supposes, that the fertility of the animals or plants has been suddenly and temporarily increased in any sensible degree. The obvious explanation is that the conditions of life have been highly favourable, and that there has consequently been less destruction of the old and young, and that nearly all the young have been enabled to breed.

Their geometrical ratio of increase, the result of which never fails to be surprising, simply explains their extraordinarily rapid increase and wide diffusion in their new homes.

In a state of nature almost every full-grown plant annually produces seed, and amongst animals there are very few which do not annually pair. Hence we may confidently assert, that all plants and animals are tending to increase at a geometrical ratio,—that all would rapidly stock every station in which they could anyhow exist,—and that this geometrical tendency to increase must be checked by destruction at some period of life. Our familiarity with the larger domestic animals tends, I think, to mislead us: we see no great destruction falling on them, but we do not keep in mind that thousands are annually slaughtered for food, and that in a state of nature an equal number would have somehow to be disposed of.

The only difference between organisms which annually produce eggs or seeds by the thousand, and those which produce extremely few, is, that the slow-breeders would require a few more years to people, under favourable conditions, a whole district, let it be ever so large. The condor lays a couple of eggs and the ostrich a score, and yet in the same country the condor may be the more numerous of the two; the Fulmar petrel lays but one egg, yet it is believed to be the most numerous bird in the world. One fly deposits hundreds of eggs, and another, like the hippobosca, a single one; but this difference does not determine how many individuals of the two species can be supported in a district. A large number of eggs is of some importance to those species which depend on a fluctuating amount of food, for it allows them rapidly to increase in number. But the real importance of a large number of eggs or seeds is to make up for much destruction at some period of life; and this period in the great majority of cases is an early one. If an animal can in any way protect its own eggs or young, a small number may be produced, and yet the average stock be fully kept up; but if many eggs or young are destroyed, many must be produced, or the species will become extinct. It would suffice to keep up the full number of a tree, which lived on an average for a thousand years, if a single seed were produced once in a thousand years, supposing that this seed were never destroyed, and could be ensured to germinate in a fitting place. So that, in all cases, the average number of any animal or plant depends only indirectly on the number of its eggs or seeds.

In looking at Nature, it is most necessary to keep the foregoing considerations always in mind—never to forget that every single organic being may be said to be striving to the utmost to increase in numbers; that each lives by a struggle at some period of its life; that heavy destruction inevitably falls either on the young or old, during each generation or at recurrent intervals. Lighten any check, mitigate the destruction ever so little, and the number of the species will almost instantaneously increase to any amount.

## Questions for Rereading, Discussing, Connecting, and Writing

### Rereading

1. The collection of subtitles that follows the title of this selection is a feature of prose not often seen in our time. These subtitles are a form of outline for the reader who wishes to scan the content of a chapter or section. After you have read this selection, go back and locate each subtitle as it occurs in the selection as a valuable way of *reviewing* a complex text.

2. Darwin has been praised among science writers for his sensitivity to not only the general principles of science but to the particular beauties of our world. As you read or reread, locate, and note some of Darwin's uses of the specific world—the details of our environment with which he illustrates his important theory.

### Discussing

3. Darwin and evolution are still controversial subjects. Discuss what evolution is—and how other views of man dispute the concept of evolution.

4. In this selection from *The Origin of Species,* Darwin asserts that the struggle for existence exists among beings—and also among beings and their environment. Which of these two relationships seems more relevant to mankind? Or do they seem equally important in our time?

5. Darwin carried out much of his research during a worldwide voyage on the HMS *Beagle* and not in the confines of a biology lab. Discuss what kinds of voyages you would like to make, and for what scientific reasons.

### Connecting

6. As a portrait of mankind, Darwin's work paints a rather grim picture of all of us in competition for food, water, shelter, and progeny. His portrait is really of *all* mankind. Contrast this large-scale portrait with others found in this book that also deal with the struggle for existence.

7. "Science writing" often deals with closely detailed accounts of discovery, or how something works or is done. Look at the Sacks (p. 92) and Walton (p. 188) selections and argue which writer, you believe, does the best job at close analysis, and why.

Writing

8. Darwin uses the woodpecker and mistletoe as examples of the struggle for existence, and how each has adapted in order to survive. Choose a plant or animal that you think has found an especially interesting way to survive either its own kind or its environment, and describe this method of survival in either analytical or story form.

9. Darwin's last sentence seems to be a warning. Read it as a caution against "fooling with Mother Nature" and then write as if a mistake has been made—and we are suffering from the consequences of an "instantaneous increase" in a species' numbers.

*Mary Cassatt*

# Girl Arranging Her Hair (1886)

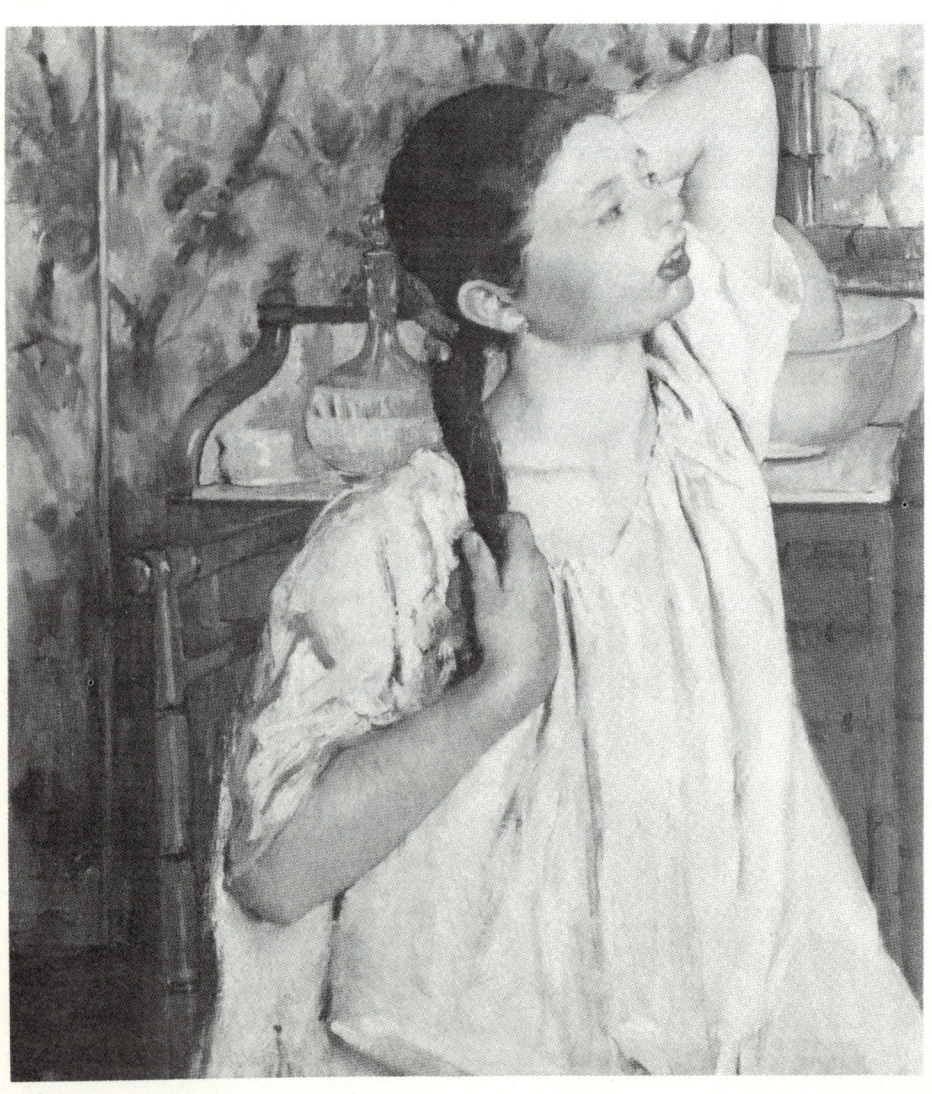

## Questions for Rereading, Discussing, Connecting, and Writing

### Rereading

**1.** A large curve dominates the composition of this painting. Try to find this shape, and consider how it unifies the main subject of the painting.

**2.** Artists can make viewers imagine more than they see on the page or canvas. What does Cassatt make us see to the right of the painting? Are there hints in the painting of what exists beyond the edges of her work?

### Discussing

**3.** What details in the painting suggest simplicity—in both the girl and her surroundings? Simplicity, some thinkers suggest, is the soul of great art.

**4.** Mary Cassatt is one of only a handful of woman artists considered to be among those that will be studied and enjoyed forever. What factors may have led to this scarcity of great woman artists? And can there be any definition of woman's art offered based on Cassatt and others—Mary Wollstonecraft Shelley (p. 192), for example, or Dorothea Lange (p. 215)?

### Connecting

**5.** A writer's attitude toward his or her subject is usually easy to discover—read Sojourner Truth's (p. 259) or John Mill's selections (p. 262), for example. But Cassatt's is more difficult. Compare her painting to Degas' and speculate on which artist is less attached, less involved with his or her subject. Point to specific elements in the paintings.

**6.** Imagine a roundtable of authors and artists on the subject of women, women's rights, women's abilities. You might select three or four women from this book—and add several men, either real or imagined—and write a dialogue using several points of view to establish conflict or debate.

### Writing

**7.** Why is this girl arranging her hair? Speculate on what comes next in the day of this girl.

**8.** Some critics suggest that this girl of Cassatt's painting is unattractive. Argue for or against this statement, using *your* definition of beauty.

**9.** Transform this nineteenth century girl into a twentieth century girl. Show us how different this scene would be as she prepares her hair.

Meridel LeSueur

# Women on the Breadlines (1932)

*I* am sitting in the city free employment bureau. It's the woman's section. We have been sitting here now for four hours. We sit here every day, waiting for a job. There are no jobs. Most of us have had no breakfast. Some have had scant rations for over a year. Hunger makes a human being lapse into a state of lethargy, especially city hunger. Is there any place else in the world where a human being is supposed to go hungry amidst plenty without an outcry, without protest, where only the boldest steal or kill for bread, and the timid crawl the streets, hunger like the beak of a terrible bird at the vitals?

We sit looking at the floor. No one dares think of the coming winter. There are only a few more days of summer. Everyone is anxious to get work to lay up something for that long siege of bitter cold. But there is no work. Sitting in the room we all know it. That is why we don't talk much. We look at the floor dreading to see that knowledge in each other's eyes. There is a kind of humiliation in it. We look away from each other. We look at the floor. It's too terrible to see this animal terror in each other's eyes.

So we sit hour after hour, day after day, waiting for a job to come in. There are many women for a single job. A thin sharp woman sits inside the wire cage looking at a book. For four hours we have watched her looking at that book. She has a hard little eye. In the small bare room there are half a dozen women sitting on the benches waiting. Many come and go. Our faces are all familiar to each other, for we wait here everyday.

This is a domestic employment bureau. Most of the women who come here are middle-aged, some have families, some have raised their families and are now alone, some have men who are out of work. Hard times and the man leaves to hunt for work. He doesn't find it. He drifts on. The woman probably doesn't hear from him for a long time. She expects it. She isn't surprised. She struggles alone to feed the many mouths. Sometimes she gets help from the charities. If she's clever she can get herself a good living from the charities, if she's naturally a lick-spittle, naturally a little docile and cunning. If she's proud then she starves silently, leaving her children to find work, coming home after a day's searching to wrestle with her house, her children.

Some such story is written on the faces of all these women. There are young girls too, fresh from the country. Some are made brazen too soon by the city. There is a great exodus of girls from the farms into the city now. Thousands of farms have been vacated completely in Minnesota. The girls are trying to get work. The prettier ones can get jobs in the stores when there are any, or waiting on table, but these jobs are only for the attractive and the adroit, the others, the real peasants have a more difficult time.

Bernice sits next me. She is a large Polish woman of thirty-five. She has been working in peoples' kitchens for fifteen years or more. She is large, her great body in mounds, her face brightly scrubbed. She has a peasant mind and finds it hard even yet to understand the maze of the city where trickery is worth more than brawn. Her blue eyes are not clever but slow and trusting. She suffers from loneliness and lack of talk. When you speak to her her face lifts and brightens as if you had spoken through a great darkness and she talks magically of little things, as if the weather were magic or tells some crazy tale of her adventures on the city streets, embellishing them in bright colors until they hang heavy and thick like some peasant embroidery. She loves the city anyhow. It's exciting to her, like a bazaar. She loves to go shopping and get a bargain, hunting out the places where stale bread and cakes can be had for a few cents. She likes walking the streets looking for men to take her to a picture show. Sometimes she goes to five picture shows in one day, or she sits through one the entire day until she knows all the dialogue by heart.

She came to the city a young girl from a Wisconsin farm. The first thing that happened to her a charlatan dentist took out all her good shining teeth and the fifty dollars she had saved working in a canning factory. After that she met men in the park who told her how to look out for herself, corrupting her peasant mind, teaching her to mistrust everyone. Sometimes now she forgets to mistrust everyone and gets taken in. They taught her to get what she could for nothing, to count her change, to go back if she found herself cheated, to demand her rights.

She lives alone in little rooms. She bought seven dollars worth of second-hand furniture eight years ago. She rents a room for perhaps three dollars a month in an attic, sometimes in a cold house. Once the house where she stayed was condemned and everyone else moved out and she lived there all winter alone on the top floor. She spent only twenty-five dollars all winter.

She wants to get married but she sees what happens to her married friends, being left with children to support, worn out before their time. So she stays single. She is virtuous. She is slightly deaf from hanging out clothes in winter. She has done people's washings and cooking for fifteen years and in that time she saved thirty dollars. Now she hasn't worked steady for a year and she has spent the thirty dollars. She dreamed of having a little house or a houseboat perhaps with a spot of ground for a few chickens. This dream she will never realize.

She has lost all her furniture now along with the dream. A married friend whose husband is gone gives her a bed for which she pays by doing a great deal of work for the woman. She comes here every day now sitting bewildered, her pudgy hands folded in her lap. She is hungry. Her great flesh has begun to hang in folds. She has been living on crackers. Sometimes a box of crackers lasts a week. She has a friend who's a baker and he sometimes steals the stale loaves and brings them to her.

A girl we have seen every day all summer went crazy yesterday at the Y. W. She went into hysterics, stamping her feet and screaming.

She hadn't had work for eight months. "You've got to give me something," she kept saying. The woman in charge flew into a rage that probably came from days and days of suffering on her part, because she is unable to give jobs, having none. She flew into a rage at the girl and there they were facing each other in a rage both helpless, helpless. This woman told me once that she could hardly bear the suffering she saw, hardly hear it, that she couldn't eat sometimes and had nightmares at night.

So they stood there the two women in a rage, the girl weeping and the woman shouting at her. In the eight months of unemployment she had gotten ragged, and the woman was shouting that she would not send her out like that. "Why don't you shine your shoes," she kept scolding the girl, and the girl kept sobbing and sobbing because she was starving.

"We can't recommend you like that," the harassed Y.W.C.A. woman said, knowing she was starving, unable to do anything. And the girls and the women sat docilely their eyes on the ground, ashamed to look at each other, ashamed of something.

Sitting here waiting for a job, the women have been talking in low voices about the girl Ellen. They talk in low voices with not too much pity for her, unable to see through the mist of their own torment. "What happened to Ellen?" one of them asks. She knows the answer already. We all know it.

A young girl who went around with Ellen tells about seeing her last evening back of a cafe downtown outside the kitchen door, kicking, showing her legs so that the cook came out and gave her some food and some men gathered in the alley and threw small coin on the ground for a look at her legs. And the girl says enviously that Ellen had a swell breakfast and treated her to one too, that cost two dollars.

A scrub woman whose hips are bent forward from stooping with hands gnarled like water soaked branches clicks her tongue in disgust. No one saves their money, she says, a little money and these foolish young things buy a hat, a dollar for breakfast, a bright scarf. And they do. If you've ever been without money, or food, something very strange happens when you get a bit of money, a kind of madness. You don't care. You can't remember that you had no money before, that the money will be gone. You can remember nothing but that there is the money for which you have been suffering. Now here it is. A lust takes hold of you. You see food in the windows. In imagination you eat hugely; you taste a thousand meals. You look in windows. Colours are brighter; you buy something to dress up in. An excitement takes hold of you. You know it is suicide but you can't help it. You must have food, dainty, splendid food and a bright hat so once again you feel blithe, rid of that ratty gnawing shame.

"I guess she'll go on the street now," a thin woman says faintly and no one takes the trouble to comment further. Like every commodity now the body is difficult to sell and the girls say you're lucky if you get fifty cents.

It's very difficult and humiliating to sell one's body.

Perhaps it would make it clear if one were to imagine having to go out on the street to sell, say, one's overcoat. Suppose you have to sell your coat so you can have breakfast and a place to sleep, say, for fifty cents. You decide to sell your only coat. You take it off and put it on your arm. The street, that has before been just a street, now becomes a mart, something entirely different. You must approach someone now and admit you are destitute and are now selling your clothes, your most intimate possessions. Everyone will watch you talking to the stranger showing him your overcoat, what a good coat it is. People will stop and watch curiously. You will be quite naked on the street. It is even harder to try and sell one's self, more humiliating. It is even humiliating to try and sell one's labour. When there is no buyer.

The thin woman opens the wire cage. There's a job for a nursemaid, she says. The old gnarled women, like old horses, know that no one will have them walk the streets with the young so they don't move. Ellen's friend gets up and goes to the window. She is unbelievably jaunty. I know she hasn't had work since last January. But she has a flare of life in her that glows like a tiny red flame and some tenacious thing, perhaps only youth, keeps it burning bright. Her legs are thin but the runs in her old stockings are neatly mended clear down her flat shank. Two bright spots of rouge conceal her palor. A narrow belt is drawn tightly around her thin waist, her long shoulders stoop and the blades show. She runs wild as a colt hunting pleasure, hunting sustenance.

It's one of the great mysteries of the city where women go when they are out of work and hungry. There are not many women in the bread line. There are no flop houses for women as there are for men, where a bed can be had for a quarter or less. You don't see women lying on the floor at the mission in the free flops. They obviously don't sleep in the jungle or under newspapers in the park. There is no law I suppose against their being in these places but the fact is they rarely are.

Yet there must be as many women out of jobs in cities and suffering extreme poverty as there are men. What happens to them? Where do they go? Try to get into the Y.W. without any money or looking down at heel. Charities take care of very few and only those that are called "deserving." The lone girl is under suspicion by the virgin women who dispense charity.

I've lived in cities for many months broke, without help, too timid to get in bread lines. I've known many women to live like this until they simply faint on the street from privations, without saying a word to anyone. A woman will shut herself up in a room until it is taken away from her, and eat a cracker a day and be as quiet as a mouse so there are no social statistics concerning her.

I don't know why it is, but a woman will do this unless she has dependents, will go for weeks verging on starvation, crawling in some hole, going through the streets ashamed, sitting in libraries, parks, going for days without speaking to a living soul like some exiled beast; keeping the runs mended in her stockings, shut up in terror in her own misery, until she becomes too supersensitive and timid to even ask for a job.

Bernice says even strange men she has met in the park have sometimes, that is in better days, given her a loan to pay her room rent. She has always paid them back.

In the afternoon the young girls, to forget the hunger and the deathly torture and fear of being jobless, try and pick up a man to take them to a ten-cent show. They never go to more expensive ones, but they can always find a man willing to spend a dime to have the company of a girl for the afternoon.

Sometimes a girl facing the night without shelter will approach a man for lodging. A woman always asks a man for help. Rarely another woman. I have known girls to sleep in men's rooms for the night, on a pallet without molestation, and given breakfast in the morning.

It's no wonder these young girls refuse to marry, refuse to rear children. They are like certain savage tribes, who, when they have been conquered refuse to breed.

Not one of them but looks forward to starvation, for the coming winter. We are in a jungle and know it. We are beaten, entrapped. There is no way out. Even if there were a job, even if that thin acrid woman came and gave everyone in the room a job for a few days, a few hours, at thirty cents an hour, this would all be repeated tomorrow, the next day and the next.

Not one of these women but knows, that despite years of labour there is only starvation, humiliation in front of them.

Mrs. Grey, sitting across from me is a living spokesman for the futility of labour. She is a warning. Her hands are scarred with labour. Her body is a great puckered scar. She has given birth to six children, buried three, supported them all alive and dead, bearing them, burying them, feeding them. Bred in hunger they have been spare, susceptible to disease. For seven years she tried to save her boy's arm from amputation, diseased from tuberculosis of the bone. It is almost too suffocating to think of that long close horror of years of child bearing, child feeding, rearing, with the bare suffering of providing a meal and shelter.

Now she is fifty. Her children, economically insecure, are drifters. She never hears of them. She doesn't know if they are alive. She doesn't know if she is alive. Such subtleties of suffering are not for her. For her the brutality of hunger and cold, the bare bone of life. That is enough. These will occupy a life. Not until these are done away with can those subtle feelings that make a human being be indulged.

She is lucky to have five dollars ahead of her. That is her security. She has a tumour that she will die of. She is thin as a worn dime with her tumour sticking out of her side. She is brittle and bitter. Her face is not the face of a human being. She has borne more than it is possible for a human being to bear. She is reduced to the least possible denominator of human feelings.

It is terrible to see her little bloodshot eyes like a beaten hound's, fearful in terror.

We cannot meet her eyes. When she looks at any of us we look away. She is like a woman drowning and we turn away. We must ignore those eyes that are surely the eyes of a person drowning, doomed. She doesn't cry out. She goes down decently. And we all look away.

The young ones know though. I don't want to marry. I don't want any children. So they all say. No children. No marriage. They arm themselves alone, keep up alone. The man is helpless now. He cannot provide. If he propagates he cannot take care of his young. The means are not in his hands. So they live alone. Get what fun they can. The life risk is too horrible now. Defeat is too clearly written on it.

So we sit in this room like cattle, waiting for a nonexistent job, willing to work to the farthest atom of energy, unable to work, unable to get food and lodging, unable to bear children; here we must sit in this shame looking at the floor, worse than beasts at a slaughter.

It is appalling to think that these women sitting so listless in the room may work as hard as it is possible for a human being to work, may labour night and day, like Mrs. Gray wash street cars from midnight to dawn and offices in the early evening, scrubbing for fourteen and fifteen hours a day, sleeping only five hours or so, doing this their whole lives, and never earn one day of security, having always before them the pit of the future. The endless labour, the bending back, the water soaked hands, earning never more than a week's wages, never having in their hands more life than that.

It's not the suffering, not birth, death, love that the young reject, but the suffering of endless labour without dream, eating the spare bread in bitterness, a slave without the security of a slave.

*Questions for Rereading, Discussing, Connecting, and Writing*

## REREADING

1. The collective "we" as the subject of writing is rare, relative to "I" or "they" or "she" or "he." As you read, try to determine just who "we" is in LeSueur's essay. Does this "we" change as you read?

2. An anecdote is a brief story used to illustrate a general point. Note anecdotes as you read. Which is the most impressive, and why?

3. How is the audience convinced that the characters in this essay are really "down and out"? Point or note specific details in your reading that are particularly vivid to you.

## Discussing

4. "Looking for a job" does not seem like a promising subject for a memorable essay. But making a common situation also *universal* is a key to effective writing. How does LeSueur make the common seem especially universal?

5. Our daily lives—the common events, the common places, the common people—are all, as one writer wrote, we have to work with. Discuss how this "commonality" in our writing can appeal to the reader.

6. "Humiliation," "suffering," "bitterness"—these are some of LeSueur's terms for the fate of the jobless. Discuss how some or all of these feelings have been experienced in our own daily lives—and discuss how we deal with them. Is writing about them one way of dealing with them?

## Connecting

7. LeSueur's emotions are clearly expressed. Find other selections for this emotional content—Truth, for example (p. 259)—and others that lack emotional content—Darwin, for example (p. 75). When is emotion appropriate in our writing?

8. Is Cassatt's "Girl Arranging Her Hair" (p. 82) waiting for a job? Why, or why not?

9. LeSueur's piece can be read as *the raising of a question.* What other texts raise questions? And what texts *provide answers*—to these questions and other questions?

## Writing

10. Write about a time of bitterness or disappointment in your life. If it was shared with others, use "we" as the subject.

11. Continue the story of Bernice, or the story of Ellen or Mrs. Grey. Or tell their stories as if they lived today, waiting for a job.

12. Analyze the employment situation today. Is it different from that of LeSueur's day? Could she write as negative a piece today as 60 years ago?

Oliver Sacks

# Hands (1986)

Madeleine J. was admitted to St. Benedict's Hospital near New York City in 1980, her sixtieth year, a congenitally blind woman with cerebral palsy, who had been looked after by her family at home throughout her life. Given this history, and her pathetic condition—with spasticity and athetosis, i.e., involuntary movements of both hands, to which was added a failure of the eyes to develop—I expected to find her both retarded and regressed.

She was neither. Quite the contrary: she spoke freely, indeed eloquently (her speech, mercifully, was scarcely affected by spasticity), revealing herself to be a high-spirited woman of exceptional intelligence and literacy.

'You've read a tremendous amount,' I said. 'You must be really at home with Braille.'

'No, I'm not,' she said. 'All my reading has been done for me—by talking-books or other people. I can't read Braille, not a single word. I can't do *anything* with my hands—they are completely useless.'

She held them up, derisively. 'Useless godforsaken lumps of dough—they don't even feel part of me.'

I found this very startling. The hands are not usually affected by cerebral palsy—at least, not essentially affected: they may be somewhat spastic, or weak, or deformed, but are generally of considerable use (unlike the legs, which may be completely paralysed—in that variant called Little's disease, or cerebral diplegia).

Miss J.'s hands were *mildly* spastic and athetotic, but her sensory capacities—as I now rapidly determined—were completely intact: she immediately and correctly identified light touch, pain, temperature, passive movement of the fingers. There was no impairment of elementary sensation, as such, but, in dramatic contrast, there was the profoundest impairment of perception. She could not recognise or identify anything whatever—I placed all sorts of objects in her hands, including one of my own hands. She could not identify—and she did not explore; there were no active 'interrogatory' movements of her hands—they were, indeed, as inactive, as inert, as useless, as 'lumps of dough.'

This is very strange, I said to myself. How can one make sense of all this? There is no gross sensory 'deficit.' Her hands would seem to have the potential of being perfectly good hands—and yet they are not. Can it be that they are functionless—'useless'—because she had never used them? Had being 'protected,' 'looked after,' 'babied' since birth prevented her from the normal exploratory use of the hands which all infants learn in the first months of life? Had she been carried about, had everything done for her, in a manner that had prevented her from developing a normal pair of hands? And if this were the case—it seemed far-fetched, but was the only hypothesis I could think of—could she now, in her sixtieth year, acquire what she should have acquired in the first weeks and months of life?

Was there any precedent? Had anything like this ever been described—or tried? I did not know, but I immediately thought of a possible parallel—what was described by Leont'ev and Zaporozhets in their book *Rehabilitation of Hand Function* (Eng. tr. 1960). The condition they were describing was quite different in origin: they described a similar 'alienation' of the hands in some two hundred soldiers following massive injury and surgery—the injured hands felt 'foreign,' 'lifeless,' 'useless,' 'stuck on,' despite elementary neurological and sensory intactness. Leont'ev and Zaporozhets spoke of how the 'gnostic systems' that allow 'gnosis,' or perceptive use of the hands, to take place, could be 'dissociated' in such cases as a consequence of injury, surgery and the weeks- or months-long hiatus in the use of the hands that followed. In Madeleine's case, although the phenomenon was identical—'uselessness,' 'lifelessness,' 'alienation'—it was lifelong. She did not need just to recover her hands, but to discover them—to acquire them, to achieve them—for the first time: not just to regain a dissociated gnostic system, but to construct a gnostic system she had never had in the first place. Was this possible?

The injured soldiers described by Leont'ev and Zaporozhets had normal hands before injury. All they had to do was to 'remember' what had been 'forgotten,' or 'dissociated,' or 'inactivated,' through severe injury. Madeleine, in contrast, had no repertoire of memory for she had never used her hands—and she felt she *had* no hands— or arms either. She had never fed herself, used the toilet by herself, or reached out to help herself, always leaving it for others to help her. She had behaved, for sixty years, as if she were a being without hands.

This then was the challenge that faced us: a patient with perfect elementary sensations in the hands, but, apparently, no power to integrate these sensations to the level of perceptions that were related to the world and to herself; no power to say, 'I perceive, I recognise, I will, I act,' so far as her 'useless' hands went. But somehow or other (as Leont'ev and Zaporozhets found with their patients), we had to get her to act and to use her hands actively, and, we hoped, in so doing, to achieve integration: 'The integration is in the action,' as Roy Campbell said.

Madeleine was agreeable to all this, indeed fascinated, but puzzled and not hopeful. 'How *can* I do anything with my hands,' she asked, 'when they are just lumps of putty?'

'In the beginning is the deed,' Goethe writes. This may be so when we face moral or existential dilemmas, but not where movement and perception have their origin. Yet here too there is always something sudden: a first step (or a first word, as when Helen Keller said 'water'), a first movement, a first perception, a first impulse—total, 'out of the blue,' where there was nothing, or nothing with sense before. 'In the beginning is the impulse.' Not a deed, not a reflex, but an 'impulse,' which is both more obvious and more mysterious than either . . . We could not say to Madeleine 'Do it!' but we might hope for an impulse; we might hope for, we might solicit, we might even provoke one . . .

I thought of the infant as it reached for the breast. 'Leave Madeleine her food, as if by accident, slightly out of reach on occasion,' I suggested to her nurses. 'Don't starve her, don't tease her, but show less than your usual alacrity in feeding her.' And one day it happened—what had never happened before: impatient, hungry, instead of waiting passively and patiently, she reached out an arm, groped, found a bagel, and took it to her mouth. This was the first use of her hands, her first manual act, in sixty years, and it marked her birth as a 'motor individual' (Sherrington's term for the person who emerges through acts). It also marked her first manual perception, and thus her birth as a complete 'perceptual individual.' Her first perception, her first recognition, was of a bagel, or 'bagelhood'—as Helen Keller's first recognition, first utterance, was of water ('waterhood').

After this first act, this first perception, progress was extremely rapid. As she had reached out to explore or touch a bagel, so now, in her new hunger, she reached out to explore or touch the whole world. Eating led the way—the feeling, the exploring, of different foods, containers, implements, etc. 'Recognition' had somehow to be achieved by a curiously roundabout sort of inference or guesswork, for having been both blind and 'handless' since birth, she was lacking in the simplest internal images (whereas Helen Keller at least had tactile images). Had she not been of exceptional intelligence and literacy, with an imagination filled and sustained, so to speak, by the images of others, images conveyed by language, by the *word*, she might have remained almost as helpless as a baby.

A bagel was recognised as round bread, with a hole in it; a fork as an elongated flat object with several sharp lines. But then this preliminary analysis gave way to an immediate intuition, and objects were instantly recognised as themselves, as immediately familiar in character and 'physiognomy,' were immediately recognised as unique, as 'old friends.' And this sort of recognition, not analytic, but synthetic and immediate, went with a vivid delight, and a sense that she was discovering a world full of enchantment, mystery and beauty.

The commonest objects delighted her—delighted her and stimulated a desire to reproduce them. She asked for clay and started to make models: her first model, her first sculpture, was of a shoehorn, and even this, somehow imbued with a peculiar power and humour, with flowing, powerful, chunky curves reminiscent of an early Henry Moore.

And then—and this was within a month of her first recognitions —her attention, her appreciation, moved from objects to people. There were limits, after all, to the interest and expressive possibilities of things, even when transfigured by a sort of innocent, ingenuous and often comical genius. Now she needed to explore the human face and figure, at rest and in motion. To be 'felt' by Madeleine was a remarkable experience. Her hands, only such a little while ago inert, doughy, now seemed charged with a preternatural animation and sensibility. One was not merely being recognised, being scrutinised, in a way more intense and searching than any visual scrutiny, but being 'tasted' and appreciated meditatively, imaginatively and aesthetically, by a born (a newborn) artist. They were, one felt, not just the hands of a blind woman exploring, but of a blind artist, a meditative and creative mind, just opened to the full sensuous and spiritual reality of the world. These explorations too pressed for representation and reproduction as an external reality.

She started to model heads and figures, and within a year was locally famous as the Blind Sculptress of St. Benedict's. Her sculptures tended to be half or three-quarters life size, with simple but recognisable features, and with a remarkably expressive energy. For me, for her, for all of us, this was a deeply moving, an amazing, almost a miraculous, experience. Who would have dreamed that basic powers of perception, normally acquired in the first months of life, but failing to be acquired at this time, could be acquired in one's sixtieth year? What wonderful possibilities of late learning, and learning for the handicapped, this opened up. And who could have dreamed that in this blind, palsied woman, hidden away, inactivated, over-protected all her life, there lay the germ of an astonishing artistic sensibility (unsuspected by her, as by others) that would germinate and blossom into a rare and beautiful reality, after remaining dormant, blighted, for sixty years?

## Postscript

The case of Madeleine J., however, as I was to find, was by no means unique. Within a year I had encountered another patient (Simon K.) who also had cerebral palsy combined with profound impairment of vision. While Mr K. had normal strength and sensation in his hands, he scarcely ever used them—and was extraordinarily inept at handling, exploring, or recognising anything. Now we had been alerted by Madeleine J., we wondered whether he too might not have a similar 'developmental agnosia'—and, as such, be 'treatable' in the same way. And, indeed, we soon found that what had been achieved with Madeleine could be achieved with Simon as well. Within a year he had become very 'handy' in all ways, and particularly enjoyed simple carpentry, shaping plywood and wooden blocks, and assembling them into simple wooden toys. He had no impulse to sculpt, to make reproductions—he was not a natural artist like Madeleine. But still, after a half-century spent virtually without hands, he enjoyed their use in all sorts of ways.

This is the more remarkable, perhaps, because he is mildly retarded, an amiable simpleton, in contrast to the passionate and highly gifted Madeleine J. It might be said that she is extraordinary, a Helen Keller, a woman in a million—but nothing like this could possibly be said of simple Simon. And yet the essential achievement—the achievement of hands—proved wholly as possible for him as for her. It seems clear that intelligence, as such, plays no part in the matter—that the sole and essential thing is *use*.

Such cases of development agnosia may be rare, but one commonly sees cases of acquired agnosia, which illustrate the same fundamental principle of use. Thus I frequently see patients with a severe 'glove-and-stocking' neuropathy, so-called, due to diabetes. If the neuropathy is sufficiently severe, patients go beyond feelings of numbness (the 'glove-and-stocking' feeling), to a feeling of complete nothingness or de-realisation. They may feel (as one patient put it) 'like a basket-case,' with hands and feet completely 'missing.' Sometimes they feel their arms and legs end in stumps, with lumps of 'dough' or 'plaster' somehow 'stuck on.' Typically this feeling of de-realisation, if it occurs, is absolutely sudden . . . and the return of reality, if it occurs, is equally sudden. There is, as it were, a critical (functional and ontological) threshold. It is crucial to get such patients to *use* their hands and feet—even, if necessary, to 'trick' them into so doing. With this there is apt to occur a sudden re-realisation—a sudden leap back into subjective reality and 'life' . . . provided there is sufficient physiological potential (if the neuropathy is total, if the distal parts of the nerves are quite dead, no such re-realisation is possible).

For patients with a severe but sub-total neuropathy, a modicum of use is literally vital, and makes all the difference between being a 'basket-case' and reasonably functional (with excessive use, there may be fatigue of the limited nerve function, and sudden de-realisation again).

It should be added that these subjective feelings have precise objective corelates: one finds 'electrical silence,' locally, in the muscles of the hands and feet; and, on the sensory side, a complete absence of any 'evoked potentials', at every level up to the sensory cortex. As soon as the hands and feet are re-realised, with use, there is a complete reversal of the physiological picture.

A similar feeling of deadness and unrealness, is described above in Chapter Three, 'The Disembodied Lady.'

*Questions for Rereading, Discussing, Connecting, and Writing*

REREADING

1. The author of this essay is a neurologist. A term like *clinical psychologist* probably makes us expect a certain kind of writing. As you read, note what terms or phrases fulfill your expectations about the essay—and what features surprise you.

2. Occasionally, taking notes or writing down questions as we read a difficult piece of writing can help us comprehend special languages outside our usual daily vocabularies. After reading "Hands" reread and note words you

d a dictionary to understand. Then go to a dictionary and write brief definitions for those words that puzzle you.

3. As you read, note where you believe the writing of this essay really began. In the author's experiences recorded in the essay, which occurred first, which second, and so on? Do they occur in this order in the finished essay, or has the author reorganized them?

## Discussing

4. Madeleine J. is an elderly woman with a handicap that is eventually overcome. Discuss what handicaps can mean in our lives, and ways you may know of overcoming them.

5. The author uses Helen Keller as an example of a person overcoming a great hurdle in her life. Recall what parts of Helen Keller's life you are familiar with, and how it compares—or contrasts—to Madeleine J.'s life.

6. Speculate on the importance of hunger or food—in this case, a breakfast bagel—in arousing what the author calls the "impulse" to use our hands, and even to defeat a handicap.

## Connecting

7. When the author asks himself "How can one make sense of all this?" he is asking a question all writers face. The answers to Sacks' question could be "close observation" and "experimentation." What other selections in this book also provide one or both of these answers?

8. Madeleine J. is vividly profiled by the author. Compare your impression of her with other elderly figures portrayed in this book—for example, Mrs. Grey in the LeSueur essay (see p. 84) and the old people in the Kingston selection (see p. 154). What can you suggest are the possible advantages—and disadvantages—of our growing old?

## Writing

9. Blindness affects millions of persons. Imagine, in writing, the world of the blind.

10. With a partner as your guide, close your eyes and take a short walk in a familiar or unfamiliar (but always *safe*) area. Afterwards, describe your sensations, and how they differed from a normal walk with your eyes open.

11. "Hands" is a portrait of a person's sudden growth through the discovery of natural abilities. Keeping in mind the author's emphasis on *use*, write your own profile of someone using his or her abilities to create something memorable.

# Three

# *Journeys*

**W**riting isn't just a way to report on experience or knowledge or observation. Writing can also be a way to make experience meaningful—a tool for learning. The calculator, for example, helps us figure out our monthly expenses, or the best way to finance a college education. Without this tool, we might fumble along without ever getting to answers. Writing can be this kind of tool, too.

Often when we are asked to write we begin with the first thing that comes into our heads; we have no good idea of where we are going. We only know that we have to start somewhere and we have faith that we will eventually get to the end. We can look at this process of starting in the dark and getting into the light as "learning by writing." Ideas are put down on paper, and put in order, and supplemented by others, and bolstered by evidence. Titles are thought up, interesting beginnings, strong endings—all seem to "come to us" as we work our way through the writing task. We can see this task as a journey we take; language is the vehicle or the tool that allows us to discover meanings as we go.

The Chinese saying, "The journey of a thousand miles begins with a single step" applies very well to our reading as well as our writing. There has to be a starting point. In our reading, that starting point is a single word or image or mark that catches our eyes, our interest. In our writing, an idea can be a starting point, or a detail, or a single word that suggests the next word, and the next word, and the next word. If we were able to ask Homer why he wrote *The Odyssey*, he might reply, "to discover the meaning of discovery." We might reply, after looking at this chapter, that discovery has many meanings, not only for the adventurer, but for the writer of the adventure.

We usually think of discovery as grand, heroic, special. Adventure is something great people did in other times, other places, when the world still had secrets. We think of Marco Polo, journeying for years among the great unknown spaces of Asia, and returning to tell the fabulous details of that journey. Or we think of Ulysses, sailing into fantastic predicaments, escaping one only to fall into another. Monsters and madmen are not unusual features of such adventures. But even these heroes on a grand scale have something more to tell us than how to be heroes. Marco Polo, as a writer, spent years painstakingly recreating his journeys. It is not known whether he is, in fact, completely accurate about them—but we sense that he invested as much energy into his writing as he did in his travels. The halls of the great Chinese emperors described by Polo are as real as our own homes. Marco Polo used writing not only to recreate, but to make sense of a land so different from his own. The world was full of unknowns, and Marco Polo wished to make it all fit together. Homer, too, describes a great journey, while the reader (and the characters in the poem) learn the meanings of courage, and faith, and a place called home.

But discovery need not be of such grandiose proportions. The selections by Kingston and Orwell demonstrate that for many of us just figuring out what we must do each day is in itself a "journey" into taking that first step and the next step and the next. Kingston's journey is into dreams and the traditions of her race, while Orwell's journey takes him into a land of moral dilemma and apartness where language is difficult and guns are used to speak with.

Maps are not always available to us as we discover things. We can set off into the woods and use our intelligence and luck to get out again; in our writing, we can't always outline the journey and follow it step-by-step. We need to learn to trust how generative writing is: how putting things on paper generates more things, and out of these raw materials come ideas. We have learned something about our subject by seeing it in our own words; as we read our words, either for the first time or as we rewrite, we continue to discover better ways to make meanings clear. These "better ways" may be nothing more than changing the order of paragraphs and crossing out several words—but we are persuaded to make these changes because meanings have been found, and we want to make them discoverable for the reader.

The reader's journey will follow, of course, and while it is fun sometimes to throw monsters and madmen at the reader, we must still be sure that the journey of reading will ultimately yield the kind of learning found in the travels of our own pens or pencils across the empty page.

# Homer

# "New Coasts and Poseidon's Son," from Book Nine, The Odyssey (8th Century B.C.)

What of my sailing, then, from Troy?
What of those years
of rough adventure, weathered under Zeus?
The wind that carried west from Ilion
brought me to Ismaros, on the far shore,
a strongpoint on the coast of the Kikonês.
I stormed that place and killed the men who fought.
Plunder we took, and we enslaved the women,
to make division, equal shares to all—
but on the spot I told them: 'Back, and quickly!
Out to sea again!' My men were mutinous,
fools, on stores of wine. Sheep after sheep
they butchered by the surf, and shambling cattle,
feasting,—while fugitives went inland, running
to call to arms the main force of Kikonês.
This was an army, trained to fight on horseback
or, where the ground required, on foot. They came
with dawn over that terrain like the leaves
and blades of spring. So doom appeared to us,
dark word of Zeus for us, our evil days.
My men stood up and made a fight of it—
backed on the ships, with lances kept in play,
from bright morning through the blaze of noon
holding our beach, although so far outnumbered;
but when the sun passed toward unyoking time,
then the Akhaians, one by one, gave way.
Six benches were left empty in every ship
that evening when we pulled away from death.
And this new grief we bore with us to sea:
our precious lives we had, but not our friends.
No ship made sail next day until some shipmate

had raised a cry, three times, for each poor ghost
unfleshed by the Kikonês on that field.

Now Zeus the lord of cloud roused in the north
a storm against the ships, and driving veils
of squall moved down like night on land and sea.
The bows went plunging at the gust; sails
cracked and lashed out strips in the big wind.
We saw death in that fury, dropped the yards,
unshipped the oars, and pulled for the nearest lee:
then two long days and nights we lay offshore
worn out and sick at heart, tasting our grief,
until a third Dawn came with ringlets shining.
Then we put up our masts, hauled sail, and rested,
letting the steersmen and the breeze take over.

I might have made it safely home, that time,
but as I came round Malea the current
took me out to sea, and from the north
a fresh gale drove me on, past Kythera.
Nine days I drifted on the teeming sea
before dangerous high winds. Upon the tenth
we came to the coastline of the Lotos Eaters,
who live upon that flower. We landed there
to take on water. All ships' companies
mustered alongside for the mid-day meal.
Then I sent out two picked men and a runner
to learn what race of men that land sustained.
They fell in, soon enough, with Lotos Eaters,
who showed no will to do us harm, only
offering the sweet Lotos to our friends—

but those who ate this honeyed plant, the Lotos,
never cared to report, nor to return:
they longed to stay forever, browsing on
that native bloom, forgetful of their homeland.
I drove them, all three wailing, to the ships,
tied them down under their rowing benches,
and called the rest: 'All hands aboard;
come, clear the beach and no one taste
the Lotos, or you lose your hope of home.'
Filing in to their places by the rowlocks
my oarsmen dipped their long oars in the surf,
and we moved out again on our sea faring.

## Questions for Rereading, Discussing, Connecting, and Writing

### Rereading

1. Given as much reading as we do, we often have to settle for excerpts or isolated sections of larger works. This can place a strain upon our abilities to comprehend a piece of text. This section from *The Odyssey* is just such a case; as you jump into this long narrative epic, what do you bring with you to the reading? What do you know of Ulysses? What do you know of Troy? Zeus? the Lotos Eaters? Does this excerpt fit your expectations—or are you surprised at certain points? Consider how this reading has altered your view of the Homeric world—or if your knowledge has been reinforced.

2. What movement do you perceive or sense in your reading of this excerpt? What can be said to be the points of focus or foregrounding in your reading? If you were to provide a bare outline of this excerpt, what would be your major entries?

3. "The Lotos Eaters" is among the most famous of all the episodes in *The Odyssey*, yet of the approximately 6000 lines of the epic, this episode comprises less than 2 dozen. Speculate, upon rereading, whether this fame rests on the episode itself—or its place within the epic, or its relationship to the whole. Think of reasons to support either view.

### Discussing

4. Many of us have heard of Troy and the great battle fought there. But Homer's reference to Zeus, and the years "weathered under Zeus" can lead to a discussion of what the gods were to the ancient civilization of Greece, and what role Zeus plays in this excerpt. In the simplest terms, what were the gods to mankind—and what was mankind to the gods?

5. What incident angers Ulysses—who is telling his own tale at this point in the poem—and what principle or rule of conduct do you think this incident violates? Discuss conduct and responsibility among the men of this voyage, and point to evidence in this excerpt.

6. *The Odyssey*, like most ancient poetry, was performed, not read. Many times the oral performance would be accompanied by mimes or actors, who would illustrate and embellish upon the words of the speaker. Devise some dramatic illustrations for this excerpt involving two or three "actors," the simple props they would require, and the specific gestures needed to help make this excerpt not only an entertainment for its audience but a teaching device as well.

## Connecting

7. The excerpt ends with reference to "our sea faring." Compare this sea faring with the "rough adventures" of the Anglo-Saxon "seafarer" (p. 105).

8. Epic poetry seems to have passed out of the contemporary world, at least as a viable form of artistic expression. If you were to try to renew this form, what events in your life—or in the life of the nation or world—do you think might contain all the adventure needed for a new epic poem?

## Writing

9. The Lotos Eaters are perfectly silent. Give them a voice, and make a reader of your choice understand them.

10. Zeus, too, is silent, but it is he who brings down "doom" upon many of the Akhaians who sail with Ulysses. Let Zeus explain, in writing, his motives.

11. Is there a "sweet Lotos" in our time? If so, persuade us of its dangers.

*Anonymous*

# The Seafarer (7th or 8th Century)

A song I sing of my sea-adventure,
The strain of peril, the stress of toil,
Which oft I endured in anguish of spirit
Through weary hours of aching woe.
My bark was swept by the breaking seas;
Bitter the watch from the bow by night
As my ship drove on within sound of the rocks.
My feet were numb with the nipping cold,
Hunger sapped a sea-weary spirit,
And care weighed heavy upon my heart.
   Little the landlubber, safe on shore,
Knows what I've suffered in icy seas
Wretched and worn by the winter storms,
Hung with icicles, stung by hail,
Lonely and friendless and far from home.
In my ears no sound but the roar of the sea,
The icy combers, the cry of the swan;
In place of the mead-hall and laughter of men
My only singing the sea-mew's call,
The scream of the gannet, the shriek of the gull;
Through the wail of the wild gale beating the bluffs
The piercing cry of the ice-coated petrel,
The storm-drenched eagle's echoing scream.
In all my wretchedness, weary and lone,
I had no comfort of comrade or kin.
   Little indeed can he credit, whose town-life
Pleasantly passes in feasting and joy,
Sheltered from peril, what weary pain
Often I've suffered in foreign seas.
Night shades darkened with driving snow
From the freezing north, and the bonds of frost
Firm-locked the land, while falling hail,
Coldest of kernels, encrusted earth.
   Yet still, even now, my spirit within me
Drives me seaward to sail the deep,

To ride the long swell of the salt sea-wave.
Never a day but my heart's desire
Would launch me forth on the long sea-path,
Fain of far harbors and foreign shores.
Yet lives no man so lordly of mood,
So eager in giving, so ardent in youth,
So bold in his deeds, or so dear to his lord,
Who is free from dread in his far sea-travel,
Or fear of God's purpose and plan for his fate.
The beat of the harp, and bestowal of treasure,
The love of woman, and worldly hope,
Nor other interest can hold his heart
Save only the sweep of the surging billows;
His heart is haunted by love of the sea.
   Trees are budding and towns are fair,
Meadows kindle and all life quickens,
All things hasten the eager-hearted,
Who joyeth therein, to journey afar,
Turning seaward to distant shores.
The cuckoo stirs him with plaintive call,
The herald of summer, with mournful song,
Foretelling the sorrow that stabs the heart.
Who liveth in luxury, little he knows
What woe men endure in exile's doom.
   Yet still, even now, my desire outreaches,
My spirit soars over tracts of sea,
O'er the home of the whale, and the world's expanse.
Eager, desirous, the lone sprite returneth;
It cries in my ears and it urges my heart
To the path of the whale and the plunging sea.

## Questions for Rereading, Discussing, Connecting, and Writing

### REREADING

1. Poems in ancient cultures were composed before printing, and were both preserved and changed through countless oral presentations. Read "The Seafarer" aloud, and imagine the settings for such oral readings in the ancient culture of the Anglo-Saxons.

2. The sections that begin "Yet still, even now" describe the strange combination of emotion that always accompanies the seafaring man. What are these conflicting emotions, and how do they alternate as the poem's focus?

## Discussing

**3.** The excitement of a journey is often colored by expectations of the new and unknown. Discuss various journeys you have made, and how "The Seafarer" has captured some of that complex excitement.

**4.** Sea voyages, to judge from "The Seafarer," were lonely and dangerous undertakings. Is this danger gone now from exploration—or does it exist in different kinds of exploration?

**5.** Debate in groups the central ambivalence of the seafaring man. One side can take the pleasures of the life on land; the other can take the dangers and challenges of the voyage on the sea. Which way is the "better" way to live? How would the seafarer vote?

## Connecting

**6.** "The Seafarer" is called an elegy because it honors something—a way of life—in deep felt terms. What writing in this book can be called "honorings" of people, places, things, events? One example is Lincoln's Gettysburg Address (p. 66). Point to specific details in these works to support your choices.

**7.** The seafarer would fit many of our versions of what a hero is; but to many he lacks some essential qualities. Try to construct what the word "hero" means to you, gathering bits and pieces of your definition from selections in this book. Homer (p. 101), Markham (p. 35), and Mercator (p. 108) might provide starting points.

## Writing

**8.** After noting some of the detail relating to the world of the lonely ocean voyage, try to write a parallel piece—either prose or poetry—about a land journey. You might refer to Marco Polo for raw material; Homer, too, writes of the peculiar dangers of travel in strange lands.

**9.** As a translation of Anglo-Saxon, "The Seafarer" contains words that we may not often hear in common speech; "oft" in line 3 is one example. Translate "The Seafarer" into a contemporary American prose piece while retaining the dignity and vividness of this mid-twentieth century translation.

## Gerardus Mercator

# Map of the World (1569)

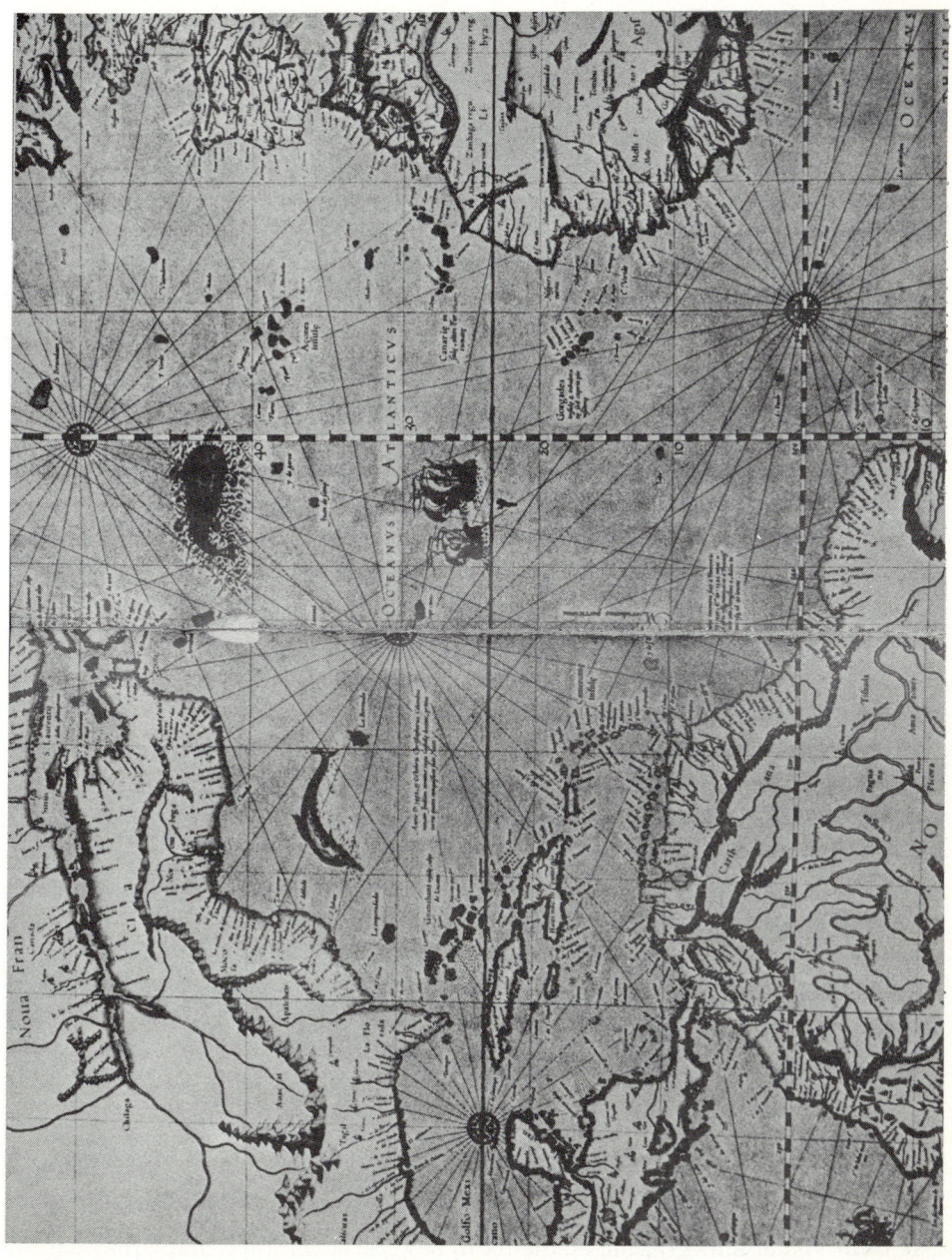

## Questions for Rereading, Discussing, Connecting, and Writing

### Rereading

1. "Reading a map" is a popular and accepted act, while "reading a painting" is not. As you read this map, note why "reading" is an accurate description of what we do as we sit in our cars, classrooms, or jets and unfold a map on our laps. What is being read? Is it the name on the street, or the word next to a mountain or lake? Or are we also reading the shape of a river, the arrangements of cities upon a great shoreline? How does map-reading resemble story-reading—and how does it differ?

2. Our present readings are always influenced by our past readings, and maps are no exception. Note any inaccuracies you find as you read this early map of the world. How do you know this map is inaccurate? Is this knowledge based on personal experience, observation, or the testimony of others?

### Discussing

3. The Mercator projection is now more than 400 years old, and it is still the most popular form of land representation on a flat "plane" or surface. What were some of the uses of maps—given the emphases found in Mercator's early map—in the sixteenth and seventeenth centuries?

4. According to a Mercator map (what we usually put on our walls), Greenland is about the size of South America, when, in fact, South America is nine times as large. How can such a distortion be accepted by navigators for centuries? You may want to investigate the special methods of navigation that "the readers of the sea" have used to explore the world.

### Connecting

5. Compare Mercator's map to the map of Africa on page 267. Has Africa changed or have our ways of making and reading maps changed? What might Mercator have added to the map of Africa, given the distinctive features of his world map of 1569?

6. Devise maps for some of the other selections in the chapter of "Journeys." Use both visual and graphic elements to suggest a "literary map" that we as readers could enjoy as we read the written texts.

## Writing

**7.** Select a map from any source and describe the process you believe went into its preparation.

**8.** Select another map from any source and use that map to write a narrative that a reader could recognize as having taken place within the borders of the map.

Marco Polo

# "The Imperial Palace of Kanbalu," from The Travels of Marco Polo (1295)

*Of the great and admirable palace of the grand khan, near to the city of Kanbalu.*

The grand khan usually resides during three months of the year, namely, December, January, and February, in the great city of Kanbalu, situated towards the north-eastern extremity of the province of Cathay; and here, on the southern side of the new city, is the site of his vast palace, the form and dimensions of which are as follows. In the first place is a square enclosed with a wall and deep ditch; each side of the square being eight miles in length, and having at an equal distance from each extremity an entrance-gate, for the concourse of people resorting thither from all quarters. Within this enclosure there is, on the four sides, an open space one mile in breadth, where the troops are stationed; and this is bounded by a second wall, enclosing a square of six miles, having three gates on the south side, and three on the north, the middle portal of each being larger than the other two, and always kept shut, excepting on the occasions of the emperor's entrance or departure. Those on each side always remain open for the use of common passengers. In the middle of each division of these walls is a handsome and spacious building, and consequently within the enclosure there are eight such buildings, in which are deposited the royal military stores; one building being appropriated to the reception of each class of stores. Thus, for instance, the bridles, saddles, stirrups, and other furniture serving for the equipment of cavalry, occupy one storehouse; the bows, strings, quivers, arrows, and other articles belonging to archery, occupy another; cuirasses, corselets, and other armour formed of leather, a third storehouse; and so of the rest. Within this walled enclosure there is still another, of great thickness, and its height is full twenty-five feet. The battlements or crenated parapets are all white. This also forms a square four miles in extent, each side being one mile, and it has six gates, disposed like those of the former enclosure. It contains in like manner eight large buildings, similarly arranged, which are appropriated to the wardrobe of the emperor. The spaces between the one wall and the other are ornamented with many handsome trees, and contain meadows in which are kept various kinds of beasts, such as stags, the animals that yield the musk, roe-bucks, fallow-deer, and others of the same class. Every interval between the walls, not occupied by buildings, is stocked in this manner. The pastures have abundant herbage. The roads across them being raised three feet above their level, and paved, no mud collects upon them, nor rain-water settles, but on the contrary runs off, and contributes to improve the vegetation. Within these walls, which constitute the boundary of four miles, stands the palace of the grand khan, the most extensive that has ever yet been known. It reaches from the northern to the southern wall, leaving only a vacant space (or court), where persons of rank and the military guards pass and repass. It has no upper floor, but the roof is very lofty. The paved foundation or platform on which it stands is raised ten spans above the level of the ground, and a wall of marble, two paces wide, is built on all sides, to the level of this pavement, within the line of which the palace is erected; so that the wall, extending beyond the ground plan of the building, and encompassing the whole, serves as a terrace, where those who walk on it are visible from without. Along the exterior edge of the wall is a handsome balustrade, with pillars, which the people are allowed to approach. The sides of the great halls and the apartments are ornamented with dragons in carved work and gilt, figures of warriors, of birds, and of beasts, with representations of battles. The inside of the roof is contrived in such a manner that nothing besides gilding and painting presents itself to the eye. On each of the four sides of the palace there is a grand flight of marble steps, by which you ascend from the level of the ground to the wall of marble which surrounds the building, and which constitute the approach to the palace itself. The grand hall is extremely long and wide, and admits of dinners being there served to great multitudes of people. The palace contains a number of separate chambers, all highly beautiful, and so admirably disposed that it seems impossible to suggest any improvement to the system of their arrangement. The exterior of the roof is adorned with a variety of colour, red, green, azure, and violet, and the sort of covering is so strong as to last for many years. The glazing of the windows is so well wrought and so delicate as to have the transparency of crystal. In the rear of the body of the palace there are large buildings containing several apartments, where is deposited the private property of the monarch, or his treasure in gold and silver bullion, precious stones, and pearls, and also his vessels of gold and silver plate. Here are likewise the apartments of his wives and concubines; and in this retired situation he despatches business with convenience, being free from every kind of interruption. On the other side of the grand palace, and opposite to that in which the emperor resides, is another palace, in every respect similar, appropriated to the residence of Chingis, his eldest son, at whose court are observed all the ceremonials belonging to that of his father, as the prince who is to succeed to the government of the empire. Not far from the palace, on the northern side, and about a bow-shot distance from the surrounding wall, is an artificial mount of earth, the height of which is full a hundred paces, and the circuit at the base about a mile. It is clothed with the most beautiful evergreen trees; for whenever his majesty receives information of a handsome tree growing in any place, he causes it to be dug up, with all its roots and the earth about them, and however large and heavy it may be, he has it transported by means of elephants to this mount, and adds it to the verdant collection. From this perpetual verdure it has acquired the appellation of the Green Mount. On its summit is erected an ornamental pavilion, which is likewise entirely green. The view of this altogether—the mount itself, the trees, and the building, form a delightful and at the same time a wonderful scene. In the northern quarter also, and equally within the precincts of the city, there is a large and deep excavation, judiciously formed, the earth from which supplied the material for raising the mount. It is furnished with water by a small rivulet, and has the appearance of a fish-pond, but its use is for watering the cattle. The stream passing from thence along an aqueduct, at the foot of the Green Mount, proceeds to fill another great and very deep excavation formed between the private palace of the emperor and that of his son Chingis; and the earth from hence equally served to increase the elevation of the mount. In this latter basin there is great store and variety of fish, from which the table of his majesty is supplied with any quantity that may be wanted. The stream discharges itself at the opposite extremity of the piece of water, and precautions are taken to prevent the escape of the fish by placing gratings of copper or iron at the places of its entrance and exit. It is stocked also with swans and other aquatic birds. From the one palace to the other there is a communication by means of a bridge thrown across the water. Such is the description of this great palace. We shall now speak of the situation and circumstances of the city of Tai-du.

## Questions for Rereading, Discussing, Connecting, and Writing

### Rereading

1. Marco Polo's writing is highly descriptive; he spends much effort on making the reader see what he sees. Note what sights seem to be the most impressive to Polo—what people, places, and things he wants us to see.

2. One way to retain information while reading is to take notes or highlight passages. Another way, when reading material that contains much information about size and relationships of space, is to construct rough maps or "blueprints." As you read or reread, draw a rough blueprint of the "great and admirable palace of the grand khan."

3. It is likely that one section of this description will be especially vivid to each reader. What section do you find most vivid? Try to discover the reasons for this vividness in both Marco Polo's power of description and in your own willingness to see and feel a particular feature of the palace.

### Discussing

4. Marco Polo has been the subject of many books, movies, and debates concerning—partly—the reality or fantasy of his journey. Did Marco Polo tell us the truth? Give evidence from any source, including your own intuition, to support your answer. Does this excerpt persuade you to believe Polo? *How* does it persuade you?

5. Writing about an exotic place—where your reader has surely not been—takes a certain kind of effort, since the reader does not share knowledge of this place with the writer. Such was Marco Polo's challenge. What methods in this excerpt do you think a writer can adopt in order to write clearly and vividly about a strange place?

### Connecting

6. The description of space is a crucial part of much good writing: letting the reader know where he or she *is*. Compare the "space writing" of Polo, Twain (p. 202), Woolf (p. 270), with the visual evidence of the Chartres Cathedral (p. 344), and try to choose which writer comes closest—and why—to being a "photographic" writer.

7. Kubla Khan's palace is a result of his great power. If the khan were to have read the selections in Chapter 5 on "Power and Justice," with which selection would he be most happy? Most unhappy? Why?

WRITING

8. As detailed as this piece is, Polo leaves many questions unanswered about life in and around the palace. Write questions to Polo about matters not attended to in this excerpt. Speculate on answers.

9. Even a humble home or apartment can be made to feel like a palace if it is lovingly, and carefully, described. Take your own favorite place and describe it as if it were one of the most wonderful places on earth.

10. What journey must you make some day—and what will finally convince you to take that first step?

*Virginia Reed*

# Letter on the Donner Party (1847)

                                                    Napa Vallie
                                                    California
                                                    May 16th 1847

**M**y Dear Cousan    May <sup>the</sup>16 1847

I take this oppertunity to write to you to let you now that we are all Well at presant and hope this letter may find you all well to  My dear Cousan I am a going to Write to you about our trubels geting to Callifornia; We had good luck til we come to big Sandy thare we lost our best yoak of oxons  we come to Brigers Fort & we lost another ox we sold some of our provisions & baut a yoak of Cows & oxen & they pursuaded us to take Hastings cut of over the salt plain  thay said it saved 3 Hondred miles, we went that road & we had to go through a long drive of 40 miles With out water or grass  Hastings said it was 40 but i think it was 80 miles  We traveld a day and night & a nother day and at noon pa went on to see if he coud find Water, he had not bin gone long till some of the oxen give out and we had to leve the Wagons and take the oxen on to water  one of the men staid with us and others went on with the cattel to water  pa was a coming back to us with Water and met the men & thay was about 10 miles from water pa said thay git to water that night, and the next day to bring the cattel back for the wagons any [and] bring some Water  pa got to us about noon the man that was with us took the horse and went on to water  We wated thare thought Thay would come we wated till night and We thought we start and walk to Mr doners wagons that night  we took what little water we had and some bread and started  pa caried Thomos and all the rest of us walk  we got to Donner and thay were all a sleep so we laid down on the ground we spred one shawl down we laid doun on it and spred another over us and then put the dogs on top it was the couldes night you most ever saw the wind blew and if it haden bin for the dogs we would have Frosen  as soon as it was day we went to Miss Donners  she said we could not walk to the Water and

117

if we staid we could ride in thare wagons to the spring so pa went on to the water to see why thay did not bring the cattel  when he got thare thare was but one ox and cow thare  none of the rest had got to water  Mr Donner come out that night with his cattel and braught his Wagons and all of us in  we staid thare a week and Hunted for our cattel and could not find them so some of the companie took thare oxons and went out and brout in one wagon and cashed the other tow and a grate manie things all but what we could put in one Wagon  we had to divied our propessions out to them to get them to carie them  We got three yoak with our oxe & cow so we [went] on that way a while and we got out of provisions and pa had to go on to callifornia for provisions  we could not get along that way, in 2 or 3 days after pa left we had to cash our wagon and take Mr. graves wagon and cash some more of our things  well we went on that way a while and then we had to get Mr Eddies Wagon  we went on that way awhile and then we had to cash all our our close except a change or 2 and put them in Mr Brins Wagon and Thomos & James rode the 2 horses and the rest of us had to walk, we went on that way a Whild and we come to a nother long drive of 40 miles and then we went with Mr Donner

  We had to Walk all the time we was a travling up the truckee river  we met that and 2 Indians that we had sent out for propessions to Suter Fort  thay had met pa, not fur from Suters Fort  he looked very bad  he had not ate but 3 times in 7 days and thes days with out any thing his horse was not abel to carrie him  thay give him a horse and he went on  so we cashed some more of our things all but what we could pack on one mule and we started Martha and James road behind the two Indians  it was a raing then in the Vallies and snowing on the montains so we went on that way 3 or 4 days tell we come to the big mountain or the Callifornia Mountain  the snow then was about 3 feet deep  thare was some wagons thare  thay said thay had atempted to cross and could not, well we thought we would try it so we started and thay started again with thare wagons  the snow was then way to the muels side  the farther we went up the deeper the snow got so the wagons could not go so thay packed thare oxons and started with us carring a child a piece and driving the oxon in snow up to thare wast  the mule Martha and the Indian was on was the best one so thay went and broak the road and that indian was the Pilot so we went on that way 2 miles and the mules kept faling down in the snow head formost and the Indian said he could not find the road  we stoped and let the Indian and man go on to hunt the road thay went on and found the road to the top of the mountain and come back and said they thought we could git over if it did not snow any more   well the Woman were all so tirder caring there Children that thay could not go over that night so we made a fire and got something to eat & ma spred down a bufalorobe & we all laid down on it & spred somthing over us & ma sit up by the fire & it snowed one foot on top of the bed so we got up in the morning & the snow was so deep we could not go over & we had to go back to the cabin & build more cabins & stay thare all Winter without Pa   we had not the first thing to eat   Ma maid arrangements for some cattel giving 2 for 1 in callifornia   we seldom thot of bread for we had not had any since [blot, words not readable] & the cattel was so poor thay could note hadley git up when thay laid down   we stoped thare the 4th of November & staid till March and what we had to eat i cant hardley tell you & we had that man & Indians to feed   well thay started over a foot and had to come back so thay made snow shoes and started again & and it come on a storme & thay had to come back   it would snow 10 days before it would stop thay wated tell it stoped & started again   I was a goeing with them & I took sick & could not go—thare was 15 started & thare was 7 got throw 5 Weman & 2 men   it come a storme and thay lost the road & got out of provisions & the ones that got throwe had to eat them that Died   not long after thay started we got out of provisions & had to put Martha at one cabin James at another   Thomas at another & Ma & Elizea & Milt Eliot & I dried up what littel meat we had and started to see if we could get across & had to leve the childrin   o Mary you may think that hard to leve theme with strangers & did not now wether we would see them again or not   we could hardle get a way from them but we told theme we would bring them Bread & then thay was willing to stay   we went & was out 5 days in the mountains   Elie giv out & had to go back   we went on a day longer   we had to lay by a day & make snow shows & we went on a while and coud not find the road & we had to turn back   I could go on verry well while i thout we wer giting along but as soone as we had to turn back i coud hadley git along but we got to the cabins that night   I froze one of my feet verry bad & that same night thare was the worst storme we had that winter & if we had not come back that night we would never got back   we had nothing to eat but ox hides   o Mary I would cry and wish I had what you all wasted Eliza had to go to Mr Graves cabin & we staid at Mr Breen   thay had meat all the time & we had to kill littel cash the dog & eat him   we ate his head and feet & hide & evry thing about him   o my Dear Cousin you dont now what trubel is   yet a many a time we had on the last thing a cooking and did not now wher the next would come from but there was awl wais some way provided

there was 15 in the cabon we was in and half of us had to lay a bed all the time  thare was 10 starved to death  there we was hadley abel to walk  we lived on litle cash a week and after Mr Breen would cook his meat we would take the bones and boil them 3 or 4 days at a time  ma went down to the other caben and got half a hide carried it in snow up to her wast

it snowed and would cover the cabin all over so we could not git out for 2 or 3 days  we would have to cut pieces of the loges in sied to make a fire with  I coud hardly eat the hides and had not eat anything 3 days  Pa stated out to us with providions and then came a storme and he could not go  he cash his provision and went back on the other side of the bay to get compana of men and the San Wakien got so hye he could not crose  well thay Made up a Compana at Suters Fort and sent out  we had not ate any thing for 3 days & we had onely a half a hide and we was out on top of the cabin and we seen them a coming

O my Dear Cousin you dont now how glad i was, we run and met them  one of them we knew  we had traveled with them on the road thay staid thare 3 days to recruet a little so we could go  thare was 20 started  all of us started and went a piece and Martha and Thomas giv out & so the men had to take them back  ma and Eliza James & I come on and o Mary that was the hades thing yet to come on and leiv them thar  did not now but what thay would starve to Death  Martha said well ma if you never see me again do the best you can  the men said thay could hadly stand it  it maid them all cry but they said it was better for all of us to go on for if we was to go back we would eat that much more from them  thay give them a littel meat and flore and took them back and we come on  we went over great hye mountain as strait as stair steps in snow up to our knees  litle James walk the hole way over all the mountain in snow up to his waist  he said every step he took he was a gitting nigher Pa and somthing to eat  the Bears took the provision the men had cashed and we had but very little to eat  when we had traveld 5 days travel we met Pa with 13 men going to the cabins  o Mary you do not nou how glad we was to see him  we had not seen him for months  we thought we woul never see him again  he heard we was coming and he made some seet cakes to give us  he said he would see Martha and Thomas the next day  he went to tow days what took us 5 days  some of the compana was eating from them that Died but

Thomas & Martha had not ate any  Pa and the men started with 12 people  Hiram O Miller Carried Thomas and Pa caried Martha and thay wer caught in [unreadable word] and thay had to stop Two days  it stormed so thay could not go and the Bears took their provision and thay weer 4 days without anything  Pa and Hiram and all the men started one of Donner boys  Pa a carring Martha Hiram caring Thomas and the snow was up to thare wast and it a snowing so thay could hadley see the way  they raped the chidlren up and never took them out for 4 days & thay had nothing to eat in all that time  Thomas asked for somthing to eat once  those that thay brought from the cabins some of them was not able to come and som would not come  Thare was 3 died and the rest eat them  thay was 10 days without any thing to eat but the Dead  Pa braught Thom and pady on to where we was  none of the men was abel to go  there feet was froze very bad so they was a nother Compana went and braught them all in  thay are all in from the Mountains now but five  they was men went out after them and was caught in a storm and had to come back  thare is another compana gone  thare was half got through that was stoped thare sent to their relief thare was but families got that all of them got  we was one

O Mary I have not wrote you half of the truble we have had but I hav Wrote you anuf to let you now that you dont now whattruble is but thank the Good god we have all got throw and the onely family that did not eat human flesh  we have left every thing but i dont cair for that  we have got through but Dont let this letter dishaten anybody and never take no cutofs and hury along as fast as you can

My Dear Cousin

We are all very well pleased with Callifornia partucularly with the climate  let it be ever so hot a day thare is all wais cool nights  it is a beautiful Country it is mostley in vallies it aut to be a beautiful Country to pay us for our trubel geting there  it is the greatest place for catle and horses you ever saw  it would Just suit Charley for he could ride down 3 or 4 horses a day and he could lern to be Bocarro that one who lases cattel  the spanards and Indians are the best riders i ever say thay have a spanish sadel and woden sturups and great big spurs the wheel of them is 5 inches in diameter and thay could not manage the Callifornia horses witout the spurs, thay wont go atol if they cant hear the spurs rattle  they have littel bells to them to make them rattle  thay blindfold the horses and then sadel them and git on them and then take the blindfole of and let run and if thay cant sit on thay tie themselves on and let them run as fast as they can and go out

to a band of bullluck and throw the reatter on a wild bullluck and but it around the horn of his sadel and he can hold it as long as he wants
 a nother Indian throws his reatter on its feet and throws them and when thay git take the reatter of of them they are very dangerous  they will run after you then hook there horses and run after any person thay see  thay ride from 80 to 100 miles a day & have some of the spanard have from 6 to 7000 head of horses and from 15 to 16000 head Cattel  we are all verry fleshey  Ma waies 10040 pon and still a gaing  I weigh 80  tel Henriet if she wants to get Married for to come to Callifornia  she can get a spanyard any time  that Eliza is a going to marrie a a spanyard by the name of Armeho and Eliza weighs 10070  We have not saw uncle Cadon yet but we have had 2 letters from him he is well and is a coming here as soon as he can  Mary take this letter to uncle Gurshon and to all tha i know to all of our neighbors and tell Dochter Meniel and every girl i know and let them read it  Mary kiss little Sue and Maryann for me and give my best love to all i know to uncle James and Lida and all the rest of the famila and to uncle Gurshon aunt Percilla and all the Children and to all of our neighbors and to all she knows
 so no more at present
 pa is yerbayan [Yerba Buena]

My Dear casons<br>Virginia Elizabeth B Reed

*Questions for Rereading,*
*Discussing, Connecting, and Writing*

REREADING

1. Spelling is a convention—a set of rules that we expect to be followed in our writing and reading. How does Virginia Reed's unconventional spelling affect your reading of her letter? Can you understand her meanings in spite of her spelling—or are their places in the letter that you feel defeat your attempts at understanding?

2. Reading a letter—rather than a story or newspaper—means reading something personal, genuine, or honest. Do you find Virginia Reed's letter "personal"—and, if so, what features make it personal? If the letter does not seem personal, point to features that led you to this conclusion.

DISCUSSING

3. The Donner Party's experiences in the California Sierra Mountains of 1846 form a chilling and memorable part of American history. Discuss what

you may have heard of this story, and what makes the Donner Party's experiences a significant part of American pioneer life.

4. The author calls this episode "our trubels getting to Callifornia"; choose one or two of these troubles that you find particularly vivid in her letter and discuss how such "trubels" may be a thing of the past—or could be repeated today.

## Connecting

5. The Donner Party story is one of survival. Find references in the Darwin selection (see p. 75) that seem relevant to the struggle Virginia Reed and her party underwent on their journey across the Sierras.

6. When Reed writes to her cousin "you dont now what truble is" she is speaking for her experiences in the mountains. But trouble can be different things to different people. Find other definitions of trouble in this chapter—Ulysses and the Lotos Eaters (p. 101), for example, Nunez and the blind in the Wells short story (p. 124), or "The Seafarer"'s loneliness (p. 105)—and consider how trouble can be treated in our writing as a way of dealing with difficult experiences.

## Writing

7. Write a letter to a cousin or family member in which you narrate and describe a difficult journey. Try to retain a personal voice and to achieve a sense of honesty and immediacy in the story you tell.

8. Imagine Reed's cousin writing back to her. What could this cousin have said, in writing, after reading a letter as full of action as this?

9. The lessons of travel are sometimes difficult to define. Try to define what lesson or lessons Virginia Reed may have learned while "getting to Callifornia."

*H. G. Wells*

# The Country of the Blind *(1913)*

*T*hree hundred miles and more from Chimborazo, one hundred from the snows of Cotopaxi, in the wildest wastes of Ecuador's Andes, there lies that mysterious mountain valley, cut off from the world of men, the Country of the Blind. Long years ago that valley lay so far open to the world that men might come at last through frightful gorges and over an icy pass into its equable meadows; and thither indeed men came, a family or so of Peruvian half-breeds fleeing from the lust and tyranny of an evil Spanish ruler. Then came the stupendous outbreak of Mindobamba, when it was night in Quito for seventeen days, and the water was boiling at Yaguachi and all the fish floating dying even as far as Guayaquil; everywhere along the Pacific slopes there were land-slips and swift thawings and sudden floods, and one whole side of the old Arauca crest slipped and came down in thunder, and cut off the Country of the Blind for ever from the exploring feet of men. But one of these early settlers had chanced to be on the hither side of the gorges when the world had so terribly shaken itself, and he perforce had to forget his wife and his child and all the friends and possessions he had left up there, and start life over again in the lower world. He started it again but ill, blindness overtook him, and he died of punishment in the mines; but the story he told begot a legend that lingers along the length of the Cordilleras of the Andes to this day.

He told of his reason for venturing back from that fastness, into which he had first been carried lashed to a llama, beside a vast bale of gear, when he was a child. The valley, he said, had in it all that the heart of man could desire—sweet water, pasture, and even climate, slopes of rich brown soil with tangles of a shrub that bore an excellent fruit, and on one side great hanging forests of pine that held the avalanches high. Far overhead, on three sides, vast cliffs of grey-green rock were capped by cliffs of ice; but the glacier stream came not to them but flowed away by the farther slopes, and only now and then huge ice masses fell on the valley side. In this valley it neither rained nor snowed, but the abundant springs gave a rich green pasture, that irrigation would spread over all the valley space. The settlers did well indeed there. Their beasts did well and multiplied, and but one thing marred their happiness. Yet it was enough to mar it greatly. A strange disease had come upon them, and had made all the children born to them there—and indeed, several older children also—blind. It was to seek some charm or antidote against this plague of blindness that he had with fatigue and danger and difficulty returned down the gorge. In those days, in such cases, men did not think of germs and infections but of sins; and it seemed to him that the reason of this affliction must lie in the negligence of these priestless immigrants to set up a shrine so soon as they entered the valley. He wanted a shrine—a handsome, cheap, effectual shrine—to be erected in the valley; he wanted relics and such-like potent things of faith, blessed objects and mysterious medals and prayers. In his wallet he had a bar of native silver for which he would not account; he insisted there was none in the valley with something of the insistence of an inexpert liar. They had all clubbed their money and ornaments together, having little need for such treasure up there, he said, to buy them holy help against their ill. I figure this dim-eyed young mountaineer, sunburnt, gaunt, and anxious, hat-brim clutched feverishly, a man all unused to the ways of the lower world, telling this story to some keen-eyed, attentive priest before the great convulsion; I can picture him presently seeking to return with pious and infallible remedies against that trouble, and the infinite dismay with which he must have faced the tumbled vastness where the gorge had once come out. But the rest of his story of mischances is lost to me, save that I know of his evil death after several years. Poor stray from that remoteness! The stream that had once made the gorge now bursts from the mouth of a rocky cave, and the legend his poor, ill-told story set going developed into the legend of a race of blind men somewhere "over there" one may still hear to-day.

And amidst the little population of that now isolated and forgotten valley the disease ran its course. The old became groping and purblind, the young saw but dimly, and the children that were born to them saw never at all. But life was very easy in that snow-rimmed basin, lost to all the world, with neither thorns nor briars, with no evil insects nor any beasts save the gentle breed of llamas they had lugged and thrust and followed up the beds of the shrunken rivers in the gorges up which they had come. The seeing had become purblind so gradually that they scarcely noted their loss. They guided the sightless youngsters hither and thither until they knew the whole valley marvellously, and when at last sight died out among them the race lived on. They had even time to adapt themselves to the blind control of fire, which they made carefully in stoves of stone. They were a simple strain of people at the first, unlettered, only slightly touched with the Spanish civilisation, but with something of a tradition of the arts of old Peru and of its lost philosophy. Generation followed generation. They forgot many things; they devised many things. Their tradition of the greater world they came from became mythical in colour and uncertain. In all things save sight they were strong and able, and presently the chance of birth and heredity sent one who had an original mind and who could talk and persuade among them, and then afterwards another. These two passed, leaving their effects, and the little community grew in numbers and in understanding, and met and settled social and economic problems that arose. Generation followed generation. Generation followed generation. There came a time when a child was born who was fifteen generations from that ancestor who went out of the valley with a bar of silver to seek God's aid, and who never returned. Thereabouts it chanced that a man came into this community from the outer world. And this is the story of that man.

He was a mountaineer from the country near Quito, a man who had been down to the sea and had seen the world, a reader of books in an original way, an acute and enterprising man, and he was taken on by a party of Englishmen who had come out to Ecuador to climb mountains, to replace one of their three Swiss guides who had fallen ill. He climbed here and he climbed there, and then came the attempt on Parascotopetl, the Matterhorn of the Andes, in which he was lost to the outer world. . . .

As the morning broke they saw the traces of his fall. It seems impossible he could have uttered a sound. He had slipped eastward towards the unknown side of the mountain; far below he had struck a steep slope of snow, and ploughed his way down it in the midst of a snow avalanche. His track went straight to the edge of a frightful precipice, and beyond that everything was hidden. Far, far below, and hazy with distance, they could see trees rising out of a narrow, shut-in valley—the lost Country of the Blind. But they did not know it was the lost Country of the Blind, nor distinguish it in any way from any other narrow streak of upland valley. . . .

And the man who fell survived. . . .

After a great interval of time he became aware that he was near the lower edge of the snow. Below, down what was now a moonlit and practicable slope, he saw the dark and broken appearance of rock-strewn turf. He struggled to his feet, aching in every joint and limb, got down painfully from the heaped loose snow about him, went downward until he was on the turf, and there dropped rather than lay beside a boulder, drank deep from the flask in his inner pocket, and instantly fell asleep. . . .

He was awakened by the singing of birds in the trees far below.

He sat up and perceived he was on a little alp at the foot of a vast precipice, that was grooved by the gully down which he and his snow had come. Over against him another wall of rock reared itself against the sky. The gorge between these precipices ran east and west and was full of the morning sunlight, which lit to the westward the mass of fallen mountain that closed the descending gorge. Below him it seemed there was a precipice equally steep, but behind the snow in the gully he found a sort of chimney-cleft dripping with snow-water down which a desperate man might venture. He found it easier than it seemed, and came at last to another desolate alp, and then after a rock climb of no particular difficulty to a steep slope of trees. He took his bearings and turned his face up the gorge, for he saw it opened out above upon green meadows, among which he now glimpsed quite distinctly a cluster of stone huts of unfamiliar fashion. At times his progress was like clambering along the face of a wall, and after a time the rising sun ceased to strike along the gorge, the voices of the singing birds died away, and the air grew cold and dark about him. But the distant valley with its houses was all the brighter for that. He came presently to talus, and among the rocks he noted—for he was an observant man—an unfamiliar fern that seemed to clutch out of the crevices with intense green hands. He picked a frond or so and gnawed its stalk and found it helpful.

About midday he came at last out of the throat of the gorge into the plain and the sunlight. He was stiff and weary; he sat down in the shadow of a rock, filled up his flask with water from a spring and drank it down, and remained for a time resting before he went on to the houses.

They were very strange to his eyes, and indeed the whole aspect of that valley became, as he regarded it, queerer and more unfamiliar. The greater part of its surface was lush green meadow, starred with many beautiful flowers, irrigated with extraordinary care, and bearing evidence of systematic cropping piece by piece. High up and ringing the valley about was a wall, and what appeared to be a circumferential water-channel, from which the little trickles of water that fed the meadow plants came, and on the higher slopes above this flocks of llamas cropped the scanty herbage. Sheds, apparently shelters or feeding-places for the llamas, stood against the boundary wall here and there. The irrigation streams ran together into a main channel down the centre of the valley, and this was enclosed on either side by a wall breast high. This gave a singularly urban quality to this secluded place, a quality that was greatly enhanced by the fact that a number of paths paved with black and white stones, and each with a curious little kerb at the side, ran hither and thither in an orderly manner. The houses of the central village were quite unlike the casual and higgledy-piggledy agglomeration of the mountain villages he knew; they stood in a continuous row on either side of a central street of astonishing cleanness; here and there their parti-coloured façade was pierced by a door, and not a solitary window broke their even frontage. They were parti-coloured with extraordinary irregularity, smeared with a sort of plaster that was sometimes grey, sometimes drab, sometimes slate-coloured or dark brown; and it was the sight of this wild plastering first brought the word "blind" into the thoughts of the explorer. "The good man who did that," he thought, "must have been as blind as a bat."

He descended a steep place, and so came to the wall and channel that ran about the valley, near where the latter spouted out its surplus contents into the deeps of the gorge in a thin and wavering thread of cascade. He could now see a number of men and women resting on piled heaps of grass, as if taking a siesta, in the remoter part of the meadow, and nearer the village a number of recumbent children, and then nearer at hand three men carrying pails on yokes along a little path that ran from the encircling wall towards the houses. These latter were clad in garments of llama cloth and boots and belts of leather, and they wore caps of cloth with back and ear flaps. They followed one another in single file, walking slowly and yawning as they walked, like men who have been up all night. There was something so reassuringly prosperous and respectable in their bearing that after a moment's hesitation Nunez stood forward as conspicuously as possible upon his rock, and gave vent to a mighty shout that echoed round the valley.

The three men stopped, and moved their heads as though they were looking about them. They turned their faces this way and that, and Nunez gesticulated with freedom. But they did not appear to see him for all his gestures, and after a time, directing themselves towards the mountains far away to the right, they shouted as if in answer. Nunez bawled again, and then once more, and as he gestured ineffectually the word "blind" came up to the top of his thoughts. "The fools must be blind," he said.

When at last, after much shouting and wrath, Nunez crossed the stream by a little bridge, came through a gate in the wall, and approached them, he was sure that they were blind. He was sure that this was the Country of the Blind of which the legends told. Conviction had sprung upon him, and a sense of great and rather enviable adventure. The three stood side by side, not looking at him, but with their ears directed towards him, judging him by his unfamiliar steps. They stood close together like men a little afraid, and he could see their eyelids closed and sunken, as though the very balls beneath had shrunk away. There was an expression near awe on their faces.

"A man," one said, in hardly recognisable Spanish—"a man it is—a man or a spirit—coming down from the rocks."

But Nunez advanced with the confident steps of a youth who enters upon life. All the old stories of the lost valley and the Country of the Blind had come back to his mind, and through his thoughts ran this old proverb, as if it were a refrain—

"In the Country of the Blind the One-eyed Man is King."

"In the Country of the Blind the One-eyed Man is King."

And very civilly he gave them greeting. He talked to them and used his eyes.

"Where does he come from, brother Pedro?" asked one.

"Down out of the rocks."

"Over the mountains I come," said Nunez, "out of the country beyond there—where men can see. From near Bogota, where there are a hundred thousands of people, and where the city passes out of sight."

"Sight?" muttered Pedro. "Sight?"

"He comes," said the second blind man, "out of the rocks."

The cloth of their coats Nunez saw was curiously fashioned, each with a different sort of stitching.

They startled him by a simultaneous movement towards him, each with a hand outstretched. He stepped back from the advance of these spread fingers.

"Come hither," said the third blind man, following his motion and clutching him neatly.

And they held Nunez and felt him over, saying no word further until they had done so.

"Carefully," he cried, with a finger in his eye, and found they thought that organ, with its fluttering lids, a queer thing in him. They went over it again.

"A strange creature, Correa," said the one called Pedro. "Feel the coarseness of his hair. Like a llama's hair."

"Rough he is as the rocks that begot him," said Correa, investigating Nunez's unshaven chin with a soft and slightly moist hand. "Perhaps he will grow finer." Nunez struggled a little under their examination, but they gripped him firm.

"Carefully," he said again.

"He speaks," said the third man. "Certainly he is a man."

"Ugh!" said Pedro, at the roughness of his coat.

"And you have come into the world?" asked Pedro.

"*Out* of the world. Over mountains and glaciers; right over above there, half-way to the sun. Out of the great big world that goes down, twelve days' journey to the sea."

They scarcely seemed to heed him. "Our fathers have told us men may be made by the forces of Nature," said Correa. "It is the warmth of things and moisture, and rottenness—rottenness."

"Let us lead him to the elders," said Pedro.

"Shout first," said Correa, "lest the children be afraid. This is a marvellous occasion."

So they shouted, and Pedro went first and took Nunez by the hand to lead him to the houses.

He drew his hand away. "I can see," he said.

"See?" said Correa.

"Yes, see," said Nunez, turning towards him, and stumbled against Pedro's pail.

"His senses are still imperfect," said the third blind man. "He stumbles, and talks unmeaning words. Lead him by the hand."

"As you will," said Nunez, and was led along, laughing.

It seemed they knew nothing of sight.

Well, all in good time he would teach them.

He heard people shouting, and saw a number of figures gathering together in the middle roadway of the village.

He found it taxed his nerve and patience more than he had anticipated, that first encounter with the population of the Country of the Blind. The place seemed larger as he drew near to it, and the smeared plasterings queerer, and a crowd of children and men and women (the women and girls, he was pleased to note, had some of them quite sweet faces, for all that their eyes were shut and sunken) came about him, holding on to him, touching him with soft, sensitive hands, smelling at him, and listening at every word he spoke. Some of the maidens and children, however, kept aloof as if afraid, and indeed his voice seemed coarse and rude beside their softer notes. They mobbed him. His three guides kept close to him with an effect of proprietorship, and said again and again, "A wild man out of the rocks."

"Bogota," he said. "Bogota. Over the mountain crests."

"A wild man—using wild words," said Pedro. "Did you hear that —*Bogota*? His mind is hardly formed yet. He has only the beginnings of speech."

A little boy nipped his hand. "Bogota!" he said mockingly.

"Ay! A city to your village. I come from the great world—where men have eyes and see."

"His name's Bogota," they said.

"He stumbled," said Correa, "stumbled twice as we came hither."

"Bring him to the elders."

And they thrust him suddenly through a doorway into a room as black as pitch, save at the end there faintly glowed a fire. The crowd closed in behind him and shut out all but the faintest glimmer of day, and before he could arrest himself he had fallen headlong over the feet of a seated man. His arm, outflung, struck the face of someone else as he went down; he felt the soft impact of features and heard a cry of anger, and for a moment he struggled against a number of hands that clutched him. It was a one-sided fight. An inkling of the situation came to him, and he lay quiet.

"I fell down," he said; "I couldn't see in this pitchy darkness."

There was a pause as if the unseen persons about him tried to understand his words. Then the voice of Correa said: "He is but newly formed. He stumbles as he walks and mingles words that mean nothing with his speech."

Others also said things about him that he heard or understood imperfectly.

"May I sit up?" he asked, in a pause. "I will not struggle against you again."

They consulted and let him rise.

The voice of an older man began to question him, and Nunez found himself trying to explain the great world out of which he had fallen, and the sky and mountains and sight and such-like marvels, to these elders who sat in darkness in the Country of the Blind. And they would believe and understand nothing whatever he told them, a thing quite outside his expectation. They would not even understand many of his words. For fourteen generations these people had been blind and cut off from all the seeing world; the names for all the things of sight had faded and changed; the story of the outer world was faded and changed to a child's story; and they had ceased to concern themselves with anything beyond the rocky slopes above their circling wall. Blind men of genius had arisen among them and questioned the shreds of belief and tradition they had brought with them from their seeing days, and had dismissed all these things as idle fancies, and replaced them with new and saner explanations. Much of their imagination had shrivelled with their eyes, and they had made for themselves new imaginations with their ever more sensitive ears and finger-tips. Slowly Nunez realised this; that his expectation of wonder and reverence at his origin and his gifts was not to be borne out; and after his poor attempt to explain sight to them had been set aside as the confused version of a new-made being describing the marvels of his incoherent sensations, he subsided, a little dashed, into listening to their instruction. And the eldest of the blind men explained to him life and philosophy and religion, how that the world (meaning their valley) had been first an empty hollow in the rocks, and then had come, first, inanimate things without the gift of touch, and llamas and a few other creatures that had little sense, and then men, and at last angels, whom one could hear singing and making fluttering sounds, but whom no one could touch at all, which puzzled Nunez greatly until he thought of the birds.

He went on to tell Nunez how this time had been divided into the warm and the cold, which are the blind equivalents of day and night, and how it was good to sleep in the warm and work during the cold, so that now, but for his advent, the whole town of the blind would have been asleep. He said Nunez must have been specially created to learn and serve the wisdom they had acquired, and that for all his mental incoherency and stumbling behaviour he must have courage, and do his best to learn, and at that all the people in the doorway murmured encouragingly. He said the night—for the blind call their day night—was now far gone, and it behoved every one to go back to sleep. He asked Nunez if he knew how to sleep, and Nunez said he did, but that before sleep he wanted food.

They brought him food—llama's milk in a bowl, and rough salted bread—and led him into a lonely place to eat out of their hearing, and afterwards to slumber until the chill of the mountain evening roused them to begin their day again. But Nunez slumbered not at all.

Instead, he sat up in the place where they had left him, resting his limbs and turning the unanticipated circumstances of his arrival over and over in his mind.

Every now and then he laughed, sometimes with amusement, and sometimes with indignation.

"Unformed mind!" he said. "Got no senses yet! They little know they've been insulting their heaven-sent king and master. I see I must bring them to reason. Let me think—let me think."

He was still thinking when the sun set.

Nunez had an eye for all beautiful things, and it seemed to him that the glow upon the snowfields and glaciers that rose about the valley on every side was the most beautiful thing he had ever seen. His eyes went from that inaccessible glory to the village and irrigated fields, fast sinking into the twilight, and suddenly a wave of emotion took him, and he thanked God from the bottom of his heart that the power of sight had been given him.

He heard a voice calling to him from out of the village.

"Ya ho there, Bogota! Come hither!"

At that he stood up smiling. He would show these people once and for all what sight would do for a man. They would seek him, but not find him.

"You move not, Bogota," said the voice.

He laughed noiselessly, and made two stealthy steps aside from the path.

"Trample not on the grass, Bogota; that is not allowed."

Nunez had scarcely heard the sound he made himself. He stopped amazed.

The owner of the voice came running up the piebald path towards him.

He stepped back into the pathway. "Here I am," he said.

"Why did you not come when I called you?" said the blind man. "Must you be led like a child? Cannot you hear the path as you walk?"

Nunez laughed. "I can see it," he said.

"There is no such word as *see*," said the blind man, after a pause. "Cease this folly, and follow the sound of my feet."

Nunez followed, a little annoyed.

"My time will come," he said.

"You'll learn," the blind man answered. "There is much to learn in the world."

"Has no one told you, 'In the Country of the Blind the One-eyed Man is King'?"

"What is blind?" asked the blind man carelessly over his shoulder.

Four days passed, and the fifth found the King of the Blind still incognito, as a clumsy and useless stranger among his subjects.

It was, he found, much more difficult to proclaim himself than he had supposed, and in the meantime, while he meditated his *coup d'état*, he did what he was told and learnt the manners and customs of the Country of the Blind. He found working and going about at night a particularly irksome thing, and he decided that that should be the first thing he would change.

They led a simple, laborious life, these people, with all the elements of virtue and happiness, as these things can be understood by men. They toiled, but not oppressively; they had food and clothing sufficient for their needs; they had days and seasons of rest; they made much of music and singing, and there was love among them, and little children.

It was marvellous with what confidence and precision they went about their ordered world. Everything, you see, had been made to fit their needs; each of the radiating paths of the valley area had a constant angle to the others, and was distinguished by a special notch upon its kerbing; all obstacles and irregularities of path or meadow had long since been cleared away; all their methods and procedure arose naturally from their special needs. Their senses had become marvellously acute; they could hear and judge the slightest gesture of a man a dozen paces away—could hear the very beating of his heart. Intonation had long replaced expression with them, and touches gesture, and their work with hoe and spade and fork was as free and confident as garden work can be. Their sense of smell was extraordinarily fine; they could distinguish individual differences as readily as a dog can, and they went about the tending of the llamas, who lived among the rocks above and came to the wall for food and shelter, with ease and confidence. It was only when at last Nunez sought to assert himself that he found how easy and confident their movements could be.

He rebelled only after he had tried persuasion.

He tried at first on several occasions to tell them of sight. "Look you here, you people," he said. "There are things you do not understand in me."

Once or twice one or two of them attended to him; they sat with faces downcast and ears turned intelligently towards him, and he did his best to tell them what it was to see. Among his hearers was a girl, with eyelids less red and sunken than the others, so that one could almost fancy she was hiding eyes, whom especially he hoped to persuade. He spoke of the beauties of sight, of watching the mountains, of the sky and the sunrise, and they heard him with amused incredulity that presently became condemnatory. They told him there were indeed no mountains at all, but that the end of the rocks where the llamas grazed was indeed the end of the world; thence sprang a cavernous roof of the universe, from which the dew and the avalanches fell; and when he maintained stoutly the world had neither end nor roof such as they supposed, they said his thoughts were wicked. So far as he could describe sky and clouds and stars to them it seemed to them a hideous void, a terrible blankness in the place of the smooth roof to things in which they believed—it was an article of faith with them that the cavern roof was exquisitely smooth to the touch. He saw that in some manner he shocked them, and gave up that aspect of the matter altogether, and tried to show them the practical value of sight. One morning he saw Pedro in the path called Seventeen and coming towards the central houses, but still too far off for hearing or scent, and he told them as much. "In a little while," he prophesied, "Pedro will be here." An old man remarked that Pedro had no business on path Seventeen, and then, as if in confirmation, that individual as he drew near turned and went transversely into path Ten, and so back with nimble paces towards the outer wall. They mocked Nunez when Pedro did not arrive, and afterwards, when he asked Pedro questions to clear his character, Pedro denied and outfaced him, and was afterwards hostile to him.

Then he induced them to let him go a long way up the sloping meadows towards the wall with one complacent individual, and to him he promised to describe all that happened among the houses. He noted certain goings and comings, but the things that really seemed to signify to these people happened inside of or behind the windowless houses—the only things they took note of to test him by—and of these he could see or tell nothing; and it was after the failure of this attempt, and the ridicule they could not repress, that he resorted to force. He thought of seizing a spade and suddenly smiting one or two of them to earth, and so in fair combat showing the advantage of eyes. He went so far with that resolution as to seize his spade, and then he discovered a new thing about himself, and that was that it was impossible for him to hit a blind man in cold blood.

He hesitated, and found them all aware that he had snatched up the spade. They stood alert, with their heads on one side, and bent ears towards him for what he would do next.

"Put that spade down," said one, and he felt a sort of helpless horror. He came near obedience.

Then he thrust one backwards against a house wall, and fled past him and out of the village.

He went athwart one of their meadows, leaving a track of trampled grass behind his feet, and presently sat down by the side of one of their ways. He felt something of the buoyancy that comes to all men in the beginning of a fight, but more perplexity. He began to realise that you cannot even fight happily with creatures who stand upon a different mental basis to yourself. Far away he saw a number of men carrying spades and sticks come out of the street of houses, and advance in a spreading line along the several paths towards him. They advanced slowly, speaking frequently to one another, and ever and again the whole cordon would halt and sniff the air and listen.

The first time they did this Nunez laughed. But afterwards he did not laugh.

One struck his trail in the meadow grass, and came stooping and feeling his way along it.

For five minutes he watched the slow extension of the cordon, and then his vague disposition to do something forthwith became frantic. He stood up, went a pace or so towards the circumferential wall, turned, and went back a little way. There they all stood in a crescent, still and listening.

He also stood still, gripping his spade very tightly in both hands. Should he charge them?

The pulse in his ears ran into the rhythm of "In the Country of the Blind the One-eyed Man is King!"

Should he charge them?

He looked back at the high and unclimbable wall behind—unclimbable because of its smooth plastering, but withal pierced with many little doors, and at the approaching line of seekers. Behind these others were now coming out of the street of houses.

Should he charge them?

"Bogota!" called one. "Bogota! where are you?"

He gripped his spade still tighter, and advanced down the meadows towards the place of habitations, and directly he moved they converged upon him. "I'll hit them if they touch me," he swore; "by Heaven, I will. I'll hit." He called aloud, "Look here, I'm going to do what I like in this valley. Do you hear? I'm going to do what I like and go where I like!"

They were moving in upon him quickly, groping, yet moving rapidly. It was like playing blind man's buff, with everyone blindfolded except one. "Get hold of him!" cried one. He found himself in the arc of a loose curve of pursuers. He felt suddenly he must be active and resolute.

"You don't understand," he cried in a voice that was meant to be great and resolute, and which broke. "You are blind, and I can see. Leave me alone!"

"Bogota! Put down that spade, and come off the grass!"

The last order, grotesque in its urban familiarity, produced a gust of anger.

"I'll hurt you," he said, sobbing with emotion. "By Heaven, I'll hurt you. Leave me alone!"

He began to run, not knowing clearly where to run. He ran from the nearest blind man, because it was a horror to hit him. He stopped, and then made a dash to escape from their closing ranks. He made for where a gap was wide, and the men on either side, with a quick perception of the approach of his paces, rushed in on one another. He sprang forward, and then saw he must be caught, and *swish!* the spade had struck. He felt the soft thud of hand and arm, and the man was down with a yell of pain, and he was through.

Through! And then he was close to the street of houses again, and blind men, whirling spades and stakes, were running with a sort of reasoned swiftness hither and thither.

He heard steps behind him just in time, and found a tall man rushing forward and swiping at the sound of him. He lost his nerve, hurled his spade a yard wide at his antagonist, and whirled about and fled, fairly yelling as he dodged another.

He was panic-stricken. He ran furiously to and fro, dodging when there was no need to dodge, and in his anxiety to see on every side of him at once, stumbling. For a moment he was down and they heard his fall. Far away in the circumferential wall a little doorway looked like heaven, and he set off in a wild rush for it. He did not even look round at his pursuers until it was gained, and he had stumbled across the bridge, clambered a little way among the rocks, to the surprise and dismay of a young llama, who went leaping out of sight, and lay down sobbing for breath.

And so his *coup d'état* came to an end.

He stayed outside the wall of the valley of the Blind for two nights and days without food or shelter, and meditated upon the unexpected. During these meditations he repeated very frequently and always with a profounder note of derision the exploded proverb: "In the Country of the Blind the One-eyed Man is King." He thought chiefly of ways of fighting and conquering these people, and it grew clear that for him no practicable way was possible. He had no weapons, and now it would be hard to get one.

The canker of civilisation had got to him even in Bogota, and he could not find it in himself to go down and assassinate a blind man. Of course, if he did that, he might then dictate terms on the threat of assassinating them all. But—sooner or later he must sleep! . . .

He tried also to find food among the pine trees, to be comfortable under pine boughs while the frost fell at night, and—with less confidence—to catch a llama by artifice in order to try to kill it—perhaps by hammering it with a stone—and so finally, perhaps, to eat some of it. But the llamas had a doubt of him and regarded him with distrustful brown eyes, and spat when he drew near. Fear came on him the second day and fits of shivering. Finally he crawled down to the wall of the Country of the Blind and tried to make terms. He crawled along by the stream, shouting, until two blind men came out to the gate and talked to him.

"I was mad," he said. "But I was only newly made."

They said that was better.

He told them he was wiser now, and repented of all he had done.

Then he wept without intention, for he was very weak and ill now, and they took that as a favourable sign.

They asked him if he still thought he could *"see."*

"No," he said. "That was folly. The word means nothing—less than nothing!"

They asked him what was overhead.

"About ten times ten the height of a man there is a roof above the world—of rock—and very, very smooth." . . . He burst again into hysterical tears. "Before you ask me any more, give me some food or I shall die."

He expected dire punishments, but these blind people were capable of toleration. They regarded his rebellion as but one more proof of his general idiocy and inferiority; and after they had whipped him they appointed him to do the simplest and heaviest work they had for anyone to do, and he, seeing no other way of living, did submissively what he was told.

He was ill for some days, and they nursed him kindly. That refined his submission. But they insisted on his lying in the dark, and that was a great misery. And blind philosophers came and talked to him of the wicked levity of his mind, and reproved him so impressively for his doubts about the lid of rock that covered their cosmic casserole that he almost doubted whether indeed he was not the victim of hallucination in not seeing it overhead.

So Nunez became a citizen of the Country of the Blind, and these people ceased to be a generalised people and became individualities and familiar to him, while the world beyond the mountains became more and more remote and unreal. There was Yacob, his master, a kindly man when not annoyed; there was Pedro, Yacob's nephew; and there was Medina-saroté, who was the youngest daughter of Yacob. She was little esteemed in the world of the blind, because she had a clear-cut face, and lacked that satisfying, glossy smoothness that is the blind man's ideal of feminine beauty; but Nunez thought her beautiful at first, and presently the most beautiful thing in the whole creation. Her closed eyelids were not sunken and red after the common way of the valley, but lay as though they might open again at any moment; and she had long eyelashes, which were considered a grave disfigurement. And her voice was strong, and did not satisfy the acute hearing of the valley swains. So that she had no lover.

There came a time when Nunez thought that, could he win her, he would be resigned to live in the valley for all the rest of his days.

He watched her; he sought opportunities of doing her little services, and presently he found that she observed him. Once at a rest-day gathering they sat side by side in the dim starlight, and the music was sweet. His hand came upon hers and he dared to clasp it. Then very tenderly she returned his pressure. And one day, as they were at their meal in the darkness, he felt her hand very softly seeking him, and as it chanced the fire leapt then and he saw the tenderness of her face.

He sought to speak to her.

He went to her one day when she was sitting in the summer moonlight spinning. The light made her a thing of silver and mystery. He sat down at her feet and told her he loved her, and told her how beautiful she seemed to him. He had a lover's voice, he spoke with a tender reverence that came near to awe, and she had never before been touched by adoration. She made him no definite answer, but it was clear his words pleased her.

After that he talked to her whenever he could take an opportunity. The valley became the world for him, and the world beyond the mountains where men lived in sunlight seemed no more than a fairy tale he would some day pour into her ears. Very tentatively and timidly he spoke to her of sight.

Sight seemed to her the most poetical of fancies, and she listened to his description of the stars and the mountains and her own sweet white-lit beauty as though it was a guilty indulgence. She did not believe, she could only half understand, but she was mysteriously delighted, and it seemed to him that she completely understood.

His love lost its awe and took courage. Presently he was for demanding her of Yacob and the elders in marriage, but she became fearful and delayed. And it was one of her elder sisters who first told Yacob that Medina-saroté and Nunez were in love.

There was from the first very great opposition to the marriage of Nunez and Medina-saroté; not so much because they valued her as because they held him as a being apart, an idiot, incompetent thing below the permissible level of a man. Her sisters opposed it bitterly as bringing discredit on them all; and old Yacob, though he had formed a sort of liking for his clumsy, obedient serf, shook his head and said the thing could not be. The young men were all angry at the idea of corrupting the race, and one went so far as to revile and strike Nunez. He struck back. Then for the first time he found an advantage in seeing, even by twilight, and after that fight was over no one was disposed to raise a hand against him. But they still found his marriage impossible.

Old Yacob had a tenderness for his last little daughter, and was grieved to have her weep upon his shoulder.

"You see, my dear, he's an idiot. He has delusions; he can't do anything right."

"I know," wept Medina-saroté. "But he's better than he was. He's getting better. And he's strong, dear father, and kind—stronger and kinder than any other man in the world. And he loves me—and, father, I love him."

Old Yacob was greatly distressed to find her inconsolable, and, besides—what made it more distressing—he liked Nunez for many things. So he went and sat in the windowless council-chamber with the other elders and watched the trend of the talk, and said, at the proper time, "He's better than he was. Very likely, some day, we shall find him as sane as ourselves."

Then afterwards one of the elders, who thought deeply, had an idea. He was the great doctor among these people, their medicine-man, and he had a very philosophical and inventive mind, and the idea of curing Nunez of his peculiarities appealed to him. One day when Yacob was present he returned to the topic of Nunez.

"I have examined Bogota," he said, "and the case is clearer to me. I think very probably he might be cured."

"That is what I have always hoped," said old Yacob.

"His brain is affected," said the blind doctor.

The elders murmured assent.

"Now, *what* affects it?"

"Ah!" said old Yacob.

"*This*," said the doctor, answering his own question. "Those queer things that are called the eyes, and which exist to make an agreeable soft depression in the face, are diseased, in the case of Bogota, in such a way as to affect his brain. They are greatly distended, he has eyelashes, and his eyelids move, and consequently his brain is in a state of constant irritation and distraction."

"Yes?" said old Yacob. "Yes?"

"And I think I may say with reasonable certainty that, in order to cure him completely, all that we need do is a simple and easy surgical operation—namely, to remove these irritant bodies."

"And then he will be sane?"

"Then he will be perfectly sane, and a quite admirable citizen."

"Thank Heaven for science!" said old Yacob, and went forth at once to tell Nunez of his happy hopes.

But Nunez's manner of receiving the good news struck him as being cold and disappointing.

"One might think," he said, "from the tone you take, that you did not care for my daughter."

It was Medina-saroté who persuaded Nunez to face the blind surgeons.

"*You* do not want me," he said, "to lose my gift of sight?"

She shook her head.

"My world is sight."

Her head drooped lower.

"There are the beautiful things, the beautiful little things—the flowers, the lichens among the rocks, the lightness and softness on a piece of fur, the far sky with its drifting down of clouds, the sunsets and the stars. And there is *you*. For you alone it is good to have sight, to see your sweet, serene face, your kindly lips, your dear, beautiful hands folded together. . . . It is these eyes of mine you won, these eyes that hold me to you, that these idiots seek. Instead, I must touch you, hear you, and never see you again. I must come under that roof of rock and stone and darkness, that horrible roof under which your imagination stoops. . . No; you would not have me do that?"

A disagreeable doubt had arisen in him. He stopped, and left the thing a question.

"I wish," she said, "sometimes—" She paused.

"Yes," said he, a little apprehensively.

"I wish sometimes—you would not talk like that."

"Like what?"

"I know it's pretty—it's your imagination. I love it, but *now*—"

He felt cold. "*Now?*" he said faintly.

She sat quite still.

"You mean—you think—I should be better, better perhaps—"

He was realising things very swiftly. He felt anger, indeed, anger at the dull course of fate, but also sympathy for her lack of understanding—a sympathy near akin to pity.

"*Dear,*" he said, and he could see by her whiteness how intensely her spirit pressed against the things she could not say. He put his arms about her, he kissed her ear, and they sat for a time in silence.

"If I were to consent to this?" he said at last, in a voice that was very gentle.

She flung her arms about him, weeping wildly. "Oh, if you would," she sobbed, "if only you would!"

For a week before the operation that was to raise him from his servitude and inferiority to the level of a blind citizen, Nunez knew nothing of sleep, and all through the warm sunlit hours, while the others slumbered happily, he sat brooding or wandered aimlessly, trying to bring his mind to bear on his dilemma. He had given his answer, he had given his consent, and still he was not sure. And at last work-time was over, the sun rose in splendour over the golden crests, and his last day of vision began for him. He had a few minutes with Medina-saroté before she went apart to sleep.

"To-morrow," he said, "I shall see no more."

"Dear heart!" she answered, and pressed his hands with all her strength.

"They will hurt you but little," she said; "and you are going through this pain—you are going through it, dear lover, for *me*. . . . Dear, if a woman's heart and life can do it, I will repay you. My dearest one, my dearest with the tender voice, I will repay."

He was drenched in pity for himself and her.

He held her in his arms, and pressed his lips to hers, and looked on her sweet face for the last time. "Goodbye!" he whispered at that dear sight, "good-bye!"

And then in silence he turned away from her.

She could hear his slow retreating footsteps, and something in the rhythm of them threw her into a passion of weeping.

He had fully meant to go to a lonely place where the meadows were beautiful with white narcissus, and there remain until the hour of his sacrifice should come, but as he went he lifted up his eyes and saw the morning, the morning like an angel in golden armour, marching down the steeps. . . .

It seemed to him that before this splendour he, and this blind world in the valley, and his love, and all, were no more than a pit of sin.

He did not turn aside as he had meant to do, but went on, and passed through the wall of the circumference and out upon the rocks, and his eyes were always upon the sunlit ice and snow.

He saw their infinite beauty, and his imagination soared over them to the things beyond he was now to resign for ever.

He thought of that great free world he was parted from, the world that was his own, and he had a vision of those further slopes, distance beyond distance, with Bogota, a place of multitudinous stirring beauty, a glory by day, a luminous mystery by night, a place of palaces and fountains and statues and white houses, lying beautifully in the middle distance. He thought how for a day or so one might come down through passes, drawing ever nearer and nearer to its busy streets and ways. He thought of the river journey, day by day, from great Bogota to the still vaster world beyond, through towns and villages, forest and desert places, the rushing river day by day, until its banks receded and the big steamers came splashing by, and one had reached the sea—the limitless sea, with its thousand islands, its thousands of islands, and its ships seen dimly far away in their incessant journeyings round and about that greater world. And there, unpent by mountains, one saw the sky—the sky, not such a disc as one saw it here, but an arch of immeasurable blue, a deep of deeps in which the circling stars were floating. . . .

His eyes scrutinised the great curtain of the mountains with a keener inquiry.

For example, if one went so, up that gully and to that chimney there, then one might come out high among those stunted pines that ran round in a sort of shelf and rose still higher and higher as it passed above the gorge. And then? That talus might be managed. Thence perhaps a climb might be found to take him up to the precipice that came below the snow; and if that chimney failed, then another farther to the east might serve his purpose better. And then? Then one would be out upon the amber-lit snow there, and half-way up to the crest of those beautiful desolations.

He glanced back at the village, then turned right round and regarded it steadfastly.

He thought of Medina-saroté, and she had become small and remote.

He turned again towards the mountain wall, down which the day had come to him.

Then very circumspectly he began to climb.

When sunset came he was no longer climbing, but he was far and high. He had been higher, but he was still very high. His clothes were torn, his limbs were blood-stained, he was bruised in many places, but he lay as if he were at his ease, and there was a smile on his face.

From where he rested the valley seemed as if it were in a pit and nearly a mile below. Already it was dim with haze and shadow, though the mountain summits around him were things of light and fire. The mountain summits around him were things of light and fire, and the little details of the rocks near at hand were drenched with subtle beauty—a vein of green mineral piercing the grey, the flash of crystal faces here and there, a minute, minutely-beautiful orange lichen close beside his face. There were deep mysterious shadows in the gorge, blue deepening into purple, and purple into a luminous darkness, and overhead was the illimitable vastness of the sky. But he heeded these things no longer, but lay quite inactive there, smiling as if he were satisfied merely to have escaped from the valley of the Blind in which he had thought to be King.

The glow of the sunset passed, and the night came, and still he lay peacefully contented under the cold clear stars.

## *Questions for Rereading, Discussing, Connecting, and Writing*

### REREADING

**1.** H.G. Wells is best known for his novels and short stories dealing with science and the fantastic. Highlight moments in your reading that you think have been planned by Wells to make you sense the strangeness of his tale. What are some of the words, phrases, and sentences that he uses to achieve this effect of strangeness?

**2.** To make something truly exotic, a writer must be, ironically, precise and very concrete in his or her attention to detail. What section or sections of this short story do you find especially persuasive in their clarity and precision of description—and do these sections also contain elements of fantasy and horror?

**3.** A common feature of modern fiction is the "open" ending; in other words, the story is not neatly wrapped up, but left unresolved or suspended between incidents. Does this story feel unresolved? If so, how does Wells achieve this open-endedness? Does this effect encourage you to "enter" and continue the story—or does it frustrate your reading?

### DISCUSSING

**4.** Of the five senses, sight is almost always given emphasis in writing, and it has been chosen in large surveys to be the most valuable sense we have.

Why is this sense given so much favor? Does Wells agree with this popular view? In the country of the blind *is* the one-eyed man king? Or is the one-eyed man a slave, a freak? How are you made to believe this?

5. Being deprived of sight is a terrifying possibility for most people. Discuss what living a life of blindness could mean—its effects on the other senses, especially. Refer to the short story for particular examples of this changed world of the blind person.

CONNECTING

6. Like the other journeys in this chapter, Nunez's journey to the country of the blind demarcates the known and unknown worlds. According to these accounts, how does a man or woman deal with the unknown—with courage, insight, and sensitivity, or greed, lust, and fear? Try to reach some conclusions about how we face the unknown.

7. Taking a long and arduous journey does not only help us discover the strange and exotic, it also helps us define *home,* or where we have come from. Looking at selections in this chapter, try to define what home means to these men and women of far-reaching vision and ambition.

WRITING

8. If you can read with your eyes closed—feeling your way around a room in the dark, for example—you can also write without your hands. Try tape-recording the same walk in the dark, talking about your sensations as you go. Listen to the tape later, transcribe it, and then revise it after taking the same walk in the daytime.

9. Wells was politically active in his native England, and this short story may be read as a warning against suppression of differences. Support or dispute this interpretation by referring to incidents in the story.

*George Orwell*

# Shooting an Elephant (1931)

*I*n Moulmein, in Lower Burma, I was hated by large numbers of people—the only time in my life that I have been important enough for this to happen to me. I was sub-divisional police officer of the town, and in an aimless, petty kind of way anti-European feeling was very bitter. No one had the guts to raise a riot, but if a European woman went through the bazaars alone somebody would probably spit betel juice over her dress. As a police officer I was an obvious target and was baited whenever it seemed safe to do so. When a nimble Burman tripped me up on the football field and the referee (another Burman) looked the other way, the crowd yelled with hideous laughter. This happened more than once. In the end the sneering yellow faces of young men that met me everywhere, the insults hooted after me when I was at a safe distance, got badly on my nerves. The young Buddhist priests were the worst of all. There were several thousands of them in the town and none of them seemed to have anything to do except stand on street corners and jeer at Europeans.

All this was perplexing and upsetting. For at that time I had already made up my mind that imperialism was an evil thing and the sooner I chucked up my job and got out of it the better. Theoretically—and secretly, of course—I was all for the Burmese and all against their oppressors, the British. As for the job I was doing, I hated it more bitterly than I can perhaps make clear. In a job like that you see the dirty work of Empire at close quarters. The wretched prisoners huddling in the stinking cages of the lock-ups, the grey, cowed faces of the long-term convicts, the scarred buttocks of the men who had been flogged with bamboos—all these oppressed me with an intolerable sense of guilt. But I could get nothing into perspective. I was young and ill-educated and I had had to think out my problems in the utter silence that is imposed on every Englishman in the East. I did not even know that the British Empire is dying, still less did I know that it is a great deal better than the younger empires that are going to supplant it. All I knew was that I was stuck between my hatred of the empire I served and my rage against the evil-spirited little beasts who tried to make my job impossible. With one part of my mind I thought of the British Raj as an unbreakable tyranny, as something clamped down, in *saecula saeculorum,* upon the will of prostrate peoples; with another part I thought that the greatest joy in the world would be to drive a bayonet into a Buddhist priest's guts. Feelings like these are the normal by-products of imperialism; ask any Anglo-Indian official, if you can catch him off duty.

One day something happened which in a roundabout way was enlightening. It was a tiny incident in itself, but it gave me a better glimpse than I had had before of the real nature of imperialism—the real motives for which despotic governments act. Early one morning the sub-inspector at a police station the other end of the town rang me up on the 'phone and said that an elephant was ravaging the bazaar. Would I please come and do something about it? I did not know what I could do, but I wanted to see what was happening and I got on to a pony and started out. I took my rifle, an old .44 Winchester and much too small to kill an elephant, but I thought the noise might be useful *in terrorem.* Various Burmans stopped me on the way and told me about the elephant's doings. It was not, of course, a wild elephant, but a tame one which had gone "must." It had been chained up, as tame elephants always are when their attack of "must" is due, but on the previous night it had broken its chain and escaped. Its mahout, the only person who could manage it when it was in that state, had set out in pursuit, but had taken the wrong direction and was now twelve hours' journey away, and in the morning the elephant had suddenly reappeared in the town. The Burmese population had no weapons and were quite helpless against it. It had already destroyed somebody's bamboo hut, killed a cow and raided some fruit-stalls and devoured the stock; also it had met the municipal rubbish van and, when the driver jumped out and took to his heels, had turned the van over and inflicted violences upon it.

The Burmese sub-inspector and some Indian constables were waiting for me in the quarter where the elephant had been seen. It was a very poor quarter, a labyrinth of squalid bamboo huts, thatched with palm-leaf, winding all over a steep hillside. I remember that it was a cloudy, stuffy morning at the beginning of the rains. We began questioning the people as to where the elephant had gone and, as usual, failed to get any definite information. That is invariably the case in the East; a story always sounds clear enough at a distance, but the nearer you get to the scene of events the vaguer it becomes. Some of the people said that the elephant had gone in one direction, some said that he had gone in another, some professed not even to have heard of any elephant. I had almost made up my mind that the whole story was a pack of lies, when we heard yells a little distance away. There was a loud, scandalized cry of "Go away, child! Go away this instant!" and an old woman with a switch in her hand came round the corner of a hut, violently shooing away a crowd of naked children. Some more women followed, clicking their tongues and exclaiming; evidently there was something that the children ought not to have seen. I rounded the hut and saw a man's dead body sprawling in the mud. He was an Indian, a black Dravidian coolie, almost naked, and he could not have been dead many minutes. The people said that the elephant had come suddenly upon him round the corner of the hut, caught him with its trunk, put its foot on his back and ground him into the earth. This was the rainy season and the ground was soft, and his face had scored a trench a foot deep and a couple of yards long. He was lying on his belly with arms crucified and head sharply twisted to one side. His face was coated with mud, the eyes wide open, the teeth bared and grinning with an expression of unendurable agony. (Never tell me, by the way, that the dead look peaceful. Most of the corpses I have seen looked devilish.) The friction of the great beast's foot had stripped the skin from his back as neatly as one skins a rabbit. As soon as I saw the dead man I sent an orderly to a friend's house nearby to borrow an elephant rifle. I had already sent back the pony, not wanting it to go mad with fright and throw me if it smelt the elephant.

The orderly came back in a few minutes with a rifle and five cartridges, and meanwhile some Burmans had arrived and told us that the elephant was in the paddy fields below, only a few hundred yards away. As I started forward practically the whole population of the quarter flocked out of the houses and followed me. They had seen the rifle and were all shouting excitedly that I was going to shoot the elephant. They had not shown much interest in the elephant when he was merely ravaging their homes, but it was different now that he was going to be shot. It was a bit of fun to them, as it would be to an English crowd; besides they wanted the meat. It made me vaguely uneasy. I had no intention of shooting the elephant—I had merely sent for the rifle to defend myself if necessary—and it is always unnerving to have a crowd following you. I marched down the hill, looking and feeling a fool, with the rifle over my shoulder and an ever-growing army of people jostling at my heels. At the bottom, when you got away from the huts, there was a metalled road and beyond that a miry waste of paddy fields a thousand yards across, not yet ploughed but soggy from the first rains and dotted with coarse grass. The elephant was standing eight yards from the road, his left side towards us. He took not the slightest notice of the crowd's approach. He was tearing up bunches of grass, beating them against his knees to clean them and stuffing them into his mouth.

I had halted on the road. As soon as I saw the elephant I knew with perfect certainty that I ought not to shoot him. It is a serious matter to shoot a working elephant—it is comparable to destroying a huge and costly piece of machinery—and obviously one ought not to do it if it can possibly be avoided. And at that distance, peacefully eating, the elephant looked no more dangerous than a cow. I thought then and I think now that his attack of "must" was already passing off; in which case he would merely wander harmlessly about until the mahout came back and caught him. Moreover, I did not in the least want to shoot him. I decided that I would watch him for a little while to make sure that he did not turn savage again, and then go home.

But at that moment I glanced round at the crowd that had followed me. It was an immense crowd, two thousand at the least and growing every minute. It blocked the road for a long distance on either side. I looked at the sea of yellow faces above the garish clothes—faces all happy and excited over this bit of fun, all certain that the elephant was going to be shot. They were watching me as they would watch a conjurer about to perform a trick. They did not like me, but with the magical rifle in my hands I was momentarily worth watching. And suddenly I realized that I should have to shoot the elephant after all. The people expected it of me and I had got to do it; I could feel their two thousand wills pressing me forward, irresistibly. And it was at this moment, as I stood there with the rifle in my hands, that I first grasped the hollowness, the futility of the white man's dominion in the East. Here was I, the white man with his gun, standing in front of the unarmed native crowd—seemingly the leading actor of the piece; but in reality I was only an absurd puppet pushed to and fro by the will of those yellow faces behind. I perceived in this moment that when the white man turns tyrant it is his own freedom that he destroys. He becomes a sort of hollow, posing dummy, the conventionalized figure of a sahib. For it is the condition of his rule that he shall spend his life in trying to impress the "natives," and so in every crisis he has got to do what the "natives" expect of him. He wears a mask, and his face grows to fit it. I had got to shoot the elephant. I had committed myself to doing it when I sent for the rifle. A sahib has got to act like a sahib; he has got to appear resolute, to know his own mind and do definite things. To come all that way, rifle in hand, with two thousand people marching at my heels, and then to trail feebly away, having done nothing—no, that was impossible. The crowd would laugh at me. And my whole life, every white man's life in the East, was one long struggle not to be laughed at.

But I did not want to shoot the elephant. I watched him beating his bunch of grass against his knees, with that preoccupied grandmotherly air that elephants have. It seemed to me that it would be murder to shoot him. At that age I was not squeamish about killing animals, but I had never shot an elephant and never wanted to. (Somehow it always seems worse to kill a *large* animal.) Besides, there was the beast's owner to be considered. Alive, the elephant was worth at least a hundred pounds; dead, he would only be worth the value of his tusks, five pounds, possibly. But I had got to act quickly. I turned to some experienced-looking Burmans who had been there when we arrived, and asked them how the elephant had been behaving. They all said the same thing: he took no notice of you if you left him alone, but he might charge if you went too close to him.

It was perfectly clear to me what I ought to do. I ought to walk up to within, say, twenty-five yards of the elephant and test his behavior. If he charged, I could shoot; if he took no notice of me, it would be safe to leave him until the mahout came back. But also I knew that I was going to do no such thing. I was a poor shot with a rifle and the ground was soft mud into which one would sink at every step. If the elephant charged and I missed him, I should have about as much chance as a toad under a steam-roller. But even then I was not thinking particularly of my own skin, only of the watchful yellow faces behind. For at that moment, with the crowd watching me, I was not afraid in the ordinary sense, as I would have been if I had been alone. A white man mustn't be frightened in front of "natives"; and so, in general, he isn't frightened. The sole thought in my mind was that if anything went wrong those two thousand Burmans would see me pursued, caught, trampled on and reduced to a grinning corpse like that Indian up the hill. And if that happened it was quite probable that some of them would laugh. That would never do. There was only one alternative. I shoved the cartridges into the magazine and lay down on the road to get a better aim.

The crowd grew very still, and a deep, low, happy sigh, as of people who see the theatre curtain go up at last, breathed from innumerable throats. They were going to have their bit of fun after all. The rifle was a beautiful German thing with cross-hair sights. I did not then know that in shooting an elephant one would shoot to cut an imaginary bar running from ear-hole to ear-hole. I ought, therefore, as the elephant was sideways on, to have aimed straight at his ear-hole; actually

I aimed several inches in front of this, thinking the brain would be further forward.

When I pulled the trigger I did not hear the bang or feel the kick —one never does when a shot goes home—but I heard the devilish roar of glee that went up from the crowd. In that instant, in too short a time, one would have thought, even for the bullet to get there, a mysterious, terrible change had come over the elephant. He neither stirred nor fell, but every line of his body had altered. He looked suddenly stricken, shrunken, immensely old, as though the frightful impact of the bullet had paralysed him without knocking him down. At last, after what seemed a long time—it might have been five seconds, I dare say—he sagged flabbily to his knees. His mouth slobbered. An enormous senility seemed to have settled upon him. One could have imagined him thousands of years old. I fired again into the same spot. At the second shot he did not collapse but climbed with desperate slowness to his feet and stood weakly upright, with legs sagging and head drooping. I fired a third time. That was the shot that did for him. You could see the agony of it jolt his whole body and knock the last remnant of strength from his legs. But in falling he seemed for a moment to rise, for as his hind legs collapsed beneath him he seemed to tower upward like a huge rock toppling, his trunk reaching skywards like a tree. He trumpeted, for the first and only time. And then down he came, his belly towards me, with a crash that seemed to shake the ground even where I lay.

I got up. The Burmans were already racing past me across the mud. It was obvious that the elephant would never rise again, but he was not dead. He was breathing very rhythmically with long rattling gasps, his great mound of a side painfully rising and falling. His mouth was wide open—I could see far down into caverns of pale pink throat. I waited a long time for him to die, but his breathing did not weaken. Finally I fired my two remaining shots into the spot where I thought his heart must be. The thick blood welled out of him like red velvet, but still he did not die. His body did not even jerk when the shots hit him, the tortured breathing continued without a pause. He was dying, very slowly and in great agony, but in some world remote from me where not even a bullet could damage him further. I felt that I had got to put an end to that dreadful noise. It seemed dreadful to see the great beast lying there, powerless to move and yet powerless to die, and not even to be able to finish him. I sent back for my small rifle and poured shot after shot into his heart and down his throat. They seemed to make no impression. The tortured gasps continued as steadily as the ticking of a clock.

In the end I could not stand it any longer and went away. I heard later that it took him half an hour to die. Burmans were bringing dahs and baskets even before I left, and I was told they had stripped his body almost to the bones by the afternoon.

Afterwards, of course, there were endless discussions about the shooting of the elephant. The owner was furious, but he was only an Indian and could do nothing. Besides, legally I had done the right thing, for a mad elephant has to be killed, like a mad dog, if its owner fails to control it. Among the Europeans opinion was divided. The older men said I was right, the younger men said it was a damn shame to shoot an elephant for killing a coolie, because an elephant was worth more than any damn Coringhee coolie. And afterwards I was very glad that the coolie had been killed; it put me legally in the right and it gave me a sufficient pretext for shooting the elephant. I often wondered whether any of the others grasped that I had done it solely to avoid looking a fool.

## Questions for Rereading, Discussing, Connecting, and Writing

### REREADING

1. George Orwell is often cited as having provided models for superior essay writing. One feature of these models is well-executed paragraphs that display topic sentences and development. After reading "Shooting an Elephant" choose any paragraph and locate its topic sentence. Do the sentences in that paragraph develop or follow from that topic sentence?

2. Orwell is also famous for the way he can combine self-examination and descriptive writing. In other words, while he is defining himself as "hated" and "an obvious target" and perhaps "a fool" he is also describing in vivid detail the workings of another culture and its people. Find more examples of this accomplished balance of interior and exterior detail.

### DISCUSSING

3. Orwell's initial confession of being hated "by large numbers of people" is a surprising and provocative start to his essay. What effect does this observation have upon the reader? If you were to say to a friend, "I know several people who really hate me"—what might your friend's reaction be, and why do you suppose this is a good strategy for opening an essay?

4. The isolation or alienation of the narrator of "Shooting an Elephant" is a common feeling among travelers far from home, or workers stuck in a strange place or situation. Relate any incidents in your life that may seem similar to the story's—and how your feeling of aloneness was solved or ended.

## Connecting

5. Orwell's essay is very much about the politics of east and west and how the British Empire exerted control over a good part of the world in the early part of this century. Find selections in Chapter 5 on "Power and Justice" that you think can be applied to Orwell's essay as either parallels or contrasts. Which of these selections would the Burmese people have appreciated? Which would the narrator have appreciated—or banned in Burma?

6. Not only are cultures at war in this essay, but cultures and nature as well. The elephant is a third element in the clash. Look at other works in this book—the cave painting (p. 10), Darwin (p. 75), for example, that depict nature as either victim or victor in a conflict of mankind's desire for power and nature's ability to resist that power.

## Writing

7. Find what you believe to be the topic sentence of the entire essay: can you find one sentence that seems to capture the whole? Then develop this sentence in your own words, as you have understood Orwell's essay.

8. Write an essay describing your last encounter with hatred, either directed *at* you or *from* you.

9. Write an essay about the last time you think you made a fool of yourself. Examine the reasons for your thinking this, and let the reader discover whether you were or were not acting foolishly under the circumstances of this event or situation.

*Maxine Hong Kingston*

# The Woman Warrior *(1976)*

When we Chinese girls listened to the adults talk-story, we learned that we failed if we grew up to be but wives or slaves. We could be heroines, swordswomen. Even if she had to rage across all China, a swordswoman got even with anybody who hurt her family. Perhaps women were once so dangerous that they had to have their feet bound. It was a woman who invented white crane boxing only two hundred years ago. She was already an expert pole fighter, daughter of a teacher trained at the Shao-lin temple, where there lived an order of fighting monks. She was combing her hair one morning when a white crane alighted outside her window. She teased it with her pole, which it pushed aside with a soft brush of its wing. Amazed, she dashed outside and tried to knock the crane off its perch. It snapped her pole in two. Recognizing the presence of great power, she asked the spirit of the white crane if it would teach her to fight. It answered with a cry that white crane boxers imitate today. Later the bird returned as an old man, and he guided her boxing for many years. Thus she gave the world a new martial art.

This was one of the tamer, more modern stories, mere introduction. My mother told others that followed swordswomen through woods and palaces for years. Night after night my mother would talk-story until we fell asleep. I couldn't tell where the stories left off and the dreams began, her voice the voice of the heroines in my sleep. And on Sundays, from noon to midnight, we went to the movies at the Confucius Church. We saw swordswomen jump over houses from a standstill; they didn't even need a running start.

At last I saw that I too had been in the presence of great power, my mother talking-story. After I grew up, I heard the chant of Fa Mu Lan, the girl who took her father's place in battle. Instantly I remembered that as a child I had followed my mother about the house, the two of us singing about how Fa Mu Lan fought gloriously and returned alive from war to settle in the village. I had forgotten this chant that was once mine, given me by my mother, who may not have known its power to remind. She said I would grow up a wife and a slave, but she taught me the song of the warrior woman, Fa Mu Lan. I would have to grow up a warrior woman.

The call would come from a bird that flew over our roof. In the brush drawings it looks like the ideograph for "human," two black wings. The bird would cross the sun and lift into the mountains (which look like the ideograph "mountain"), there parting the mist briefly that swirled opaque again. I would be a little girl of seven the day I followed the bird away into the mountains. The brambles would tear off my shoes and the rocks cut my feet and fingers, but I would keep climbing, eyes upward to follow the bird. We would go around and around the tallest mountain, climbing ever upward. I would drink from the river, which I would meet again and again. We would go so high the plants would change, and the river that flows past the village would become a waterfall. At the height where the bird used to disappear, the clouds would gray the world like an ink wash.

Even when I got used to that gray, I would only see peaks as if shaded in pencil, rocks like charcoal rubbings, everything so murky. There would be just two black strokes—the bird. Inside the clouds—inside the dragon's breath—I would not know how many hours or days passed. Suddenly, without noise, I would break clear into a yellow, warm world. New trees would lean toward me at mountain angles, but when I looked for the village, it would have vanished under the clouds.

The bird, now gold so close to the sun, would come to rest on the thatch of a hut, which, until the bird's two feet touched it, was camouflaged as part of the mountainside.

The door opened, and an old man and an old woman came out carrying bowls of rice and soup and a leafy branch of peaches.

"Have you eaten rice today, little girl?" they greeted me.

"Yes, I have," I said out of politeness. "Thank you."

("No, I haven't," I would have said in real life, mad at the Chinese for lying so much. "I'm starved. Do you have any cookies? I like chocolate chip cookies.")

"We were about to sit down to another meal," the old woman said. "Why don't you eat with us?"

They just happened to be bringing three rice bowls and three pairs of silver chopsticks out to the plank table under the pines. They gave me an egg, as if it were my birthday, and tea, though they were older than I, but I poured for them. The teapot and the rice pot seemed bottomless, but perhaps not; the old couple ate very little except for peaches.

When the mountains and the pines turned into blue oxen, blue dogs, and blue people standing, the old couple asked me to spend the night in the hut. I thought about the long way down in the ghostly dark and decided yes. The inside of the hut seemed as large as the outdoors. Pine needles covered the floor in thick patterns; someone had carefully arranged the yellow, green, and brown pine needles according to age. When I stepped carelessly and mussed a line, my feet kicked up new blends of earth colors, but the old man and old woman walked so lightly that their feet never stirred the designs by a needle.

A rock grew in the middle of the house, and that was their table. The benches were fallen trees. Ferns and shade flowers grew out of one wall, the mountainside itself. The old couple tucked me into a bed just my width. "Breathe evenly, or you'll lose your balance and fall out," said the woman, covering me with a silk bag stuffed with feathers and herbs. "Opera singers, who begin their training at age five, sleep in beds like this." Then the two of them went outside, and through the window I could see them pull on a rope looped over a branch. The rope was tied to the roof, and the roof opened up like a basket lid. I would sleep with the moon and the stars. I did not see whether the old people slept, so quickly did I drop off, but they would be there waking me with food in the morning.

"Little girl, you have now spent almost a day and a night with us," the old woman said. In the morning light I could see her earlobes pierced with gold. "Do you think you can bear to stay with us for fifteen years? We can train you to become a warrior."

"What about my mother and father?" I asked.

The old man untied the drinking gourd slung across his back. He lifted the lid by its stem and looked for something in the water. "Ah, there," he said.

At first I saw only water so clear it magnified the fibers in the walls of the gourd. On the surface, I saw only my own round reflection. The old man encircled the neck of the gourd with his thumb and index finger and gave it a shake. As the water shook, then settled, the colors and lights shimmered into a picture, not reflecting anything I could see around me. There at the bottom of the gourd were my mother and father scanning the sky, which was where I was. "It has happened already, then," I could hear my mother say. "I didn't expect it so soon." "You knew from her birth that she would be taken," my father answered. "We'll have to harvest potatoes without her help this year," my mother said, and they turned away toward the fields, straw baskets in their arms. The water shook and became just water again. "Mama. Papa," I called, but they were in the valley and could not hear me.

"What do you want to do?" the old man asked. "You can go back right now if you like. You can go pull sweet potatoes, or you can stay with us and learn how to fight barbarians and bandits."

"You can avenge your village," said the old woman. "You can recapture the harvests the thieves have taken. You can be remembered by the Han people for your dutifulness."

"I'll stay with you," I said.

So the hut became my home, and I found out that the old woman did not arrange the pine needles by hand. She opened the roof; an autumn wind would come up, and the needles fell in braids—brown strands, green strands, yellow strands. The old woman waved her arms in conducting motions; she blew softly with her mouth. I thought, nature certainly works differently on mountains than in valleys.

"The first thing you have to learn," the old woman told me, "is how to be quiet." They left me by streams to watch for animals. "If you're noisy, you'll make the deer go without water."

When I could kneel all day without my legs cramping and my breathing became even, the squirrels would bury their hoardings at the hem of my shirt and then bend their tails in a celebration dance. At night, the mice and toads looked at me, their eyes quick stars and slow stars. Not once would I see a three-legged toad, though; you need strings of cash to bait them.

The two old people led me in exercises that began at dawn and ended at sunset so that I could watch our shadows grow and shrink and grow again, rooted to the earth. I learned to move my fingers, hands, feet, head, and entire body in circles. I walked putting heel down first, toes pointing outward thirty to forty degrees, making the ideograph "eight," making the ideograph "human." Knees bent, I would swing into the slow, measured "square step," the powerful walk into battle. After five years my body became so strong that I could control even the dilations of the pupils inside my irises. I could copy owls and bats, the words for "bat" and "blessing" homonyms. After six years the deer let me run beside them. I could jump twenty feet into the air from a standstill, leaping like a monkey over the hut. Every creature has a hiding skill and a fighting skill a warrior can use. When birds alighted on my palm, I could yield my muscles under their feet and give them no base from which to fly away.

But I could not fly like the bird that led me here, except in large, free dreams.

During the seventh year (I would be fourteen), the two old people led me blindfolded to the mountains of the white tigers. They held me by either elbow and shouted into my ears, "Run. Run. Run." I ran and, not stepping off a cliff at the edge of my toes and not hitting my forehead against a wall, ran faster. A wind buoyed me up over the roots, the rocks, the little hills. We reached the tiger place in no time—a mountain peak three feet three from the sky. We had to bend over.

The old people waved once, slid down the mountain, and disappeared around a tree. The old woman, good with the bow and arrow, took them with her; the old man took the water gourd. I would have to survive bare-handed. Snow lay on the ground, and snow fell in loose gusts—another way the dragon breathes. I walked in the direction from which we had come, and when I reached the timberline, I collected wood broken from the cherry tree, the peony, and the walnut, which is the tree of life. Fire, the old people had taught me, is stored in trees that grow red flowers or red berries in the spring or whose leaves turn red in the fall. I took the wood from the protected spots beneath the trees and wrapped it in my scarf to keep dry. I dug where squirrels might have come, stealing one or two nuts at each place. These I also wrapped in my scarf. It is possible, the old people said, for a human being to live for fifty days on water. I would save the roots and nuts for hard climbs, the places where nothing grew, the emergency should I not find the hut. This time there would be no bird to follow.

The first night I burned half of the wood and slept curled against the mountain. I heard the white tigers prowling on the other side of the fire, but I could not distinguish them from the snow patches. The morning rose perfectly. I hurried along, again collecting wood and edibles. I ate nothing and only drank the snow my fires made run.

The first two days were gifts, the fasting so easy to do, I so smug in my strength that on the third day, the hardest, I caught myself sitting on the ground, opening the scarf and staring at the nuts and dry roots. Instead of walking steadily on or even eating, I faded into dreams about the meat meals my mother used to cook, my monk's food forgotten. That night I burned up most of the wood I had collected, unable to sleep for facing my death—if not death here, then death someday. The moon animals that did not hibernate came out to hunt, but I had given up the habits of a carnivore since living with the old people. I would not trap the mice that danced so close or the owls that plunged just outside the fire.

On the fourth and fifth days, my eyesight sharp with hunger, I saw deer and used their trails when our ways coincided. Where the deer nibbled, I gathered the fungus, the fungus of immortality.

At noon on the tenth day I packed snow, white as rice, into the worn center of a rock pointed out to me by a finger of ice, and around the rock I built a fire. In the warming water I put roots, nuts, and the fungus of immortality. For variety I ate a quarter of the nuts and roots raw. Oh, green joyous rush inside my mouth, my head, my stomach, my toes, my soul—the best meal of my life.

One day I found that I was striding long distances without hindrance, my bundle light. Food had become so scarce that I was no longer stopping to collect it. I had walked into dead land. Here even the snow stopped. I did not go back to the richer areas, where I could not stay anyway, but, resolving to fast until I got halfway to the next woods, I started across the dry rocks. Heavily weighed down by the wood on my back, branches poking maddeningly, I had burned almost all of the fuel not to waste strength lugging it.

Somewhere in the dead land I lost count of the days. It seemed as if I had been walking forever; life had never been different from this. An old man and an old woman were help I had only wished for. I was fourteen years old and lost from my village. I was walking in circles. Hadn't I been already found by the old people? Or was that yet to come? I wanted my mother and father. The old man and old woman were only a part of this lostness and this hunger.

One nightfall I ate the last of my food but had enough sticks for a good fire. I stared into the flames, which reminded me about helping my mother with the cooking and made me cry. It was very strange looking through water into fire and seeing my mother again. I nodded, orange and warm.

A white rabbit hopped beside me, and for a moment I thought it was a blob of snow that had fallen out of the sky. The rabbit and I studied each other. Rabbits taste like chickens. My mother and father had taught me how to hit rabbits over the head with wine jugs, then skin them cleanly for fur vests. "It's a cold night to be an animal," I said. "So you want some fire too, do you? Let me put on another branch, then." I would not hit it with the branch. I had learned from rabbits to kick backward. Perhaps this one was sick because normally the animals did not like fire. The rabbit seemed alert enough, however, looking at me so acutely, bounding up to the fire. But it did not stop when it got to the edge. It turned its face once toward me, then jumped into the fire. The fire went down for a moment, as if crouching in surprise, then the flames shot up taller than before. When the fire became calm again, I saw the rabbit had turned into meat, browned just right. I ate it, knowing the rabbit had sacrificed itself for me. It had made me a gift of meat.

When you have been walking through trees hour after hour—and I finally reached trees after the dead land—branches cross out everything, no relief whichever way your head turns until your eyes start to invent new sights. Hunger also changes the world—when eating can't be a habit, then neither can seeing. I saw two people made of gold dancing the earth's dances. They turned so perfectly that together they were the axis of the earth's turning. They were light; they were molten, changing gold—Chinese lion dancers, African lion dancers in midstep. I heard high Javanese bells deepen in midring to Indian bells, Hindu Indian, American Indian. Before my eyes, gold bells shredded into gold tassles that fanned into two royal capes that softened into lions' fur. Manes grew tall into feathers that shone—became light rays. Then the dancers danced the future—a machine-future—in clothes I had never seen before. I am watching the centuries pass in moments because suddenly I understand time, which is spinning and fixed like the North Star. And I understand how working and hoeing are dancing; how peasant clothes are golden, as king's clothes are golden; how one of the dancers is always a man and the other a woman.

The man and the woman grow bigger and bigger, so bright. All light. They are tall angels in two rows. They have high white wings on their backs. Perhaps there are infinite angels; perhaps I see two angels in their consecutive moments. I cannot bear their brightness and cover my eyes, which hurt from opening so wide without a blink. When I put my hands down to look again, I recognize the old brown man and the old gray woman walking toward me out of the pine forest.

It would seem that this small crack in the mystery was opened, not so much by the old people's magic, as by hunger. Afterward, whenever I did not eat for long, as during famine or battle, I could stare at ordinary people and see their light and gold. I could see their dance. When I get hungry enough, then killing and falling are dancing too.

The old people fed me hot vegetable soup. Then they asked me to talk-story about what happened in the mountains of the white tigers. I told them that the white tigers had stalked me through the snow but that I had fought them off with burning branches, and my great-grandparents had come to lead me safely through the forests. I had met a rabbit who taught me about self-immolation and how to speed up transmigration: one does not have to become worms first but can change directly into a human being—as in our own humaneness we had just changed bowls of vegetable soup into people too. That made them laugh. "You tell good stories," they said. "Now go to sleep, and tomorrow we will begin your dragon lessons."

"One more thing," I wanted to say. "I saw you and how old you really are." But I was already asleep; it came out only a murmur. I would want to tell them about that last moment of my journey; but it was only one moment out of the weeks that I had been gone, and its telling would keep till morning. Besides, the two people must already know. In the next years, when I suddenly came upon them or when I caught them out of the corners of my eyes, he appeared as a handsome young man, tall with long black hair, and she, as a beautiful young woman who ran bare-legged through the trees. In the spring she dressed like a bride; she wore juniper leaves in her hair and a black embroidered jacket. I learned to shoot accurately because my teachers held the targets. Often when sighting along an arrow, there to the side I would glimpse the young man or young woman, but when I looked directly, he or she would be old again. By this time I had guessed from their sexless manner that the old woman was to the old man a sister or a friend rather than a wife.

After I returned from my survival test, the two old people trained me in dragon ways, which took another eight years. Copying the tigers, their stalking kill and their anger, had been a wild, bloodthirsty joy. Tigers are easy to find, but I needed adult wisdom to know dragons. "You have to infer the whole dragon from the parts you can see and touch," the old people would say. Unlike tigers, dragons are so immense, I would never see one in its entirety. But I could explore the mountains, which are the top of its head. "These mountains are also *like* the tops of *other* dragons' heads," the old people would tell me. When climbing the slopes, I could understand that I was a bug riding on a dragon's forehead as it roams through space, its speed so different from my speed that I feel the dragon solid and immobile. In quarries I could see its strata, the dragon's veins and muscles; the minerals, its teeth and bone. I could touch the stones the old woman wore—its bone marrow. I had worked the soil, which is its flesh, and harvested the plants and climbed the trees, which are its hairs. I could listen to its voice in the thunder and feel its breathing in the winds, see its breathing in the clouds. Its tongue is the lightning. And the red that the lightning gives to the world is strong and lucky—in blood, poppies, roses, rubies, the red feathers of birds, the red carp, the cherry tree, the peony, the line alongside the turtle's eyes and the mallard's. In the spring when the dragon awakes, I watched its turnings in the rivers.

## Questions for Rereading, Discussing, Connecting, and Writing

### Rereading

**1.** Finding the voice of the writer as we read can be a difficult but rewarding part of comprehending and enjoying texts. Maxine Hong Kingston's "voice" is a complex one, since it is composed of several ages, several places, and several realities. Try to sort these out—these several parts of her voice—and decide which you consider to be most important in hearing Kingston's "talk-story."

**2.** Choose the most vivid incident in this short excerpt from *The Woman Warrior* and decide with as much specific analysis as possible what makes this excerpt *most* vivid. Is it sensory detail? Is it clarity of action? Is it the voices or spoken words of the characters? Is it *true*? Your analysis can be as close as arguing for *one* word being just the perfect choice.

### Discussing

**3.** The narrator of this selection is a journeyer of a different sort than those of the other selections. Define this crucial difference in the quality of the journey. Describe your last journey of this kind.

**4.** "Talking story" is another term for "oral literature" coming to life in the real world, our world. Try to talk story to a group; begin with a plot or action or character or place or time in mind, and then develop it *out loud*.

**5.** The narrator says that listening to her mother "talking-story" was "great power." Try to recall the storytelling that you have received from parents or guardians, and what those stories meant to you as a young child.

### Connecting

**6.** Compare the narrator of Kingston's selection with other women in this book—Sojourner Truth (p. 259), for example, or Beryl Markham (p. 35), or Meridel LeSueur (p. 84). Is there a single quality that binds them together?

**7.** This selection is about a "secret" of great value that is withheld from general view because it is an invention of the mind. How many other journeys in this book are secret? Look at the Lange (p. 215), Parker (p. 230), and

Goya (p. 257), for example, and find in these pieces more journeys than are just shown on the page. Try to discover the mental processes of those people in the selections.

WRITING

**8.** Write your own imaginary journey, in which you become exactly what your ideals or your dreams have shown that you should become. Persuade the reader that this is *you*, only "better."

**9.** Kingston draws on old Chinese folktales and myths for her backgrounds and actions. Draw on fairy tales or folk stories or myths that you are familiar with, and reshape your own life—or a part of your life—into a story that clearly resembles a myth or folktale that some of your readers will recognize. Has your life been like Cinderella's? Or Paul Bunyan's?

Tom Wolfe

# "The Angels," from The Right Stuff (1979)

Within five minutes, or ten minutes, no more than that, three of the others had called her on the telephone to ask her if she had heard that something had happened out there.

"Jane, this is Alice. Listen, I just got a call from Betty, and she said she heard something's happened out there. Have you heard anything?" That was the way they phrased it, call after call. She picked up the telephone and began relaying this same message to some of the others.

"Connie, this is Jane Conrad. Alice just called me, and she says something's happened . . ."

*Something* was part of the official Wife Lingo for tiptoeing blindfolded around the subject. Being barely twenty-one years old and new around here, Jane Conrad knew very little about this particular subject, since nobody ever talked about it. But the day was young! And what a setting she had for her imminent enlightenment! And what a picture she herself presented! Jane was tall and slender and had rich brown hair and high cheekbones and wide brown eyes. She looked a little like the actress Jean Simmons. Her father was a rancher in southwestern Texas. She had gone East to college, to Bryn Mawr, and had met her husband, Pete, at a debutante's party at the Gulf Mill Club in Philadelphia, when he was a senior at Princeton. Pete was a short, wiry, blond boy who joked around a lot. At any moment his face was likely to break into a wild grin revealing the gap between his front teeth. The Hickory Kid sort, he was; a Hickory Kid on the deb circuit, however. He had an air of energy, self-confidence, ambition, *joie de vivre*. Jane and Pete were married two days after he graduated from Princeton. Last year Jane gave birth to their first child, Peter. And today, here in Florida, in Jacksonville, in the peaceful year 1955, the sun shines through the pines outside, and the very air takes on the sparkle of the ocean. The ocean and a great mica-white beach are less than a mile away. Anyone driving by will see Jane's little house gleaming like a dream house in the pines. It is a brick house, but Jane and Pete painted the bricks white, so that it gleams in the sun against a great green screen of pine trees with a thousand little places where the sun peeks through. They painted the shutters black, which makes the white walls look even more brilliant. The house has only eleven hundred square feet of floor space, but Jane and Pete designed it themselves and that more than makes up for the size. A friend of theirs was the builder and gave them every possible break, so that it cost only eleven thousand dollars. Outside, the sun shines, and inside, the fever rises by the minute as five, ten, fifteen, and, finally, nearly all twenty of the wives join the circuit, trying to find out what has happened, which, in fact, means: to whose husband.

After thirty minutes on such a circuit—this is not an unusual morning around here—a wife begins to feel that the telephone is no longer located on a table or on the kitchen wall. It is exploding in her solar plexus. Yet it would be far worse right now to hear the front doorbell. The protocol is strict on that point, although written down nowhere. No woman is supposed to deliver the final news, and certainly not on the telephone. The matter mustn't be bungled!—that's the idea. No, a man should bring the news when the time comes, a man with some official or moral authority, a clergyman or a comrade of the newly deceased. Furthermore, he should bring the bad news in person. He should turn up at the front door and ring the bell and be standing there like a pillar of coolness and competence, bearing the bad news on ice, like a fish. Therefore, all the telephone calls from the wives were the frantic and portentous beating of the wings of the death angels, as it were. When the final news came, there would be a ring at the front door—a wife in this situation finds herself staring at the front door as if she no longer owns it or controls it—and outside the door would be a man . . . come to inform her that unfortunately something has happened out there, and her husband's body now lies incinerated in the swamps or the pines or the palmetto grass, "burned beyond recognition," which anyone who had been around an air base for very long (fortunately Jane had not) realized was quite an artful euphemism to describe a human body that now looked like an enormous fowl that has burned up in a stove, burned a blackish brown all over, greasy and blistered, fried, in a word, with not only the entire face and all the hair and the ears burned off, not to mention all the clothing, but also the *hands* and *feet*, with what remains of the arms and legs bent at the knees and elbows and burned into absolutely rigid angles, burned a greasy blackish brown like the bursting body itself, so that this husband, father, officer, gentleman, this *ornamentum* of some mother's eye,

His Majesty the Baby of just twenty-odd years back, has been reduced to a charred hulk with wings and shanks sticking out of it.

*My own husband*—how could this be what they were talking about? Jane had heard the young men, Pete among them, talk about other young men who had "bought it" or "augered in" or "crunched," but it had never been anyone they knew, no one in the squadron. And in any event, the way they talked about it, with such breezy, slangy terminology, was the same way they talked about sports. It was as if they were saying, "He was thrown out stealing second base." And that was all! Not one word, not in print, not in conversation—not in this amputated language!—about an incinerated corpse from which a young man's spirit has vanished in an instant, from which all smiles, gestures, moods, worries, laughter, wiles, shrugs, tenderness, and loving looks—*you, my love!*—have disappeared like a sigh, while the terror consumes a cottage in the woods, and a young woman, sizzling with the fever, awaits her confirmation as the new widow of the day.

The next series of calls greatly increased the possibility that it was Pete to whom something had happened. There were only twenty men in the squadron, and soon nine or ten had been accounted for . . . by the fluttering reports of the death angels. Knowing that the word was out that an accident had occurred, husbands who could get to a telephone were calling home to say *it didn't happen to me*. This news, of course, was immediately fed to the fever. Jane's telephone would ring once more, and one of the wives would be saying:

"Nancy just got a call from Jack. He's at the squadron and he says something's happened, but he doesn't know what. He said he saw Frank D\_\_\_\_\_ take off about ten minutes ago with Greg in back, so they're all right. What have you heard?"

But Jane has heard nothing except that other husbands, and not hers, are safe and accounted for. And thus, on a sunny day in Florida, outside of the Jacksonville Naval Air Station, in a little white cottage, a veritable dream house, another beautiful young woman was about to be apprised of the *quid pro quo* of her husband's line of work, of the tradeoff, as one might say, the subparagraphs of a contract written in no visible form. Just as surely as if she had the entire roster in front of her, Jane now realized that only two men in the squadron were unaccounted for. One was a pilot named Bud Jennings; the other was Pete. She picked up the telephone and did something that was much frowned on in a time of emergency. She called the squadron office. The duty officer answered.

"I want to speak to Lieutenant Conrad," said Jane. "This is Mrs. Conrad."

"I'm sorry," the duty officer said—and then his voice cracked. "I'm sorry . . . I . . ." He couldn't find the words! He was about to cry! "I'm—that's—I mean . . . he can't come to the phone!"

*He can't come to the phone!*

"It's very important!" said Jane.

"I'm sorry—it's impossible—" The duty officer could hardly get the words out because he was so busy gulping back sobs. *Sobs!* "He can't come to the phone."

"Why not? Where is he?"

"I'm sorry—" More sighs, wheezes, snuffling gasps. "I can't tell you that. I—I have to hang up now!"

And the duty officer's voice disappeared in a great surf of emotion and he hung up.

The duty officer! *The very sound of her voice was more than he could take!*

The world froze, congealed, in that moment. Jane could no longer calculate the interval before the front doorbell would ring and some competent long-faced figure would appear, some Friend of Widows and Orphans, who would inform her, officially, that Pete was dead.

Even out in the middle of the swamp, in this rot-bog of pine trunks, scum slicks, dead dodder vines, and mosquito eggs, even out in this great overripe sump, the smell of "burned beyond recognition" obliterated everything else. When airplane fuel exploded, it created a heat so intense that everything but the hardest metals not only *burned*—everything of rubber, plastic, celluloid, wood, leather, cloth, flesh, gristle, calcium, horn, hair, blood, and protoplasm—it not only burned, it gave up the ghost in the form of every stricken putrid gas known to chemistry. One could smell the horror. It came in through the nostrils and burned the rhinal cavities raw and penetrated the liver and permeated the bowels like a black gas until there was nothing in the universe, inside or out, except the stench of the char. As the helicopter came down between the pine trees and settled onto the bogs, the smell hit Pete Conrad even before the hatch was completely open, and they were not even close enough to see the wreckage yet. The rest of the way Conrad and the crewmen had to travel on foot. After a few steps the water was up to their knees, and then it was up to their armpits, and they kept wading through the water and the scum and the vines and the pine trunks, but it was nothing compared to the smell. Conrad, a twenty-five-year-old lieutenant junior grade, happened to be on duty as squadron safety officer that day and was supposed to make the on-site investigation of the crash. The fact was, however, that this squadron was the first duty assignment of his career, and he had never been at a crash site before and had never smelled any such revolting stench or seen anything like what awaited him.

When Conrad finally reached the plane, which was an SNJ, he found the fuselage burned and blistered and dug into the swamp with one wing sheared off and the cockpit canopy smashed. In the front seat was all that was left of his friend Bud Jennings. Bud Jennings, an amiable fellow, a promising young fighter pilot, was now a horrible roasted hulk—with no head. His head was completely gone, apparently torn off the spinal column like a pineapple off a stalk, except that it was nowhere to be found.

Conrad stood there soaking wet in the swamp bog, wondering what the hell to do. It was a struggle to move twenty feet in this freaking muck. Every time he looked up, he was looking into a delirium of limbs, vines, dappled shadows, and a chopped-up white light that came through the treetops—the ubiquitous screen of trees with a thousand little places where the sun peeked through. Nevertheless, he started wading back out into the muck and the scum, and the others followed. He kept looking up. Gradually he could make it out. Up in the treetops there was a pattern of broken limbs where the SNJ had come crashing through. It was like a tunnel through the treetops. Conrad and the others began splashing through the swamp, following the strange path ninety or a hundred feet above them. It took a sharp turn. That must have been where the wing broke off. The trail veered to one side and started downward. They kept looking up and wading through the muck. Then they stopped. There was a great green sap wound up there in the middle of a tree trunk. It was odd. Near the huge gash was . . . tree disease . . . some sort of brownish lumpy sac up in the branches, such as you see in trees infested by bagworms, and there were yellowish curds on the branches around it, as if the disease had caused the sap to ooze out and fester and congeal—except that it couldn't be sap because it was streaked with blood. In the next instant—Conrad didn't have to say a word. Each man could see it all. The lumpy sac was the cloth liner of a flight helmet, with the earphones attached to it. The curds were Bud Jennings's brains. The tree trunk had smashed through the cockpit canopy of the SNJ and knocked Bud Jennings's head to pieces like a melon.

In keeping with the protocol, the squadron commander was not going to release Bud Jennings's name until his widow, Loretta, had been located and a competent male death messenger had been dispatched to tell her. But Loretta Jennings was not at home and could not be found. Hence, a delay—and more than enough time for the other wives, the death angels, to burn with panic over the telephone lines. All the pilots were accounted for except the two who were in the woods, Bud Jennings and Pete Conrad. One chance in two, acey-deucy, one finger-two finger, and this was not an unusual day around here.

Loretta Jennings had been out at a shopping center. When she returned home, a certain figure was waiting outside, a man, a solemn Friend of Widows and Orphans, and it was Loretta Jennings who lost the game of odd and even, acey-deucy, and it was Loretta whose child (she was pregnant with a second) would have no father. It was this young woman who went through all the final horrors that Jane Conrad had imagined—*assumed!*—would be hers to endure forever. Yet this grim stroke of fortune brought Jane little relief.

On the day of Bud Jennings's funeral, Pete went into the back of the closet and brought out his bridge coat, per regulations. This was the most stylish item in the Navy officer's wardrobe. Pete had never had occasion to wear his before. It was a double-breasted coat made of navy-blue melton cloth and came down almost to the ankles. It must have weighed ten pounds. It had a double row of gold buttons down the front and loops for shoulder boards, big beautiful belly-cut collar and lapels, deep turnbacks on the sleeves, a tailored waist, and a center vent in back that ran from the waistline to the bottom of the coat. Never would Pete, or for that matter many other American males in the mid-twentieth century, have an article of clothing quite so impressive and aristocratic as that bridge coat. At the funeral the nineteen little Indians who were left—Navy boys!—lined up manfully in their bridge coats. They looked so young. Their pink, lineless faces with their absolutely clear, lean jawlines popped up bravely, correctly, out of the enormous belly-cut collars of the bridge coats. They sang an old Navy hymn, which slipped into a strange and lugubrious minor key here and there, and included a stanza added especially for aviators. It ended with: "O hear us when we lift our prayer for those in peril in the air."

Three months later another member of the squadron crashed and was burned beyond recognition and Pete hauled out the bridge coat again and Jane saw eighteen little Indians bravely going through the motions at the funeral. Not long after that, Pete was transferred from

Jacksonville to the Patuxent River Naval Air Station in Maryland. Pete and Jane had barely settled in there when they got word that another member of the Jacksonville squadron, a close friend of theirs, someone they had had over to dinner many times, had died trying to take off from the deck of a carrier in a routine practice session a few miles out in the Atlantic. The catapult that propelled aircraft off the deck lost pressure, and his ship just dribbled off the end of the deck, with its engine roaring vainly, and fell sixty feet into the ocean and sank like a brick, and he vanished, *just like that.*

Pete had been transferred to Patuxent River, which was known in Navy vernacular as Pax River, to enter the Navy's new test-pilot school. This was considered a major step up in the career of a young Navy aviator. Now that the Korean War was over and there was no combat flying, all the hot young pilots aimed for flight test. In the military they always said "flight test" and not "test flying." Jet aircraft had been in use for barely ten years at the time, and the Navy was testing new jet fighters continually. Pax River was the Navy's prime test center.

Jane liked the house they bought at Pax River. She didn't like it as much as the little house in Jacksonville, but then she and Pete hadn't designed this one. They lived in a community called North Town Creek, six miles from the base. North Town Creek, like the base, was on a scrub-pine peninsula that stuck out into Chesapeake Bay. They were tucked in amid the pine trees. (Once more!) All around were rhododendron bushes. Pete's classwork and his flying duties were very demanding. Everyone in his flight test class, Group 20, talked about how difficult it was—and obviously loved it, because in Navy flying this was the big league. The young men in Group 20 and their wives were Pete's and Jane's entire social world. They associated with no one else. They constantly invited each other to dinner during the week; there was a Group party at someone's house practically every weekend; and they would go off on outings to fish or waterski in Chesapeake Bay. In a way they could not have associated with anyone else, at least not easily, because the boys could talk only about one thing: their flying. One of the phrases that kept running through the conversation was "pushing the outside of the envelope." The "envelope" was a flight-test term referring to the limits of a particular aircraft's performance, how tight a turn it could make at such-and-such speed, and so on. "Pushing the outside," probing the outer limits, of the envelope seemed to be the great challenge and satisfaction of flight test. At first "pushing the outside of the envelope" was not a particularly terrifying phrase to hear. It sounded once more as if the boys were just talking about sports.

Then one sunny day a member of the Group, one of the happy lads they always had dinner with and drank with and went waterskiing with, was coming in for a landing at the base in an A3J fighter plane. He came in too low before lowering his flaps, and the ship stalled out, and he crashed and was burned beyond recognition. And they brought out the bridge coats and sang about those in peril in the air and put the bridge coats away, and the Indians who were left talked about the accident after dinner one night. They shook their heads and said it was a damned shame, but he should have known better than to wait so long before lowering the flaps.

Barely a week had gone by before another member of the Group was coming in for a landing in the same type of aircraft, the A3J, trying to make a ninety-degree landing, which involves a sharp turn, and something went wrong with the controls, and he ended up with one rear stabilizer wing up and the other one down, and his ship rolled in like a corkscrew from 800 feet up and crashed, and he was burned beyond recognition. And the bridge coats came out and they sang about those in peril in the air and then they put the bridge coats away and after dinner one night they mentioned that the departed had been a good man but was inexperienced, and when the malfunction in the controls put him in that bad corner, he didn't know how to get out of it.

Every wife wanted to cry out: "Well, my God! The *machine* broke! What makes *any* of you think you would have come out of it any better!" Yet intuitively Jane and the rest of them knew it wasn't right even to suggest that. Pete never indicated for a moment that he thought any such thing could possibly happen to him. It seemed not only wrong but dangerous to challenge a young pilot's confidence by posing the question. And that, too, was part of the unofficial protocol for the Officer's Wife. From now on every time Pete was late coming in from the flight line, she would worry. She began to wonder if—no! *assume!*—he had found his way into one of those corners they all talked about so spiritedly, one of those little dead ends that so enlivened conversation around here.

Not long after that, another good friend of theirs went up in an F-4, the Navy's newest and hottest fighter plane, known as the Phantom. He reached twenty thousand feet and then nosed over and dove straight into Chesapeake Bay. It turned out that a hose connection was missing in his oxygen system and he had suffered hypoxia and passed out at the high altitude. And the bridge coats came out and they lifted a prayer about those in peril in the air and the bridge coats were put away and the little Indians were incredulous. How could anybody fail to check his hose connections? And how could anybody be in such poor condition as to pass out *that quickly* from hypoxia?

A couple of days later Jane was standing at the window of her house in North Town Creek. She saw some smoke rise above the pines from over in the direction of the flight line. Just that, a column of smoke; no explosion or sirens or any other sound. She went to another room, so as not to have to think about it but there was no explanation for the smoke. She went back to the window. In the yard of a house across the street she saw a group of people . . . standing there and looking at her house, as if trying to decide what to do. Jane looked away—but she couldn't keep from looking out again. She caught a glimpse of *a certain figure* coming up the walkway toward her front door. She knew exactly who it was. She had had nightmares like this. And yet this was no dream. She was wide awake and alert. Never more alert in her entire life! Frozen, completely defeated by the sight, she simply waited for the bell to ring. She waited, but there was not a sound. Finally she could stand it no more. In real life, unlike her dream life, Jane was both too self-possessed and too polite to scream through the door: "Go away!" So she opened it. There was no one there, no one at all. There was no group of people on the lawn across the way and no one to be seen for a hundred yards in any direction along the lawns and leafy rhododendron roads of North Town Creek.

Then began a cycle in which she had both the nightmares and the hallucinations, continually. Anything could touch off an hallucination: a ball of smoke, a telephone ring that stopped before she could answer it, the sound of a siren, even the sound of trucks starting up (crash trucks!). Then she would glance out the window, and a certain figure would be coming up the walk, and she would wait for the bell. The only difference between the dreams and the hallucinations was that the scene of the dreams was always the little white house in Jacksonville. In both cases, the feeling that *this time it has happened* was quite real.

The star pilot in the class behind Pete's, a young man who was the main rival of their good friend Al Bean, went up in a fighter to do some power-dive tests. One of the most demanding disciplines in flight test was to accustom yourself to making precise readings from the control panel in the same moment that you were pushing the outside of the envelope. This young man put his ship into the test dive and was still reading out the figures, with diligence and precision and great discipline, when he augered straight into the oyster flats and was burned beyond recognition. And the bridge coats came out and they sang about those in peril in the air and the bridge coats were put away, and the little Indians remarked that the departed was a swell guy and a brilliant student of flying; a little too *much* of a student, in fact; he hadn't bothered to look out the window at the real world soon enough. Beano—Al Bean—wasn't quite so brilliant; on the other hand, he was still here.

Like many other wives in Group 20 Jane wanted to talk about the whole situation, the incredible series of fatal accidents, with her husband and the other members of the Group, to find out how they were taking it. But somehow the unwritten protocol forbade discussions of this subject, which was the fear of death. Nor could Jane or any of the rest of them talk, really *have a talk,* with anyone around the base. You could talk to another wife about being worried. But what good did it do? Who *wasn't* worried? You were likely to get a look that said: *"Why dwell on it?"* Jane might have gotten away with divulging the matter of the nightmares. But *hallucinations?* There was no room in Navy life for any such anomalous tendency as that.

By now the bad string had reached ten in all, and almost all of the dead had been close friends of Pete and Jane, young men who had been in their house many times, young men who had sat across from Jane and chattered like the rest of them about the grand adventure of military flying. And the survivors still sat around *as before*—with the same inexplicable exhilaration! Jane kept watching Pete for some sign that his spirit was cracking, but she saw none. He talked a mile a minute, kidded and joked, laughed with his Hickory Kid cackle. He always had. He still enjoyed the company of members of the group like Wally Schirra and Jim Lovell. Many young pilots were taciturn and cut loose with the strange fervor of this business only in the air. But Pete and Wally and Jim were not reticent; not in any situation. They loved to kid around. Pete called Jim Lovell "Shaky," because it was the last thing a pilot would want to be called. Wally Schirra was outgoing to the point of hearty; he loved practical jokes and dreadful puns, and so on. The three of them—*even in the midst of this bad string!*—would love to get on a subject such as accident-prone Mitch Johnson. Accident-prone Mitch Johnson, it seemed, was a Navy pilot whose life was in the hands of two angels, one of them bad and the other one good. The bad angel would put him into accidents that would have annihilated any ordinary pilot, and the good angel would bring him out of them without a scratch. Just the other day—this was the sort of story Jane would hear them tell—Mitch Johnson was coming in to land on a carrier. But he came in short, missed the flight deck, and crashed into the fantail, below the deck. There was a tremendous explosion, and the rear half of the plane fell into the water in flames. Everyone on the flight deck said, "Poor Johnson. The good angel was off duty." They were still debating how to remove the debris and his mortal remains when a phone rang on the bridge. A somewhat dopey voice said, "This is Johnson. Say, listen, I'm down here in the supply hold and the hatch is locked and I can't find the lights and I can't see a goddamned thing and I tripped over a cable and I think I hurt my leg." The officer on the bridge slammed the phone down, then vowed to find out what morbid sonofabitch could pull a phone prank at a time like this. Then the phone rang again, and the man with the dopey voice managed to establish the fact that he was, indeed, Mitch Johnson. The good angel had not left his side. When he smashed into the fantail, he hit some empty ammunition drums, and they cushioned the impact, leaving him groggy but not seriously hurt. The fuselage had blown to pieces; so he just stepped out onto the fantail and opened a hatch that led into the supply hold. It was pitch black in there, and there were cables all across the floor, holding down spare aircraft engines. Accident-prone Mitch Johnson kept tripping over these cables until he found a telephone. Sure enough, the one injury he had was a bruised shin from tripping over a cable. The man was accident-prone! Pete and Wally and Jim absolutely cracked up over stories like this. It was amazing. Great sports yarns! Nothing more than that.

 A few days later Jane was out shopping at the Pax River commissary on Saunders Road, near the main gate to the base. She heard the sirens go off at the field, and then she heard the engines of the crash trucks start up. This time Jane was determined to keep calm. Every instinct made her want to rush home, but she forced herself to stay in the commissary and continue shopping. For thirty minutes she went through the motions of completing her shopping list. Then she drove home to North Town Creek. As she reached the house, she saw a figure going up the sidewalk. It was a man. Even from the back there was no question as to who he was. He had on a black suit, and there was a white band around his neck. It was her minister, from the Episcopal Church. She stared, and this vision did not come and go. The figure kept on walking up the front walk. She was not asleep now, and she was not inside her house glancing out the front window. She was outside in her car in front of her house. She was not dreaming, and she was not hallucinating, and the figure kept walking up toward her front door.

 The commotion at the field was over one of the most extraordinary things that even veteran pilots had ever seen at Pax River. And they had all seen it, because practically the entire flight line had gathered out on the field for it, as if it had been an air show.

Conrad's friend Ted Whelan had taken a fighter up, and on takeoff there had been a structural failure that caused a hydraulic leak. A red warning light showed up on Whelan's panel, and he had a talk with the ground. It was obvious that the leak would cripple the controls before he could get the ship back down to the field for a landing. He would have to bail out; the only question was where and when, and so they had a talk about that. They decided that he should jump at 8,100 feet at such-and-such a speed, directly over the field. The plane would crash into the Chesapeake Bay, and he would float down to the field. Just as coolly as anyone could have asked for it, Ted Whelan lined the ship up to come across the field at 8,100 feet precisely and he punched out, ejected.

Down on the field they all had their faces turned up to the sky. They saw Whelan pop out of the cockpit. With his Martin-Baker seat-parachute rig strapped on, he looked like a little black geometric lump a mile and a half up in the blue. They watched him as he started dropping. Everyone waited for the parachute to open. They waited a few more seconds, and then they waited some more. The little shape was getting bigger and bigger and picking up tremendous speed. Then there came an unspeakable instant at which everyone on the field who knew anything about parachute jumps knew what was going to happen. Yet even for them it was an unearthly feeling, for no one had ever seen any such thing happen so close up, from start to finish, from what amounted to a grandstand seat. Now the shape was going so fast and coming so close it began to play tricks on the eyes. It seemed to stretch out. It became much bigger and hurtled toward them at a terrific speed, until they couldn't make out its actual outlines at all. Finally there was just a streaking black blur before their eyes, followed by what seemed like an explosion. Except that it was not an explosion; it was the tremendous *crack* of Ted Whelan, his helmet, his pressure suit, and his seat-parachute rig smashing into the center of the runway, precisely on target, right in front of the crowd; an absolute bull's-eye. Ted Whelan had no doubt been alive until the instant of impact. He had had about thirty seconds to watch the Pax River base and the peninsula and Baltimore County and continental America and the entire comprehensible world rise up to smash him. When they lifted his body up off the concrete, it was like a sack of fertilizer.

Pete took out the bridge coat again and he and Jane and all the little Indians went to the funeral for Ted Whelan. That it hadn't been Pete was not solace enough for Jane. That the preacher had not, in fact, come to her front door as the Solemn Friend of Widows and Orphans, but merely for a church call . . . had not brought peace and relief. That Pete still didn't show the slightest indication of thinking that any unkind fate awaited him no longer lent her even a moment's courage. The next dream and the next hallucination, and the next and the next, merely seemed more real. For she now *knew.* She now knew the subject and the essence of this enterprise, even though not a word of it had passed anybody's lips. She even knew why Pete—the Princeton boy she met at a deb party at the Gulf Mill Club!—would never quit, never withdraw from this grim business, unless in a coffin. And God knew, and she knew, there was a coffin waiting for each little Indian.

Seven years later, when a reporter and a photographer from *Life* magazine actually stood near her in her living room and watched her face, while outside, on the lawn, a crowd of television crewmen and newspaper reporters waited for a word, an indication, anything—perhaps a glimpse through a part in a curtain!—waited for some sign of what she felt—when one and all asked with their ravenous eyes and, occasionally, in so many words: "How do you feel?" and "Are you scared?"—America wants to know!—it made Jane want to laugh, but in fact she couldn't even manage a smile.

"Why ask *now?*" she wanted to say. But they wouldn't have had the faintest notion of what she was talking about.

## Questions for Rereading, Discussing, Connecting, and Writing

### REREADING

**1.** The first paragraph of this chapter from *The Right Stuff* contains several "indefinites"—"five minutes, or ten minutes . . . others . . . her . . . something . . . out there." Sometimes being "fuzzy" like this can be criticized in writing. What effect does Wolfe's indefiniteness have on you as you read this selection's opening?

**2.** Wolfe is noted for his attention to sense-detail; he allows us to sense experience not only through sight or vision, but through the other four senses. Note Wolfe's attention to these senses as you read, and note what objects or events are drawn more lifelike because of this attention.

**3.** Death and injury—and the fear of both—are vividly drawn in this selection. Find examples as you read or reread, and try to discover what details are particularly powerful, and why.

## Discussing

**4.** The astronauts of America's space program are called heroes. Why?

**5.** The journeys of America's astronauts since the early sixties have been the focus of great public attention. Why are these journeys valued by the public—and should they continue to be?

**6.** Has technology increased the safety of today's space travelers—as compared to the travelers of other times—or has it increased the jeopardy of space travelers? Point to examples in Wolfe's piece as evidence.

## Connecting

**7.** Homer (p. 101) might approve of the attention Wolfe pays to the wives of the astronauts, and to their own heroism. Why?

**8.** Does the character of Pete Conrad, and the other astronauts, resemble the character of other travelers in this chapter? Can you find a common denominator in these selections that can unite the travelers written of?

**9.** Travelers often visit strange lands; what words used by Polo (p. 112), Kingston (p. 154), and Wells (p. 124) can also be used to describe outer space?

## Writing

**10.** Waiting for news of a loved one is a common experience; the waiting can go on for hours, days, or weeks. Write your own account of *waiting*. What does it mean in terms of fear, loneliness, or overactive imagination?

**11.** The space program has suffered some setbacks in recent years. Write an argument for or against its continued existence as a government program.

**12.** Should humans take part in space exploration? Or should robots replace humans in space? Argue for or against these questions.

# Four

# Work and Play

$A$ composer sits at her desk thinking about a writing task. She draws a circle in the middle of a sheet of paper and writes a word in it. From that central circle, she draws a series of lines outward, and as she thinks of additional ideas she writes other words or phrases in smaller circles clustered around the central one. When she begins to write, this composer will not necessarily use everything she has written in this cluster of words, but playing with language in this way helps her generate ideas she can develop and use as she begins drafting.

Another composer sits at his word processor typing. He has been sitting there for two hours, and he has promised himself that he will stay there until he has produced a complete first draft. The words do not always come easily, and he deletes much of what he writes, but he keeps typing, not allowing himself to think about the beautiful fall day and the soccer game he is missing. When he finally stands up after another two hours his muscles are stiff, and he feels exhausted, but he has a first draft.

Composing, as these two vignettes illustrate, encompasses a mixture of work and play, with the combination leading to effective texts. The generation of ideas is frequently playful as composers draw unusual connections, develop exaggerated versions, or make sketches of their ideas. The play of composing may occur at the beginning of a writing project or anywhere in its development. Decisions about sentence shape—whether, for example, to connect two short sentences with a semicolon or to leave them separate—can be as playful as generating ideas.

The work of composing likewise occurs throughout the writing process. John McPhee, author of one of the selections included in this chapter, talks about forcing himself to sit in his office and write for more than eight hours a day. Sometimes these long hours yield little actual writing, because he is generating ideas or discards sections he has written. For most composers, the real work of writing comes with *revision*. Meaning literally to "re-see," revision requires composers to reconceptualize a whole topic. Frequently, this requires adding major sections, deleting favorite sentences, and making major organizational changes.

Revision enables composers to emphasize different aspects of a subject. This chapter's three paintings by Degas illustrate how one composer's revisions bring different elements of the same situation into focus. We can, as Degas suggests, consider an entire scene or look at a single individual within that scene. Similarly, we can, by changing the background of what we present, change the reader's perception of our subject. Revision in writing provides us opportunities to reconsider what we want to emphasize or minimize, in what order we want readers to encounter material.

Revision is one of the most powerful processes available to writers, and it is also one of the most difficult to understand. The work of revision is not often visible in the final composition. We don't see the many pencil sketches, the multiple drawings, or the discarded canvasses that go into a single painting. Similarly, we do not see the erasures, the arrows and lines covering a rough draft, or the crumpled sheets that lead to a piece of writing. We see the final printed copy with its neat margins and forget the messy drafts that preceded it. Most writing can be improved through revision, and without it ideas often remain undeveloped and concepts unclear. Revision is the hard work of writing that transforms ideas generated through language play into finished texts.

The selections in this chapter offer insight into the nature of both work and play. Laye and Parker, for example, show us something about the ritualistic aspect of work. The goldsmith who purifies his body before working and the pianist who writes in her journal every day before practicing remind us of the composer who must sharpen six pencils and arrange all the books on the desk before beginning to write. Far from trivial activities, these rituals play an important role in work, whether the work of fashioning gold or of writing.

Taken together, the selections in this chapter suggest the range of activities that can be included under the title of "work." Dancing, piloting a steamboat, and playing basketball may not be the first occupations that come to mind when the word "work" is mentioned, but this chapter's treatment of these and other occupations offers a way to broaden the meaning of a word usually associated with labor or toil. In addition to suggesting the variety of forms work can take, selections included here offer detailed examinations of what constitutes work of various sorts. Bacon's careful definition of studies, Amman's portrayal of the carpenter, and the Foxfire account of the shoemaker show, in very different ways, what it means to do a particular kind of work.

Some selections explore the emotional freight surrounding work. The shoemaker's pride in his craft, Mary Shelley's uncertainties about the value of her work, and Dorothea Lange's portrayal of the bindlestiff's (farm laborer's) search for work all demonstrate the close connection between feelings and work. These emotions are not, of course, exclusive to work. Selections such as Walton's discussion of fishing and McPhee's portrayal of Bill Bradley illustrate the immense commitment that can accompany what we call play.

Finally, the lines between work and play blur. Playful doodling to develop an idea merges into laborious completion of a draft, and that, in turn, opens the way to the play of a new turn of phrase. Play transforms itself into work as easily as work becomes play. The backyard baseball player becomes a professional paid to hit and field. The pianist decides to make music for her own pleasure. Writers alternating between visions and revisions can see in this chapter a reflection of the oscillation between work and play that marks their own composing.

*Jost Amman*

# The Carpenter (1568)

Ich Zimmermann / mach starck gebeuw /
In Schlösser / Heusser / alt vnd neuw /
Ich mach auch mancherley Mülwerck /
Auch Windmüln oben auff die Berg /
Uber die Wasser starcke Brückn /
Auch Schiff vnd Flöß / von freyen stückn /
Blochheusser zu der gegenwehr /
Dedalus gab mir diese Lehr.

The Carpenter builds houses, mills, bridges, ships, rafts, block-houses; Daedalus invented the art.

## Questions for Rereading, Discussing, Connecting, and Writing

### REREADING

**1.** Reading a woodcut is different from reading an essay or poem or story, but there are similarities too. When you first turned to "The Carpenter," how did you read or "take in" the picture?

**2.** We often read images without noticing *how*. If you were unaware of the way you read "The Carpenter," go back and note how your eyes move up, down, and across the picture as you put its elements or "pieces" together. What pieces catch your eye over and over—and what can this tell you about the picture?

**3.** No matter what we read, we expect to find a certain amount of *information* in the text. As you reread "The Carpenter" now, try to record the information in the picture, substituting word for picture. You may end up with a diagram that, like a wiring manual for a television, turns images into lines and words and symbols.

### DISCUSSING

**4.** "The Carpenter" is one of 75 arts, crafts, and trades depicted in a Renaissance text published in 1568. Consider the nature of carpentry. How do you think it can be construed as an art, craft, or trade?

**5.** The book's author considered his woodcuts "exact descriptions." Point to details—for example, the sawhorse—in the print that seem "exact" to you. How do they contribute to your understanding of "The Carpenter"?

**6.** What is puzzling or unclear to you in the woodcut? Identify those details or areas of uncertainty—for example, the items in the right front corner—then speculate on possible clarifications.

### CONNECTING

**7.** Consider "The Carpenter" in concert with some other selections dealing with descriptions of arts, crafts, and trades—for example, Degas' "The Dancing School" (p. 197) and Lange's farm laborer "Bindle Stiff" (p. 215). How does each treat its main character—with sympathy, criticism, admiration, love? How are these qualities communicated to the reader? Write captions for Degas and Lange in the style of Amman's caption for "The Carpenter."

**8.** Work and play are common subjects of our composing. Look at Amman, Degas (p. 197), Lange (p. 215), and McPhee (p. 218) and discover some common methods in composing about work and play. How, for example, is action handled? Choose the one you think best uses action—and give your reasons why.

9. Look for the subjects of work and play in other selections. How, for example, can the computer program (p. 372) be "enlarged" by you into a narrative or essay about work? Or the baseball box score (p. 235) be transformed into a narrative about play?

WRITING

10. The woodcut seems to be depicting not only a scene, but action as well. What can you say about the actions of each of the five people portrayed here? Narrate the essential action you can discover in the woodcut. Assume various points of view—the artist's, each of the figures', the Renaissance viewer's.

11. A freely rendered English summary of the German poem appears below the woodcut. How would you describe the relationship between the poem and the woodcut? What is the effect of the last line? Write your own text to "illustrate" the point—as you see it—of the woodcut.

12. Transform the print into a contemporary scene of a carpenter. Describe your carpenter and put this carpenter in an equivalent scene we might encounter in real life today.

*Francis Bacon*

# Of Studies (1597)

Studies serve for delight, for ornament, and for ability. Their chief use for delight is in privateness and retiring; for ornament, is in discourse; and for ability, is in the judgment and disposition of business; for expert men can execute, and perhaps judge of particulars, one by one; but the general counsels, and the plots and marshaling of affairs come best from those that are learned. To spend too much time in studies is sloth; to use them too much for ornament is affectation; to make judgment wholly by their rules is the humor of a scholar. They perfect nature, and are perfected by experience; for natural abilities are like natural plants, that need pruning by study; and studies themselves do give forth directions too much at large, except they be bounded in by experience. Crafty men contemn studies, simple men admire them, and wise men use them; for they teach not their own use; but that is a wisdom without them and above them, won by observation. Read not to contradict and confute, nor to believe and take for granted, nor to find talk and discourse, but to weigh and consider. Some books are to be tasted, others to be swallowed, and some few to be chewed and digested; that is, some books are to be read only in parts; others to be read but not curiously, and some few to be read wholly, and with diligence and attention. Some books also may be read by deputy, and extracts made of them by others; but that would be only in the less important arguments and the meaner sort of books; else distilled books are, like common distilled waters, flashy things. Reading maketh a full man; conference a ready man; and writing an exact man. And, therefore, if a man write little, he had need have a great memory; if he confer little, he had need have a present wit; and if he read little, he had need have much cunning, to seem to know that he doth not. Histories make men wise; poets, witty; the mathematics, subtle; natural philosophy, deep; moral, grave; logic and rhetoric, able to contend: *Abeunt studia in mores*! Nay, there is no stand or impediment in the wit but may be wrought out by fit studies; like as diseases of the body may have appropriate exercises. Bowling is good for the stone and reins, shooting for the lungs and breast, gentle walking for the stomach, riding for the head, and the like. So if a man's wit be wandering, let him study the mathematics; for in demonstrations, if his wit be called away never so little, he must begin again. If his wit be not apt to distinguish or find differences, let him study the schoolmen; for they are *cymini sectores*! If he be not apt to beat over matters, and to call up one thing to prove and illustrate another, let him study the lawyers' cases. So every defect of the mind may have a special receipt.

## Questions for Rereading, Discussing, Connecting, and Writing

### REREADING

1. "Of Studies" comes from Bacon's collection of essays—works written in journals as a relief from more serious writing. To what extent would you characterize this essay as "serious"?

2. Bacon's first sentence states the main point of his essay. What draws you to read on? How is your continued reading rewarded? When you have read this selection through at least twice, what can you say about Bacon's views on studies?

3. Francis Bacon was both a statesman and a scholar. He served as Lord Chancellor under King James I of England and wrote philosophical works that helped advance scientific development. As you read, consider the ways these two careers make themselves felt in this selection.

### DISCUSSING

4. This essay contains a number of pithy statements which have been quoted repeatedly. Identify a phrase that strikes you as memorable. Compare your phrase with those chosen by others and explain and discuss your choices.

5. Bacon identifies three purposes for study—delight, ornament, and ability. What other reasons can you think of for studying? Why, for example, do you study? Discuss your responses along with those of your classmates.

6. Although he acknowledges the value of studies, Bacon warns against too much study. Do you find his argument against excessive study convincing?

## Connecting

7. As a student, you no doubt have your own view of studies. In what ways do your experiences as a student lead you to agree or disagree with Bacon?

8. Although Bacon does not mention work or play specifically, he addresses both indirectly. Look at several other selections in this chapter and identify one that takes a similar attitude toward work and play.

9. Bacon discusses studies in terms of their ability to cure various defects of the mind. In what ways might other types of work—such as shoemaking, dancing, or writing—be considered cures? What might they cure?

## Writing

10. Drawing on your own experience as a student, write a contemporary version of "On Studies." Begin, as Bacon does, by identifying three purposes for study and then develop your explanation.

11. Bacon comments on the nature of reading and writing as he claims that reading makes one "full" and writing makes one "exact." Write an explanation of what these statements mean.

12. Bacon claims that to spend too much time on studies is laziness. Write an essay in which you argue either for or against this statement.

*Izaak Walton*

# The Complete Angler (1653)

Now for Flies, which is the third bait wherewith Trouts are usually taken. You are to know, that there are so many sorts of flies as there be of fruits: I will name you but some of them; as the Dun-fly, the Stone-fly, the Red-fly, the Moor-fly, the Tawny-fly, the Shell-fly, the Cloudy or Blackish-fly, the Flag-fly, the Vine-fly: there be of flies, Caterpillars, and Canker-flies, and Bear-flies; and indeed too many either for me to name or for you to remember: and their breeding is so various and wonderful, that I might easily amaze myself and tire you in relation of them.

And yet I will exercise your promised patience by saying a little of the Caterpillar, or the Palmer-fly or worm, that by them you may guess what a work it were in a discourse but to run over those very many flies, worms, and little living creatures with which the sun and summer adorn and beautify the river-banks and meadows, both for the recreation and contemplation of us Anglers: pleasures which, I think, myself enjoy more than any other man that is not of my profession.

Pliny holds an opinion, that many have their birth or being from a dew, that in the spring falls upon the leaves of trees; and that some kinds of them are from a dew left upon herbs or flowers; and others from a dew left upon coleworts or cabbages; all which kinds of dews being thickened and condensed, are by the sun's generative heat most of them hatched, and in three days made living creatures: and these of several shapes and colors; some being hard and tough, some smooth and soft; some are horned in their head, some in their tail, some have none: some have hair, some none: some have sixteen feet, some less, and some have none: but, as our Topsel hath, with great diligence, observed, those which have none move upon the earth, or upon broad leaves, their motion being not unlike to the waves of the sea. Some of them he also observes to be bred of the eggs of other caterpillars, and that those in their time turn to be butterflies; and again, that their eggs turn the following year to be caterpillars. And some affirm, that every plant has his particular fly or caterpillar, which it breeds and feeds. I have seen, and may therefore affirm it, a green caterpillar, or worm, as big as a small peascod, which had fourteen legs; eight on the belly, four under the neck, and two near the tail. It was found on a hedge of privet; and was taken thence, and put into a large box, and a little branch or two of privet put to it, on which I saw it feed as sharply as a dog gnaws a bone: it lived thus five or six days, and thrived, and changed the color two or three times; but, by some neglect in the keeper of it, it then died and did not turn to a fly: but if it had lived, it had doubtless turned to one of those flies that some call Flies-of-prey, which those that walk by the rivers may, in summer, see fasten on smaller flies, and, I think, make them their food. And 'tis observable, that, as there be these Flies-of-prey which be very large, so there be others, very little, created, I think, only to feed them, and breed out of I know not what; whose life, they say, Nature intended not to exceed an hour; and yet that life is thus made shorter by other flies, or accident.

'Tis endless to tell you what the curious searchers into Nature's productions have observed of these worms and flies: but yet I shall tell you what Aldrovandus, our Topsel, and others, say of the Palmer-worm or Caterpillar: that whereas others content themselves to feed on particular herbs or leaves,—for most think those very leaves that gave them life and shape give them a particular feeding and nourishment, and that upon them they usually abide;—yet he observes that this is called a Pilgrim or Palmerworm, for his very wandering life and various food; not contenting himself, as others do, with any one certain place for his abode, nor any certain kind of herb or flower for his feeding; but will boldly and disorderly wander up and down, and not endure to be kept to a diet, or fixed to a particular place.

Nay, the very colors of Caterpillars are, as one has observed, very elegant and beautiful. I shall, for a taste of the rest, describe one of them, which I will some time the next month show you feeding on a willow-tree, and you shall find him punctually to answer this very description: his lips and mouth somewhat yellow, his eyes black as jet, his forehead purple, his feet and hinder parts green, his tail two-forked and black; the whole body stained with a kind of red spots which run along the neck and shoulder-blade, not unlike the form of Saint Andrew's cross, or the letter X, made thus crosswise, and a white line drawn down his back to his tail; all which add much beauty to his whole body. And it is to me observable, that at a fixed age this Caterpillar gives over to eat, and towards winter comes to be covered over with a strange shell or crust, called an Aurelia; and so lives a kind of dead life, without eating, all the winter. And, as others of several kinds turn to be several kinds of flies and vermin the spring following, so this caterpillar then turns to be a painted butterfly.

## Questions for Rereading, Discussing, Connecting, and Writing

### Rereading

1. This selection from Walton's book addresses the reader directly as "you." As you read, speculate on how the nature of the "you" addressed in 1653 differs from the "you" of today.

2. Walton refers frequently to the work of others in this selection—Pliny (a Roman scholar who lived in the first century AD and wrote, among other things, a 37 volume natural history); Aldrovandus (an Italian naturalist of the sixteenth century); and Bacon (a sixteenth-century English philosopher and author, see p. 184). Consider the effect of Walton's mentioning the work of these individuals in his discussion.

3. As you read this selection, speculate on the relationship between science and art. Walton's subject suggests science, but the style suggests art. What relationship do you see between the two?

### Discussing

4. In her study of the development of the printing press, Elizabeth Eisenstein observes that printing enabled scientists to form a community across time and space as they read about one another's work. Discuss the role of community in Walton's work.

5. The subtitle of *The Complete Angler* is "The Contemplative Man's Recreation." Discuss the appropriateness of this subtitle with regard to fishing and this selection.

6. The sentences of this selection are much longer than most sentences written today. Discuss the effect of these lengthy sentences upon contemporary readers.

### Connecting

7. Walton discusses flies in great detail here. Compare the detail of this selection with that of the Sutton Hoo buckle (p. 341).

8. Compare this selection with a passage about insects in a contemporary science text. What similarities and differences do you find?

9. Compare Walton's description of flies with Twain's description of a river town (p. 202). How would you describe the accuracy of each selection?

WRITING

10. This selection closes with a description of a specific caterpillar. Using this description as a guide, make a sketch of this caterpillar. Then write an account of what you learned from making the sketch.

11. In addition to sentence length, there are many features that mark Walton's English as different from our own. Rewrite the first three paragraphs of this selection in a style you would describe as contemporary.

12. Although you may not fish for recreation, you undoubtedly pursue some hobby or recreation that you would describe as play. Write an account of your recreation, giving special attention to why it is play for you.

## Mary Wollstonecraft Shelley

# *Journal* (1822)

ALBATO, ITALY, 1822

Oct. 2.—On the 8th of July I finished my journal. This is a curious coincidence. The date still remains—the fatal 8th—a monument to show that all ended then. And I begin again? Oh, never! But several motives induce me, when the day has gone down, and all is silent around me, steeped in sleep, to pen as occasion wills, my reflections and feelings. First, I have no friend. For eight years I communicated, with unlimited freedom, with one whose genius, far transcending mine awakened and guided my thoughts. I conversed with him; rectified my errors of judgment; obtained new lights from him; and my mind was satisfied. Now I am alone—oh, how alone! The stars may behold my tears, and the winds drink my sighs; but my thoughts are a sealed treasure, which I can confide to none. But can I express all I feel? Can I give words to thoughts and feelings that, as a tempest, hurry me along? Is this the sand that the ever-flowing sea of thought would impress indelibly? Alas! I am alone. No eye answers mine; my voice can with none assume its natural modulation. What a change! O my beloved Shelley! how often during those happy days—happy, though chequered—I thought how superiorly gifted I had been in being united to one to whom I could unveil myself, and who could understand me! Well, then, now I am reduced to these white pages, which I am to blot with dark imagery. As I write, let me think what he would have said if, speaking thus to him, he could have answered me. Yes, my own heart, I would fain know what to think of my desolate state; what you think I ought to do, what to think. I guess you would answer thus:—"Seek to know your own heart, and, learning what it best loves, try to enjoy that." Well, I cast my eyes around, and, look forward to the bounded prospect in view; I ask myself what pleases my there? My child;—so many feelings arise when I think of him, that I turn aside to think no more. Those I most loved are gone for ever; those who held the second rank are absent; and among those near me as yet, I trust to the disinterested kindness of one alone. Beneath all this, my imagination never flags. Literary labours, the improvement of my mind, and the enlargement of my ideas, are the only occupations that elevate me from my lethargy; all events seem to lead me to that one point, and the courses of destiny having dragged me to that single resting-place, have left me. Father, mother, friend, husband, children —all made, as it were, the team that conducted me here; and now all, except you, my poor boy (and you are necessary to the continuance of my life), all are gone, and I am left to fulfil my task. So be it.

Oct. 19.—How painful all change becomes to one who, entirely and despotically engrossed by their own feelings, leads as it were an *internal* life, quite different from the outward and apparent one! Whilst my life continues its monotonous course within sterile banks, an undercurrent disturbs the smooth face of the waters, distorts all analogy either with my opinion of him, or the subject of his conversation. With another I might talk, and not for the moment think of Shelley—at least not think of him with the same vividness as if I were alone; but, when in company with Albè, I can never cease for a second to have Shelley in my heart and brain with a clearness that mocks reality—interfering even by its force with the functions of life—until, if tears do not relieve me, the hysterical feeling, analogous to that which the murmur of the sea gives me, presses painfully upon me.

Well, for the first time for about a month, I have been in company with Albè for two hours, and, coming home, I write this, so necessary is it for me to express in words the force of my feelings. Shelley, beloved! I look at the stars and at all nature, and it speaks to me of you in the clearest accents. Why cannot you answer me, my own one? Is the instrument so utterly destroyed? I would endure ages of pain to hear one tone of your voice strike on my ear!

Nov. 11.—It is better to grieve than not to grieve. Grief at least tells me that I was not always what I am now. I was once selected for happiness; let the memory of that abide by me. You pass by an old ruined house in a desolate lane, and heed it not. But if you hear that that house is haunted by a wild and beautiful spirit, it acquires an interest and beauty of its own.

I shall be glad to be more alone again; one ought to see no one, or many; and, confined to one society, I shall lose all energy except that which I possess from my own resources; and I must be alone for those to be put in activity.

A cold heart! Have I a cold heart? God knows! But none need envy the icy region this heart encircles; and at least the tears are hot which the emotions of this cold heart forces me to shed. A cold heart!

yes, it would be cold enough if all were as I wished it—cold, or burning in the flame for whose sake I forgive this, and would forgive every other imputation—that flame in which your heart, beloved, lay unconsumed. My heart is very full to-night.

I shall write his life, and thus occupy myself in the only manner from which I can derive consolation. That will be a task that may convey some balm. What though I weep? All is better than inaction and—not forgetfulness—that never is—but an inactivity of remembrance.

And you, my own Boy! I am about to begin a task which, if you live, will be an invaluable treasure to you in after times. I must collect my materials, and then, in the commemoration of the divine virtues of your Father, I shall fulfil the only act of pleasure there remains for me, and be ready to follow you, if you leave me, my task being fulfilled. I have lived; rapture, exultation, content—all the varied changes of enjoyment—have been mine. It is all gone; but still, the airy paintings of what it has gone through float by, and distance shall not dim them. If I were alone, I had already begun what I had determined to do; but I must have patience, and for those events my memory is brass, my thoughts a never-tired engraver. France—Poverty—A few days of solitude, and some uneasiness—A tranquil residence in a beautiful spot [Bishopsgate]—Switzerland—Bath—Marlow—Milan—The Baths of Lucca—Este—Venice—Rome—Naples—Rome and misery—Leghorn—Florence—Pisa—Solitude—The Williamses—The Baths—Pisa: these are the heads of chapters, and each containing a tale romantic beyond romance.

I no longer enjoy, but I love! Death cannot deprive me of that living spark which feeds on all given it, and which is now triumphant in sorrow. I love, and shall enjoy happiness again. I do not doubt that; but when?

## *Questions for Rereading, Discussing, Connecting, and Writing*

### REREADING

1. It has been said that writing can be therapeutic for persons facing trauma or loss. Mary Shelley, author of the novel *Frankenstein*, wrote these journal entries about three months after the death of her husband Percy Bysshe Shelley. What, if any, evidence do you find that Mary Shelley obtained comfort from her journal?

2. The entries included here were written over more than a month. Do you see any progression/change as you move from one to another? Does the voice, for example, seem to change?

3. Shelley uses the word "task" in reference to taking care of her Boy (the only surviving child of the four she had borne) and to writing about her husband. How does the meaning of "task" change as you move from one to the other?

DISCUSSING

4. After reading, decide whether the process of writing this journal represented work or play for Mary Shelley. Explain and discuss your decision with others.

5. July 8, the day Mary Shelley finished her journal, happened also to be the day her husband died. Discuss occasions on which seemingly unrelated events may have taken on great significance in your life.

6. Mary Shelley asserts that it is better to grieve than not to grieve. Do you agree? Discuss your response to this statement.

CONNECTING

7. If you have ever kept a journal, reflect on the similarities and differences between yours and Shelley's. If you haven't kept a journal, interview someone who has. In either event, consider whether keeping a journal can be described as work or play.

8. Selections from the journal of pianist Carol Mont Parker are included in this chapter (p. 230). How would you compare the journals of Parker and Shelley in terms of style?

9. Mary Shelley's proposed task of writing about her deceased husband could be described as a form of work. How does this work compare with other forms of work described in this chapter—with, say, the work of a carpenter or a farm laborer?

WRITING

10. In creating headings such as France, Switzerland, Bath, and so on, Mary Shelley provides what could be described as a preliminary outline of the book she plans to write. Develop a similar outline drawing upon events in your own life and write an account of one of them.

**11.** Drawing upon what you can learn from the text and from any other texts (such as biographical accounts of Mary and Percy Shelley), compose an obituary of Percy Bysshe Shelley as Mary Shelley might have written it.

**12.** Write an imaginary next entry in Mary Shelley's style.

*Edgar Degas*

# Dancers Practicing at the Bar (1876)

*Edgar Degas*

# The Rehearsal (1877)

*Edgar Degas*

# The Dancing Class (1872)

*Questions for Rereading,
Discussing, Connecting, and Writing*

REREADING

1. Degas allowed much of his unfinished work to reach public view. What relationships do you see among the sketches and the finished painting of the Dancing Class?

2. Notice where your eye moves as you look at each of these paintings. Trace your pattern of eye movement for each. What does each pattern of movement tell you about the painting under consideration?

3. Select one of these Degas paintings and enumerate in your mind an account of what is happening in it.

### Discussing

4. All three works contain a figure at the barre. What similarities and differences do you see in the three presentations of this same figure?

5. How does the shift from windows to mirrors change the atmosphere presented?

6. All of these works portray rehearsals rather than performances by dancers. Think about times when you have watched a rehearsal, perhaps of a musical group, or a practice session, perhaps by an athletic team. What is the effect of watching rehearsals or practice? How do rehearsals differ from performances or practices from games? What is the effect of portraying a rehearsal in a painting?

7. What do you find puzzling or unclear in these works? Do you, for example, have difficulty deciding what is on the chair in the central foreground of the third picture? Speculate on what Degas intended.

### Connecting

8. McPhee (p. 218) describes Bill Bradley as "not an innovator." If we take innovator to mean one who introduces new things, to what extent, if any, are these dancers innovators?

9. Twain's (p. 202) phrase, "a husbanded grandeur created with a bit of pitch pine just before arriving at a town" demonstrates his insider's knowledge of steamboat life. To what extent does Degas offer an insider's perspective on ballet?

10. Parker (p. 230) describes her fantasy of the "placard outside Carnegie." What fantasy might these dancers have?

### Writing

11. Write an essay explaining the differences between rehearsals and performances as they affect participants or spectators or both.

12. The men and women in these works wear different clothing, assume different postures, and (presumably) have different roles. Write an essay explaining the implications of these differences. Do they, for example, suggest anything about the relationship between art and life?

13. Write an explanation of what you think Degas wants to "tell" us about the dancers, . . . about dancing, . . . about dancing schools.

14. Write a narrative of the third picture from the perspective of the musician or one of the dancers, or the teacher, or Degas.

*Mark Twain*

# The Boy's Ambition (1875)

When I was a boy, there was but one permanent ambition among my comrades in our village[1] on the west bank of the Mississippi River. That was, to be a steamboatman. We had transient ambitions of other sorts, but they were only transient. When a circus came and went, it left us all burning to become clowns; the first negro minstrel show that ever came to our section left us all suffering to try that kind of life; now and then we had a hope that, if we lived and were good, God would permit us to be pirates. These ambitions faded out, each in its turn; but the ambition to be a steamboatman always remained.

Once a day a cheap, gaudy packet arrived upward from St. Louis, and another downward from Keokuk. Before these events, the day was glorious with expectancy; after them, the day was a dead and empty thing. Not only the boys, but the whole village, felt this. After all these years I can picture that old time to myself now, just as it was then: the white town drowsing in the sunshine of a summer's morning; the streets empty, or pretty nearly so; one or two clerks sitting in front of the Water Street stores, with their splint-bottomed chairs tilted back against the walls, chins on breasts, hats slouched over their faces, asleep—with shingle-shavings enough around to show what broke them down; a sow and a litter of pigs loafing along the sidewalk, doing a good business in watermelon rinds and seeds; two or three lonely little freight piles scattered about the "levee"; a pile of "skids" on the slope of the stone-paved wharf, and the fragrant town drunkard asleep in the shadow of them; two or three wood flats at the head of the wharf, but nobody to listen to the peaceful lapping of the wavelets against them; the great Mississippi, the majestic, the magnificent Mississippi, rolling its mile-wide tide along, shining in the sun; the dense forest away on the other side; the "point" above the town, and the "point" below, bounding the river-glimpse and turning it into a sort of sea, and withal a very still and brilliant and lonely one. Presently a film of dark smoke appears above one of those remote "points";

[1] Hannibal, Missouri

instantly a negro drayman, famous for his quick eye and prodigious voice, lifts up the cry, "S-t-e-a-m-boat a-comin'!" and the scene changes! The town drunkard stirs, the clerks wake up, a furious clatter of drays follows, every house and store pours out a human contribution, and all in a twinkling the dead town is alive and moving. Drays, carts, men, boys, all go hurrying from many quarters to a common center, the wharf. Assembled there, the people fasten their eyes upon the coming boat as upon a wonder they are seeing for the first time. And the boat *is* rather a handsome sight, too. She is long and sharp and trim and pretty; she has two tall, fancy-topped chimneys, with a gilded device of some kind swung between them; a fanciful pilothouse, all glass and "gingerbread," perched on top of the "texas" deck behind them; the paddle-boxes are gorgeous with a picture or with gilded rays above the boat's name; the boiler-deck, the hurricane-deck, and the texas deck are fenced and ornamented with clean white railings; there is a flag gallantly flying from the jack-staff; the furnace doors are open and the fires glaring bravely; the upper decks are black with passengers; the captain stands by the big bell, calm, imposing, the envy of all; great volumes of the blackest smoke are rolling and tumbling out of the chimneys—a husbanded grandeur created with a bit of pitch-pine just before arriving at a town; the crew are grouped on the forecastle; the broad stage is run far out over the port bow, and an envied deck-hand stands picturesquely on the end of it with a coil of rope in his hand; the pent steam is screaming through the gauge-cocks; the captain lifts his hand, a bell rings, the wheels stop; then they turn back, churning the water to foam, and the steamer is at rest. Then such a scramble as there is to get aboard, and to get ashore, and to take in freight and to discharge freight, all at one and the same time; and such a yelling and cursing as the mates facilitate it all with! Ten minutes later the steamer is under way again, with no flag on the jack-staff and no black smoke issuing from the chimneys. After ten more minutes the town is dead again, and the town drunkard asleep by the skids once more.

My father was a justice of the peace, and I supposed he possessed the power of life and death over all men, and could hang anybody that offended him. This was distinction enough for me as a general thing; but the desire to be a steamboatman kept intruding, nevertheless. I first wanted to be a cabin-boy, so that I could come out with a white apron on and shake a table-cloth over the side, where all my old comrades could see me; later I thought I would rather be the deck-hand who stood on the end of the stage-plank with the coil of rope in his hand, because he was particularly conspicuous. But these were only day-dreams—they were too heavenly to be contemplated as real possibilities. By and by one of our boys went away. He was not heard of for a long time. At last he turned up as apprentice engineer or "striker" on a steamboat. This thing shook the bottom out of all my Sunday-school teachings. That boy had been notoriously worldly, and I just the reverse; yet he was exalted to this eminence, and I left in obscurity and misery. There was nothing generous about this fellow in his greatness. He would always manage to have a rusty bolt to scrub while his boat tarried at our town, and he would sit on the inside guard and scrub it, where we all could see him and envy him and loathe him. And whenever his boat was laid up he would come home and swell around the town in his blackest and greasiest clothes, so that nobody could help remembering that he was a steamboatman; and he used all sorts of steamboat technicalities in his talk, as if he were so used to them that he forgot common people could not understand them. He would speak of the "labboard" side of a horse in an easy, natural way that would make one wish he was dead. And he was always talking about "St. Looy" like an old citizen; he would refer casually to occasions when he was "coming down Fourth Street," or when he was "passing by the Planter's House," or when there was a fire and he took a turn on the brakes of "the old Big Missouri"; and then he would go on and lie about how many towns the size of ours were burned down there that day. Two or three of the boys had long been persons of consideration among us because they had been to St. Louis once and had a vague general knowledge of its wonders, but the day of their glory was over now. They lapsed into a humble silence, and learned to disappear when the ruthless "cub"-engineer approached. This fellow had money, too, and hair-oil. Also an ignorant silver watch and a showy brass watch-chain. He wore a leather belt and used no suspenders. If ever a youth was cordially admired and hated by his comrades, this one was. No girl could withstand his charms. He "cut out" every boy in the village. When his boat blew up at last, it diffused a tranquil contentment among us such as we had not known for months. But when he came home the next week, alive, renowned, and appeared in church all battered up and bandaged, a shining hero, stared at and wondered over by everybody, it seemed to us that the partiality of Providence for an undeserving reptile had reached a point where it was open to criticism.

This creature's career could produce but one result, and it speedily followed. Boy after boy managed to get on the river. The minister's son became an engineer. The doctor's and the postmaster's sons became "mud clerks"; the wholesale liquor dealer's son became a barkeeper on a boat; four sons of the chief merchant, and two sons of the county judge, became pilots. Pilot was the grandest position of all. The pilot, even in those days of trivial wages, had a princely salary—from a hundred and fifty to two hundred and fifty dollars a month, and no board to pay. Two months of his wages would pay a preacher's salary for a year. Now some of us were left disconsolate. We could not get on the river—at least our parents would not let us.

So, by and by, I ran away. I said I would never come home again till I was a pilot and could come in glory. But somehow I could not manage it. I went meekly aboard a few of the boats that lay packed together like sardines at the long St. Louis wharf, and humbly inquired for the pilots, but got only a cold shoulder and short words from mates and clerks. I had to make the best of this sort of treatment for the time being, but I had comforting day-dreams of a future when I should be a great and honored pilot, with plenty of money, and could kill some of these mates and clerks and pay for them.

## *Questions for Rereading, Discussing, Connecting, and Writing*

### REREADING

**1.** When you first look at this selection, you may notice that it contains several long paragraphs. Indentations for paragraphs are one code writers can use to signal to readers. What significance do you attach to the length of Twain's paragraphs?

**2.** Sentence length likewise signals readers. What meaning do you find in the two long sentences in Twain's second paragraph—one begins "After all these years . . ." and the other "She is long . . ."

**3.** Shifts in tense also send signals to readers. Consider the effect of the shift from present to past tense in the third paragraph, which begins "My father . . ."

**4.** Imagine that you are an artist. What details do you have and do you need additional details to sketch Twain's Hannibal and steamboat? If so, what are they?

DISCUSSING

5. This selection is part of a collection titled *Life on the Mississippi* which, according to some readers, is mostly about the river itself. What role, in your view, does the river play in this selection?

6. Most youngsters have ambitions like Twain's—they want to become firefighters or police officers when they grow up—but few go on, as Twain did, to act on them. Twain actually worked as a steamboat pilot for a few years. How do you think Twain feels about having worked on a steamboat?

7. Twain describes the envied steamboat boy's watch as "ignorant." What is an "ignorant watch"?

CONNECTING

8. Twain's account emphasizes the ambition that motivated him to seek employment on a steamboat. Compare Twain's ambition with that of Bill Bradley (as described by McPhee) (p. 218) or Carol Mont Parker (p. 230). Does play have a role in the accomplishments of any of them?

9. Both Amman and Twain make specific reference to physical labor in their selections. How are their references similar or different?

10. This selection resembles Foxfire (p. 223) in describing a world that is no more. Compare the attitudes of these two narrators toward the past.

WRITING

11. Parents often have ambitions for their children, hoping the children will "better" themselves. Write a response to Twain's boyhood ambition from the viewpoint of Twain's father, the Justice of the Peace.

12. Twain describes the youth who first went on a steamboat as "cordially admired and hated by his comrades." Write an essay explaining how it is possible to simultaneously admire and hate someone.

13. Write about your own childhood ambition from the perspective of your present knowledge of the world. Do you still see that ambition the same way?

Rube Goldberg

# Professor Butts' Moth Exterminator (1931)

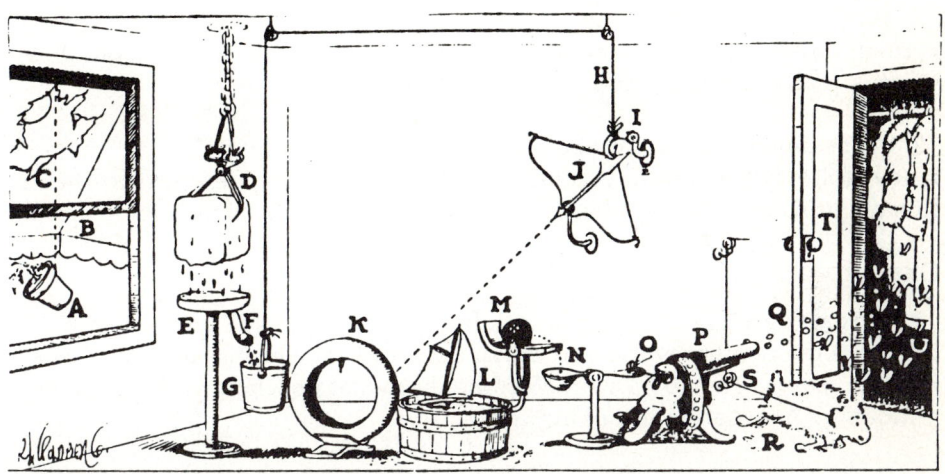

The Professor emerges from the goofy booth with a device for the extermination of moths.
Start singing. Lady upstairs, when sufficiently annoyed, throws flower pot(A) through awning(B). Hole(C) allows sun to come through and melt cake of ice(D). Water drips into pan(E) running through pipe(F) into pail(G). Weight of pail causes cord(H) to release hook(I) and allow arrow(J) to shoot into tire (K). Escaping air blows against toy sailboat(L) driving it against lever(M) and causing ball to roll into spoon(N) and pull string(O) which sets off machine gun(P) discharging camphor balls(Q). Report of gun frightens lamb(R) which runs and pulls cord(S), opening closet door(T). As moths(U) fly out to eat wool from lamb's back they are killed by the barrage of moth balls.

If any of the moths escape and there is danger of their returning, you can fool them by moving.

## Questions for Rereading, Discussing, Connecting, and Writing

REREADING

1. Different kinds of texts very often are required to interact with each other. This cartoon by Goldberg is an excellent example of the *caption*, in which a visual text is supplemented by a written text. How is your attention divided between cartoon and caption—and how does the mood of one match the mood of the other?

2. Why is this selection funny? Or is it? Point to features in either text—cartoon or caption—that you believe have a comic effect. Can you pin down what is really "comical" about these features?

3. What devices does Goldberg employ to make absolutely sure that the reader follows the action, or understands what will happen next in the action about to begin? Note these simple markers in both cartoon and caption.

DISCUSSING

4. Cartoons are not always comical, but they are "playful" in the sense that they take the familiar world and critique it for us. The professor's moth exterminator may, in fact, be a workable one, but what or whom is the cartoonist critiquing? At what is he poking fun?

5. It has been said that if we have fun while we work, then our work becomes play. Discuss how a difficult task has become "play" because you found pleasure or surprise or satisfaction in doing or completing it.

6. Professor Butts is famous for his crazy inventions—like an automatic collar-buttoning machine, or a pancake flipper—that are certainly ingenious but also ridiculous. What exactly is wrong with Professor Butts' moth exterminator—and how could you improve on his invention?

CONNECTING

7. "How to do something" is often the essence of good work—and good play. Learning a skill well is a key ingredient to success. If you could assign Professor Butts two readings from this section on work and play, which would they be—and why? What fundamental skill do you think the professor may lack?

8. Goldberg—as a social commentator—may have been satirizing the modern world's apparent admiration for complex machinery. Or he may have wanted us just to laugh at our own inventiveness. Look at the Swift (p. 296),

Dickenson (p. 320), Twain (p. 202), and Springsteen (p. 47) selections for the ways in which different people at different times in different places manage to be serious and playful (to get work done while having some fun). Which do you consider most successful at balancing work and play?

WRITING

9. What Goldberg has given us is a sort of skeleton or outline of the action about to happen. Write out this action, and remember to invent a good central character.

10. Conduct a serious cause-and-effect analysis of this moth exterminator. Answer the question, in precise language, "How does the professor's invention work?" Remember that your reader will not have the benefit of the cartoon.

11. Describe something in our lives that you consider overly complicated. Point to the cause of this complication, and then suggest a way to overcome it. In short, solve the problem.

12. You, too, enter the professor's "goofy booth" and dream up your own moth exterminator. You believe it works; describe it in a narrative that takes your reader through the workings of your new invention.

Camara Laye

# The Dark Child *(1954)*

At a sign from my father the apprentices began working two sheepskin bellows. The skins were on the floor, on opposite sides of the forge, connected to it by earthen pipes. While the work was in progress the apprentices sat in front of the bellows with crossed legs. That is, the younger of the two sat, for the elder was sometimes allowed to assist. But the younger—this time it was Sidafa—was only permitted to work the bellows and watch while waiting his turn for promotion to less rudimentary tasks. First one and then the other worked hard at the bellows: the flame in the forge rose higher and became a living thing, a genie implacable and full of life.

Then my father lifted the clay pot with his long tongs and placed it on the flame.

Immediately all activity in the workshop almost came to a halt. During the whole time that the gold was being smelted, neither copper nor aluminum could be worked nearby, lest some particle of these base metals fall into the container which held the gold. Only steel could be worked on such occasions, but the men, whose task that was, hurried to finish what they were doing, or left it abruptly to join the apprentices gathered around the forge. There were so many, and they crowded so around my father, that I, the smallest person present, had to come near the forge in order not to lose track of what was going on.

If he felt he had inadequate working space, my father had the apprentices stand well away from him. He merely raised his hand in a simple gesture: at that particular moment he never uttered a word, and no one else would: no one was allowed to utter a word. Even the go-between's voice was no longer raised in song. The silence was broken only by the panting of the bellows and the faint hissing of the gold. But if my father never actually spoke, I know that he was forming words in his mind. I could tell from his lips, which kept moving, while, bending over the pot, he stirred the gold and charcoal with a bit of wood that kept bursting into flame and had constantly to be replaced by a fresh one.

What words did my father utter? I do not know. At least I am not certain what they were. No one ever told me. But could they have been anything but incantation? On these occasions was he not invoking the genies of fire and gold, of fire and wind, of wind blown by the blast-pipes of the forge, of fire born of wind, of gold married to fire? Was it not their assistance, their friendship, their espousal that he besought? Yes. Almost certainly he was invoking these genies, all of whom are equally indispensable for smelting gold.

The operation going on before my eyes was certainly the smelting of gold, yet something more than that: a magical operation that the guiding spirits could regard with favor or disfavor. That is why, all around my father, there was absolute silence and anxious expectancy. Though only a child, I knew there could be no craft greater than the goldsmith's. I expected a ceremony; I had come to be present at a ceremony; and it actually was one, though very protracted. I was still too young to understand why, but I had an inkling as I watched the almost religious concentration of those who followed the mixing process in the clay pot.

When finally the gold began to melt I could have shouted aloud—and perhaps we all would have if we had not been forbidden to make a sound. I trembled, and so did everyone else watching my father stir the mixture—it was still a heavy paste—in which the charcoal was gradually consumed. The next stage followed swiftly. The gold now had the fluidity of water. The genies had smiled on the operation!

"Bring me the brick!" my father would order, thus lifting the ban that until then had silenced us.

The brick, which an apprentice would place beside the fire, was hollowed out, generously greased with Galam butter. My father would take the pot off the fire and tilt it carefully, while I would watch the gold flow into the brick, flow like liquid fire. True, it was only a very sparse trickle of fire, but how vivid, how brilliant! As the gold flowed into the brick, the grease sputtered and flamed and emitted a thick smoke that caught in the throat and stung the eyes, leaving us all weeping and coughing.

But there were times when it seemed to me that my father ought to turn this task over to one of his assistants. They were experienced, had assisted him hundreds of times, and could certainly have performed the work well. But my father's lips moved and those inaudible, secret words, those incantations he addressed to one we could not see or hear, was the essential part. Calling on the genies of fire, of wind, of gold and exorcising the evil spirits—this was a knowledge he alone possessed.

By now the gold had been cooled in the hollow of the brick, and my father began to hammer and stretch it. This was the moment when his work as a goldsmith really began. I noticed that before embarking on it he never failed to stroke the little snake stealthily as it lay coiled up under the sheepskin. I can only assume that this was his way of gathering strength for what remained to be done, the most trying part of his task.

But was it not extraordinary and miraculous that on these occasions the little black snake was always coiled under the sheepskin? He was not always there. He did not visit my father every day. But he was always present whenever there was gold to be worked. His presence was no surprise to *me*. After that evening when my father had spoken of the guiding spirit of his race I was no longer astonished. The snake was there intentionally. He knew what the future held. Did he tell my father? I think that he most certainly did. Did he tell him everything? I have another reason for believing firmly that he did.

The craftsman who works in gold must first of all purify himself. That is, he must wash himself all over and, of course, abstain from all sexual commerce during the whole time. Great respecter of ceremony as he was, it would have been impossible for my father to ignore these rules. Now, I never saw him make these preparations. I saw him address himself to his work without any apparent preliminaries. From that moment it was obvious that, forewarned in a dream by his black guiding spirit of the task which awaited him in the morning, my father must have prepared for it as soon as he arose, entering his workshop in a state of purity, his body smeared with the secret potions hidden in his numerous pots of magical substances; or perhaps he always came into his workshop in a state of ritual purity. I am not trying to make him out a better man than he was—he was a man and had his share of human frailties—but he was always uncompromising in his respect for ritual observance.

## Questions for Rereading, Discussing, Connecting, and Writing

### Rereading

1. Camara Laye grew up in Guinea, a country in West Africa, and wrote this autobiography when he was in his twenties. In what ways does this selection seem like an autobiography to you? Does it resemble another form such as, say, a novel?

2. As you read, note places that raise questions in your mind. What kinds of things do you have difficulty understanding? How can you make sense of these passages?

3. Laye mentions that he moves near the forge to keep track of what's going on. As you read, define for yourself what is going on in this selection. Would you describe the action as work or play? Why?

### Discussing

4. Laye wrote this autobiography when he was in France studying engineering. In what ways does it become easier to write an autobiography when living at some distance from one's childhood home?

5. In the section preceding this one Laye identifies himself as about six at the time of these events. Discuss the ways a child's perspective is evident in this text.

6. Laye associates the snake under the sheepskin with the guiding spirit of his father's race. What does this assertion mean to you? Discuss meanings developed by you and your peers.

### Connecting

7. Laye describes his father's ritual of preparation in some detail. What rituals of preparation do you observe as you work or play? What rituals have you observed among players or workers around you?

8. The word "genie" appears several times in this text. What associations do you have with this word? How are these associations changed by the use of genie here?

9. How would you describe Laye's definition of work? What comparison can you make between this and the work described in selections by Twain (p. 202), Amman (p. 182), and McPhee (p. 218)?

## Writing

**10.** This text offers a careful account of a complicated set of actions. Think about actions you have observed and write your own careful account of an activity.

**11.** Consider the way Laye presents his father and speculate on what this account reveals about relations between father and son. Write an essay in which you explain your perception of this relationship (remembering, among other things, that Laye went on to study engineering in Europe).

**12.** What Laye describes here could be characterized as a technical/chemical process. Write an essay in which you explore the losses and gains of presenting technology as Laye does.

Dorothea Lange

# Bindle Stiff (1937)

## Questions for Rereading, Discussing, Connecting, and Writing

REREADING

1. The title of this photograph, "Bindle Stiff," is a slang term for migrant workers who carry their own bedrolls. Does this seem an appropriate title? Can you suggest others?

2. As you look at this photograph, make a list of the information it provides. What can you say about the person and the place pictured?

3. The date of the photograph places it during what is called the Great Depression in the United States. What does this photograph contribute to what you already know about the Depression?

DISCUSSING

4. Many photographs show a frontal view of subjects. What does Lange achieve by showing this subject from the rear?

5. Lange took this photograph as part of a large project recording what she called the "American Exodus" forced by drought in the Southwest. What happens to people who are forced to migrate?

6. Migrant workers continue to provide farm labor in the United States today. How does what you know about contemporary farm workers contribute to what you see in this photograph?

CONNECTING

7. Compare the composition of this photograph with that of the Degas (p. 197) and Goya (p. 257) paintings. How, for example, does each use the central space? What effect does each achieve by hiding faces of subjects?

8. The term "exodus" has been used to describe the migrations of many different peoples. What meanings do you attach to the term "exodus"? What texts do you associate with the word?

WRITING

9. Write a narrative, from the perspective of the worker pictured here, recounting his life thus far.

**10.** Lange and this worker must have talked with one another as she took his picture. Write a dialogue of their conversation.

**11.** It is said that a picture is worth 1000 words. Write 1000 words explaining the "worth" of this picture.

*John McPhee*

# *A Sense of Where You Are: A Profile of Bill Bradley at Princeton* (1965)

*A*ll shots in basketball are supposed to have names—the set, the hook, the lay-up, the jump shot, and so on—and one weekend last July, while Bradley was in Princeton working on his senior thesis and putting in some time in the Princeton gymnasium to keep himself in form for the Olympics, I asked him what he called his over-the-shoulder shot. He said that he had never heard a name for it, but that he had seen Oscar Robertson, of the Cincinnati Royals, and Jerry West, of the Los Angeles Lakers, do it, and had worked it out for himself. He went on to say that it is a much simpler shot than it appears to be, and, to illustrate, he tossed a ball over his shoulder and into the basket while he was talking and looking me in the eye. I retrieved the ball and handed it back to him. "When you have played basketball for a while, you don't need to look at the basket when you are in close like this," he said, throwing it over his shoulder again and right through the hoop. "You develop a sense of where you are."

Bradley is not an innovator. Actually, basketball has had only a few innovators in its history—players like Hank Luisetti, of Stanford, whose introduction in 1936 of the running one-hander did as much to open up the game for scoring as the forward pass did for football; and Joe Fulks, of the old Philadelphia Warriors, whose twisting two-handed heaves, made while he was leaping like a salmon, were the beginnings of the jump shot, which seems to be basketball's ultimate weapon. Most basketball players appropriate fragments of other players' styles, and thus develop their own. This is what Bradley has done, but one of the things that set him apart from nearly everyone else is that the process has been conscious rather than osmotic. His jump shot, for example, has had two principal influences. One is Jerry West, who has one of the best jumpers in basketball. At a summer basketball camp in Missouri some years ago, West told Bradley that he always gives an extra hard bounce to the last dribble before a jump shot, since this seems to catapult him to added height. Bradley has been doing that ever since. Terry Dischinger, of the Detroit Pistons, has told Bradley that he always slams his foot to the floor on the last step before a jump shot, because this stops his momentum and thus prevents drift. Drifting while aloft is the mark of a sloppy jump shot.

Bradley's graceful hook shot is a masterpiece of eclecticism. It consists of the high-lifted knee of the Los Angeles Lakers' Darrall Imhoff, the arms of Bill Russell, of the Boston Celtics, who extends his idle hand far under his shooting arm and thus magically stabilizes the shot, and the general corporeal form of Kentucky's Cotton Nash, a rookie this year with the Lakers. Bradley carries his analyses of shots further than merely identifying them with pieces of other people. "There are five parts to the hook shot," he explains to anyone who asks. As he continues, he picks up a ball and stands about eighteen feet from a basket. "Crouch," he says, crouching, and goes on to demonstrate the other moves. "Turn your head to look for the basket, step, kick, follow through with your arms." Once, as he was explaining this to me, the ball curled around the rim and failed to go in.

"What happened then?" I asked him.

"I didn't kick high enough," he said.

"Do you always know exactly why you've missed a shot?"

"Yes," he said, missing another one.

"What happened that time?"

"I was talking to you. I didn't concentrate. The secret of shooting is concentration."

His set shot is borrowed from Ed Macauley, who was a St. Louis University All-American in the late forties and was later a star member of the Boston Celtics and the St. Louis Hawks. Macauley runs the basketball camp Bradley first went to when he was fifteen. In describing the set shot, Bradley is probably quoting a Macauley lecture. "Crouch like Groucho Marx," he says. "Go off your feet a few inches. You shoot with your legs. Your arms merely guide the ball." Bradley says that he has more confidence in his set shot than in any other. However, he seldom uses it, because he seldom has to. A set shot is a long shot, usually a twenty-footer, and Bradley, with his speed and footwork, can almost always take some other kind of shot, closer to the basket. He will take set shots when they are given to him, though. Two seasons ago, Davidson lost to Princeton, using a compact zone defense that ignored the remoter areas of the court. In one brief sequence, Bradley sent up seven set shots, missing only one. The missed one happened to rebound in Bradley's direction, and he leaped up, caught it with one hand, and scored.

Even his lay-up shot has an ancestral form; he is full of admiration for "the way Cliff Hagan pops up anywhere within six feet of the basket," and he tries to do the same. Hagan is a former Kentucky star who now plays for the St. Louis Hawks. Because opposing teams always do everything they can to stop Bradley, he gets an unusual number of foul shots. When he was in high school, he used to imitate Bob Pettit, of the St. Louis Hawks, and Bill Sharman of the Boston Celtics, but now his free throw is more or less his own. With his left foot back about eighteen inches—"wherever it feels comfortable," he says—he shoots with a deep-bending rhythm of knees and arms, one-handed, his left hand acting as a kind of gantry for the ball until the moment of release. What is most interesting, though, is that he concentrates his attention on one of the tiny steel eyelets that are welded under the rim of the basket to hold the net to the hoop—on the center eyelet, of course—before he lets fly. One night, he scored over twenty points on free throws alone; Cornell hacked at him so heavily that he was given twenty-one free throws, and he made all twenty-one, finishing the game with a total of thirty-seven points.

When Bradley, working out alone, practices his set shots, hook shots, and jump shots, he moves systematically from one place to another around the basket, his distance from it being appropriate to the shot, and he does not permit himself to move on until he has made at least ten shots out of thirteen from each location. He applies this standard to every kind of shot, with either hand, from any distance. Many basketball players, including reasonably good ones, could spend five years in a gym and not make ten out of thirteen left-handed hook shots, but that is part of Bradley's daily routine. He talks to himself while he is shooting, usually reminding himself to concentrate but sometimes talking to himself the way every high-school j.v. basketball player has done since the dim twenties—more or less imitating a radio announcer, and saying, as he gathers himself up for a shot, "It's pandemonium in Dillon Gymnasium. The clock is running out. He's up with a jumper. Swish!"

Last summer, the floor of the Princeton gym was being resurfaced, so Bradley had to put in several practice sessions at the Lawrenceville School. His first afternoon at Lawrenceville, he began by shooting fourteen-foot jump shots from the right side. He got off to a bad start, and he kept missing them. Six in a row hit the back rim of the basket and bounced out. He stopped, looking discomfited, and seemed to be making an adjustment in his mind. Then he went up for another jump shot from the same spot and hit it cleanly. Four more shots went in without a miss, and then he paused and said, "You want to know something? That basket is about an inch and a half low." Some weeks later, I went back to Lawrenceville with a steel tape, borrowed a stepladder, and measured the height of the basket. It was nine feet ten and seven-eighths above the floor, or one and one-eighth inches too low.

## Questions for Rereading, Discussing, Connecting, and Writing

### Rereading

1. As you read this selection, consider the author's attitude toward Bill Bradley. What does McPhee say that tells you how he feels about Bradley?

2. If you are not actively interested in basketball (you don't follow teams and players regularly), what in this piece captures your interest? If you are a basketball fan, how does this selection compare with your usual readings on the sport?

3. McPhee reports much of what Bradley says, but in only one section does he use direct quotations. What differences do you find between direct and indirect quotations of Bradley's statements?

### Discussion

4. Objectivity is sometimes cited as a virtue in writing, but this selection cannot be described as objective. What are the benefits of McPhee's obvious admiration for Bradley? What would be the effect if he took a more "objective" view of his subject? That is, what would be the effect if McPhee seemed less enthusiastic about Bradley?

5. In the introduction to the book from which this selection comes, McPhee explains that Bradley had been described by basketball regulars as an extraordinary player. On the basis of reading this selection, how would you describe Bradley? Refer to particular words or phrases in the essay.

6. McPhee describes the borrowing (of several individuals' shots) and coordination (of different movements) that go into a single shot (such as a hook shot). Discuss the borrowing and coordination necessary in an activity you know well; you may want to think of "borrowing" as "imitating" or "learning from others."

CONNECTING

7. Basketball, like piano and baseball are often prefaced by the word "playing," yet many people who engage in these activities are paid and could be described as "working." Explain the various definitions of work and play presented by McPhee, Parker (p. 230), and the box score (p. 235).

8. McPhee's portrayal of Bradley tells us about his subject's human qualities as well as about Bradley as a basketball player. Compare these revelations with what you learn about the subject in selections by Lange, (p. 215), Amman (p. 182), Shakespeare (p. 23), and Sacks (p. 92).

9. McPhee uses words to "show" physical action. Compare the action McPhee shows with that shown by Amman (p. 182), Lange (p. 215), Cassatt (p. 82), and Eisenstein (p. 32).

WRITING

10. One of the direct quotations McPhee includes is Bradley's imitation of a radio announcer describing an exciting moment in a basketball game. Using this quotation—and perhaps your own experience of listening to sports reports—as a model, write an account of Bradley practicing in the Lawrenceville gym.

11. This selection makes clear that McPhee spent considerable time watching and talking with Bradley. Write an account of what it must have been like for McPhee to spend so much time hanging around gyms and retrieving Bradley's shots.

12. Although this selection tells us a great deal about Bradley, it does not reveal what he is thinking. Take Bradley's perspective and write an account of the events reported here.

Foxfire

# Shoemaking (1980)

To make a pair of shoes, the first step, of course, is to get the leather. Neighbors would slaughter a beef and bring the raw hides in to my father and he would tan them on the shares—tan the hide and take one half as his fee and give them the other half. That was a common setup back when I was a child. Then he'd sell his half of the hide, or work it into shoes or harness or whatever he wanted to use it for to get his money out of his labor. And there was more to tanning a hide than you might think. My father always figured that it took about a year from beginning to end because there was a lot of lost time in there. He'd never promise a finished hide in less than a year.

I remember the process they used. They'd take the raw hides when they first came off the animal and put them in a strong solution of lime water. That was made with unslaked lime shoveled into water in a big vat dug out in the ground. The vat measured about eight feet wide by ten feet long—big enough so the hides would go in flat—and it was lined with heavy oak or locust boards. Every tannery would have five or six of those vats.

They'd usually process more than one hide at a time, and those hides would be pegged together by their ends with wooden pegs. They'd be set in the vat accordion-fashion, and there was a windlass over the vats. Every day they'd wind the hides out—since they were pegged together, they'd follow each other out in a long string—and then stir up the solution with a long pole with a paddle on the end of it. Get it stirred up good and then wind the hides back in again.

The hides would stay in that lime water about three to five days—whatever it took for the hair to come loose. Then they'd put the hide over a special bench. Usually it was made out of a log. They'd go to the woods and find a big log—hollow if possible, as this would cut down the weight a lot—and peel the bark off of it and have it smooth. Then they'd cut about a six-foot section out and put two legs into one end. The legs would be long enough so that that end would be about waist high. The other end would be cut at an angle so that it would fit flush against the floor. They'd drape the hide over that and, leaning against the end of the log, they'd push the hair off with a special knife that had a blade about two feet long. The knife had a dull blade, and the log was oval and smooth, so the hide wouldn't be cut in any way.

When the hair was off, they'd turn the hide over and push the flesh off the same way. Then they'd put those hides into a clear, strong saltwater solution in another vat for three or four days. They'd still be wet, and they'd be pinned together like before. That step was called pickling.

Then they'd take them out of there and put them in another vat that was set up so that fresh water ran through it constantly. Sometimes they'd run a creek through it. That would wash the hides and get all the salt and lime out of the pores of the hide.

Then they'd grind up tan bark, which was either chestnut oak or hemlock bark that was gathered in the spring of the year when the sap first came out. People would peel that bark off and haul it into the tanneries, and the tanneries would buy enough of that in the spring to run them for the complete year. And the bark mill that they ground the bark up with was pulled by a mule hooked to a long sweep, and the mule would walk in a circle around and around that mill (just like making syrup) and the man would drop bark down in the hopper of the mill and it would come out down at the bottom ground up real fine.

I guess they used those particular trees because the tannic acid in them was stronger in their bark than it was in any other trees in the area. They'd cut those trees and get the bark off of them and then let the logs lay there and rot—or they'd burn them. Just the bark was what they were after. Then a *few* of them would drag the logs out to sawmills, but not many. That was a real waste.

Then they'd take that ground bark and put it in another vat in a layer, and then put in a hide, and then more bark and then another hide and keep building that up with hides and bark until it was full. The hides would still be pinned together like before. Then they'd run water in over that and keep those hides in there for about ninety days. Every few days they'd wind the hides out and add a little more bark and water and stir it up and put the hides back in. The ooze out of that bark made a liquid that penetrated the pores of the skins and that's what tanned them.

Then they'd take the hides out and hang them up to dry just like clothes on a clothesline, and then put them on a big table and work grease into them to soften them and make them pliable. That grease was mostly a mixture of fish oil and tallow rendered out of any animal like a beef. The hides had to be dry, though, before they'd take that oil.

Then if they were going to make black leather, they'd use lampblack, also, and later they'd work that into the grain side—or the side the hair had come off of. They'd work that in by hand on a big table where they could spread the whole hide out.

Then they'd split that hide right down the back following where the backbone had been. They'd make two pieces out of it, and each one was called a side.

Now to make a good pair of shoes, the leather has to be carefully selected. Where the best steaks come out of the animal is where the best quality of leather is. For instance, on the hips, that makes better sole leather. Down in the belly and flanks (the cull leather)—that went into harness, bridles, blinders, and stuff like that. It wasn't too good quality, but it worked. But the leather off the hips was better quality and would wear longer and had more form and didn't have near the stretch in it that the thinner leather had. It would hold its shape better.

The thread used was made from flax. I still use flax thread here. It's made in Louisiana or Mississippi, I believe. Cotton thread will work, but it doesn't have nearly the durability as flax has. And the old shoemakers, they'd twist that thread together to make heavier strands, and then they'd run that over a chunk of wax to make the strands hold together so they could sew with it.

For shoelaces, they'd cut a narrow strip of leather out of the soft part of the hide. It would be a square strip—not round, of course. And then some people used ground-hog hide for laces. They tanned it the same way, and it was supposed to be the toughest and the stoutest of any hide.

In making shoes, Dad used mostly hand tools such as hammers and knives, nippers, pegging awls, etc. Nippers are used to pull the upper of the shoe over the last to shape it before attaching the sole. Pegging awls are used to make the holes to drive the wooden pegs in. The hammers or mallets are used to drive the awls with. It's all hand work. There weren't any mechanized tools at all at that time. You did the sewing by hand with two needles that were steel needles or bristles. Bristles out of a hog's back. Wax that on the end and it will follow the hole you made with the awl—even if it was a curved hole. That was the object in using a bristle. It was flexible and would follow that curved hole. I hunted for some here yesterday. I've got a pack somewhere that I've had for years, but I never did find them. I wouldn't know of anybody anymore now that'd know how to put a wax thread on a bristle and make it stay so they could sew with it.

Now many people had their own lasts—that's the wooden form in the shape of a foot that the shoe is shaped around. They'd find a shoe that fit them and they'd tear that shoe apart when it was worn out and make a wooden last to fit that foot. Then they'd save that and bring their lasts when they brought their hide in to have it tanned to have their shoes made.

If they didn't have lasts, the shoemaker would measure their feet and try to find a pattern that fit. They'd use the lasts they had. My father had patterns. Back when he made shoes he had to have patterns for different sizes and so on. I can remember patterns hanging in the shop against the wall for different size shoes, different styles, whatever he had orders for. And I remember when he had tables full of lasts—I guess all you could haul in a pickup truck—all different sizes. But there weren't many styles. Mostly they were all just plain lace-up shoes. A lot of women's shoes had buttons on them. And then there were rough, heavy work shoes called brogans. In the morning sometimes it would be so cold you couldn't put them on stiff. On those, the leather for the uppers would be turned inside out with the flesh side or the fuzzy side to the outside, and the smooth side next to the foot. They'd turn water better if the leather was turned inside out. I don't know why, but it would turn water better. And it makes the shoes smoother inside, too, to turn the outside in.

A shoe usually had four main pieces of leather not counting the sole, the insole, or the heel. That's the vamp (or the toe and tongue part), the two quarters, and the leather cap that covered the toe. For the vamp, he'd select the best part of the leather. That's where almost all of the wear comes because that's where the shoe bends and wrinkles. An inferior piece of leather would give way.

Here's how you put a shoe together: You stitch the vamp and the quarters together first. Then the quarters are sewed together in the back of the shoe with the edges out (or the flaps out), and then a small strip would be added up the back of the shoe to cover that seam where the two pieces are joined.

Then the insole is cut out to fit the last. Actually, you can cut the insole out first, fit it to the last, then sew the two quarters together with your flax thread and then add the vamp. If you use a cap on the toe it goes across next. Then you start shaping the upper over the last. Wet it and stretch it to conform to the shape of the last and the size of the shoe you want. When you get that stretched and shaped over the last, you should have about a half-inch to three-quarters-inch lap on the underside of the last to attach the sole through. On the bottom of the last, the insole piece comes first and is tacked down in place with a couple of tacks (one in the toe and one in the heel). Then the upper is lapped around, and as it is stretched into place, it is tacked down through the insole into the last. The sole goes onto the top of that; and if you want a heel, you add that onto the top of the sole.

Before the sole is put on, you remove the tacks that are in the insole, as you wouldn't be able to get at them to take them out after the sole is in place. As you draw the upper over the last, you can begin putting on the sole, pegging it down right through the lap of the upper and the insole as you go through holes punched with the pegging awl. Or you can fasten the upper's lap with wooden pegs as you shape it, and then as you add the sole, remove the wooden pegs and replace them with new ones that go through the sole and the upper. That way you only have one row of wooden pegs all the way around the shoe, and not double and triple rows. As tacks are removed and replaced with pegs, the tacks are kept for the next job. The heel is made of layers of leather pegged to the sole with longer pegs.

For stitching the uppers, holes for the thread are punched through the leather with the sewing awl. They didn't do any more of that than they had to. When you're doing it by hand, you don't want an excessive amount of stitching—decorative stitching would be left off completely. Nor would there be any stitching around the top of the uppers—that would be left plain.

Where the eyelets went, they'd double the leather over and stitch the back part inside the shoe. Holes would be punched through for the laces. If the leather was real heavy, that section wouldn't have to be doubled at all. To soften the leather on the shoes, Neat's-foot oil was often used, or fish oil or mutton tallow.

How long the shoes lasted depended on how much you wore them, but most people figured on getting a year out of a pair of shoes. If you wore them out before the year was out, you went barefooted until you got another pair.

*Questions for Rereading,
Discussing, Connecting, and Writing*

### REREADING

1. This selection was developed from an interview with the speaker, Ernest Riddle, and it preserves some features of oral language. What can you discover about differences between speaking and writing by reading the selection?

**2.** Knowing something well often leads us to assume our audience shares our knowledge, and we fail to include all the necessary details and explanations. What knowledge do the authors of this selection assume you have?

**3.** Reading directions or explanations of how to do something frequently involves assimilating new information. As you read "Shoemaking," what new information do you encounter? Try to record this new information in ways other than writing.

DISCUSSING

**4.** This selection results from the collective efforts of Ernest Riddle; Tina Smith, Karen Jones, and John Bowen, the high school students who interviewed him; and of Eliot Wiggington, the high school teacher who developed the *Foxfire* concept of encouraging students to interview older people about local culture and who served as editor of the collection in which "Shoemaking" is included. This collaboration raises questions about authorship because we usually think of an author as an individual or (occasionally) a couple of individuals. Explain the rationale for describing each of the individuals listed above as an author.

**5.** In the first edition of *Foxfire*, Wiggington described his goal as one of preserving the folkways of his region of the country. Given this one selection, to what extent do you think has he achieved this goal?

**6.** In the introduction to this selection, Ernest Riddle expresses skepticism about whether his interviewers could explain the process of shoemaking clearly: "I don't care how many books you read . . . it takes actual experience to really know how to make a pair." To what extent do you agree?

CONNECTING

**7.** This selection, like that by Degas (p. 197) or Parker (p. 230), offers insight into learning how to do something. Each conveys a slightly different message about what is involved in this kind of learning. What similarities and differences do you find?

**8.** "Shoemaking" could be included in Amman's book of arts, crafts, and trades. Draw on this selection to create an entry that could appear next to "The Carpenter" (p. 182).

**9.** Like Twain's (p. 202), this selection is recounted from the perspective of an adult looking back at work done when he was a child. How do "Shoemaking" and "The Boy's Ambition" differ in their portrayal of fast-disappearing forms of work?

## WRITING

**10.** Ernest Riddle and his collaborators seem to share Wiggington's goal of preserving cultural folkways. Decide on the "goal" of another selection in this chapter and write an introduction to it that explains this goal.

**11.** As this selection demonstrates, interviewing can yield a great deal of information for writers. Identify an expert whom you know, interview that person about this area of expertise, and write an account of how to do what your interviewee has described.

**12.** Write directions for something you know how to do well.

Carol Mont Parker

# The Anatomy of a New York City Debut: A Chronicle (1982)

### August

Tonight I want to consider the whole question of Beethoven's music, who plays it, and how. It's been suggested to me that I am suicidal to play Beethoven in New York. Why? First of all, there's the notion of being sufficiently ripe to tackle it; and second, the fact that everyone likes his Beethoven a different way, and you can never please everyone, and, chances are, especially not the guy who's sitting out there with his pencil and paper. Josef Fidelman (one of my two fine teachers) told me if I'm doing this thing for reviews, forget it. Don't do it. You don't play to one person who may or may not be a "cabbage." You go into it doing your best, you don't stake your ego and your future ego on this guy's whims. You know what you are beforehand and afterwards. Along with this, I feel I must play what I love.

This morning, it feels particularly lonely at the piano. It's as though the piano and I are condemned to each other for better or for worse. The phone is deathly silent, my friends being respectfully obedient to the 8 A.M. to 12 noon moratorium. The concentration needs harnessing back to the focal points, and even the dogs (the little one curled up right on my feet at the pedals) are no comfort.

Shall I admit in writing that one of my favorite fantasies these days is the image of The Placard outside Carnegie, plastered up with my likeness on it, for all the sophisticated 57th Street passers-by to see for one long important week? And the ad in the *Times* the Sunday before would be another agreeable notion, if I didn't know how shockingly through-the-nose one pays to place it.

A vanity exists between the pianist and his instrument, even if it's "a child only a mother could love."

The great black mass that is my piano has immense beauty to me. All that potential, standing stodgily on three strategic legs and capable of the widest reaches and varieties of sound of any instrument in the world. I once realized that I am so vain about my piano that I would sooner hear a compliment about its virtues than mine.

Years ago when I had first begun to read the Schumann Études Symphoniques, I was so enchanted by the fifth Anhang variation that I must have played it twenty times on end in one session. My daughter Kim, a fine flutist, who was very little then, quietly came, and left a note on the piano while I was playing, and disappeared. When I stopped to look at it, I read the following rhapsody: "O Mommy, that piece is so beautiful! And you are so beautiful, I love you! It sounds like birdies having a funeral. Love, Kim." This, complete with a sketch of a bevy of tearful birds around a bird-sized coffin.

Today, four days before my first recital in the series, I'm having a good case of why I haven't chosen to do more playing in public. In spite of the fact that the program went smoothly for Josef a couple of days ago, and in spite of all the positive thinking, I am being plagued by the all too familiar signs of nervous tension: stomach unrest, a lump in the throat, hallucinations of musical disasters, self-scrutiny, the works. One gorgeous package.

## December

Impressions in a backstage closet:
The facilities leave something to be desired. I find myself at 2:10 P.M. in a no-exit 7' x 9' sterile chamber with cement-block walls, three chairs, a pitcher of water, my music, and a crossword puzzle. Beyond the wall there is the increasing murmur of the audience filling the seats in the room. I expect, momentarily, a short buzzer to signal that the lights have been dimmed and my appearance on the stage is being awaited. Two-thirty and no signal. My hands are alternately perspiring and cold to the touch. My stomach is churning to beat the band, and no matter how hard I "meditate," with due respects to all the yogis, or concentrate on the crossword puzzle, the good old nerves are in full bloom.

Then, ten insufferably eternal minutes later, the piercing buzz startles me and I find myself entering, smiling confidently, and seating myself at the keyboard.

I was looking idly at my hands for a long time today, and I find I like them. They would never appeal to anyone by the usual standards of feminine contours or embellishment, and I am often self-consciously aware of them at a dinner table. They are not slim, graceful hands with tapered manicured nails, lily white and smooth. They are strong, developed, working hands which in some way always seem to have on them a hint of whatever I am involved in. In the springtime there is the roughness from working the soil; during periods when I am painting, there are signs of the more permanent pigments, so hard to remove from the pores; and in this, the Year of the Piano, my hands are quite visibly changed: networks of developed muscles, bones and veins close to the surface, and the components of the machinery clearly seen through the thin skin holding it all together. The nails are exactly to the ends of the fingers, and the fingers' ends are somewhat blunted with the slightest indications of calluses. The element of ivory ( or its synthetics) is no more foreign to them than the air itself.

If there is anything which is as sensually satisfying to the touch as the keyboard these days, it is my dogs' heads. Probably the only interruption I do not resent, and actually welcome, is a soft muzzle, and soulful eyes suddenly looking up at me from under the piano.

What is the magic of the N. Y. *Times* that the appearance of one's name in BLOCK LETTERS, in an ad that one pays for oneself, can, nevertheless, be so exciting? That concert page, like a counterpane of assorted-size boxes filled with some of the most illustrious names, shoulder to shoulder with the "unknowns," is like a joyous tintinnabulation of all the various concerts being played at once.

## January

Someday I am going to write a book called "Pianos I've Known." The old instruments we have to play on sometimes seem as though they've been dredged up from the *Titanic*! Today's specimen in the college recital hall where my last pre-recital takes place will go down as the Dead Middle. This nine-foot Steinway is an old baby that has been through the wars. The panel behind the keyboard is literally gouged to bits by the passionate fingernails of hundreds of pianists.

## February 9

Today I don't know how to discuss brain waves or brain activity in intelligent, scientific terms, but if they have a gauge to measure it, mine would certainly register over the deep end. I feel supercharged electronically. My stream of consciousness is dragging me through every human mood from the most fearsome insecurity to the most cocky sureness, and back down again. The roller-coaster ride is no fun at all.

## February 10

My first glimpse of Carnegie last evening after the long and tense drive was almost surrealistic. The marquee of the Great Carnegie and the elegant, canopied entrance to the Recital Hall seemed more brilliantly illuminated and grander than ever. I dashed across 57th Street in my blue jeans and pea jacket, with my black velvet formal ensemble and white silk blouse flapping wildly on the hanger, and stopped short on the way in to grin secretly at my poster in the showcase at the entrance, under the sign which read "TONIGHT."

## *Questions for Rereading, Discussing, Connecting, and Writing*

### REREADING

1. This selection draws on a journal Parker kept next to her piano during the six months before her Carnegie Hall recital. As you move from one entry to another, what kinds of progression do you find? How do you think Parker feels about playing the recital by the time the long-awaited date arrives?

2. Journal entries are one way of representing experience, just as novels and paintings are others. Each genre contains its own set of possibilities and limitations. What, in your view, are the possibilities of the journal as Parker uses it? In other words, what is she able to do by writing a journal that she would not be able to do in another genre?

3. Parker did not include all her journal entries here; she selected a smaller number from the larger whole. What, as you see it, unifies these entries?

### DISCUSSING

4. As Parker describes her situation, there seems to be little extrinsic reward for her hard work. She even has to pay for her own newspaper advertisement. Discuss what motivates her to play at the recital.

**5.** Because a limited number of entries is included in this selection, we do not have all the details of Parker's six-month preparation. What is the effect of including the parts that deal with her dog and her daughter?

**6.** Parker's relationship to her instrument is primary in her recital preparation. Consider Parker's various descriptions of and discussions of pianos and define this relationship.

## CONNECTING

**7.** Although she takes a different approach, Parker resembles Lange (p. 215), Twain (p. 202), and *Foxfire* (p. 223) in giving her readers insight into the feelings that underlie her work. Consider the similarities and differences in four expressions of feelings about work.

**8.** The process of composing often leads one into additional projects as happens when Parker says "Someday I am going to write a book called 'Pianos I've Known.'" Look for the suggestion of additional projects in selections by Degas (p. 197), Updike (p. 377), and others of your choosing.

**9.** Both money-lending and giving piano recitals can be described as work. Consider the various definitions of work implicit in the Parker and Amman (p. 182) selections.

## WRITING

**10.** Write a journal entry from the perspective of Parker's daughter.

**11.** Parker offers some explanation of her reasons for doing the recital, for honoring this commitment to herself. Write an essay in which you explain a commitment you have made or would like to make in your own life.

**12.** Write an entry that might appear in Parker's journal the day after the recital.

*Box Score*

# Baseball (1989)

## BOX SCORE

### American League

### Athletics 9, Angels 5

| CALIFORNIA | ab | r | h | bi | OAKLAND | ab | r | h | bi |
|---|---|---|---|---|---|---|---|---|---|
| Washngtn rf | 4 | 0 | 0 | 0 | R.Hndrsn lf | 5 | 1 | 2 | 2 |
| Ray 2b | 4 | 2 | 2 | 0 | Lansfrd 3b | 5 | 0 | 2 | 1 |
| White cf | 5 | 0 | 3 | 1 | Parker dh | 5 | 1 | 2 | 0 |
| Joyner 1b | 3 | 1 | 1 | 1 | McGwir 1b | 4 | 1 | 2 | 0 |
| Downng dh | 5 | 0 | 0 | 0 | Javier lb | 0 | 1 | 0 | 0 |
| Davis lf | 4 | 1 | 2 | 2 | D.Hndrsn cf | 4 | 2 | 3 | 2 |
| Schroedr c | 3 | 0 | 0 | 0 | Canseco rf | 4 | 0 | 0 | 0 |
| Howell 3b | 4 | 0 | 0 | 0 | Hassey c | 4 | 2 | 2 | 1 |
| Schofild ss | 3 | 1 | 2 | 1 | Phillips 2b | 3 | 0 | 1 | 1 |
|  |  |  |  |  | Gallego ss | 3 | 1 | 0 | 2 |
| Totals | 35 | 5 | 10 | 5 | Totals | 37 | 9 | 14 | 9 |

California 102 000 110—5
Oakland    100 400 04x—9

E—Steinbach, Schroeder. DP—Oakland 1. LOB—California 9, Oakland 6. 2B—D.Henderson, McGwire, Davis. HR—R.Henderson (7). SB—Schofield (8), Washington (7), R.Henderson (41), Lansford (17). S—Schroeder. SF—Gallego.

|  | IP | H | R | ER | BB | SO |
|---|---|---|---|---|---|---|
| **California** |  |  |  |  |  |  |
| Witt L,7-8 | 7 | 11 | 7 | 6 | 0 | 6 |
| Montlne | 2/3 | 3 | 2 | 2 | 1 | 1 |
| McClure | 1/3 | 0 | 0 | 0 | 0 | 1 |
| **Oakland** |  |  |  |  |  |  |
| Moore | 6 1/3 | 6 | 4 | 4 | 2 | 8 |
| Honeycutt | 1/3 | 1 | 0 | 0 | 2 | 1 |
| Burns | 1 | 2 | 1 | 1 | 0 | 0 |
| Young W,1-3 | 1/3 | 0 | 0 | 0 | 1 | 0 |
| Eckersley | 1 | 1 | 0 | 0 | 0 | 0 |

WP—M.Young. Umpires—Home, Clark; First, Johnson; Second, Phillips; Third, Reed. T—3:25. A—44,588.

*Questions for Rereading, Discussing, Connecting, and Writing*

REREADING

**1.** Box scores were developed by sports reporters of the 1800s who needed an efficient way to get the most important information about a baseball game into newspapers. As you look at the box score, what evidence of efficiency in conveying information do you find? Take a single number from the box score and note what it tells you about the game.

**2.** If you are a baseball fan you probably read box scores without thinking about all the special language they contain. If you do not read them regularly, you may need help decoding abbreviations such as *GWRBI* and *LOB*. Whether or not you are familiar with the box score, make an inventory of all the codes necessary to understanding everything included here.

3. One of the costs of efficiency is that it can leave important things out. As you read the box score, consider what it does not include. If you have difficulty thinking about what is missing, look at a newspaper account of a baseball game.

DISCUSSING

4. Baseball is called *the* American sport; it has been played in the United States since 1846. In what ways is baseball "American"? How does baseball compare with, say, football or some other major league sports played in the United States?

5. The information contained in this or any box score refers to a specific set of actions on a given day. What does this information reveal about baseball in general?

6. The information contained in a box score comes from statistics collected by sportswriters during a game. Who, in your view, can be described as the author(s) of this particular box score?

CONNECTING

7. The box score can be described as a text written in a highly abbreviated language. Compare the box score language with that used by Mozart (p. 349) and Amman (p. 182).

8. Like the box score, "Shoemaking" (p. 223) has multiple authors. Compare the effects achieved by the several authors of these two selections.

9. The box score is not the only statistical code that appears regularly in our culture. In a newspaper, find a text that resembles the box score in its economy—you might look at financial pages as well as sports pages. What similarities and differences do you find?

WRITING

10. Translate the box score into another code by writing a narrative of the game described in the box score.

11. One of the statistics included in the box score is attendance. Write an essay in which you explain why it is important to know the number of people present at a given baseball game.

12. Develop an efficient code for describing some activity you know well—perhaps a college class or a game. Write an essay explaining your code.

# Five

# Power and Justice

One of the assumptions behind writing in the classroom can be put in the form of a question: "Whom do I want to reach, and what effect do I want to make?" The audience for a piece of writing must be identified at some point in the composing process, as well as what the writer would like the audience to think or feel or do when it reads this piece of writing. We can think of the composing process, then, as an *exercise in power*.

"Power" is a general term for *influence* when we speak of it in writing class. And influence can be seen as *effect*—what our words will do out there in the world when a reader gets hold of them. Sometimes only one reader—the teacher—will encounter your work. You can consider the teacher as your audience, and work on influencing that teacher with your work, to make him or her see its *power*—or any of those terms we usually associate with "good writing," like clarity, precision, well-developed thought, and originality.

But an audience can extend far beyond the classroom—and so can the effect of reaching an intended audience. Thomas Jefferson's *Declaration of Independence* is an example of a work that started rather modestly—short pieces scribbled in Jefferson's "daybooks" (or journals) for the sake of straightening out his thinking on some important issues. Slowly these pieces evolved from journal work to the tremendously influential document we know the declaration to be. The "power" in Jefferson's work did not make itself evident until the document was circulated, and then it contributed to the establishing of the United States of America. Jefferson, as the work's author, gradually revised his work so that its audience could feel the full force of his intended effect.

Similarly, John Stuart Mill's selection in this chapter, "The Subjection of Women," clearly has as its intended audience those who would ponder his charges—legislators, for example—and who could make changes in the treatment of women in nineteenth-century England. Mill was just as interested as Jefferson in establishing "power" or "effect" over those who could change a social condition. The politics of the situation were fully felt by Mill.

This chapter on power and politics can also be used by the writer as a place to find examples of work that exert power far beyond their authors' intended audiences. Jefferson had the citizenry of colonial America—and the oppressors from England—in mind when he circulated his declaration, yet the piece has great power even today. Goya's painting of a rebel's death, "The Third of May," can be seen not only as the painter's commentary on Spanish politics, but also as a more general statement to any audience about the suffering of the accused, or the humanity of victims.

In contrast, what can we make of a photograph like Adam's, taken with the split-second impulse of the professional journalist? The photographer's job requires that super-awareness of events happening around him or her, and in this famous case the photographer was ready with the camera. The photograph became famous in a matter of hours, and its effect was felt just as quickly; the antiwar movement used it most forcefully to show what could happen under the stress of war. What is most important to us writers, viewing this example of journalism, is that we realize simply being "open" to events around us may help us be that "lightning rod" to events that can change history, politics, society.

Power and politics tend to be subjects that are so common we can overlook them. Every moment of every day we are either exerting power or feeling it exerted upon us. Whether we are about to vote for president or are simply reading the front page of the daily newspaper, we are in the middle of power and politics. We exert power in order to get an increase in our salaries, and sometimes we get embroiled, for example, in the politics of neighborhood development. Influence—and getting influenced—is a timeless occupation, and the selections in this chapter are chosen to show the variety of contexts in which we can view these occupations, whether they are the *conquering* role of the European nations in Africa, circa 1876, or a slave woman's eloquent plea for human dignity and worth, as in Sojourner Truth's "Ain't I a Woman?".

In this chapter are examples of power found and lost, politics fair and unfair. This chapter can provide inspiration for the common man or woman writing of the uncommon moment, or the universal truth. The audience may at first be only ourselves, but the possibilities of audience, and influence, are endless.

## The Prophet Amos

# *The Bible* *(760 B.C.)*

3 Hear this word that the LORD has spoken against you, O people of Israel, against the whole family which I brought up out of the land of Egypt:
2 "You only have I known
 of all the families of the earth;
 therefore I will punish you
 for all your iniquities.

3 "Do two walk together,
 unless they have made an appointment?
4 Does a lion roar in the forest,
 when he has no prey?
 Does a young lion cry out from his den,
 if he has taken nothing?
5 Does a bird fall in a snare on the earth,
 when there is no trap for it?
 Does a snare spring up from the ground,
 when it has taken nothing?
6 Is a trumpet blown in a city,
 and the people are not afraid?
 Does evil befall a city,
 unless the LORD has done it?
7 Surely the Lord GOD does nothing,
 without revealing his secret
 to his servants the prophets.
8 The lion has roared;
 who will not fear?
 The Lord GOD has spoken;
 who can but prophesy?"

9 Proclaim to the strongholds in Assyria,
 and to the strongholds in the land of Egypt,
 and say, "Assemble yourselves upon the mountains of Sama´ria,
 and see the great tumults within her,
 and the oppressions in her midst."
10 "They do not know how to do right," says the LORD,
 "those who store up violence and robbery in their strongholds."

11 Therefore thus says the Lord GOD:
"An adversary shall surround the land,
and bring down your defenses from you,
and your strongholds shall be plundered."

12 Thus says the LORD: "As the Shepherd rescue from the mouth of the lion two legs, or a piece of an ear, so shall the people of Israel who dwell in Sama′ria be rescued, with the corner of a couch and part of a bed."

13 "Hear, and testify against the house of Jacob,"
    says the Lord GOD, the God of hosts,
14 "that on the day I punish Israel for his transgressions,
    I will punish the altars of Bethel,
and the horns of the altar shall be cut off
    and fall to the ground.
15 I will smite the winter house with the summer house;
    and the houses of ivory shall perish,
and the great houses shall come to an end,"
                                                        says the LORD.

4 "Hear this word, you cows of Bashan,
    who are in the mountain of Sama′ria,
who oppress the poor, who crush the needy,
    who say to their husbands, 'Bring, that we may drink!'
2 The Lord GOD has sworn by his holiness
    that, behold, the days are coming upon you,
when they shall take you away with hooks,
    even the last of you with fishhooks.
3 And you shall go out through the breaches,
    every one straight before her;
and you shall be cast forth into Harmon,"
                                                        says the LORD.

4 "Come to Bethel, and transgress;
    to Gilgal, and multiply transgression;
bring your sacrifices every morning,
    your tithes every three days;
5 offer a sacrifice of thanksgiving of that which is leavened,
    and proclaim freewill offerings, publish them;
for so you love to do, O people of Israel!"
                                                    says the Lord GOD.

6 "I gave you cleanness of teeth in all your cities,
    and lack of bread in all your places,
yet you did not return to me,"
                                                        says the LORD.

7 "And I also withheld the rain from you
   when there were yet three months to the harvest;
 I would send rain upon one city,
   and send no rain upon another city;
 one field would be rained upon,
   and the field on which it did not rain withered;
8 so two or three cities wandered to one city
   to drink water, and were not satisfied;
 yet you did not return to me,"
                                               says the LORD.

9 "I smote you with blight and mildew;
   I laid waste your gardens and your vineyards;
   your fig trees and your olive trees the locust devoured;
 yet you did not return to me,"
                                               says the LORD.

10 "I sent among you a pestilence after the manner of Egypt;
   I slew your young men with the sword;
 I carried away your horses;
   and I made the stench of your camp go up into your nostrils;
 yet you did not return to me,"
                                               says the LORD.

11 "I overthrew some of you,
   as when God overthrew Sodom and Gomor'rah,
   and you were as a brand plucked out of the burning;
 yet you did not return to me,"
                                               says the LORD.

12 "Therefore thus I will do to you, O Israel;
   because I will do this to you,
   prepare to meet your God, O Israel!"

13 For lo, he who forms the mountains, and creates the wind,
     and declares to man what is his thought;
   who makes the morning darkenss,
     and treads on the heights of the earth—
   the LORD, the God of hosts, is his name!

5 Hear this word which I take up over you in lamentation, O house of Israel:
2 "Fallen, no more to rise,
   is the virgin Israel;
 forsaken on her land,
   with none to raise her up."

3 For thus says the Lord GOD:
"The city that went forth a thousand
shall have a hundred left,
and that which went forth a hundred
shall have ten left
to the house of Israel."

4 For thus says the LORD to the house of Israel:
"Seek me and live;
5 but do not seek Bethel,
and do not enter into Gilgal
or cross over to Beer-sheba;
for Gilgal shall surely go into exile,
and Bethel shall come to nought."

6 Seek the LORD and live,
lest he break out like fire in the house of Joseph,
and it devour, with none to quench it for Bethel,
7 O you who turn justice to wormwood,
and cast down righteousness to the earth!

8 He who made the Pleiades and Orion,
and turns deep darkness into the morning,
and darkens the day into night,
who calls for the waters of the sea,
and pours them out upon the surface of the earth,
the LORD is his name,
9 who makes destruction flash forth against the strong,
so that destruction comes upon the fortress.

10 They hate him who reproves in the gate,
and they abhor him who speaks the truth.
11 Therefore because you trample upon the poor
and take from him exactions of wheat,
you have built houses of hewn stone,
but you shall not dwell in them;
you have planted pleasant vineyards,
but you shall not drink their wine.
12 For I know how many are your transgressions,
and how great are your sins—
you who afflict the righteous, who take a bribe,
and turn aside the needy in the gate.
13 Therefore he who is prudent will keep silent in such a time;
for it is an evil time.

14 Seek good, and not evil,
>    that you may live;
> and so the Lord, the God of hosts, will be with you,
>    as you have said.
15 Hate evil, and love good,
>    and establish justice in the gate;
> it may be that the Lord, the God of hosts,
>    will be gracious to the remnant of Joseph.

16 Therefore thus says the Lord, the God of hosts, the Lord:
> "In all the squares there shall be wailing;
>    and in all the streets they shall say, 'Alas! alas!'
> They shall call the farmers to mourning
>    and to wailing those who are skilled in lamentation,
17 and in all vineyards there shall be wailing,
>    for I will pass through the midst of you,"

                                                                says the Lord.

18 Woe to you who desire the day of the Lord!
>    Why would you have the day of the Lord?
> It is darkness, and not light;
19 as if a man fled from a lion,
>    and a bear met him;
> or went into the house and leaned with his hand against the wall,
>    and a serpent bit him.
20 Is not the day of the Lord darkness, and not light,
>    and gloom with no brightness in it?

21 "I hate, I despise your feasts,
>    and I take no delight in your solemn assemblies.
22 Even though you offer me your burnt offerings and cereal offerings,
>    I will not accept them,
> and the peace offerings of your fatted beasts
>    I will not look upon.
23 Take away from me the noise of your songs;
>    to the melody of your harps I will not listen.
24 But let justice roll down like waters,
>    and righteousness like an ever-flowing stream.

25 "Did you bring to me sacrifices and offerings the forty years in the wilderness, O house of Israel? 26 You shall take up Sakkuth your king, and Kaiwan your star-god, your images, which you made for yourselves; 27 therefore I will take you into exile beyond Damascus," says the Lord, whose name is the God of hosts.

## Questions for Rereading, Discussing, Connecting, and Writing

### Rereading

**1.** The prophetic literature of the Bible, of which this selection is a part, has its own distinctive features. As you read, notice the effect of some of these features. What, for example is the effect of several questions appearing in succession, of the imperative verbs such as "hear," proclaim," and "come," or of images from nature?

**2.** Amos prophesied to his fellow Isrealites during a time of peace and prosperity. What is the effect of his frequent references to the material comforts Isrealites enjoy?

**3.** As a prophet, Amos claims to be speaking God's word. Consider how the language of God and the language of Amos are represented in this selection.

### Discussing

**4.** Much of Amos's prophecy centers on God's concern about the Israelites' injustices to the poor. Discuss the difficulty of making this kind of prophecy when most people live in relative comfort.

**5.** Consider the structure of the argument Amos makes. A typical argument will make a claim and then offer evidence to support it. Discuss the ways that this selection does and does not represent a typical argument.

**6.** Even though this selection was composed over 2500 years ago, its central concern—the plight of the poor—is still with us. Discuss the problems of the poor in today's world.

### Connecting

**7.** Like Sojourner Truth (p. 259) and John Stuart Mill (p. 262), Amos is concerned with the rights of the oppressed. What are the similarities and differences in the concerns expressed by these three composers?

**8.** The contempory world does not lack for prophets, even though their words may not be recorded in a holy book. Whom would you identify as a prophet of our time? What issues concern contemporary prophets?

## Writing

**9.** Amos and the employment officer represented in the LeSueur selection (p. 84) exhibit very different attitudes toward the poor. Write a dialogue of what Amos and the employment officer might say to one another about the poor.

**10.** Write your own version of this selection, presenting the essence of what Amos says. What differences do you notice between your version and the original selection?

**11.** Select a contemporary issue about which you feel strongly, one to which society should respond. Write a prophecy, loosely based on the model of Amos, about this issue and what you think society should do.

## Niccolo Machiavelli

# *The Prince* (1532)

*XXV. How far human affairs are governed by fortune, and how fortune can be opposed*

I am not unaware that many have held and hold the opinion that events are controlled by fortune and by God in such a way that the prudence of men cannot modify them, indeed, that men have no influence whatsoever. Because of this, they would conclude that there is no point in sweating over things, but that one should submit to the rulings of chance. This opinion has been more widely held in our own times, because of the great changes and variations, beyond human imagining, which we have experienced and experience every day. Sometimes, when thinking of this, I have myself inclined to this same opinion. Nonetheless, so as not to rule out our free will, I believe that it is probably true that fortune is the arbiter of half the things we do, leaving the other half or so to be controlled by ourselves. I compare fortune to one of those violent rivers which, when they are enraged, flood the plains, tear down trees and buildings, wash soil from one place to deposit it in another. Everyone flees before them, everybody yields to their impetus, there is no possibility of resistance. Yet although such is their nature, it does not follow that when they are flowing quietly one cannot take precautions, constructing dykes and embankments so that when the river is in flood they would keep to one channel or their impetus be less wild and dangerous. So it is with fortune. She shows her potency where there is no well regulated power to resist her, and her impetus is felt where she knows there are no embankments and dykes built to restrain her. If you consider Italy, the theatre of those changes and variations I mentioned, which first appeared here, you will see that she is a country without embankments and without dykes: for if Italy had been adequately reinforced, like Germany, Spain, and France, either this flood would not have caused the great changes it has, or it would not have swept in at all.

I want what I have said to suffice, in general terms, on the question of how to oppose fortune. But, confining myself now to particular circumstances, I say that we see that some princes flourish one day and come to grief the next, without appearing to have changed in character or any other way. This I believe arises, first, for the reasons discussed at length earlier on, namely, that those princes who are utterly dependent on fortune come to grief when their fortune changes. I also believe that the one who adapts his policy to the times prospers, and likewise that the one whose policy clashes with the demands of the times does not. It can be observed that men use various methods in pursuing their own personal objectives, that is glory and riches. One man proceeds with circumspection, another impetuously; one uses violence, another stratagem; one man goes about things patiently, another does the opposite; and yet everyone, for all this diversity of method, can reach his objective. It can also be observed that with two circumspect men, one will achieve his end, the other not; and likewise two men succeed equally well with different methods, one of them being circumspect and the other impetuous. This results from nothing else except the extent to which their methods are or are not suited to the nature of the times. Thus it happens that, as I have said, two men, working in different ways, can achieve the same end, and of two men working in the same way one gets what he wants and the other does not. This also explains why prosperity is ephemeral; because if a man behaves with patience and circumspection and the time and circumstances are such that this method is called for, he will prosper; but if time and circumstances change he will be ruined because he does not change his policy. Nor do we find any man shrewd enough to know how to adapt his policy in this way; either because he cannot do otherwise than what is in character or because, having always prospered by proceeding one way, he cannot persuade himself to change. Thus a man who is circumspect, when circumstances demand impetuous behaviour, is unequal to the task, and so he comes to grief. If he changed his character according to the time and circumstances, then his fortune would not change.

Pope Julius II was impetuous in everything; and he found the time and circumstances so favourable to his way of proceeding that he always met with success. Consider his first campaign, against Bologna, when messer Giovanni Bentivogli was still living. The Venetians mistrusted it: so did the king of Spain; and Julius was still arguing about the enterprise with France. Nonetheless, with typical forcefulness and impetuosity, he launched the expedition in person. This move disconcerted and arrested Spain and the Venetians, the latter because they were afraid and the former because of the king's ambition to reconquer all the kingdom of Naples. On the other hand, he drew the king of France after him. This was because the king, seeing Julius go into action, and anxious for his support in subduing the Venetians, decided he could not refuse him troops without doing him a manifest disservice. With that impetuous move of his, therefore, Julius achieved what no other pontiff, with the utmost human prudence, would have achieved. Because had Julius delayed setting out from Rome until all his plans and negotiations were completed, as any other pontiff would have done, he would never have succeeded. The king of France would have found a hundred and one excuses, and the others would have inspired Julius with a hundred and one fears. I shall not discuss his other deeds, which were all like this and which all met with success. The brevity of his pontifical life did not let him experience the contrary. If there had come a time when it was necessary for him to act with circumspection he would have come to grief: he would never have acted other than in character.

I conclude, therefore, that as fortune is changeable whereas men are obstinate in their ways, men prosper so long as fortune and policy are in accord, and when there is a clash they fail. I hold strongly to this: that it is better to be impetuous than circumspect; because fortune is a woman and if she is to be submissive it is necessary to beat and coerce her. Experience shows that she is more often subdued by men who do this than by those who act coldly. Always, being a woman, she favours young men, because they are less circumspect and more ardent; and because they command her with greater audacity.

*Questions for Rereading, Discussing, Connecting, and Writing*

### REREADING

**1.** Machiavelli, an Italian statesman, wrote the book from which this selection comes after he retired from public life, having been deprived of office and imprisoned briefly. As you read, consider how Machiavelli's position as a retired statesman (as opposed to an active one) contributes to what he says about governance.

**2.** You may know the name Machiavellian and associate it with something sinister or evil. Consider, as you read, what, if anything, contributes to this association of the name Machiavelli with evil qualities.

**3.** As you read consider the relationship between the title of this selection and the text that follows. How does the title contribute to your reading of the text?

## Discussing

**4.** Machiavelli claims that fortune controls half of what happens in our lives and that we can control the other half. Discuss both the claim and the proportion. Do you agree with the claim? Does the ratio seem right?

**5.** The metaphor of a violent river describes fortune. Consider other metaphors that might be used to describe fortune. What effect would they have?

**6.** Although it was written in 1513, *The Prince* was not published until after Machiavelli's death in 1527. Speculate on this delay in publication. What audience do you think Machiavelli wrote for?

## Connecting

**7.** Machiavelli acknowledges that many people assume that humans have no influence on events and that there is no point in "sweating over things." Many people today take a similar position. Cite evidence—from sayings or expressions, from various media, from any source you can find—that demonstrates the contemporary nature of this view.

**8.** Like Machiavelli, Thomas Jefferson concerns himself with the nature of governance. After looking at the Declaration of Independence (p. 251), speculate on what response Jefferson would have to Machiavelli's statements.

**9.** Machiavelli concludes by describing fortune as a woman. Note the characteristics he attributes to women and consider how Mill (p. 262) or Truth (p. 259) or Woolf (p. 270) might respond to this description of women.

## Writing

**10.** The degree to which humans can control the events in their own lives is debated as much today as it was in Machiavelli's time. Think of a time in your own life when you felt strongly either that you did or did not have control over what happened. Use this experience in your own life as a point of departure to explain your own views on how much humans can shape the events of their lives.

**11.** Implicit in much of what Machiavelli says is the idea that the ends justify the means, that it doesn't matter how you achieve your goals as long as you achieve them. Write an essay in which you explore the relationship between ends and means, focusing on a contemporary issue.

**12.** Machiavelli urges political leaders to act impetuously rather than cautiously and offers examples and arguments to support his view. Write an essay in which you support either the impetuous or cautious approach to leadership, drawing on contemporary evidence to support your position.

*Thomas Jefferson*

# Declaration of Independence (1776)

When in the Course of human events, it becomes necessary for one people to dissolve the political bands which have connected them with another, and to assume among the powers of the earth, the separate and equal station to which the Laws of Nature and of Nature's God entitle them, a decent respect to the opinions of mankind requires that they should declare the causes which impel them to the separation.—We hold these truths to be self-evident, that all men are created equal, that they are endowed by their Creator with certain unalienable Rights, that among these are Life, Liberty and the pursuit of Happiness.—That to secure these rights, Governments are instituted among Men, deriving their just powers from the consent of the governed,—That whenever any Form of Government becomes destructive of these ends, it is the Right of the People to alter or to abolish it, and to institute new Government, laying its foundation on such principles and organizing its powers in such forms, as to them shall seem most likely to effect their Safety and Happiness. Prudence, indeed, will dictate that Governments long established should not be changed for light and transient causes; and accordingly all experience hath shown, that mankind are more disposed to suffer, while evils are sufferable, than to right themselves by abolishing the forms to which they are accustomed. But when a long train of abuses and usurpations, pursuing invariably the same Object evinces a design to reduce them under absolute Despotism, it is their right, it is their duty, to throw off such Government, and to provide new Guards for their future security. —Such has been the patient sufferance of these Colonies; and such is now the necessity which constrains them to alter their former Systems of Government. The history of the present King of Great Britain is a history of repeated injuries and usurpations, all having in direct object the establishment of an absolute Tyranny over these States. To prove this, let Facts be submitted to a candid world.—He has refused his

Assent to Laws, the most wholesome and necessary for the public good.—He has forbidden his Governors to pass Laws of immediate and pressing importance, unless suspended in their operation till his Assent should be obtained; and when so suspended, he has utterly neglected to attend to them.—He has refused to pass other Laws for the accommodation of large districts of people, unless those people would relinquish the right of Representation in the Legislature, a right inestimable to them and formidable to tyrants only.—He has called together legislative bodies at places unusual, uncomfortable, and distant from the depository of their public Records, for the sole purpose of fatiguing them into compliance with his measures.—He has dissolved Representative Houses repeatedly, for opposing with manly firmness his invasions on the rights of the people.—He has refused for a long time, after such dissolutions, to cause others to be elected; whereby the Legislative powers, incapable of Annihilation, have returned to the People at large for their exercise; the State remaining in the mean time exposed to all the dangers of invasion from without, and convulsions within.—He has endeavoured to prevent the population of these States; for that purpose obstructing the Laws for Naturalization of Foreigners; refusing to pass others to encourage their migration hither, and raising the conditions of new Appropriations of Lands.—He has obstructed the Administration of Justice, by refusing his Assent to Laws for establishing Judiciary powers.—He has made Judges dependent on his Will alone, for the tenure of their offices, and the amount and payment of their salaries.—He has erected a multitude of New Offices, and sent hither swarms of Officers to harrass our people, and eat out their substance.—He has kept among us, in times of peace, Standing Armies, without the Consent of our legislatures.—He has affected to render the Military independent of and superior to the Civil power.—He has combined with others to subject us to a jurisdiction foreign to our constitution, and unacknowledged by our laws; giving his Assent to their Acts of pretended Legislation:—For quartering large bodies of armed troops among us:—For protecting them, by a mock Trial, from punishment for any Murders which they should commit on the Inhabitants of these States:—For cutting off our Trade with all parts of the world:—For imposing Taxes on us without our Consent:—For depriving us in many cases, of the benefits of Trial by Jury:—For transporting us beyond Seas to be tried for pretended offences:—For abolishing the free System of English Laws in a neighbouring Province, establishing therein an Arbitrary government, and enlarging its Boundaries so as to render it at once an example and fit instrument for introducing the same absolute rule into these Colonies:—For taking away our Charters, abolishing our most valuable Laws, and altering fundamentally the Forms of our Governments:—For suspending our own Legislatures, and declaring themselves invested with power to legislate for us in all cases whatsoever.—He has abdicated Government here, by declaring us out of his Protection and waging War against us.—He has plundered our seas, ravaged our Coasts, burnt our towns, and destroyed the lives of our people.—He is at this time transporting large Armies of foreign Mercenaries to compleat the works of death, desolation and tyranny, already begun with circumstances of Cruelty & perfidy scarcely paralleled in the most barbarous ages, and totally unworthy the Head of a civilized nation.—He has constrained our fellow Citizens taken Captive on the high Seas to bear Arms against their Country, to become the executioners of their friends and Brethren, or to fall themselves by their Hands.—He has excited domestic insurrections amongst us, and has endeavoured to bring on the inhabitants of our frontiers, the merciless Indian Savages, whose known rule of warfare, is an undistinguished destruction of all ages, sexes and conditions. In every stage of these Oppressions We have Petitioned for Redress in the most humble terms: Our repeated Petitions have been answered only by repeated injury. A Prince, whose character is thus marked by every act which may define a Tyrant, is unfit to be the ruler of a free people. Nor have We been wanting in attentions to our British brethren. We have warned them from time to time of attempts by their legislature to extend an unwarrantable jurisdiction over us. We have reminded them of the circumstances of our emigration and settlement here. We have appealed to their native justice and magnanimity, and we have conjured them by the ties of our common kindred to disavow these usurpations, which, would inevitable interrupt our connections and correspondence. They too have been deaf to the voice of justice and of consanguinity. We must, therefore, acquiesce in the necessity, which denounces our Separation, and hold them, as we hold the rest of mankind, Enemies in War, in Peace Friends.—

WE, THEREFORE, the REPRESENTATIVES of the UNITED STATES OF AMERICA, in General Congress, Assembled, appealing to the Supreme Judge of the world for the rectitude of our intentions, do, in the Name, and by Authority of the good People of these Colonies, solemnly publish and declare, That these United Colonies are, and of Right ought to be FREE AND INDEPENDENT STATES; that they are Absolved from all Allegiance to the British Crown, and that all political connection between them and the State of Great Britain, is and ought to be totally dissolved; and that as Free and Independent States, they have full Power to levy War, conclude Peace, contract Alliances, establish Commerce, and to do all other Acts and Things which Independent States may of right do.—And for the support of this Declaration, with a firm reliance on the protection of Divine Providence, we mutually pledge to each other our Lives, our Fortunes and our sacred Honor.

JOHN HANCOCK.

Josiah Bartlett,
Wm. Whipple,
Matthew Thornton.

Saml. Adams,
John Adams,
Robt. Treat Paine,
Elbridge Gerry.

Step. Hopkins,
William Ellery.

Roger Sherman,
Sam'el Huntington,
Wm. Williams,
Oliver Wolcott.

Wm. Floyd,
Phil. Livingston,
Frans. Lewis,
Lewis Morris.

Richd. Stockton,
Jno. Witherspoon,
Fras. Hopkinson,
John Hart,
Abra. Clark.

Robt. Morris,
Benjamin Rush,
Benja. Franklin,
John Morton,
Geo. Clymer,
Jas. Smith,
Geo. Taylor,
James Wilson,
Geo. Ross.

Caesar Rodney,
Geo. Read,
Tho. M'Kean.

Samuel Chase,
Wm. Paca,
Thos. Stone,
Charles Carroll
  of Carrollton.

George Wythe,
Richard Henry Lee,
Th. Jefferson,
Benja. Harrison,
Ths. Nelson, Jr.,
Francis Lightfoot Lee,
Carter Braxton.

Wm. Hooper,
Joseph Hewes,
John Penn.

Edward Rutledge,
Thos. Heyward, Junr.,
Thomas Lynch, Junr.,
Arthur Middleton.

Button Gwinnett,
Lyman Hall,
Geo. Walton.

## Questions for Rereading, Discussing, Connecting, and Writing

### Rereading

**1.** The Declaration of Independence is one of the most important documents in American history. Jefferson is its primary author; Ben Franklin and John Adams are also given credit for its composition. Given these simple facts—the work's place in time and its joint authorship—speculate upon the problems that might have arisen in "group writing" and how a cause—a real motive for writing—may have helped solve them.

**2.** Most readers today could identify this document as noncontemporary; it "sounds" almost archaic. Point to particular phrases and sentences that support this view. Note conventions of writing—such as paragraphing, capitalization, and sentence length—that differ from contemporary form. What clues enable you to read this particularly archaic language?

**3.** The subject designations "we," "they," and "he" appear dozens of times in this document. Investigate this structural triangle and purpose to which the authors employed it.

### Discussing

**4.** The ideas expressed in the Declaration are timeless. Choose two or three of the facts "submitted to a candid world" and discuss how these, too, are timeless conditions under which men and women live. Refer to events in our time.

**5.** Given the facts of the Declaration's place in time, discuss how the particular pressure of current events affects writing. How is the force of history evident in this text?

**6.** The word "author," derived from the word "authority," implies singularity of production. How can a work have several authors?

### Connecting

**7.** When we call a text a "document" we mean something factual, self-contained. But a document can be filled with emotion, color and the "music" of conflict. Consider the selections by Swift (p. 296), and Goya (p. 257) as both art and document.

**8.** Like the Declaration, "The Seafarer" (p. 105) and the Sioux Indian myth (p. 25) had multiple authors, but they remain anonymous. Read these two selections and compare the effects achieved by anonymous authors with those achieved by Jefferson and his collaborators.

**9.** The Declaration can be described as both a timeless and time-specific document. Timeless because it deals with universal questions and time-specific because it addresses a particular set of historical events. Consider the advertisement (p. 357), and the baseball box score (p. 235) in terms of their timeless and time-specific qualities.

WRITING

**10.** Jefferson and his co-authors explicitly stake their lives on the necessity of freedom—and fighting for that freedom. This "power of the pen" did, in fact, affect the lives of millions. Describe the last time you felt under the power of the pen.

**11.** Select a portion of the Declaration that contains phrases that strike you as particularly archaic, and translate it into the common written English of today. How does this translation help you to understand the Declaration of Independence?

**12.** Take a current news story about which opinion is divided and write about it persuasively, trying to convince your reader—as the authors of the Declaration do—to adopt your point of view.

*Francisco Jose de Goya*

# The 3rd of May, 1808 (1814)

*Questions for Rereading,
Discussing, Connecting, and Writing*

REREADING

1. Images—especially those consciously arranged as paintings are—tend to have points of focus just as written texts do. What is the point of focus in Goya's painting? What can you identify in the painting that directs your eyes to that point?

2. We think very often of good and evil in terms of white and black; we have been conditioned to think this way just as Goya seems to be using light

and shadows to indicate what he admires and what he abhors or dislikes. Can you therefore interpret the artist's opinion of the act or actions depicted in the painting?

## DISCUSSING

3. The human face is always of interest in an image; in Goya's painting, the face tells us much about the subject of the painting. What is this subject?

4. On the other hand, the executioners' placement, which does not allow us to see faces, may mean that our inability to see these faces is just as important to the painting's meaning. Discuss these "missing" faces—and their reasons for being obscured from sight.

5. Why is the painting's time-sense placed at night? What might the night symbolize as we read this image? What other details in the shadows can you discover, and how do you interpret them?

## CONNECTING

6. This painting describes a decisive moment in what is obviously a series of events having to do with crime and punishment, and perhaps with revolution. If Machiavelli (p. 246) were shown this painting, what might his response be? Why?

7. Heroes and villains may be depicted in this painting. Discover other heroes and villains in this book and, taking them as types, what features are necessary to their being called heroes or villains?

## WRITING

8. The faceless executioners are as real in this painting as their victims are. Tell their stories.

9. To what *use* can any reader put a painting like Goya's? It seems to be protesting a certain event in the past—but how can you make the painting affect our own history as a letter to the editor might?

10. Argue for the justice or injustice of execution. Keep in mind cultural differences toward crime and punishment. Research into the matter of capital punishment might strengthen such an essay.

*Sojourner Truth*

# Ain't I a Woman? *(1851)*

Well, children, where there is so much racket there must be something out of kilter. I think that 'twixt the negroes of the South and the women at the North, all talking about rights, the white men will be in a fix pretty soon. But what's all this here talking about?

That man over there says that women need to be helped into carriages, and lifted over ditches, and to have the best place everywhere. Nobody ever helps me into carriages, or over mud-puddles, or gives me any best place! And ain't I a woman? Look at me! Look at my arm! I have ploughed and planted, and gathered into barns, and no man could head me! And ain't I a woman? I could work as much and eat as much as a man—when I could get it—and bear the lash as well! And ain't I a woman? I have borne thirteen children, and seen them most all sold off to slavery, and when I cried out with my mother's grief, none but Jesus heard me! And ain't I a woman?

Then they talk about this think in the head; what's this they call it? (Intellect, someone whispers.) That's it, honey. What's that got to do with women's rights or negro's rights? If my cup won't hold but a pint, and yours holds a quart, wouldn't you be mean not to let me have my little half-measure full?

Then that little man in black there, he says women can't have as much rights as men, 'cause Christ wasn't a woman! Where did your Christ come from? Where did your Christ come from? From God and a woman! Man had nothing to do with Him.

If the first woman God ever made was strong enough to turn the world upside down all alone, these women together ought to be able to turn it back, and get it right side up again! And now they is asking to do it, the men better let them.

Obliged to you for hearing me, and now old Sojourner ain't got nothing more to say.

## Questions for Rereading, Discussing, Connecting, and Writing

### Rereading

1. This selection comes from a speech that was transcribed at the Women's Rights Convention in Akron, Ohio. Sojourner Truth, the speaker, was born a slave, received her freedom when she was a young woman and was active in the move to abolish slavery. Although the narrative of her life was a popular book at the time, Sojourner never learned to read and write. What oral qualities do you find in her language?

2. Sojourner made this speech in response to several ministers who appeared at the Women's Rights Convention to argue for Biblical and theological justifications of the inferiority of women, and the men she refers to in her speech are these ministers. Consider Sojourner's strategy for opposing their insistence on women's inferiority.

3. Women who attended this Convention expressed concern that women's rights would become confused with the abolition of slavery as Sojourner spoke. In what ways does this speech confirm and refute their fears?

### Discussing

4. This speech was made 10 years before the Civil War began and over 60 years before women in the United States received the right to vote. Discuss the ways the historical context in which Sojourner lived contributed to her speech.

5. Sojourner's experiences as a slave underlie her recurring question "Ain't I a woman?" What is the effect of this recounting upon her argument that men "better let" women have rights?

6. Sojourner Truth was the name taken by a slave named Isabelle (her last name had always been that of her master) after she was freed and decided to stop serving white people. Discuss the implications of changing one's name and how that change may have contributed to Sojourner's speaking ability.

### Connecting

7. Virginia Woolf (p. 270), John Stuart Mill (p. 262), and Sojourner Truth all address the issue of women's rights. What similarities and differences do you find in their approaches?

**8.** Like the Sioux Indian myth (p. 25), Homer's "Lotos Eaters" (p. 101), and the prophecy of Amos (p. 239), this selection comes from an oral tradition. Read Sojourner's speech and one of these other selections aloud and compare the effects they achieve.

**9.** Both Sojourner Truth and Thomas Jefferson (p. 251) raise issues of justice. What differences in style and content characterize their statements?

WRITING

**10.** Imagine that you were a newspaper reporter attending the Akron Women's Rights Convention. Write an account of the meeting, including reference to Sojourner's speech.

**11.** As it stands, Sojourner's speech contains many features of oral language. Write a "translation" that presents the content of the speech in standard written English.

**12.** The ministers who spoke at the Akron Convention clearly differed with Sojourner on the issue of women's rights. Write a response to her speech from the viewpoint of one of them.

*John Stuart Mill*

# The Subjection of Women (1869)

The object of this essay is to explain as clearly as I am able, the grounds of an opinion which I have held from the very earliest period when I had formed any opinions at all on social or political matters, and which, instead of being weakened or modified, has been constantly growing stronger by the progress of reflection and the experience of life: That the principle which regulates the existing social relations between the two sexes—the legal subordination of one sex to the other—is wrong in itself, and now one of the chief hindrances to human improvement; and that it ought to be replaced by a principle of perfect equality, admitting no power or privilege on the one side, nor disability on the other. [Mill goes on to compare the status of women to slaves and other oppressed groups and then continues . . . ]

But, it will be said, the rule of men over women differs from all these others in not being a rule of force: it is accepted voluntarily; women make no complaint, and are consenting parties to it. In the first place, a great number of women do not accept it. Ever since there have been women able to make their sentiments known by their writings (the only mode of publicity which society permits to them), an increasing number of them have recorded protests against their present social condition: and recently many thousands of them, headed by the most eminent women known to the public, have petitioned Parliament for their admission to the Parliamentary Suffrage. The claim of women to be educated as solidly, and in the same branches of knowledge, as men, is urged with growing intensity, and with a great prospect of success; while the demand for their admission into professions and occupations hitherto closed against them, becomes every year more urgent. Though there are not in this country, as there are in the United States, periodical Conventions and an organized party to agitate for the Rights of Women, there is a numerous and active Society organized and managed by women, for the more limited object of obtaining the political franchise. Nor is it only in our own country and in America that women are beginning to protest, more or less collectively, against the disabilities under which they labour. France, and Italy, and Switzerland, and Russia now afford examples of the same thing. How many more women there are who silently cherish similar aspirations, no one can possibly know; but there are abundant tokens how many *would* cherish them, were they not so strenuously taught to repress them as contrary to the proprieties of their sex. It must be remembered, also, that no enslaved class ever asked for complete liberty at once. When Simon de Montfort called the deputies of the commons to sit for the first time in Parliament, did any of them dream of demanding that an assembly, elected by their constituents, should make and destroy ministries, and dictate to the king in affairs of state? No such thought entered into the imagination of the most ambitious of them. The nobility had already these pretensions; the commons pretended to nothing but to be exempt from arbitrary taxation, and from the gross individual oppression of the king's officers. It is a political law of nature that those who are any power of ancient origin, never begin by complaining of the power itself, but only of its oppressive exercise. There is never any want of women who complain of ill usage by their husbands. There would be infinitely more, if complaint were not the greatest of all provocatives to a repetition and increase of the ill usage. It is this which frustrates all attempts to maintain the power but protect the woman against its abuses. In no other case (except that of a child) is the person who has been proved judicially to have suffered an injury, replaced under the physical power of the culprit who inflicted it. Accordingly wives, even in the most extreme and protracted cases of bodily ill usage, hardly ever dare avail themselves of the laws made for their protection: and if, in a moment of irrepressible indignation, or by the interference of neighbours, they are induced to do so, their whole effort afterwards is to disclose as little as they can, and to beg off their tyrant from his merited chastisement.

All causes, social and natural, combine to make it unlikely that women should be collectively rebellious to the power of men. They are so far in a position different from all other subject classes, that their masters require something more from them than actual service. Men do not want solely the obedience of women, they want their sentiments. All men, except the most brutish, desire to have, in the woman most nearly connected with them, not a forced slave but a willing one, not a slave merely, but a favourite. They have therefore put everything in practice to enslave their minds. The masters of all other slaves rely, for maintaining obedience, on fear; either fear of themselves, or religious fears. The masters of women wanted more than simple obedience, and they turned the whole force of education to effect their purpose. All women are brought up from the very earliest years in the belief that their ideal of character is the very opposite to that of men; not self-will, and government by self-control, but submission, and yielding to the control of others. All the moralities tell them that it is the duty of women, and all the current sentimentalities that it is their nature, to live for others; to make complete abnegation of themselves, and to have no life but in their affections. And by their affections are meant the only ones they are allowed to have—those to the men with whom they are connected, or to the children who constitute an additional and indefeasible tie between them and a man. When we put together three things—first, the natural attraction between opposite sexes; secondly, the wife's entire dependence on the husband, every privilege or pleasure she has being either his gift, or depending entirely on his will; and lastly, that the principal object of human pursuit, consideration, and all objects of social ambition, can in general be sought or obtained by her only through him, it would be a miracle if the object of being attractive to men had not become the polar star of feminine education and formation of character. And, this great means of influence over the minds of women having been acquired, an instinct of selfishness made men avail themselves of it to the utmost as a means of holding women in subjection, by representing to them meekness, submissiveness, and resignation of all individual will into the hands of a man, as an essential part of sexual attractiveness. Can it be doubted that any of the other yokes which mankind have succeeded in breaking, would have subsisted till now if the same means had existed, and had been as sedulously used, to bow down their minds to it? If it had been made the object of the life of every young plebeian to find personal favour in the eyes of some patrician, of every young serf with some seigneur; if domestication with him, and a share of his personal affections, had been held out as the prize which they all should look out for, the most gifted and aspiring being able to reckon on the most desirable prizes; and if, when this prize had been obtained, they had been shut out by a wall of brass from all interests not centering in him, all feelings and desires but those which he shared or inculcated; would not serfs and seigneurs, plebeians and patricians, have been as broadly distinguished at this day as men and women are? And would not all but a thinker here and there, have believed the distinction to be a fundamental and unalterable fact in human nature?

The preceding considerations are amply sufficient to show that custom, however universal it may be, affords in this case no presumption, and ought not to create any prejudice, in favour of the arrangements which place women in social and political subjection to men. But I may go farther, and maintain that the course of history, and the tendencies of progressive human society, afford not only no presumption in favour of this system of inequality of rights, but a strong one against it; and that, so far as the whole course of human improvement up to this time, the whole stream of modern tendencies, warrants any inference on the subject, it is, that this relic of the past is discordant with the future, and must necessarily disappear.

## Questions for Rereading, Discussing, Connecting, and Writing

### Rereading

1. John Stuart Mill was a philosopher and economist who wrote on a number of political topics—one of his most famous works being *System of Logic*. As you read, identify one economic or philosophical issue that contributes to what Mill says about the relations of men and women.

2. Those who knew him claimed that Mill possessed an extraordinarily logical mind. What evidence of logical thinking do you find in this selection?

3. Speculate on what would motivate Mill, a man who had no direct experience of the subjection he describes, to write on behalf of women's rights.

### Discussing

4. In the first paragraph, Mill claims that the subjection of women is "one of the chief hindrances to human improvement." Does this claim make sense to you? Can you think of instances where the subjection of one group hinders human progress, or do you think Mill is over-stating the case?

5. Speculate on the benefits and liabilities that result when a non-oppressed individual takes up the cause of an oppressed group and argues, as Mill does, on behalf of a group to which he does not belong.

6. Most of Mill's claims about the plight of women are based on the assumption that women are wives who must depend entirely upon their husbands for pleasures and privileges. To what extent is Mill's argument weakened by his lack of attention to single women?

CONNECTING

**7.** One form of subjection to which Mill gives attention is physical abuse. The existence of community shelters for battered women suggests that this form of subjection exists today just as it did over 100 years ago. Find a current account of domestic violence in a local or national publication and compare its claims with those made by Mill.

**8.** Mill's long-time friend and eventual wife Harriet assisted in all his writing and he sought, unsuccessfully, to list her as a co-author. This selection could, then, be described as a collaborative effort. Compare its effect with collaborative works such as the Declaration of Independence attributed to Jefferson (p. 251).

**9.** Mill describes women in terms that emphasize their powerlessness and vulnerability to the power of others. Compare this view of women with that offered by Markham (p. 35), Cassatt (p. 82), and LeSueur (p. 84).

WRITING

**10.** Although today's women enjoy more political freedom than the women of Mill's time did, there are still ways in which contemporary women lack the rights and privileges accorded men. Select an area in which you feel women lack equality and write about this form of subjection of women.

**11.** Conditions in Mill's England indicate that most people did not share his view that women should enjoy equality with men. Imagine that you are a man living in the 1860s. Write a letter of negative response to Mill's essay.

**12.** Mill takes exception to the view that custom justifies continuation of a given practice, but "we have always done it this way" is the nearly universal response to proposals for change within any institution. Write an essay in which you argue for changing some established custom trying, as Mill did, to counter the objections of your audience.

# Africa Map (1876)

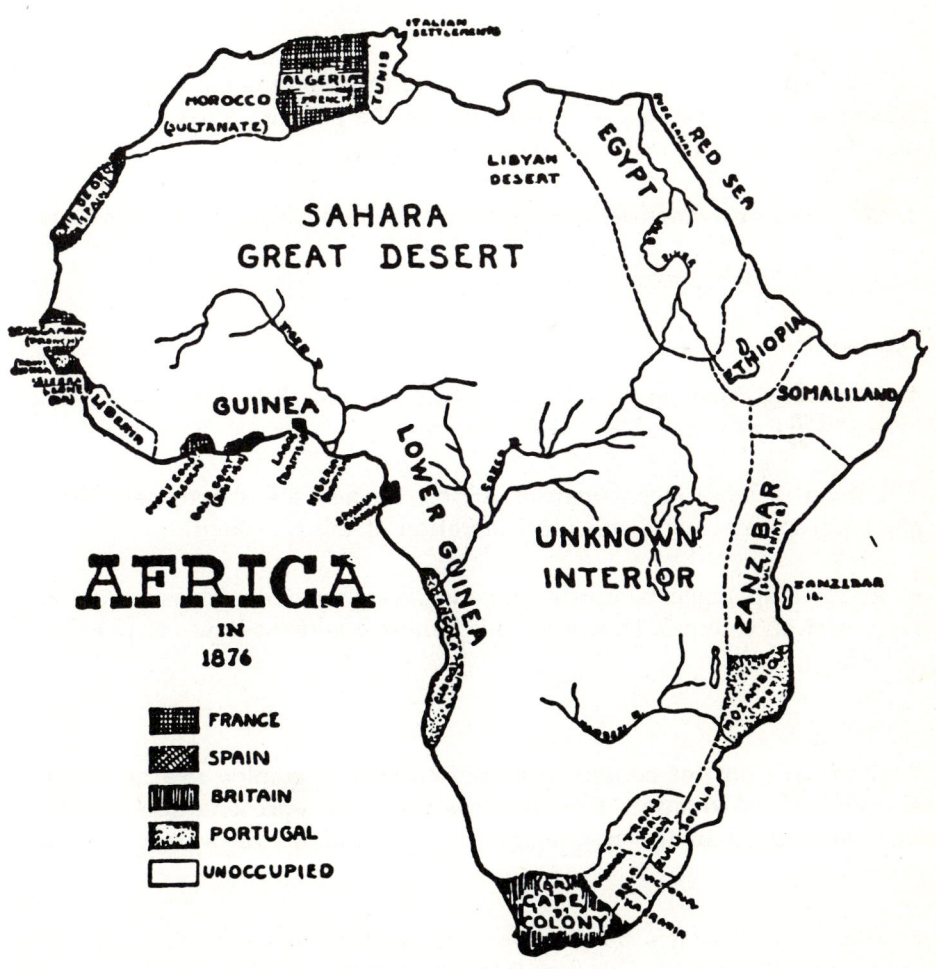

## Questions for Rereading, Discussing, Connecting, and Writing

### REREADING

1. Maps offer one way to see and understand parts of our world. As you read this map, consider what one can learn from maps and from this map in particular.

2. Not only does a map use special ways of representing information, it also assumes a certain amount of knowledge on the part of its readers. What do you need to know in order to read this map?

3. What does this map tell you about the relationship of Europe to Africa during the nineteenth century? What, for example, is the significance of the designation "unoccupied" in the key?

### DISCUSSING

4. In reading this map, you probably learned something new about Africa. Discuss what you have learned from this map.

5. Look at a more recent map of Africa. Discuss the differences between contemporary maps and this representation of the continent.

6. As the map suggests, European countries competed with one another to create African colonies. How does this behavior address issues of power and justice?

### CONNECTING

7. Maps are not, of course, the only texts that employ special ways of representing information. Compare the forms of representation used here with those used in the box score (p. 235) and in the Mozart selection (p. 349).

8. This map illustrates the European colonial influence, but African place names are still present. Can you think of a place you have lived or visited where place names represented people who had been oppressed or who had disappeared from the area?

9. Compare this map with the Mercator map (p. 108). What similarities and differences do you find?

WRITING

**10.** Translate this map into writing that explains. Begin by considering the implied relationship between Europe and Africa and among the European countries mentioned on the map. What does this say about political events in 1876 in Africa?

**11.** A large portion of this map is designated as "unoccupied" even though people native to Africa lived there, which suggests the European perspective of the mapmaker. Write a description of the African map that might have been made in 1876 by someone native to Africa.

**12.** Africa was often called the "Dark Continent" during the nineteenth century, partly because much of it was unknown, partly because Europeans who went there risked deathly diseases such as malaria, and partly because it was populated by blacks. Decide on a descriptive name for the continent of North America today and write an explanation of your choice.

*Virginia Woolf*

# *A Room of One's Own* (1928)

But, you may say, we asked you to speak about women and fiction—what has that got to do with a room of one's own? I will try to explain. When you asked me to speak about women and fiction I sat down on the banks of a river and began to wonder what the words meant. They might mean simply a few remarks about Fanny Burney; a few more about Jane Austen; a tribute to the Brontës and a sketch of Haworth Parsonage under snow; some witticisms if possible about Miss Mitford; a respectful allusion to George Eliot; a reference to Mrs. Gaskell and one would have done. But at second sight the words seemed not so simple. The title women and fiction might mean, and you may have meant it to mean, women and what they are like; or it might mean women and the fiction that they write; or it might mean women and the fiction that is written about them; or it might mean that somehow all three are inextricably mixed together and you want me to consider them in that light. But when I began to consider the subject in this last way, which seemed the most interesting, I soon saw that it had one fatal drawback. I should never be able to come to a conclusion. I should never be able to fulfil what is, I understand, the first duty of a lecturer—to hand you after an hour's discourse a nugget of pure truth to wrap up between the pages of your notebooks and keep on the mantelpiece for ever. All I could do was to offer you an opinion upon one minor point—a woman must have money and a room of her own if she is to write fiction; and that, as you will see, leaves the great problem of the true nature of woman and the true nature of fiction unsolved. I have shirked the duty of coming to a conclusion upon these two questions—women and fiction remain, so far as I am concerned, unsolved problems. But in order to make some amends I am going to do what I can to show you how I arrived at this opinion about the room and the money. I am going to develop in your presence as fully and freely as I can the train of thought which led me to think this. Perhaps if I lay bare the ideas, the prejudices, that lie behind this statement you will find that they have some bearing upon women and some upon fiction. At any rate, when a subject is highly controversial—and any question about sex is that—one cannot hope to tell the truth. One can only show how one came to hold whatever opinion one does hold. One can only give one's audience the chance of drawing their own conclusions as they observe the limitations, the prejudices, the idiosyncrasies of the speaker. Fiction here is likely to contain more truth than fact. Therefore I propose, making use of all the liberties and licences of a novelist, to tell you the story of the two days that preceded my coming here—how, bowed down by weight of the subject which you have laid upon my shoulders, I pondered it, and made it work in and out of my daily life. I need not say that what I am about to describe has no existence; Oxbridge is an invention; so is Fernham: "I" is only a convenient term for somebody who has no real being. Lies will flow from my lips, but there may perhaps be some truth mixed up with them; it is for you to seek out this truth and to decide whether any part of it is worth keeping. If not, you will of course throw the whole of it into the wastepaper basket and forget all about it.

Here then was I (call me Mary Beton, Mary Seton, Mary Carmichael or by any name you please—it is not a matter of importance) sitting on the banks of a river a week or two ago in fine October weather, lost in thought. That collar I have spoken of, women and fiction, the need of coming to some conclusion on a subject that raises all sorts of prejudices and passions, bowed my head to the ground. To the right and left bushes of some sort, golden and crimson, glowed with colour, even it seemed burnt with the heat, of fire. On the further bank the willows wept in perpetual lamentation, their hair about their shoulders. The river reflected whatever it chose of sky and bridge and burning tree, and when the undergraduate had oared his boat through the reflections they closed again, completely, as if he had never been. There one might have sat the clock round lost in thought. Thought—to call it by a prouder name than it deserved—had let its line down into the stream. It swayed, minute after minute, hither and thither among the reflections and the weeds, letting the water lift it and sink it, until—you know the little tug—the sudden conglomeration of an idea at the end of one's line: and then the cautious hauling of it in, and the careful laying of it out? Alas, laid on the grass how small, how insignificant this thought of mine looked; the sort of fish that a good fisherman puts back into the water so that it may grow fatter and be one day worth cooking and eating. I will not trouble you with that thought now, though if you look carefully you may find it for yourselves in the course of what I am going to say.

But however small it was, it had, nevertheless, the mysterious property of its kind- -put back into the mind, it became at once very exciting, and important; and as it darted and sank, and flashed hither and thither, set up such a wash and tumult of ideas that it was impossible to sit still. It was thus that I found myself walking with extreme rapidity across a grass plot. Instantly a man's figure rose to intercept me. Nor did I at first understand that the gesticulations of a curious-looking object, in a cut-away coat and evening shirt, were aimed at me. His face expressed horror and indignation. Instinct rather than reason came to my help; he was a Beadle; I was a woman. This was the turf; there was the path. Only the Fellows and Scholars are allowed here; the gravel is the place for me. Such thoughts were the work of a moment. As I regained the path the arms of the Beadle sank, his face assumed its usual repose, and though turf is better walking than gravel, no very great harm was done. The only charge I could bring against the Fellows and Scholars of whatever the college might happen to be was that in protection of their turf, which has been rolled for 300 years in succession, they had sent my little fish into hiding.

What idea it had been that had sent me so audaciously trespassing I could not now remember. The spirit of peace descended like a cloud from heaven, for if the spirit of peace dwells anywhere, it is in the courts and quadrangles of Oxbridge on a fine October morning. Strolling through those colleges past those ancient halls the roughness of the present seemed smoothed away; the body seemed contained in a miraculous glass cabinet through which no sound could penetrate, and the mind, freed from any contact with facts (unless one trespassed on the turf again), was at liberty to settle down upon whatever meditation was in harmony with the moment. As chance would have it, some stray memory of some old essay about revisiting Oxbridge in the long vacation brought Charles Lamb to mind—Saint Charles, said Thackeray, putting a letter of Lamb's to his forehead. Indeed, among all the dead (I give you my thoughts as they came to me), Lamb is one of the most congenial; one to whom one would have liked to say, Tell me then how you wrote your essays? For his essays are superior even to Max Beerbohm's, I thought, with all their perfection, because of that wild flash of imagination, that lightning crack of genius in the middle of them which leaves them flawed and imperfect, but starred with poetry. Lamb then came to Oxbridge perhaps a hundred years ago. Certainly he wrote an essay—the name escapes me—about the manuscript of one of Milton's poems which he saw here. It was *Lycidas* perhaps, and Lamb wrote how it shocked him to think it possible that any word in *Lycidas* could have been different from what it is. To think of Milton changing the words in that poem seemed to him a sort of sacrilege. This led me to remember what I could of *Lycidas* and to amuse myself with guessing which word it could have been that Milton had altered, and why. It then occurred to me that the very manuscript itself which Lamb had looked at was only a few hundred yards away, so that one could follow Lamb's footsteps across the quadrangle to that famous library where the treasure is kept. Moreover, I recollected, as I put this plan into execution, it is in this famous library that the manuscript of Thackeray's *Esmond* is also preserved. The critics often say that *Esmond* is Thackeray's most perfect novel. But the affection of the style, with its imitation of the eighteenth century, hampers one, so far as I remember; unless indeed the eighteenth-century style was natural to Thackeray—a fact that one might prove by looking at the manuscript and seeing whether the alterations were for the benefit of the style or of the sense. But then one would have to decide what is style and what is meaning, a question which—but here I was actually at the door which leads into the library itself. I must have opened it, for instantly there issued, like a guardian angel barring the way with a flutter of black gown instead of white wings, a deprecating, silvery, kindly gentleman, who regretted in a low voice as he waved me back that ladies are only admitted to the library if accompanied by a Fellow of the College or furnished with a letter of introduction.

That a famous library has been cursed by a woman is a matter of complete indifference to a famous library. Venerable and calm, with all its treasures safe locked within its breast, it sleeps complacently and will, so far as I am concerned, so sleep for ever. Never will I wake those echoes, never will I ask for that hospitality again, I vowed as I descended the steps in anger. Still an hour remained before luncheon, and what was one to do? Stroll on the meadows? sit by the river? Certainly it was a lovely autumn morning; the leaves were fluttering red to the ground; there was no great hardship in doing either. But the sound of music reached my ear. Some service or celebration was going forward. The organ complained magnificently as I passed the chapel door. Even the sorrow of Christianity sounded in that serene air more like the recollection of sorrow than sorrow itself; even the groaning of the ancient organ seemed lapped in peace. I had no wish to enter had I the right, and this time the verger might have stopped me, demanding perhaps my baptismal certificate, or a letter of introduction from the Dean. But the outside of these magnificent buildings is often as beautiful as the inside. Moreover, it was amusing enough to watch the congregation assembling, coming in and going out again, busying themselves at the door of the chapel like bees at the mouth of a hive. Many were in cap and gown; some had tufts of fur on their shoulders; others were wheeled in bath-chairs; others, though not past middle age, seemed creased and crushed into shapes so singular that one was reminded of those giant crabs and crayfish who heave with difficulty across the sand of an aquarium. As I leant against the wall the University indeed seemed a sanctuary in which are preserved rare types which would soon be obsolete if left to fight for existence on the pavement of the Strand. Old stories of old deans and old dons came back to mind, but before I had summoned up courage to whistle—it used to be said that at the sound of a whistle old Professor _____ instantly broke into a gallop—the venerable congregation had gone inside. The outside of the chapel remained. As you know, its high domes and pinnacles can be seen, like a sailing-ship always voyaging never arriving, lit up at night and visible for miles, far away across the hills. Once, presumably, this quadrangle with its smooth lawns, its massive buildings, and the chapel itself was marsh too, where the grasses waved and the swine rootled. Teams of horses and oxen, I thought, must have hauled the stone in wagons from far countries, and then with infinite labour the grey blocks in whose shade I was now standing were poised in order one on top of another, and then the painters brought their glass for the windows, and the masons were busy for centuries up on that roof with putty and cement, spade and trowel. Every Saturday somebody must have poured gold and silver out of a leathern purse into their ancient fists, for they had their beer and skittles presumably of an evening. An unending stream of gold and silver, I thought, must have flowed into this court perpetually to keep the stones coming and the masons working; to level, to ditch, to dig and to drain. But it was then the age of faith, and money was poured liberally to set these stones on a deep foundation, and when the stones were raised, still more money was poured in from the coffers of kings and queens and great nobles to ensure that hymns should be sung here and scholars taught. Lands were granted; tithes were paid. And when the age of faith was over and the age of reason had come, still the same flow of gold and silver went on; fellowships were founded; lectureships endowed; only the gold and silver flowed now, not from the coffers of the king, but from the chests of merchants and manufacturers, from the purses of men who had made, say, a fortune from industry, and returned, in their wills, a bounteous share of it to endow more chairs, more lectureships, more fellowships in the university where they had learnt their craft. Hence the libraries and laboratories; the observatories; the splendid equipment of costly and delicate instruments which now stands on glass shelves, where centuries ago the grasses waved and the swine rootled. Certainly, as I strolled round the court, the foundation of gold and silver seemed deep enough; the pavement laid solidly over the wild grasses. Men with trays on their heads went busily from staircase to staircase. Gaudy blossoms flowered in window-boxes. The strains of the gramophone blared out from the rooms within. It was impossible not to reflect—the reflection whatever it may have been was cut short. The clock struck. It was time to find one's way to luncheon.

It is a curious fact that novelists have a way of making us believe that luncheon parties are invariably memorable for something very witty that was said, or for something very wise that was done. But they seldom spare a word for what was eaten. It is part of the novelist's convention not to mention soup and salmon and ducklings, as if soup and salmon and ducklings were of no importance whatsoever, as if nobody every smoked a cigar or drank a glass of wine. Here, however, I shall take the liberty to defy that convention and to tell you that the lunch on this occasion began with soles, sunk in a deep dish, over which the college cook had spread a counterpane of the whitest cream, save that it was branded here and there with brown spots like the spots on the flanks of a doe. After that came the partridges, but if this suggest a couple of bald, brown birds on a plate you are mistaken. The partridges, many and various, came with all their retinue of sauces and salads, the sharp and the sweet, each in its order; their potatoes, thin as coins but not so hard; their sprouts, foliated as rosebuds but more succulent. And no sooner had the roast and its retinue been done with than the silent serving-man, the Beadle himself perhaps in a milder manifestation, set before us, wreathed in napkins, a confection which rose all sugar from the waves. To call it pudding and so relate it to rice and tapioca would be an insult. Meanwhile the wineglasses had flushed yellow and flushed crimson; had been emptied; had been filled. And thus by degrees was lit, halfway down the spine, which is the seat of the soul, not that hard little electric light which we call brilliance, as it pops in and out upon our lips, but the more profound, subtle and subterrranean glow, which is the rich yellow flame of rational intercourse. No need to hurry. No need to sparkle. No need to be anybody but oneself. We are all going to heaven and Vandyck is of the company—in other words, how good life seemed, how sweet its rewards, how trivial this grudge or that grievance, how admirable friendship and the society of one's kind, as, lighting a good cigarette, one sunk among the cushions in the window-seat.

If by good luck there had been an ash-tray handy, if one had not knocked the ash out of the window in default, if things had been a little different from what they were, one would not have seen, presumably, a cat without a tail. The sight of that abrupt and truncated animal padding softly across the quadrangle changed by some fluke of the subconscious intelligence the emotional light for me. It was as if some one had let fall a shade. Perhaps the excellent hock was relinquishing its hold. Certainly, as I watched the Manx cat pause in the middle of the lawn as if it too questioned the universe, something seemed lacking, something seemed different. But what was lacking, what was different, I asked myself, listening to the talk. And to answer that question I had to think myself out of the room, back into the past, before the war indeed, and to set before my eyes the model of another luncheon party held in rooms not very far distant from these; but different. Everything was different. Meanwhile the talk went on among the guests, who were many and young, some of this sex, some of that; it went on swimmingly, it went on agreeably, freely, amusingly. And as it went on I set it against the background of that other talk, and as I matched the two together I had no doubt that one was the descendant, the legitimate heir of the other. Nothing was changed; nothing was different save only—here I listened with all my ears not entirely to what was being said, but to the murmur or current behind it. Yes, that was it—the change was there. Before the war at a luncheon party like this people would have said precisely the same things but they would have sounded different, because in those days they were accompanied by a sort of humming noise, not articulate, but musical, exciting, which changed the value of the words themselves. Could one set that humming noise to words? Perhaps with the help of the poets one could. A book lay beside me and, opening it, I turned casually enough to Tennyson. And here I found Tennyson was singing:

> There has fallen a splendid tear
>   From the passion-flower at the gate.
> She is coming, my dove, my dear;
>   She is coming, my life, my fate;
> The red rose cries, "She is near, she is near";
>   And the white rose weeps, "She is late";
> The larkspur listens, "I hear, I hear";
>   And the lily whispers, "I wait."

Was that what men hummed at luncheon parties before the war? And the women?

> My heart is like a singing bird
>    Whose nest is in a water'd shoot;
> My heart is like an apple tree
>    Whose boughs are bent with thick-set fruit;
> My heart is like a rainbow shell
>    That paddles in a halcyon sea;
> My heart is gladder than all these
>    Because my love is come to me.

Was that what women hummed at luncheon parties before the war?

There was something so ludicrous in thinking of people humming such things even under their breath at luncheon parties before the war that I burst out laughing, and had to explain my laughter by pointing at the Manx cat, who did look a little absurd, poor beast, without a tail, in the middle of the lawn. Was he really born so, or had he lost his tail in an accident? The tailless cat, though some are said to exist in the Isle of Man, is rarer than one thinks. It is a queer animal, quaint rather than beautiful. It is strange what a difference a tail makes—you know the sort of things one says as a lunch party breaks up and people are finding their coats and hats.

This one, thanks to the hospitality of the host, had lasted far into the afternoon. The beautiful October day was fading and the leaves were falling from the trees in the avenue as I walked through it. Gate after gate seemed to close with gentle finality behind me. Innumerable beadles were fitting innumerable keys into well-oiled locks; the treasure-house was being made secure for another night. After the avenue one comes out upon a road—I forget its name—which leads you, if you take the right turning, along to Fernham. But there was plenty of time. Dinner was not till half-past seven. One could almost do without dinner after such a luncheon. It is strange how a scrap of poetry works in the mind and makes the legs move in time to it along the road. Those words—

> There has fallen a splendid tear
>    From the passion-flower at the gate.
> She is coming, my dove, my dear—

sang in my blood as I stepped quickly along towards Headingley. And then, switching off into the other measure, I sang, where the waters are churned up by the weir:

> *My heart is like a singing bird*
> *Whose nest is in a water'd shoot;*
> *My heart is like an apple tree . . .*

What poets, I cried aloud, as one does in the dusk, what poets they were!

In a sort of jealousy, I suppose, for our own age, silly and absurd though these comparisons are, I went on to wonder if honestly one could name two living poets now as great as Tennyson and Christina Rossetti were then. Obviously it is impossible, I thought, looking into those foaming waters, to compare them. The very reason why the poetry excites one to such abandonment, such rapture, is that it celebrates some feeling that one used to have (at luncheon parties before the war perhaps), so that one responds easily, familiarly, without troubling to check the feeling, or to compare it with any that one has now. But the living poets express a feeling that is actually being made and torn out of us at the moment. One does not recognize it in the first place; often for some reason one fears it; one watches it with keenness and compares it jealously and suspiciously with the old feeling that one knew. Hence the difficulty of modern poetry; and it is because of this difficulty that one cannot remember more than two consecutive lines of any good modern poet. For this reason—that my memory failed me—the argument flagged for want of material. But why, I continued, moving on towards Headingley, have we stopped humming under our breath at luncheon parties? Why has Alfred ceased to sing

> *She is coming, my dove, my dear?*

Why has Christina ceased to respond

> *My heart is gladder than all these*
> *Because my love is come to me?*

Shall we lay the blame on the war? When the guns fired in August 1914, did the faces of men and women show so plain in each other's eyes that romance was killed? Certainly it was a shock (to women in particular with their illusions about education, and so on) to see the faces of our rulers in the light of the shell-fire. So ugly they looked—German, English, French—so stupid. But lay the blame where one will, on whom one will, the illusion which inspired Tennyson and Christina Rossetti to sing so passionately about the coming of their loves is far rarer now than then. One has only to read, to look, to listen, to remember. But why say "blame"? Why, if it was an illusion, not praise the catastrophe, whatever it was, that destroyed illusion and put truth in its place? For truth . . . those dots mark the spot where, in search of truth I missed the turning up to Fernham. Yes indeed, which was truth and which was illusion, I asked myself. What was the truth about these houses, for example, dim and festive now with their red windows in the dusk, but raw and red and squalid, with their sweets and their boot-laces, at nine o'clock in the morning? And the willows and the river and the gardens that run down to the river, vague now with the mist stealing over them, but gold and red in the sunlight—which was the truth, which was the illusion about them? I spare you the twists and turns of my cogitations, for no conclusion was found on the road to Headingley, and I ask you to suppose that I soon found out my mistake about the turning and retraced my steps to Fernham.

As I have said already that it was an October day, I dare not forfeit your respect and imperil the fair name of fiction by changing the season and describing lilacs hanging over garden walls, crocuses, tulips and other flowers of spring. Fiction must stick to facts, and the truer the facts the better the fiction—so we are told. Therefore it was still autumn and the leaves were still yellow and falling, if anything, a little faster than before, because it was now evening (seven twenty-three to be precise) and a breeze (from the southwest to be exact) had risen. But for all that there was something odd at work:

> *My heart is like a singing bird*
>   *Whose nest is in a water'd shoot;*
> *My heart is like an apple tree*
>   *Whose boughs are bent with thick-set fruit—*

perhaps the words of Christina Rossetti were partly responsible for the folly of the fancy—it was nothing of course but a fancy—that the lilac was shaking its flowers over the garden walls, and the brimstone butterflies were scudding hither and thither, and the dust of the pollen was in the air. A wind blew, from what quarter I know not, but it lifted the half-grown leaves so that there was a flash of silver grey in the air. It was the time between the lights when colours undergo their intensification and purples and golds burn in window-panes like the beat of an excitable heart; when for some reason the beauty of the world revealed and yet soon to perish (here I pushed into the garden, for, unwisely, the door was left open and no beadles seemed about), the beauty of the world which is so soon to perish, has two edges, one of laughter, one of anguish, cutting the heart asunder. The gardens of Fernham lay before me in the spring twilight, wild and open, and in the long grass, sprinkled and carelessly flung, were daffodils and bluebells, not orderly perhaps at the best of times, and now wind-blown and waving as they tugged at their roots. The windows of the building, curved like ships' windows among generous waves of red brick, changed from lemon to silver under the flight of the quick spring clouds. Somebody was in a hammock, somebody, but in this light they were phantoms only, half guessed, half seen, raced across the grass—would no one stop her?—and then on the terrace, as if popping out to breathe the air, to glance at the garden, came a bent figure, formidable yet humble, with her great forehead and her shabby dress—could it be the famous scholar, could it be J_____ H_____ herself? All was dim, yet intense too, as if the scarf which the dusk had flung over the garden were torn asunder by star or sword—the flash of some terrible reality leaping, as its way is, out of the heart of the spring. For youth _____

Here was my soup. Dinner was being served in the great dining-hall. Far from being spring it was in fact an evening in October. Everybody was assembled in the big dining-room. Dinner was ready. Here was the soup. It was a plain gravy soup. There was nothing to stir the fancy in that. One could have seen through the transparent liquid any pattern that there might have been on the plate itself. But there was no pattern. The plate was plain. Next came beef with its attendant greens and potatoes—a homely trinity, suggesting the rumps of cattle in a muddy market, and sprouts curled and yellowed at the edge, and bargaining and cheapening, and women with string bags on Monday morning. There was no reason to complain of human nature's daily food, seeing that the supply was sufficient and coal-miners doubtless were sitting down to less. Prunes and custard followed. And if any one complains that prunes, even when mitigated by custard, are an uncharitable vegetable (fruit they are not), stringy as a miser's heart and exuding a fluid such as might run in misers' veins who have denied themselves wine and warmth for eighty years and yet not given to the poor, he should reflect that there are people whose charity embraces even the prune. Biscuits and cheese came next, and here the water-jug was liberally passed round, for it is the nature of biscuits to be dry, and these were biscuits to the core. That was all. The meal was over. Everybody scraped their chairs back; the swing-doors swung violently to and fro; soon the hall was emptied of every sign of food and made ready no doubt for breakfast next morning. Down corridors and up staircases the youth of England went banging and singing. And was it for a guest, a stranger (for I had no more right here in Fernham than in Trinity or Somerville or Girton or Newnham or Christchurch), to say, "The dinner was not good," or to say (we were now, Mary Seton and I, in her sitting-room), "Could we not have dined up here alone?" for if I had said anything of the kind I should have been prying and searching into the secret economies of a house which to the stranger wears so fine a front of gaiety and courage. No, one could say nothing of the sort. Indeed, conversation for a moment flagged. The human frame being what it is, heart, body and brain all mixed together, and not contained in separate compartments as they will be no doubt in another million years, a good dinner is of great importance to good talk. One cannot think well, love well, sleep well, if one has not dined well. The lamp in the spine does not light on beef and prunes. We are all *probably* going to heaven, and Vandyck is, we *hope*, to meet us round the next corner—that is the dubious and qualifying state of mind that beef and prunes at the end of the day's work breed between them. Happily my friend, who taught science, had a cupboard where there was a squat bottle and little glasses—(but there should have been sole and partridge to begin with)—so that we were able to draw up to the fire and repair some of the damages of the day's living. In a minute or so we were slipping freely in and out among all those objects of curiosity and interest which form in the mind in the absence of a particular person, and are naturally to be discussed on coming together again— how somebody has married, another has not; one thinks this, another that; one has improved out of all knowledge, the other most amazingly gone to the bad—with all those speculations upon human nature and the character of the amazing world we live in which spring naturally from such beginnings. While these things were being said, however, I became shamefacedly aware of a current setting in of its own accord and carrying everything forward to an end of its own. One might be talking of Spain or Portugal, of book or racehorse, but the real interest of whatever was said was none of those things, but a scene of masons on a high roof some five centuries ago. Kings and nobles brought treasure in huge sacks and poured it under the earth. This scene was for ever coming alive in my mind and placing itself by another of lean cows and a muddy market and withered greens and the stringy hearts of old men—these two pictures, disjointed and disconnected and nonsensical as they were, were for ever coming together and combating each other and had me entirely at their mercy. The best course, unless the whole talk was to be distorted, was to expose what was in my mind to the air, when with good luck it would fade and crumble like the head of the dead king when they opened the coffin at Windsor. Briefly, then, I told Miss Seton about the masons who had been all those years on the roof of the chapel, and about the kings and queens and nobles bearing sacks of gold and silver on their shoulders, which they shovelled into the earth; and then how the great financial magnates of our own time came and laid cheques and bonds, I suppose, where the others had laid ingots and rough lumps of gold. All that lies beneath the colleges down there, I said; but this college, where we are now sitting, what lies beneath its gallant red brick and the wild unkempt grasses of the garden? What force is behind the plain china off which we dined, and (here it popped out of my mouth before I could stop it) the beef, the custard and the prunes?

Well, said Mary Seton, about the year 1860—Oh, but you know the story, she said, bored, I suppose, by the recital. And she told me—rooms were hired. Committees met. Envelopes were addressed. Circulars were drawn up. Meetings were held; letters were read out; so-and-so has promised so much; on the contrary, Mr. _____ won't give a penny. The *Saturday Review* has been very rude. How can we raise a fund to pay for offices? Shall we hold a bazaar? Can't we find a pretty girl to sit in the front row? Let us look up what John Stuart Mill said on the subject. Can any one persuade the editor of the _____ to print a letter? Can we get Lady _____ to sign it? Lady _____ is out of town. That was the way it was done, presumably, sixty years ago, and it was a prodigious effort, and a great deal of time was spent on it. And it was only after a long struggle and with the utmost difficulty that they got thirty thousand pounds together. So obviously we cannot have wine and partridges and servants carrying tin dishes on their heads, she said. We cannot have sofas and separate rooms. "The amenities," she said, quoting from some book or other, "will have to wait."

At the thought of all those women working, year after year and finding it hard to get two thousand pounds together, and as much as they could do to get thirty thousand pounds, we burst out in scorn at the reprehensible poverty of our sex. What had our mothers been doing then that they had no wealth to leave us? Powdering their noses? Looking in at shop windows? Flaunting in the sun at Monte Carlo? There were some photographs on the mantel-piece. Mary's mother—if that was her picture—may have been a wastrel in her spare time (she had thirteen children by a minister of the church), but if so her gay and dissipated life had left too few traces of its pleasures on her face. She was a homely body; an old lady in a plaid shawl which was fastened by a large cameo; and she sat in a basket-chair, encouraging a spaniel to look at the camera, with the amused, yet strained expression of one who is sure that the dog will move directly the bulb is pressed. Now if she had gone into business; had become a manufacturer of artificial silk or a magnate on the Stock Exchange; if she had left two or three hundred thousand pounds to Fernham, we could have been sitting at our ease tonight and the subject of our talk might have been archaelogy, botany, anthropology, physics, the nature of the atom, mathematics, astronomy, relativity, geography. If only Mrs. Seton and her mother and her mother before her had learnt the great art of making money and had left their money, like their fathers and their grandfathers before them, to found fellowships and lectureships and prizes and scholarships appropriated to the use of their own sex, we might have dined very tolerably up here alone off a bird and a bottle of wine; we might have looked forward without undue confidence to a pleasant and honourable lifetime spent in the shelter of one of the liberally endowed professions. We might have been exploring or writing; mooning about the venerable places of the earth; sitting contemplative on the steps of the Parthenon, or going at ten to an office and coming home comfortably at half-past four to write a little poetry. Only, if Mrs. Seton and her like had gone into business at the age of fifteen, there would have been—that was the snag in the argument—no Mary. What, I asked, did Mary think of that? There between the curtains was the October night, calm and lovely, with a star or two caught in the yellowing trees. Was she ready to resign her share of it and her memories (for they had been a happy family, though a large one) of games and quarrels up in Scotland, which she is never tired of praising for the fineness of its air and the quality of its cakes, in order that Fernham might have been endowed with fifty thousand pounds or so by a stroke of the pen? For, to endow a college would necessitate the suppression of families altogether. Making a fortune and bearing thirteen children—no human being could stand it. Consider the facts, we said. First there are nine months before the baby is born. Then the baby is born. Then there are three or four months spent in feeding the baby. After the baby is fed there are certainly five years spent in playing with the baby. You cannot, it seems, let children run about the streets. People who have seen them running wild in Russia say that the sight is not a pleasant one. People say, too, that human nature takes its shape in the years between one and five. If Mrs. Seton, I said, had been making money, what sort of memories would you have had of games and quarrels? What would you have known of Scotland, and its fine air and cakes and all the rest of it? But it is useless to ask these questions, because you would never have come into existence at all. Moreover, it is equally useless to ask what might have happened if Mrs. Seton and her mother and her mother before her had amassed great wealth and laid it under the foundations of college and library, because, in the first place, to earn money was impossible for them, and in the second, had it been possible, the law denied them the right to possess what money they earned. It is only for the last forty-eight years that Mrs. Seton has had a penny of her own. For all the centuries before that it would have been her husband's property—a thought which, perhaps, may have had its share in keeping Mrs. Seton and her mothers off the Stock Exchange. Every penny I earn, they may have said, will be taken from me and disposed of according to my husband's wisdom—perhaps to found a scholarship or to endow a fellowship in Balliol or Kings, so that to earn money, even if I could earn money, is not a matter that interests me very greatly. I had better leave it to my husband.

At any rate, whether or not the blame rested on the old lady who was looking at the spaniel, there could be no doubt that for some reason or other our mothers had mismanaged their affairs very gravely. Not a penny could be spared for "amenities"; for partridges and wine, beadles and turf, books and cigars, libraries and leisure. To raise bare walls out of the bare earth was the utmost they could do.

So we talked standing at the window and looking, as so many thousands look every night, down on the domes and towers of the famous city beneath us. It was very beautiful, very mysterious in the autumn moonlight. The old stone looked very white and venerable. One thought of all the books that were assembled down there; of the pictures of old prelates and worthies hanging in the panelled rooms; of the painted windows that would be throwing strange globes and crescents on the pavement; of the tablets and memorials and inscriptions; of the fountains and the grass; of the quiet rooms looking across the quiet quadrangles. And (pardon me the thought) I thought, too, of the admirable smoke and drink and the deep armchairs and the pleasant carpets: of the urbanity, the geniality, the dignity which are the offspring of luxury and privacy and space. Certainly our mothers had not provided us with anything comparable to all this—our mothers who found it difficult to scrape together thirty thousand pounds, our mothers who bore thirteen children to ministers of religion at St. Andrews.

So I went back to my inn, and as I walked through the dark streets I pondered this and that, as one does at the end of the day's work. I pondered why it was that Mrs. Seton had no money to leave us; and what effect poverty has on the mind; and what effect wealth has on the mind; and I thought of the queer old gentlemen I had seen that morning with tufts of fur upon their shoulders; and I remembered how if one whistled one of them ran; and I thought of the organ booming in the chapel and of the shut doors of the library; and I thought how unpleasant it is to be locked out; and I thought how it is worse perhaps to be locked in; and, thinking of the safety and prosperity of the one sex and of the poverty and insecurity of the other and of the effect of tradition and of the lack of tradition upon the mind of a writer, I thought at last that it was time to roll up the crumpled skin of the day, with its arguments and its impressions and its anger and its laughter, and cast it into the hedge. A thousand stars were flashing across the blue wastes of the sky. One seemed alone with an inscrutable society. All human beings were laid asleep—prone, horizontal, dumb. Nobody seemed stirring in the streets of Oxbridge. Even the door of the hotel sprang open at the touch of an invisible hand—not a boots was sitting up to light me to bed, it was so late.

## *Questions for Rereading, Discussing, Connecting, and Writing*

### REREADING

1. This selection comes from a paper read to a women's group. As you read, consider how these words might have been received by women over 60 years ago.

2. Some of the conditions of women have changed since Virginia Woolf wrote this essay. Which of her claims seem outdated for contemporary women and which still have relevance today?

3. Woolf claims that much of what she says here is based on lies but "there may perhaps be some truth mixed up with them." What truths do you find as you read?

## Discussing

**4.** As she contrasts the meals at the imaginary Fernham and Oxbridge, Woolf asserts that "one cannot think well, love well, sleep well, if one has not dined well." Implicit in this statement is the idea expressed earlier that a woman must have money as well as a room of her own in order to write fiction. What is your response to this insistence upon material things for creativity?

**5.** In concluding, Woolf notes that it is unpleasant to be locked out but "it is worse perhaps to be locked in." Consider the relative merits and difficulties of being locked in or locked out.

**6.** How would the effect of Woolf's essay be changed if she told more truths, wrote about actual places, people, and events?

## Connecting

**7.** When asked about the origins of Fernham, the imaginary Mary Seton cites the year 1860 as the time when it was founded. Considering the dates of Mill's (p. 262) and Truth's (p. 259) selections, speculate on the historical truth underlying Seton's statement.

**8.** Woolf looks at the women of Fernham in terms of what they lack. Consider composers such as Lange (p. 215), LeSueur (p. 84), and Woolf in terms of their ability to portray subjects who lack something.

## Writing

**9.** Sometimes lies with "truth mixed up with them" can convey an issue more effectively than straight truth. Select an issue that you feel needs attention and present it in ficitional form.

**10.** For Woolf the tailess Manx cat—even though it was seemingly unrelated to the Oxbridge scene—changed the emotional atmosphere. Write about a time when your feelings changed significantly because of something you happened to see.

**11.** Imagine that someone who has not read this essay poses the question with which Woolf begins: What has a room of one's own to do with women and fiction? Write a response to the question.

# Eddie Adams

## Vietnam Photograph (1968)

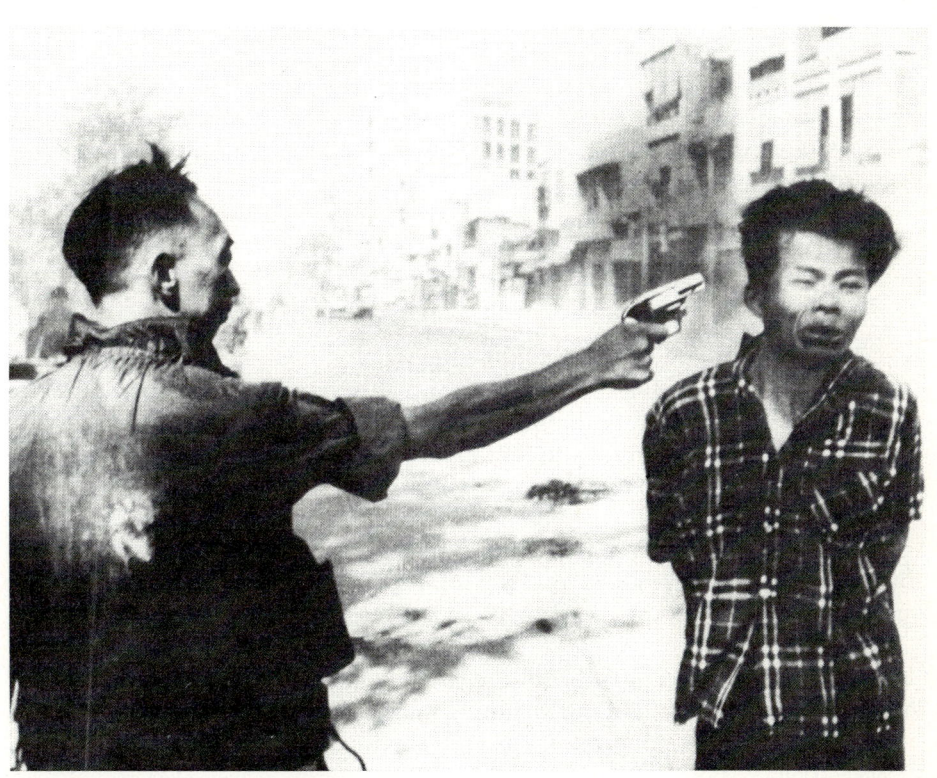

## Questions for Rereading, Discussing, Connecting, and Writing

### Rereading

1. This photograph taken during the Vietnam War is generally considered to be one of the most shocking documents of that war. As you look at the photograph, speculate on the reasons for the act that you perceive being committed in a street of Saigon.

2. The man firing the gun is a South Vietnamese police chief. The man being shot is a suspected Viet Cong. The attitudes of these two men are in sharp contrast; what can you conclude from these attitudes about the political situation at the time?

3. There is another observer in the photograph besides ourselves. Who is he, and what—do you think—is he feeling?

### Discussing

4. To take a memorable or great photograph sometimes is simply a case of luck. Discuss what may be behind this "luck" that so many artists seem to possess, such as a willingness to take chances, to be open to adventures, to be ready to look and listen and act.

5. If there had been no photographer present at this execution, how might the news of it have reached the world? What other ways are there for the spread of news?

6. What image in your life do you wish you could have photographed? Why? Can you construct that image in words? Why? Why not?

### Connecting

7. The arm and hand raised against a human being in this photograph can be thought of as a symbol of power, or justice, or injustice. Look at the selections by Jefferson (p. 251), Mill (p. 262), and Darwin (p. 75) and try to trace our thinking on why there must be the powerful and the powerless—and why, perhaps, there should *not* be the powerful and the powerless.

8. The situation in this photograph bears a strong resemblance to the Goya painting (p. 257). Compare the two. Which, do you think, is the more effective depiction of the carrying out of a sentence. Give several reasons for your opinion.

WRITING

**9.** There are two viewpoints besides the victim's in this photograph: the police chief's and the soldier's (on the left). One is a participant's viewpoint; one is a spectator's viewpoint. Choose one and describe this viewpoint.

**10.** The victim, in the moments before the act captured in the photograph, was led up to photographers in order to publicize the event. Write an essay from the victim's point of view, speculating on the reasons for his fate—or his feelings toward the cameras and the photographers.

**11.** Write an essay explaining why you think—or why you do not think—there are things or actions in the world that should not be described, seen, or photographed. Consider the argument that has existed for centuries between our right to know—and our right to privacy.

# Six

# *Humor and Irony*

Composing in writing, like composing in any other part of life, involves variety. Just as we resist living our lives in a deadening routine, so we resist monotonous writing. As readers, we turn away exclaiming, "That's boring." As writers we search for ways to enliven our work. One strategy available to us is use of voice. Writing, like speaking, can articulate itself in many voices.

We can employ a serious voice, one analogous to the speaking voice we use when explaining a late paper to a professor, or we can employ a sympathetic voice, one analogous to the one we use when talking with a friend who has just lost a parent. Writers can employ a wide variety of voices, each suited to the situation and audience being addressed.

As this chapter illustrates, a single voice—in this case a comic voice—can take many forms, ranging from the sarcasm of Swift to the satire of Dickenson. One source of this variety is the degree of formality employed by the author. Degree of formality can be compared to clothing: We do not wear exactly the same clothes for every occasion because we want to present ourselves differently according to the circumstances. Our various outfits—for cleaning the house, for going to school, for attending a formal wedding—resemble the various voices we can use in writing. Depending upon the audience and purpose of our writing, we can employ casual, informal, or formal language.

Selections included in this chapter illustrate the variety. When Gore Vidal, for example, writes that "the pushers got kids hooked on heroin," he is using a relatively casual voice. Judy Syfers, who writes,

"I want a wife who will plan the menus, do the necessary grocery shopping, prepare the meals, serve them pleasantly, and then do the cleaning up while I do my studying," employs an informal voice. Jonathan Swift, in contrast, uses a formal voice when he writes, "I grant this food will be somewhat dear, and therefore very proper for landlords, who, as they have already devoured most of the parents, seem to have the best title to the children."

Thinking carefully about the audience and purpose for writing is usually the best way to decide what degree of formality to employ in a piece of writing. A desire to impress a distant or potentially hostile audience dictates a relatively formal approach, while a desire to convey a sense of warmth or to create a sense of intimacy with an audience mandates something more casual. As the three quotations above illustrate, distant or unknown audiences (all three of these authors wrote for widely circulated publications) does not preclude using casual or informal language. Similarly, some occasions—such as writing an angry letter to a spouse—may call for a formal tone with a familiar audience.

Despite the great variety possible within a single type of voice, there are common qualities within types. The comic voice, as this chapter illustrates, enables the composer to take a new or fresh perspective on a subject. As readers, we may smile or laugh, but at the same time we recognize that we have just been presented with a new thought. We can see evidence of this as we look at the Igbo Tortoise Story and Magritte's *Key of Dreams*. Each deals with questions of identity. In playing with the relationship between a word and the thing it represents, Magritte makes us think again about how language works. The Igbo story encourages us to reconsider the way we describe ourselves.

The comic voice in writing frequently employs irony, the technique of saying one thing while meaning another. Irony enables writers to make more compelling statements than would a serious tone. Swift's proposed solution to problems of starvation in Ireland illustrates the cruelties of British policy more graphically than any exhortation could do. Similarly, Fanny Fern and Judy Syfers make eloquent statements about relationships between men and women by using irony.

The comic voice gives writers distance from their subjects. The objectivity fostered by comedy encourages composers to play with language—both verbal and graphic language—thereby stretching the limits of the possible. Pushing past the possible enables both readers and writers to see things in new ways, to extend their horizons. The Igbo tale, cartoons, and Dickenson's account of ironing the telephone book all push us beyond usual boundaries of credibility, thereby enlarging our sense of the world and creating new possibilities for writing.

## Aesop

# The Fox and the Hedgehog (550 B.C.)

A Fox, swimming across a river, was drifted along by the stream, and carried by an eddy into a nook on the opposite bank. He lay there exhausted and unable for a time to scramble up. To add to his misfortunes a swarm of Flies settled upon his head and stung and plagued him grievously. A Hedgehog, that happened to be near the edge of the water, offered to drive away the Flies that molested and teased him in that sad manner. "Nay," cried the Fox, "pray let them alone. Those that are now upon me are already full almost to bursting with my blood. If you drive them away, a fresh swarm of hungry rascals will take their places, and I shall not have a drop of blood left in my body."

*Questions for Rereading, Discussing, Connecting, and Writing*

### REREADING

1. Animal stories designed to reveal or comment on human qualities have developed in many cultures. The animal stories commonly known as Aesop's Fables were collected by Demetrius Phalereus, founder of the Alexandria Library, who lived about 200 years after Aesop. Some of the fables may have been told in Aesop's time or even told by Aesop, but others came from different sources. What, in your view, is the effect of assigning authorship of these fables to Aesop?

2. Aesop lived in Greece during a period (around 550 BC) when free speech was politically dangerous. Fables were frequently used to express political views that were unsafe to state openly. What political implications can you find in "The Fox and the Hedgehog?"

3. What difference does it make to your reading of Aesop's fables to know that Aesop was a slave who was killed in accordance with the oracle at Delphi?

## Discussing

**4.** After they were originally collected in 300 BC, Aesop's fables underwent a series of translations during succeeding years so that they would be available to other cultures. What, in your view, would have motivated the head of the Alexandria Library to collect the fables in the first place, and why would it have been important to later generations to translate and preserve them?

**5.** You have undoubtedly heard animal stories other than "The Fox and the Hedgehog." Think about these other fables and consider what they have in common.

**6.** When fables or other stories are repeated from one person to another, the wording frequently changes with each telling. After you and others in your discussion group are sufficiently familiar with "The Fox and the Hedgehog" have a couple of people tell this fable in their own words. What differences do you notice between versions?

## Connecting

**7.** It has been said that the fable is at once too simple and too roundabout to be a satisfactory form of literary expression in today's world. The same might be said about cartoons. Look at Smith's cartoon (p. 318) or MAL's (p. 334) and consider the ways in which cartoons are both simple and roundabout.

**8.** The Igbo story of the tortoise (p. 305) could be described as a fable. What similarities and differences do you see as you look at the Aesop and Igbo texts together?

**9.** Aesop's fables come from the same culture (although from a later period) as Homer's "Lotos Eaters" (p. 101). Do you find common features in these two selections?

## Writing

**10.** Decide what "message" this fable was intended to convey and write an essay in which you present the same point without the use of an animal story. What differences do you notice between your version and Aesop's?

**11.** Imagine that the Hedgehog portrayed in this story reports his meeting with the Fox to his friends. Write an account of how the Hedgehog might narrate this meeting.

**12.** The fact that Aesop's fables remain in print over two thousand years after they were originally composed suggests that they contain timeless qualities. Write an essay explaining the timelessness of fables.

Jonathan Swift

# A Modest Proposal (1729)

It is a melancholy object to those who walk through this great town, or travel in the country, when they see the streets, the roads, and cabin-doors crowded with beggars of the female sex, followed by three, four, or six children all in rags, and importuning every passenger for an alms. These mothers, instead of being able to work for their honest livelihood, are forced to employ all their time in strolling, to beg sustenance for their helpless infants, who, as they grow up, either turn thieves for want of work, or leave their dear native country to fight for the Pretender in Spain, or sell themselves to the Barbadoes.

I think it is agreed by all parties that this prodigious number of children, in the arms, or on the backs, or at the heels of their mothers, and frequently of their fathers, is in the present deplorable state of the kingdom a very great additional grievance; and therefore whoever could find out a fair, cheap, and easy method of making these children sound and useful members of the commonwealth would deserve so well of the public as to have his statue set up for a preserver of the nation.

But my intention is very far from being confined to provide only for the children of professed beggars; it is of a much greater extent, and shall take in the whole number of infants at a certain age who are born of parents in effect as little able to support them as those who demand our charity in the streets.

As to my own part, having turned my thoughts for many years upon this important subject, and maturely weighed the several schemes of other projectors, I have always found them grossly mistaken in their computation. It is true a child just dropped from its dam may be suported by her milk for a solar year with little other nourishment, at most not above the value of two shillings, which the mother may certainly get, or the value in scraps, by her lawful occupation of begging, and it is exactly at one year old that I propose to provide for them, in such a manner as, instead of being a charge upon their parents, or the parish, or wanting food and raiment for the rest of their lives, they shall, on the contrary, contribute to the feeding and partly to the clothing of many thousands.

There is likewise another great advantage in my scheme, that it will prevent those voluntary abortions, and that horrid practice of women murdering their bastard children, alas, too frequent among us, sacrificing the poor innocent babes, I doubt, more to avoid the expense than the shame, which would move tears and pity in the most savage and inhuman breast.

The number of souls in Ireland being usually reckoned one million and a half, of these I calculate there may be about two hundred thousand couples whose wives are breeders, from which number I subtract thirty thousand couples who are able to maintain their own children, although I apprehend there cannot be so many under the present distresses of the kingdom, but this being granted, there will remain an hundred and seventy thousand breeders. I again subtract fifty thousand for those women who miscarry, or whose children die by accident or disease within the year. There only remain an hundred and twenty thousand children of poor parents annually born: the question therefore is, how this number shall be reared, and provided for, which, as I have already said, under the present situation of affairs is utterly impossible by all the methods hitherto proposed, for we can neither employ them in handicraft or agriculture; we neither build houses (I mean in the country), nor cultivate land: they can very seldom pick up a livelihood by stealing until they arrive at six years old, except where they are of towardly parts, although I confess they learn the rudiments much earlier, during which time they can however be properly looked upon only as probationers, as I have been informed by a principal gentleman in the County of Cavan, who protested to me that he never knew above one or two instances under the age of six, even in a part of the kingdom so renowned for the quickest proficiency in the art.

I am assured by our merchants that a boy or a girl before twelve years old, is no saleable commodity, and even when they come to this age, they will not yield above three pounds, or three pounds and half-a-crown at most on the Exchange, which cannot turn to account either to the parents or the kingdom, the charge of nutriment and rags having been at least four times that value.

I shall now therefore humbly propose my own thoughts, which I hope will not be liable to the least objection.

I have been assured by a very knowing American of my acquaintance in London, that a young healthy child well nursed is at a year old a most delicious, nourishing and wholesome food, whether stewed, roasted, baked, or boiled, and I make no doubt that it will equally serve in a fricassee, or a ragout.

I do therefore humbly offer it to public consideration, that of the hundred and twenty thousand children already computed, twenty thousand may be reserved for breed, whereof only one fourth part to be males, which is more than we allow to sheep, black-cattle, or swine, and my reason is that these children are seldom the fruits of marriage, a circumstance not much regarded by our savages, therefore one male will be sufficient to serve four females. That the remaining hundred thousand may at a year old be offered in sale to the persons of quality, and fortune, through the kingdom, always advising the mother to let them suck plentifully in the last month, so as to render them plump, and fat for a good table. A child will make two dishes at an entertainment for friends, and when the family dines alone, the fore or hind quarter will make a reasonable dish, and seasoned with a little pepper or salt will be very good boiled on the fourth day, especially in winter.

I have reckoned upon a medium, that a child just born will weigh twelve pounds, and in a solar year if tolerably nursed increaseth to twenty-eight pounds.

I grant this food will be somewhat dear, and therefore very proper for landlords, who, as they have already devoured most of the parents, seem to have the best title to the children.

Infant's flesh will be in season throughout the year, but more plentiful in March, and a little before and after, for we are told by a grave author, an eminent French physician, that fish being a prolific diet, there are more children born in Roman Catholic countries about nine months after Lent than at any other season; therefore reckoning a year after Lent, the markets will be more glutted than usual, because the number of Popish infants is at least three to one in this kingdom, and therefore it will have one other collateral advantage by lessening the number of Papists among us.

I have already computed the charge of nursing a beggar's child (in which list I reckon all cottagers, labourers, and four-fifths of the farmers) to be about two shillings per annum, rags included, and I believe no gentleman would repine to give ten shillings for the carcass of a good fat child, which, as I have said, will make four dishes of excellent nutritive meat, when he hath only some particular friend or his own family to dine with him. Thus the Squire will learn to be a good landlord and grow popular among his tenants, the mother will have eight shillings net profit, and be fit for work until she produces another child.

Those who are more thrifty (as I must confess the times require) may flay the carcass; the skin of which artificially dressed, will make admirable gloves for ladies, and summer boots for fine gentlemen.

As to our city of Dublin, shambles may be appointed for this purpose, in the most convenient parts of it, and butchers we may be assured will not be wanting, although I rather recommend buying the children alive, and dressing them hot from the knife, as we do roasting pigs.

A very worthy person, a true lover of his country, and whose virtues I highly esteem, was lately pleased, in discoursing on this matter to offer a refinement upon my scheme. He said that many gentlemen of this kingdom, having of late destroyed their deer, he conceived that the want of venison might be well supplied by the bodies of young lads and maidens, not exceeding fourteen years of age, nor under twelve, so great a number of both sexes in every country being now ready to starve, for want of work and service: and these to be disposed of by their parents if alive, or otherwise by their nearest relations. But with due deference to so excellent a friend, and so deserving a patriot, I cannot be altogether in his sentiments. For as to the males, my American acquaintance assured me from frequent experience that their flesh was generally tough and lean, like that of our schoolboys, by continual exercise, and their taste disagreeable, and to fatten them would not answer the charge. Then as to the females, it would, I think with humble submission, be a loss to the public, because they soon would become breeders themselves: and besides, it is not improbable that some scrupulous people might be apt to censure such a practice (although indeed very unjustly) as a little bordering upon cruelty, which I confess, hath always been with me the strongest objection against any project, howsoever well intended.

But in order to justify my friend, he confessed that this expedient was put into his head by the famous Psalmanazar, a native of the island Formosa, who came from thence to London, above twenty years ago, and in conversation told my friend that in his country when any young person happened to be put to death, the executioner sold the carcass to persons of quality, as a prime dainty, and that, in his time, the body of a plump girl of fifteen, who was crucified for an attempt to poison the emperor, was sold to his Imperial Majesty's Prime Minister of State, and other great Mandarins of the Court, in joints from the gibbet, at four hundred crowns. Neither indeed can I deny that if the same use were made of several plump young girls in this town who, without one single groat to their fortunes, cannot stir abroad without a chair, and appear at the playhouse and assemblies in foreign fineries, which they never will pay for, the kingdom would not be the worse.

Some persons of a desponding spirit are in great concern about that vast number of poor people, who are aged, diseased, or maimed, and I have been desired to employ my thoughts what course may be taken to ease the nation of so grievous an encumbrance. But I am not in the least pain upon that matter, because it is very well known that they are every day dying, and rotting, by cold, and famine, and filth, and vermin, as fast as can be reasonably expected. And as to the younger labourers they are now in almost as hopeful a condition. They cannot get work, and consequently pine away from want of nourishment, to a degree that if at any time they are accidentally hired to common labour, they have not strength to perform it; and thus the country and themselves are in a fair way of being soon delivered from the evils to come.

I have too long digressed, and therefore shall return to my subject. I think the advantages by the proposal which I have made are obvious and many, as well as of the highest importance.

For first, as I have already observed, it would greatly lessen the number of Papists, with whom we are yearly overrun, being the principal breeders of the nation, as well as our most dangerous enemies, and who stay at home on purpose with a design to deliver the kingdom to the Pretender, hoping to take their advantage by the absence of so many good Protestants, who have chosen rather to leave their country than stay at home and pay tithes against their conscience to an idolatrous Episcopal curate.

Secondly, the poorer tenants will have something valuable of their own, which by law may be made liable to distress, and help to pay their landlord's rent, their corn and cattle being already seized, and money a thing unknown.

Thirdly, whereas the maintenance of an hundred thousand children, from two years old, and upwards, cannot be computed at less than ten shillings a piece per annum, the nation's stock will be thereby increased fifty thousand pounds per annum, besides the profit of a new dish, introduced to the tables of all gentlemen of fortune in the kingdom, who have any refinement in taste, and the money will circulate among ourselves, the goods being entirely of our own growth and manufacture.

Fourthly, the constant breeders, besides the gain of eight shillings sterling per annum, by the sale of their children, will be rid of the charge of maintaining them after the first year.

Fifthly, this food would likewise bring great custom to taverns, where the vintners will certainly be so prudent as to procure the best receipts for dressing it to perfection, and consequently have their houses frequented by all the fine gentlemen, who justly value themselves upon their knowledge in good eating; and a skilful cook, who understands how to oblige his guests, will contrive to make it as expensive as they please.

Sixthly, this would be a great inducement to marriage, which all wise nations have either encouraged by rewards, or enforced by laws and penalties. It would increase the care and tenderness of mothers towards their children, when they were sure of a settlement for life, to the poor babes, provided in some sort by the public to their annual profit instead of expense. We should soon see an honest emulation among the married women, which of them could bring the fattest child to the market. Men would become as fond of their wives, during the time of their pregnancy, as they are now of their mares in foal, their cows in calf, or sows when they are ready to farrow, nor offer to beat or kick them (as it is too frequent a practice) for fear of a miscarriage.

Many other advantages might be enumerated. For instance, the addition of some thousand carcasses in our exportation of barrelled beef; the propagation of swine's flesh, and improvement in the art of making good bacon, so much wanted among us by the great destruction of pigs, too frequent at our tables, and no way comparable in taste or magnificence to a well-grown, fat yearling child which roasted whole will make a considerable figure at a Lord Mayor's feast, or any other public entertainment. But this and many others I omit, being studious of brevity.

Supposing that one thousand families in this city would be constant customers for infants' flesh, besides others who might have it at merry meetings, particularly weddings and christenings; I compute that Dublin would take off annually about twenty thousand carcasses, and the rest of the kingdom (where probably they will be sold somewhat cheaper) the remaining eighty thousand.

I can think of no one objection that will possibly be raised against this proposal, unless it should be urged that the number of people will be thereby much lessened in the kingdom. This I freely own, and it was indeed one principal design in offering it to the world. I desire the reader will observe, that I calculate my remedy for this one individual Kingdom of Ireland, and for no other that ever was, is, or, I think, ever can be upon earth. Therefore let no man talk to me of other expedients: Of taxing our absentees at five shillings a pound: Of using neither clothes, nor household furniture, except what is of our own growth and manufacture: Of utterly rejecting the materials and instruments that promote foreign luxury: Of curing the expensiveness of pride, vanity, idleness, and gaming in our women: Of introducing a vein of parsimony, prudence, and temperance: Of learning to love our country, wherein we differ even from Laplanders, and the inhabitants of Topinamboo: Of quitting our animosities and factions, nor act any longer like the Jews, who were murdering one another at the very moment their city was taken: Of being a little cautious not to sell our country and consciences for nothing: Of teaching landlords to have at least one degree of mercy towards their tenants. Lastly, of putting a spirit of honesty, industry, and skill into our shopkeepers, who, if a resolution could now be taken to buy only our native goods, would immediately unite to cheat and exact upon us in the price, the measure and the goodness, nor could ever yet be brought to make one fair proposal of just dealing, though often and earnestly invited to it.

Therefore I repeat, let no man talk to me of these and the like expedients, till he hath at least a glimpse of hope that there will ever be some hearty and sincere attempt to put them in practice.

But as to myself, having been wearied out for many years with offering vain, idle, visionary thoughts, and at length utterly despairing of success, I fortunately fell upon this proposal, which as it is wholly new, so it hath something solid and real, of no expense and little trouble, full in our own power, and whereby we can incur no danger in disobliging England. For this kind of commodity will not bear exportation, the flesh being of too tender a consistence to admit a long continuance in salt, although perhaps I could name a country which would be glad to eat up our whole nation without it.

After all I am not so violently bent upon my own opinion as to reject any offer, proposed by wise men, which shall be found equally innocent, cheap, easy and effectual. But before some thing of that kind shall be advanced in contradiction to my scheme, and offering a better, I desire the author, or authors, will be pleased maturely to consider two points. First, as things now stand, how they will be able to find food and raiment for a hundred thousand useless mouths and backs? And secondly, there being a round million of creatures in human figure, throughout this kingdom, whose whole subsistence put into a common stock would leave them in debt two millions of pounds sterling; adding those who are beggars by profession, to the bulk of farmers, cottagers, and labourers with their wives and children, who are beggars in effect; I desire those politicians who dislike my overture, and may perhaps be so bold to attempt an answer, that they will first ask the parents of these mortals whether they would not at this day think it a great happiness to have been sold for food at a year old, in the manner I prescribe, and thereby have avoided such a perpetual scene of misfortunes as they have since gone through, by the oppression of landlords, the impossibility of paying rent without money or trade, the want of common sustenance, with neither house nor clothes to cover them from the inclemencies of weather, and the most inevitable prospect of entailing the like, or greater miseries upon their breed for ever.

I profess in the sincerity of my heart that I have not the least personal interest in endeavouring to promote this necessary work, having no other motive than the public good of my country, by advancing our trade, providing for infants, relieving the poor, and giving some pleasure to the rich. I have no children by which I can propose to get a single penny; the youngest being nine years old, and my wife past child-bearing.

## Questions for Rereading, Discussing, Connecting, and Writing

### REREADING

1. Swift wrote this essay in response to the economic situation in Ireland during the early eighteenth century. England had passed laws that restricted Irish agriculture and, thereby, food production. Absentee landlords drew off more than half of Irish resources, and between 1725 and 1728 Irish crops had failed, leading to near famine in the country. What references to these conditions do you find embedded throughout the essay?

2. The "great town" to which Swift refers is Dublin. As you read, you will probably find other references that puzzle you or are difficult for you to understand. Note these and consider how they influence your reading.

3. We commonly talk about words in terms of their ability to communicate ideas, but words also function to convey the opposite of what they say. Sarcasm, humor, and irony all depend upon the reader/listener's ability to understand the difference between what is said and what is meant. Speculate on what Swift means (as opposed to what he says).

## Discussing

4. Humor often serves to make a serious point. Consider what point Swift wants to make by using satire.

5. Swift offers a great number of details to make his proposal convincing. Can you think of issues he fails to consider? Why do you suppose Swift fails to address these?

6. In concluding, Swift offers a list of "advantages" for his proposal. Generate a list of disadvantages that might be offered in response.

## Connecting

7. Swift's proposal resembles Syfer's "I Want A Wife" (p. 330) in that it approaches serious social conditions in a humorous way. Consider the similarities and differences of the humor in these two selections.

8. The Konica advertisement (p. 374) resembles Swift's essay in its presentation of images (lions running copy machines) that the audience is not expected to take literally. What differences do you see between the two in the way they treat their audiences?

9. Many of the texts included in this book make proposals about social issues just as Swift's does. Compare his approach with that of Amos (p. 239), Thomas Jefferson (p. 251), or John Stuart Mill (p. 262).

## Writing

10. Swift chose the essay form for presenting his case on behalf of Ireland. Select another form and make the same argument. You might, for example, compose a poem, a ballad, an advertisement, a collage, or a cartoon.

11. Although it takes the form of a satire, Swift's essay can be regarded as an argument. Write a rebuttal to his argument.

12. You can undoubtedly think of many contemporary issues that need changing. Write a "modest proposal" recommending a change that will improve the situation.

## The Igbo People

# The Tortoise's Friendship with the Birds (19th Century)

There was a time when the Birds and the Beasts of the land battled against each other. The Beasts, who were much more vicious than the Birds, declared that anyone who could exterminate the Birds would be crowned King. As a result each of the Beasts sought for a way to destroy the Birds. All of them, except for the Tortoise, laid their plans publicly. The Tortoise kept his a closely guarded secret.

The Birds were well aware of the deep-rooted hatred which the Beasts felt for them. Therefore one day the Birds held a meeting, which was attended by every single one of them, to devise a means for defending themselves against the wicked plans of the non-winged animals. As they were deliberating, the Tortoise was ushered in by one of his avian friends. In his characteristic manner, he playfully teased the Birds and shortly felt at home in their midst.

Tortoise's friend asked the Birds to gather together to hear him speak of the Tortoise's promise. "My friend the Tortoise," he said, "has heard from me the story of our predicament. He has kindly undertaken to be our spy among his kinsmen. He will bring us regular reports about the evil designs of the non-winged animals. And the wonder of it all is that my good friend the Tortoise has agreed to discharge this responsibility without any fee to us."

The Birds went wild with joy and applauded and saluted the Tortoise over and over again.

In the following days the Tortoise furnished the Birds with insignificant or outdated information. Nevertheless the Birds continued to trust him. When the Tortoise knew for certain that the Birds had complete confidence in him, he announced his plan to celebrate his mother's second burial.

The ceremony was to be in his home in the land of the non-winged animals and he invited all the Birds to the festival. When some of the more suspicious Birds wondered if they would be safe in the realm of their enemies, the Tortoise assured them. He said that because his kinsmen so feared his wrath, they would not dare to harm a feather of any of his guests. Besides, he said, he had provided adequate security measures. All the Birds would be entertained in one large hall with only one entrance which was also the only exit. It had neither windows nor cracks. Once the door was securely barred, no one else could possibly get in.

The Tortoise warned the Birds that they would have to remain in the hall for as long as the celebration lasted for his kinsmen would be firing their guns and cannons outside as part of the ceremony. Indeed he would not be pleased to have any of his guests hit by accident. That is why, he repeated, all of them must remain inside. After his kinsmen had done their shooting and gone home, he would unbar the door and let the Birds out.

In this manner the Tortoise convinced the Birds of their safety in the land of their enemies.

On the day of the festival, the Birds arrived long before the first group of the non-winged animals reached the Tortoise's premises. The Tortoise locked all the Birds inside the hall and set food and palm wine before them. When some of his kinsmen arrived, he told them to return home for the ceremony was not to begin until he had finished attending to his august visitors from a distant place. He told them to come back for the ceremony in one hour.

As soon as these non-winged animals left, the Tortoise set the hall in which the Birds were feasting on fire. The fire blazed fiercely. The Birds chirped and flapped their wings desperately but there was no escape for them. Flames flashed like lightning and smoke ascended into the sky in thick columns. All the non-winged animals saw the flashing flames and the rising smoke, and ran towards the Tortoise's compound, each with palm leaves to quench the fire.

When they arrived the Tortoise laughed at them and said, "My people, throw away your leaves, rest your nerves, recover your breath, and get ready to feast. After the celebration of the death of all the Birds, then you will celebrate the second burial of the mother of your King. For I have not only killed all the Birds but I have also prepared them as meat for your feasting."

The Beasts stood dumbfounded with admiration and surprise. They ate the meat, played their part in the burial ceremony, and finally crowned the Tortoise King over all the other non-winged animals.

*Questions for Rereading,*
*Discussing, Connecting, and Writing*

REREADING

1. This selection comes from the African tradition of trickster tales, tales in which animals such as the tortoise play major roles. This tale first appeared in oral form among the Igbo people of what is now Nigeria. Speculate on how its oral origin shapes the language of this tale.

2. At what point in your reading did you become aware of the tortoise's plan to trick the birds? What clues did you rely upon?

3. Do the animals in this tale seem human to you? Why or why not?

DISCUSSING

4. Tortoise is a character who appears frequently in trickster tales. Discuss why this animal might be selected for such a role. What attributes qualify him?

5. Discuss the use of "friendship" in the title. What does this use of the word contribute to the humor/irony of the story?

6. Tortoise might be described as the hero of the tale. Discuss the narrator's attitude toward him. What is your attitude toward tortoise?

CONNECTING

7. This tale shares many elements with the Sioux Indian myth (p. 25) but it is also distinctly different. What similarities and differences can you discover?

8. Much of the humor of this tale is achieved at the expense of the birds. How does this type of humor compare with that found in Aesop's fable (p. 294).

WRITING

9. Using this story as a model, write your own trickster tale.

10. Write a prose description of an illustration that might accompany this tale.

11. Describe tortoise's reign as king (after the end of the tale). What would he do as king? How do you know?

*Fanny Fern*

# Tom Pax's Conjugal Soliloquy (1856)

MRS. PAX is an authoress. I knew it when I married her. I liked the idea. I had not tried it then. I had not a clear idea what it was to have one's wife belong to the public. I thought marriage was marriage, brains not excepted. I was mistaken. Mrs. Pax is very kind: I don't wish to say that she is not. Very obliging: I would not have you think the contrary; but when I put my arm round Mrs. Pax's waist, and say, "Mary, I love you," she smiles in an absent, moonlight-kind of a way, and says, "Yes, to-day is Wednesday, is it not? I must write an article for 'The Weekly Monopolizer' to-day." That dampens my ardor; but presently I say again, being naturally affectionate, "Mary, I love you;" she replies (still abstractedly), "Thank you, how do you think it will do to call my next article for 'The Weekly Monopolizer,' 'The Stray Waif?'"

Mrs. Pax sews on all my shirt-buttons with the greatest good humor: I would not have you think she does not; but with her thoughts still on "The Weekly Monopolizer," she sews them on the flaps, instead of the wristbands. This is inconvenient; still Mrs. Pax is kindness itself; I make no complaint.

I am very fond of walking. After dinner I say to Mrs. Pax, "Mary, let us take a walk." She says, "Yes, certainly, I must go down town to read the proof of my article for 'The Monopolizer.'" So, I go down town with Mrs. Pax. After tea I say, "Mary, let us go to the theater to-night;" she says, "I would be very happy to go, but the atmosphere is so bad there, the gas always escapes, and my head must be clear to-morrow, you know, for I have to write the last chapter of my forthcoming work, 'Prairie Life.'" So I stay at home with Mrs. Pax, and as I sit down by her on the sofa, and as nobody comes in, I think that this, after all, is better, (though I must say my wife looks well at the Opera, and I like to take her there). I put my arm around Mrs. Pax. It is a habit I have. In comes the servant; and brings a handful of letters for her by mail, directed to "Julia Jesamine!" (that's my wife's *nom-de-plume*). I remove my arm from her waist, because she says "they are probably business letters which require immediate notice." She sits down at the table, and breaks the seals. Four of them are from fellows who want "her autograph." *Mrs. Pax's* autograph! The fifth is from a gentlemen who, delighted with her last book, which he says "mirrored his own soul" (how do you suppose Mrs. Pax found out how to "mirror *his* soul?") requests "permission to correspond with the charming authoress." "Charming!" my wife! "his soul!" Mrs. Pax! The sixth is from a gentleman who desires "the loan of five hundred dollars, as he has been unfortunate in business, and has heard that her works have been very remunerative." Five hundred dollars for John Smith, from my wife! The seventh letter is from a man at the West, offering her her own price to deliver a lecture before the Pigtown Young Men's Institute. *I like that!*

Mrs. Pax opens her writing desk; it is one I gave her; takes some delicate buff note-paper; I gave her that, too; dips her gold pen (my gift) into the inkstand, and writes—writes till eleven o'clock. Eleven! and I, her husband, Tom Pax, sit there and wait for her.

The next morning when I awake, I say, "Mary dear?" She says, "Hush! don't speak, I've just got a capital subject to write about for 'The Weekly Monopolizer.'" Not that I am *complaining* of Mrs. Pax, not at all; not that I don't like my wife to be an authoress; I do. To be sure I can't say that I knew *exactly* what it involved. I did not know, for instance, that the Press in speaking of her by her *nom-de-plume* would call her "OUR Julia," but I would not have you think I object to her being literary. On the contrary, I am not sure that I do not rather like it; but I ask the Editor of "The Weekly Monopolizer," as a man—as a Christian—as a husband—if he thinks it right—if it is doing as he would be done by—to monopolize my wife's thoughts as early as five o'clock in the morning? I merely ask for information. I trust I have no resentful feelings toward the animal.

## Questions for Rereading, Discussing, Connecting, and Writing

### Rereading

1. Fanny Fern was the pen name of Sara Payson Willis, a widowed woman who wrote to support herself and her children in a time when most women depended upon fathers and/or husbands for their livelihood. What response do you have to the name Fanny Fern? As you read, speculate on why the author chose this name.

2. Consider the proper names—such as Pax and "The Weekly Monopolizer"—used in this selection. What effect do they have?

3. This selection, written by a woman from a man's perspective, raises questions about attitude toward the subject. What do you take to be Tom's attitude toward Mrs. Pax? What attitude does the author have toward both the Paxes?

### Discussing

4. Although this selection was written more than 100 years ago, the issue of women in the work force is still with us. Discuss the ways this selection does and does not have something to say to today's world.

5. As the title suggests, this selection deals with the topic of marriage. What, in your view, is the author's view of marriage?

6. The soliloquy is often used to reveal the inner thoughts of a character in a play. Imagine Tom Pax as an actor in a play and describe the action that would surround his speech.

### Connecting

7. Both Judy Syfers (p. 330), and Fanny Fern comment on relationships between husbands and wives. What comparisons can you make about the style and substance of these two commentaries?

8. One function, among others, of this selection is to reveal something about the writer's work. How would you describe the work of writing as it is presented here? How does it compare with the kinds of work portrayed in Chapter 4?

9. Samuel Clemens, like Sara Payson Willis, took a pen name. What similarities and differences do you see in motivations behind and effects of the names Mark Twain and Fanny Fern?

WRITING

**10.** This selection says a great deal about Tom Pax's expectations of marriage, even though it is softened by a comic voice. Adopt a more serious voice and write an account of these expectations.

**11.** Tom Pax invites a response from the Editor of "The Weekly Monopolizer." Write that response.

**12.** Take the perspective of Mrs. Pax and write a soliloquy from her point of view. How might she describe her marriage?

## Apollinaire

# It's Raining (1916)

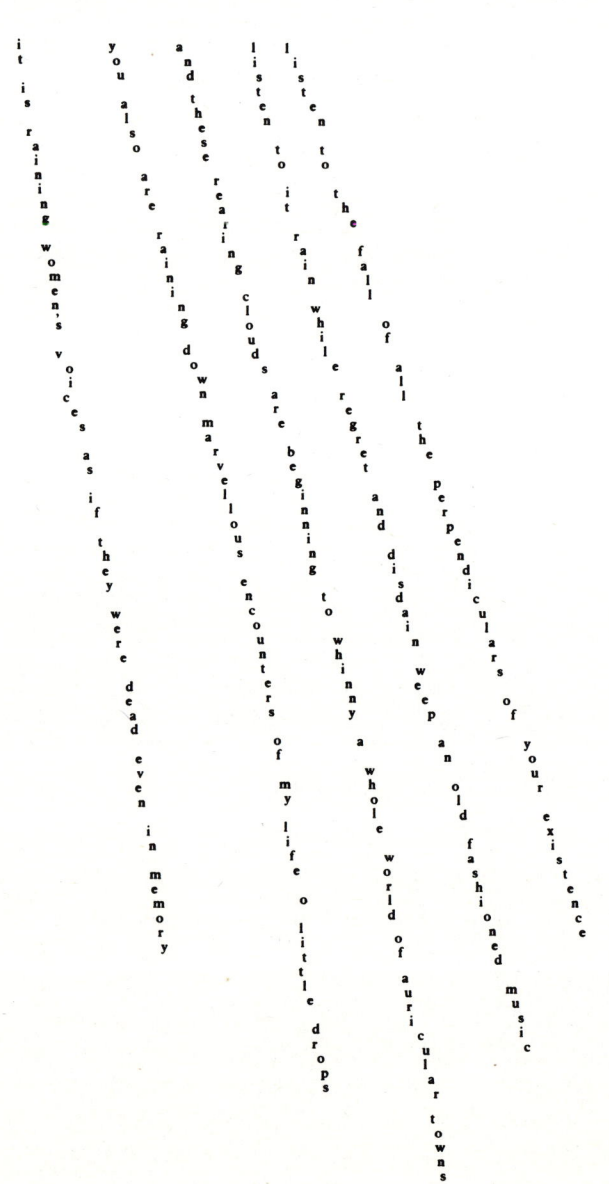

it is raining women's voices as if they were dead even in memory

you also are raining down marvellous encounters of my life o little drops

and these rearing clouds are beginning to whinny a whole world of auricular towns

listen to it rain while regret and disdain weep an old fashioned music

listen to the fall of all the perpendiculars of your existence

## Questions for Rereading, Discussing, Connecting, and Writing

### Rereading

1. When you first look at this poem, you probably focus on its form. As you read it, consider what other shapes Apollinaire might have selected to represent rain and then speculate on why he chose this one.

2. Although the visual form is most obvious at first glance, Apollinaire has also given attention to aural features. Try reading this selection aloud and then describe the rhythms you hear.

3. As you read through the poem, what emotional shifts do you notice? How would you describe the emotional tone of "dead even in memory" as compared with "listen to the fetters falling that bind you high and low"?

### Discussing

4. Identify parts of the poem that surprise you, that make an unexpected move or contain an unusual turn of phrase. Discuss the effect of these parts. What new insights or ways of seeing do they generate?

5. Each line in a poem adds something new to the effect of the whole. Discuss how this poem would be different if it ended after line 1, or line 2 or line 3 or line 4.

6. In one way this poem can be described as free from structure because it employs a form different from that of many poems, but in another way it can be described as highly structured. Discuss how function and structure both operate here.

### Connecting

7. Like the cartoon on page 334, "It's Raining" plays with language to achieve an effect. What other similarities do you see between this poem and the cartoon?

8. Poems shaped like what they represent have been created by a number of poets and artists. If you have seen a poem like this, consider how it does or does not capture the essence of "It's Raining." Alternatively, compare "It's Raining" with other poems or ads that unite form and content.

## Writing

**9.** Using "It's Raining" as a model, write a poem that unites content and form. You might, for example, write a poem about rainbows, football, or hearts.

**10.** Copy Apollinaire's poem into traditional stanza form, insert conventional punctuation and capitalization, and then write an essay exploring the difference between this and the form Apollinaire chose.

**11.** Select one of the puzzling or surprising phrases in this poem and write an explanation of it.

### René Magritte

# The Key of Dreams (1936)

## Questions for Rereading, Discussing, Connecting, and Writing

### Rereading

1. As you first look at this painting, what features catch your attention immediately? Where do you look first, second, and so on? Does anything here surprise or puzzle you?

2. In looking at the four objects and four phrases represented in this painting, you probably see nothing unfamiliar. You have probably seen the objects and words many times before. But you may not have seen them in this combination. How do these particular combinations affect your "reading" of this painting?

3. Four seemingly separate sections comprise this painting. What relationships do you see among the parts? How would the painting be changed if one section were removed?

### Discussing

4. This painting is part of a series in which the French artist Magritte explored the relationship between language and physical objects. Consider what this particular painting says about the relationship between words and objects.

5. Although the four-part division invites us to look at this painting in parts, consider it as a whole piece and speculate on the significance of its title. In what (if any) ways can this work be described as a "Key of Dreams"?

6. Common words such as door and bird are often surprisingly complicated to understand. To see evidence of this complexity, ask several people to explain in detail the specific creature that comes to mind when the word "bird" is mentioned. Pay particular attention to how prior experiences have contributed to the meanings individuals attach to this word.

### Connecting

7. Although they employ different means, both Magritte and Swift (p. 296) use language to make statements that we do not take as literally true. We do not assume that Magritte has confused a pitcher with a bird any more than we assume that Swift actually wants to eat Irish children. In what ways does the effect of Magritte's work resemble that of Swift's?

**8.** Work by Degas, another French painter, is included on page 197. What similarities do you see as you compare the three versions of "The Dancing School" with "The Key of Dreams"? Specifically, what strategies do these painters employ to represent their subjects?

**9.** Arrangement of words and images is central to the humor of Magritte's painting. Apollinaire (p. 313) likewise arranges words in unconventional ways. Compare the effects of these two unconventional forms of arrangement.

WRITING

**10.** Magritte's combination of words and images can be described as a way of playing with language. You can probably think of other forms of language play such as puns, jokes, and words with unusual sounds. Write an essay in which you consider play as one of the functions (along with communication) of language.

**11.** The relationship between this painting and its title is not immediately apparent. Explore, in writing, the meaning of the title "The Key of Dreams."

**12.** One could describe an effect of Magritte's painting as forcing us to look more closely at common objects and concepts. The combination of words such as "the door" and "the wind" with images of a horse and a clock causes us to take a second look at our ideas of both. Write an account of an experience that forced you to look more closely at some object. If you have difficulty thinking of such an experience, you might begin by trying to draw a telephone dial without looking at one.

Dorman Smith

# Cartoon *(1938)*

Dorman H. Smith, ca. 1938. © New York American.

*Questions for Rereading,
Discussing, Connecting, and Writing*

REREADING

1. Consider the allocation of space and relative size of figures in this cartoon. What effects are achieved by these proportions?

**2.** This cartoon captures a moment of action between two characters. Describe what happened just before this moment.

**3.** The figures in the cartoon wear labels. How do these labels influence your reading of the cartoon?

## Discussing

**4.** Consider what you know about the year 1938. What might "Hard Boiled World" mean in this context? What does this cartoon tell you about 1938?

**5.** The artist uses the technique of personification to portray the world. How does this personification add to the cartoon?

## Connecting

**6.** This cartoon resembles Swift's "A Modest Proposal" (p. 296) in offering a commentary on the world. What similarities and differences do you see as you compare the two texts?

**7.** Like the Igbo tale of the tortoise (p. 305), this cartoon represents events that cannot be described as ordinary. What does this quality contribute to the humor of both selections?

## Writing

**8.** Write an essay in which you discuss this cartoon's appropriateness for today's graduates.

**9.** Write an account of the graduate's contest with the world from the graduate's perspective.

*Fred Dickenson*

# How to Iron a Telephone Book (1959)

*I*f you have been putting off ironing your telephone book, you need no longer hesitate. I can tell you how it's done. I recently ironed the Manhattan Directory—all eighteen hundred and thirty-six pages. This stimulating adventure had its beginning when our electric dishwasher accidentally turned itself on—a little caprice caused, we later found out, by a short in some inscrutable automatic control. Nobody was home except our beagle, Lucky. There were no dishes or soap in the machine, but these details are really irrelevant. What *is* important is that the top was up. Dishwashers are not supposed to turn themselves on, in the first place, and, in the second place, there are all sorts of safety devices that shut them off when the cover is raised, but apparently a short circuit takes care of this safeguard nonsense easily.

We live in Chappaqua, thirty-two miles north of New York City. My wife was at the supermarket, the children were in school, and I was at my office, in New York, when our dishwasher started automatically flooding the kitchen. When my wife returned home and opened the kitchen door, she was met by a cloud of steam and by the beagle, who, although slightly parboiled, was still able to fly. He set a new dash record from kitchen door to driveway, and vanished under our car.

My wife turned off the machine and settled down at the telephone, first calling the repairman, who said that the dishwasher could not possibly have turned itself on by accident. Then she called me. "The kitchen looks like one of those Kentucky caves" was the picturesque way she put it. "Water is dripping from the ceiling. I never saw so much water in my life. I found a double boiler full of water inside a closed cabinet."

By the time I got home that night, the paper on the kitchen walls and ceiling had dried, leaving only a faint fragrance of old paste, and everything else had been emptied or mopped up. The only important damage was to our precious new 1958–59 Manhattan Telephone Directory. Both the Manhattan and the Westchester telephone books, which nestle on a shelf near the dishwasher (it now sullenly refused to do *anything*), were sopping. I must explain that, as resident of Chappaqua, we are entitled only to the Westchester County book. This, I knew, we could have replaced by simply calling the phone company. But a Manhattan book can only be obtained free in the suburbs by borrowing it from one's own office in the city when nobody is looking, and hauling it all the way home on the train. It had taken me two years to find the exact moment when this nervy maneuver could be executed. And now, within a few weeks, the fruit of my endeavors was a sodden mass.

"Maybe it will dry out by itself," I said hopefully the next morning. "We'll leave it as it is."

A week later, the book had swollen to almost twice its normal size and was threatening to force the phone itself off the shelf. A quick flip—or flop—through the pages showed them to be as wet as ever.

"We'll dry it in the oven," my wife said brightly. "If you can make bricks that way, you certainly ought to be able to dry a telephone book. I'd say about two hundred and fifty degrees, so it won't get too well done on the outside."

The oven was turned on, and we slipped the book in tenderly. Five hours later, you still couldn't get a fork into it. It steamed merrily but damply, and now we were alarmed to notice that it was beginning to wrinkle. We took it out and set it on a window sill to cool.

"There's only one thing to do," my wife said. "We've got to iron it. How many pages are there?"

I looked. "One thousand eight hundred and thirty-six."

She made a rapid calculation. We have three teen-age daughters. The beagle, of course, could not be counted upon. "That means three hundred and sixty-seven pages each," she said.

What we did not realize was that teen-age daughters cannot be counted upon, either, especially when it comes to ironing telephone books. They simply do not seem to grasp the challenge. When they came home from school, my wife told them gaily, "Tonight we are all going to take turns ironing the telephone book!"

They regarded her steadily, with that terrible candor of the teenager, and asked for a repeat. When the full import of her plan struck home, the response was loud and negative—so negative, in fact, that I, in disgust, said I would do the entire job, all by myself. I expected a chorus of protests to greet this suggestion. I was wrong. Ironing is woman's work, but, for some reason, all the ladies in my family seemed to take the attitude that ironing a telephone book is a masculine undertaking, like carpentry or car washing.

Pioneering this little-known field, I believe I picked up a few pointers that should be passed on to those who may come after. First of all, when you are ironing a telephone book the size of the Manhattan Directory, it is important that you be properly dressed. I chose sneakers, tennis socks, brown chino trousers, and a T shirt. Although I ironed in the evenings, I found that even a cool basement laundry room heats up long before you have completed a hundred pages, and I was grateful that I had had the foresight to select an outfit that provided maximum comfort and freedom of movement.

The heat dial of the iron should be set for Cotton. Rayon is not hot enough, and Linen is apt to scorch around the edges, particularly if you get to watching for lady chiropractors, Arabian delicatessens, and the like.

Begin at the back. For some reason, it helps to think of yourself as on page 1836, rather than page 1. I will never again see a Manhattan Directory without recalling the ZzzyZzy Ztamp Ztudioz Co., the last entry in the book, and the first your iron touches under these circumstances.

You may sit down while ironing, but only during the earlier stages. I used my workbench stool for a while, but I soon found that as the ironed pages grew higher, it was increasingly difficult to exert sufficient downward pressure to smooth out the more stubborn wrinkles.

Dismiss from your mind any timesaving ideas that may occur to you. It is impossible to iron a wet telephone book quickly and still maintain a high standard of workmanship. There is no use trying to iron more than one page at a time. Purely in the interests of science, and not because of any weakening in my resolve, I tried this short cut as early as the "T"s, taking first four pages, then three, and finally settling for two, but the bottom one will not dry. (In the course of this experiment, I kept the iron on one page too long, and was warned just in time by a tiny spiral of smoke. A half column of Thompsons in my book are now the color of toast.)

And don't think you can speed things up by holding the wet pages in one hand and flipping them down one by one, as needed. It won't work. The moisture causes the pages to stick together, and they have to be separated, with both hands, which means, of course, that you have to put the iron down nine hundred and eighteen times.

For one wild moment, along about the mid-"O"s, I considered using the mangle (*"They laughed when I sat down at the mangle, but . . ."*), and I did take a brief respite to study the machine. You operate a mangle with your knees, of course, and this would have been a welcome change, for my hand had begun to cramp around the handle of the iron. However, it was obvious that I would have to hold the book, feed in one page at a time, and release the roller at precisely the right instant. The danger of tearing the pages was too great, and I went back to hand labor, comforting myself with the thought that the best places always advertise that type of work.

Since there are no short cuts to success in this rather special field, I suggest that you allow at least two nights for the job. I ended my first ironing session around 2 A.M. The next evening was almost a complete loss. Just as I was starting on the "K"s, some friends asked us over, and my wife was too embarrassed—as well she might have been—to say that we couldn't go because I was down in the cellar ironing the telephone book. The upshot was that I had to change out of my ironing costume and play games for the rest of the evening. I finally finished the job at one-fifteen the following night.

Ironing the Manhattan Directory is not mentally stimulating. From time to time, my wife would come down to see how I was doing, or one of the children would call down the stairs to ask me for information about ancient Egyptian civilization. The dog also came to visit, nervously sniffing the unusual mixture of steam, paper, and ink. But even with occasional visitors the hours do not fly by, and I suggest that you try to think of yourself as on a scenic tour of the glittering metropolis. On my magic iron, I glided through the West Side Zuckermans, passed the Yale Club and the Woolworth Bldg., and appreciated for the first time the sprawling bureaucracy of the United States Government—"WEATHER BUR." through "ADVISORY GROUP ON ELECTRON TUBES." There was the United Nations (Yugoslavia through Afghanistan), Trinity Church, the Stork Club, the Smiths (seven and a half pages of them), and the Original Crispy Pizza Crust Co. My iron smoothed the furrowed brows of Merrill Lynch Pierce Fenner & Smith, paused at Luchow's, pressed on to the Joneses (only four pages of them), and dropped into El Morocco for a nightcap. The whole vast panorama of Manhattan (smelling only slightly of hot paper) passed before me, until finally I ironed the last wrinkle from page 1— "Emergency Calls."

A cautionary note: When ironing a telephone book, you will find that several beers not only enhance the tour but also diminish the importance of any little burns or muscular aches picked up along the way. The quantity of beer consumed must be carefully regulated. I erred on the side of generosity the first evening, and by the time I reached the "Mc"s, I noticed that the quality of my work had deteriorated. In fact, I had to sprinkle the "McD"s and iron them all over again.

## Questions for Rereading, Discussing, Connecting, and Writing

### Rereading

1. As you look at the title of this selection, what is your first reaction? Does this reaction change as you read the text?

2. Who do you take to be the "you" addressed by this text? How does this form of address contribute to your reading?

3. The author includes a number of direct quotations. What effect do they achieve? In what ways would the text change if these quotations were paraphrased?

4. This selection contains a number of references to New York City. What effect do these have on your reading?

### Discussing

5. How would you describe the author's attitude toward the topic of ironing telephone books? Discuss your view with others.

6. This selection can be described as a narrative account. Which details strike you as realistic and which seem unrealistic? What does this combination contribute to the narrative?

7. What is the effect of the concluding cautionary note? Propose other possible endings for this selection.

### Connecting

8. Self-help books are among the most popular in the United States, as a look at the list of best-sellers will verify. If you have not read a self-help book previously, look at one and compare it with this selection. In particular, consider the voice in which the two are written.

9. Look at this selection in relation to all the others included in this chapter. Which would you identify as closest in purpose or aim?

Writing

**10.** Imagine that you are a graphic artist assigned to produce copy to accompany this text. Write a description of what you would create.

**11.** As Dickenson illustrates, one way to achieve a comic effect is to treat a ridiculous topic seriously. Identify a topic as silly as ironing telephone books and write an essay in which you treat it seriously.

**12.** Before it was published, this selection was reviewed by an editor. Write the letter the editor might have sent to Dickenson in response to "How to Iron a Telephone Book."

*Gore Vidal*

# *Drugs* (1970)

*I*t is possible to stop most drug addiction in the United States within a very short time. Simply make all drugs available and sell them at cost. Label each drug with a precise description of what effect—good and bad—the drug will have on the taker. This will require heroic honesty. Don't say that marijuana is addictive or dangerous when it is neither, as millions of people know—unlike "speed," which kills most unpleasantly, or heroin, which is addictive and difficult to kick.

For the record, I have tried—once—almost every drug and liked none, disproving the popular Fu Manchu theory that a single sniff of opium will enslave the mind. Nevertheless many drugs are bad for certain people to take and they should be told why in a sensible way.

Along with exhortation and warning, it might be good for our citizens to recall (or learn for the first time) that the United States was the creation of men who believed that each man has the right to do what he wants with his own life as long as he does not interfere with his neighbor's pursuit of happiness (that his neighbor's idea of happiness is persecuting others does confuse matters a bit).

This is a startling notion to the current generation of Americans. They reflect a system of public education which has made the Bill of Rights, literally, unacceptable to a majority of high school graduates (see the annual Purdue reports) who now form the "silent majority"—a phrase which that underestimated wit Richard Nixon took from Homer who used it to describe the dead.

Now one can hear the warning rumble begin: if everyone is allowed to take drugs everyone will and the GNP will decrease, the Commies will stop us from making everyone free, and we shall end up a race of Zombies, passively murmuring "groovie" to one another. Alarming thought. Yet it seems most unlikely that any reasonably sane person will become a drug addict if he knows in advance what addiction is going to be like.

Is everyone reasonably sane? No. Some people will always

become drug addicts just as some people will always become alcoholics, and it is just too bad. Every man, however, has the power (and should have the legal right) to kill himself if he chooses. But since most men don't, they won't be mainliners either. Nevertheless, forbidding people things they like or think they might enjoy only makes them want those things all the more. This psychological insight is, for some mysterious reason, perennially denied our governors.

It is a lucky thing for the American moralist that our country has always existed in a kind of time-vacuum: we have no public memory of anything that happened before last Tuesday. No one in Washington today recalls what happened during the years alcohol was forbidden to the people by a Congress that thought it had a divine mission to stamp out Demon Rum—launching, in the process, the greatest crime wave in the country's history, causing thousands of deaths from bad alcohol, and creating a general (and persisting) contempt among the citizenry for the laws of the United States.

The same thing is happening today. But the government has learned nothing from past attempts at prohibition, not to mention repression.

Last year when the supply of Mexican marijuana was slightly curtailed by the Feds, the pushers got the kids hooked on heroin and deaths increased dramatically, particularly in New York. Whose fault? Evil men like the Mafiosi? Permissive Dr. Spock? Wild-eyed Dr. Leary? No.

The Government of the United States was responsible for those deaths. The bureaucratic machine has a vested interest in playing cops and robbers. Both the Bureau of Narcotics and the Mafia want strong laws against the sale and use of drugs because if drugs are sold at cost there would be no money in it for anyone.

If there was no money in it for the Mafia, there would be no friendly playground pushers, and addicts would not commit crimes to pay for the next fix. Finally, if there was no money in it, the Bureau of Narcotics would wither away, something they are not about to do without a struggle.

Will anything sensible be done? Of course not. The American people are as devoted to the idea of sin and its punishment as they are to making money—and fighting drugs is nearly as big a business as pushing them. Since the combination of sin and money is irresistible (particularly to the professional politician), the situation will only grow worse.

## Questions for Rereading, Discussing, Connecting, and Writing

### REREADING

**1.** Although this selection is not very old, it contains slang terms and specific references that date it. As you read, note terms that strike you as old-fashioned or confusing. Which of Vidal's references remain entirely obscure to you? How do these influence your recognition of this selection?

**2.** As you read, notice the attitude Vidal expresses toward politicians and the general public. How would you describe his attitude? Is it significant that Vidal has run (unsuccessfully) for public office?

**3.** Vidal begins this selection with a direct assertion. As you read, consider the extent to which he convinces you. What is the effect of the final paragraph?

### DISCUSSING

**4.** A good argument anticipates the opposition's views. Consider the extent to which Vidal has anticipated what the opposition might say about his proposal. Do you find any inadequacies in his arguments? Does he fail to address any opposing viewpoints?

**5.** Vidal bases much of his argument on the law's failure to prohibit alcohol in the United States. How far does the analogy between drugs and alcohol extend? Do you see any problems with basing an argument on this view?

### CONNECTING

**6.** Like Jonathan Swift (p. 296), Vidal proposes a solution for a social problem. What similarities and differences do you see in the way these two writers treat their subjects?

**7.** Vidal's use of slang and his reference to specific people give this selection a timely (as opposed to timeless) quality. What timeless features do you see in this selection? How does it compare with timeless selections such as the Igbo tale (p. 305), the Declaration of Independence (p. 251), and the prophecy of Amos (p. 239)?

**8.** Like Syfers (p. 330), Vidal proposes social conditions quite different from those we now know. Consider the similarities and differences in what Syfers and Vidal propose.

WRITING

**9.** A proposal like Vidal's invites rejoinder. Write a response from the opposite point of view, pointing to the weaknesses and potential problems in his proposal. If it helps you focus your thinking, you might imagine that you are writing a newspaper editorial.

**10.** Identify a current social problem and write a proposal for solving it, using "Drugs" as a model.

**11.** Vidal clearly believes in the freedom of the individual. Write an essay in which you explore the implications of this belief for a current controversial issue such as gun control or abortion.

## Judy Syfers

# I Want A Wife (1971)

*I* belong to that classification of people known as wives. I am A Wife. And, not altogether incidentally, I am a mother.

Not too long ago a male friend of mine appeared on the scene fresh from a recent divorce. He had one child, who is, of course, with his ex-wife. He is obviously looking for another wife. As I thought about him while I was ironing one evening, it suddenly occurred to me that I, too, would like to have a wife. Why do I want a wife?

I would like to go back to school so that I can become economically independent, support myself, and, if need be, support those dependent upon me. I want a wife who will work and send me to school. And while I am going to school I want a wife to take care of my children. I want a wife to keep track of the children's doctor and dentist appointments. And to keep track of mine, too. I want a wife to make sure my children eat properly and are kept clean. I want a wife who will wash the children's clothes and keep them mended. I want a wife who is a good nurturant attendant to my children, who arranges for their schooling, makes sure that they have an adequate social life with their peers, takes them to the park, the zoo, etc. I want a wife who takes care of the children when they are sick, a wife who arranges to be around when the children need special care, because, of course, I cannot miss classes at school. My wife must arrange to lose time at work and not lose the job. It may mean a small cut in my wife's income from time to time, but I guess I can tolerate that. Needless to say, my wife will arrange and pay for the care of the children while my wife is working.

I want a wife who will take care of *my* physical needs. I want a wife who will keep my house clean. A wife who will pick up after me. I want a wife who will keep my clothes clean, ironed, mended, replaced when need be, and who will see to it that my personal things are kept in their proper place so that I can find what I need the minute I need it. I want a wife who cooks the meals, a wife who is a *good* cook. I want a wife who will plan the menus, do the necessary grocery shopping, prepare the meals, serve them pleasantly, and then do the cleaning up while I do my studying. I want a wife who will care for me when I am sick and sympathize with my pain and loss of time from school. I want a wife to go along when our family takes a vacation so that someone can continue to care for me and my children when I need a rest and change of scene.

I want a wife who will not bother me with rambling complaints about a wife's duties. But I want a wife who will listen to me when I feel the need to explain a rather difficult point I have come across in my course of studies. And I want a wife who will type my papers for me when I have written them.

I want a wife who will take care of the details of my social life. When my wife and I are invited out by my friends, I want a wife who will take care of the babysitting arrangements. When I meet people at school that I like and want to entertain, I want a wife who will have the house clean, will prepare a special meal, serve it to me and my friends, and not interrupt when I talk about the things that interest me and my friends. I want a wife who will have arranged that the children are fed and ready for bed before my guests arrive so that the children do not bother us. I want a wife who takes care of the needs of my guests so that they feel comfortable, who makes sure that they have an ashtray, that they are passed the hors d'oeuvres, that they are offered a second helping of the food, that their wine glasses are replenished when necessary, that their coffee is served to them as they like it. And I want a wife who knows that sometimes I need a night out by myself.

I want a wife who is sensitive to my sexual needs, a wife who makes love passionately and eagerly when I feel like it, a wife who makes sure that I am satisfied. And, of course, I want a wife who will not demand sexual attention when I am not in the mood for it. I want a wife who assumes the complete responsibility for birth control, because I do not want more children. I want a wife who will remain sexually faithful to me so that I do not have to clutter up my intellectual life with jealousies. And I want a wife who understands that *my* sexual needs may entail more than strict adherence to monogamy. I must, after all, be able to relate to people as fully as possible.

If, by chance, I find another person more suitable as a wife than the wife I already have, I want the liberty to replace my present wife with another one. Naturally I will expect a fresh, new life; my wife will take the children and be solely responsible for them so that I am left free.

When I am through with school and have a job, I want my wife to quit working and remain at home so that my wife can more fully and completely take care of a wife's duties.

My God, who *wouldn't* want a wife?

## Questions for Rereading, Discussing, Connecting, and Writing

### Rereading

**1.** It is possible to tell something about the intended audience for a given selection by considering the assumptions it makes. As you read Syfers' work, notice what she assumes about her readers and speculate on the audience for which she wrote.

**2.** Although dictionary definitions tell us something about the meaning of words, we each have our own definitions of words based on our experience. The word "dog," for example, will mean warm, loving, family pet for someone who lived with an even-tempered Golden Retriever while it will mean fierce, sharp-toothed attacker to someone who has been bitten by a Pit Bull Terrier. What definition of the word "wife" would you ascribe to Syfers?

**3.** Trying to guess an author's intentions is never a reliable practice, and sometimes authors are themselves unclear about why they have written something. With that proviso, speculate on what Syfers intended to accomplish by writing this essay.

### Discussing

**4.** Because each of us has different experiences, the definitions we develop often seem, when viewed by another, to be missing something. Discuss what, if anything, is missing from Syfers' definition of the word "wife."

**5.** Meanings of words are shaped by cultural context as well as individual experience. To an Eskimo who depends on his dog team for transportation, the word "dog" has a different meaning than it does for a city dweller who has a dog for companionship. What evidence do you find to support the claim that Syfers has been shaped by her culture? You might approach this issue by thinking about how a writer from India or Iran might define "wife."

**6.** Most essays demonstrate a progression in that they move from one point to another. Describe the progression of Syfers' essay. How does the final paragraph differ from early ones? What, for example, is the effect of the absence of gendered pronouns after the first two paragraphs?

## Connecting

**7.** Syfers makes what could be described as a "modest proposal" in declaring that she would like a wife. What similarities and differences do you see as you compare this essay with Swift's (p. 296)?

**8.** Although they were written over 100 years apart, Syfers' essay deals with some of the same questions raised by Sojourner Truth (p. 259). What differences do you see in the issues raised and in the way these two women address the issues?

**9.** Many of the selections in this chapter play with language by saying one thing when they mean another. What similarities do you find between this and other selections in this chapter with regard to this kind of play?

## Writing

**10.** After considering what Syfers has omitted from her definition of wife, write an essay that incorporates these omissions into an opposing perspective and write an essay titled "I Don't Want a Wife."

**11.** Syfers defines wife by describing some of the things a person in this role does. Write an essay in which you define a term such as "student," "mother," or "teacher" in similar fashion.

**12.** Select a topic about which you have strong feelings. It may be a topic dealing with roles commonly assigned to men or women or something entirely different. Write an opinion piece in which you avoid all use of gendered pronouns.

*Mal Inc.*

# Cartoon (1987)

*Questions for Rereading, Discussing, Connecting, and Writing*

### Rereading

1. Both the written text and the position of the two figures suggest that this cartoon is one frame in a continuing series of actions. As you look at the cartoon, imagine the words and actions that occur on either side of it.

2. As you consider the written text of this cartoon, think about political events of 1987 and how these events contribute to making this cartoon humorous.

### Discussing

3. The humor of this cartoon hinges on seeing obfuscation or lack of clarity as something to be avoided in arguments. Discuss whether clarity is always a virtue in arguments. Are there occasions when it is better to be less than clear?

4. Cartoonists draw on both graphic and verbal resources. Consider how the two work together here. What, for example, would be the effect of removing the nose-to-nose figures? What might be substituted for them?

## Connecting

5. Simplicity of design characterizes this cartoon with its plain block-lettered text and unadorned figures. How is the simplicity of this cartoon similar to and different from the simplicity of Magritte's "Key of Dreams" (p. 315)?

6. This cartoon portrays an argument. Selections such as Mills "The Subjection of Women" (p. 262) and the Konica ad (p. 374) also portray arguments. In what ways do these various arguments resemble one another?

## Writing

7. Write an essay in which you explore ways that cartoons can be described as art.

8. Write an essay in which you explain the cartoonist's attitude toward his subject. Would you describe the artist as sympathetic, mocking, what?

# Seven

# Worlds of Language

We use language for many purposes—to delight, to inform, to persuade, to demonstrate. Underlying all of these purposes is the common aim of communication. Language enables us to share our view of the world with others, to understand the world view of persons very different from ourselves. At the mention of "language," our first thoughts often take us to the written word, but, as this book illustrates, language also takes graphic form. Earlier chapters have demonstrated how forms as different as cave paintings, the earliest known human texts, and contemporary cartoons function to communicate meaning. The selections in this chapter enlarge upon this definition to include other forms of language.

A gold buckle, for example, tells us about the Angles and Saxons who invaded the British Isles between AD 500 and 800. Advertisements from various periods in history communicate about the culture that produced them as well as the products they display. Architecture from the medieval period contains messages about the people who designed and constructed it, along with information about a period of time distant from our own. Inscriptions, musical scores, and dance notation likewise function as languages because they communicate meanings about persons and activities.

Many forms of language included here require precision from the composer, both in writing and reading. A single wrong symbol or a single misreading in a wiring diagram or a house plan or a computer program can render the whole text useless. The precision required by such languages resembles the precision of *diction* or word choice necessary to good writing. When we compose in writing we search carefully for exactly the "right" word, knowing the immense difference between a close approximation and the precise one. Consider, for example, the effect of John Updike's choice of "the illustrative itch" for his title. How does it compare to alternatives such as "the illustrative desire" or "the illustrative urge?"

All languages represent specialized codes. Our alphabet is as much a code as is musical notation. Codes require the reader not only to decode the symbols but to bring enough meaning to the code to make sense of it. It is not enough, for example, to know that the black dot on the second space of the treble musical staff represents the note A; one must also know something about the relationship of A to other notes and have some idea of how to produce an A with voice or instrument. *Conventions* or agreed-upon systems of representation aid our use of codes. Musicians the world over know that the dot on the second space of the treble staff always represents A, not D or G. Conventions likewise play an important role in writing. Readers and writers can communicate effectively as long as both follow conventions of spelling, punctuation, and usage. Consider, for example, the effect if Updike had written "words become plant and expressive" rather than "words become pliant and expressive."

A number of the languages included here contain directives for action. Although they differ in many ways, dance notation, computer programs, musical scores, and advertisements tell readers to do something. The prescribed activity ranges from buying a product to performing an intricate set of body movements, but the function remains the same—these languages imply action for the reader. In a larger sense, all languages are designed to move the reader in some way. As writers, for example, we seek to induce actions even if only to make the reader smile or nod in agreement.

In this chapter, the reader will find many types of language, each employing its own precise code and following its own conventions. Like all languages, the ones included here imply action as they communicate. By working with these languages and reading reflections (such as Updike's and Ruskin's) upon them, we can become more sensitive to the language of our own writing.

# *Trajan Inscription* (2nd Century)

*Questions for Rereading,
Discussing, Connecting, and Writing*

### Rereading

**1.** Without a knowledge of Latin, the words of the Trajan inscription are indecipherable; but as works of sculpture, there is much to see in them. Note as you consider these letters and words (which are each about four and one-half inches high) the varying form of a single letter—A, for example—and the difference between our alphabet today and these inscriptions of the second century.

**2.** The inscription begins, "The senate and the people of Rome to the Imperial Caesar . . . " and enumerates Caesar's titles and years in office. Does the character of the words and letters—the way they *look*—indicate this subject? How does the inscription's presentation indicate the qualities of the subject matter?

## Discussing

**3.** One historian—Donald Anderson—calls the Trajan inscription "the most celebrated piece of writing in the history of written language." Speculate on Anderson's reason for this opinion and dispute his opinion with your own nomination for "the most celebrated piece of writing in the history of written language."

**4.** This inscription was outdoors for the public to see. What examples of "outdoor writing" can you cite—and what are their uses? Does a common thread exist in them that could include the power behind the Trajan inscription?

## Connecting

**5.** Find other written works in this book that you think could have been or should be inscribed in stone. Give your reasons why *permanence* can be a positive outcome of technology.

**6.** Compare the Trajan inscription with the Sutton Hoo gold buckle (p. 341) and speculate on the differences between the two. How can we then draw inferences about the culture and civilization out of which these two emerged?

## Writing

**7.** The process of inscribing in stone has three parts—the writing *on* the stone, the cutting of the stone, and the painting of the letters. Describe the process by which *we* put words on paper, remembering such mechanical elements as the production of the pen and ink and paper.

**8.** No one knows who the scribe of this famous inscription was. Tell his or her story.

**9.** If you could have 25 words or less inscribed in stone, what would they be, where would they be, and why?

## Sutton Hoo Excavation
# Gold Buckle (A.D. C400)

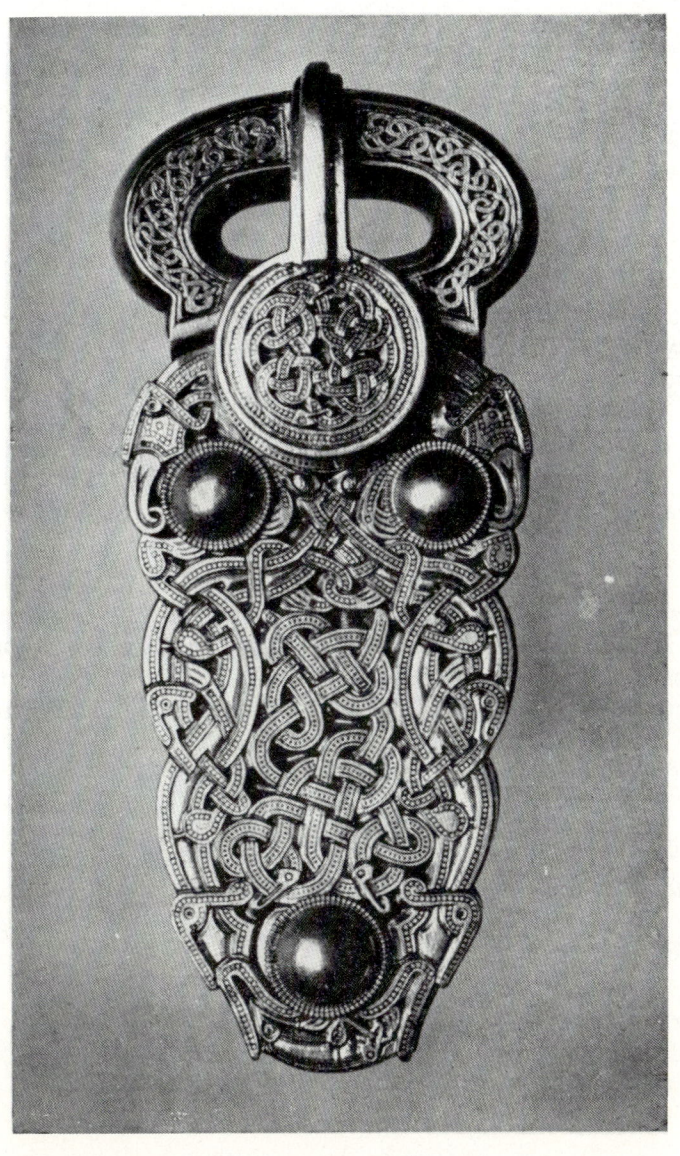

## Questions for Rereading, Discussing, Connecting, and Writing

### REREADING

1. This belt buckle was made by a goldsmith of the Angles and Saxons, Germanic groups who invaded the British Isles between AD 200 and 600. It was found in a burial chamber located in what is now southern England. Read this piece as a text from the past to determine what it can tell you about the culture from which it comes.

2. There are a number of intricate designs on this buckle. Try "reading" one of the designs and then shift to another portion of the buckle and do the same thing. What is the effect of these various designs? How would the buckle be changed if, say, the three smooth circular pieces were removed?

### DISCUSSING

3. This buckle is actually 5 inches long and it weighs 14 ounces. What kind of person might have worn such a buckle? How might it have been worn and on what occasions?

4. At the same time that it is an object of art, this buckle also serves a function. It unites with a belt to hold clothing in place. Discuss the relationship between art and function or use. What role do museums play in this relationship?

5. Some archaeologists believe that objects such as this buckle should be considered in and of themselves, as artifacts of a culture we can never fully know or understand. Other archaeologists believe that it is important to try to understand the psychological and social dimensions of the cultures from which such objects come. Consider both points of view using this buckle as a case in point.

### CONNECTING

6. This buckle was one of 26 pieces of gold jewelry found in the Sutton Hoo excavation. Speculate on what other kinds of jewelry might have been included in this collection.

7. Compare this belt buckle with others you have seen. How is it similar to and different from buckles you have worn or seen on others? How does it compare with other types of contemporary jewelry?

**8.** Unlike art such as Degas' "The Dancing Class" (p. 197) or the cave painting (p. 10), this buckle does not portray action directly. At the same time it is not exactly a static piece. Explore the "action" of this buckle and compare it with the action of other forms of art.

WRITING

**9.** Imagine that you have just found this buckle and you want to share your find with a distant friend. Write a description detailed enough to help your friend "see" the buckle.

**10.** It is frequently claimed that art imitates nature. Write an essay in which you explore the ways this buckle imitates nature.

**11.** Write the narrative of this buckle. Include details of its production, its use by its owner(s), and explain how it came to be included in the burial chamber where it was found.

## Chartres Cathedral
# *Nave* (1194)

# Questions for Rereading, Discussing, Connecting, and Writing

## Rereading

1. This photograph is a two-dimensional representation of a three-dimensional space. Try to read the third dimension into the photograph. You might begin by imagining yourself standing at various points in the structure.

2. Chartres Cathedral represents the Gothic style of architecture. What differences do you notice between this structure and buildings constructed in the United States during the past 20 years?

3. Buildings, like writing, frequently make statements. As you look at this cathedral, consider what statement it makes. Can you put this statement into words?

## Discussing

4. This cathedral was built nearly 800 years ago without the aid of modern machinery. The walls are over 100 feet tall, and the ceiling extends across 75 feet. Discuss the kinds of logistical problems and financial investments required for such a building at such a time. Then speculate on the motivations for undertaking such an effort.

5. The architects of Chartres, like most architects of the time, were guided by religious leaders whose ecclesiastical authority included pronouncements on beauty, harmony, and fitness in architecture. Speculate on the kinds of authorities who guide today's architects.

6. The dimensions of this building extend well beyond human scale. Discuss how humans are likely to feel when standing in a building nearly 20 times taller than they. Then speculate on why this scale was employed.

## Connecting

7. Gothic architecture originated in France as part of a Catholic bishop's effort to unite religious and political power in symbolic terms. Think about a modern building you have seen and speculate on the motivations that lie behind it.

## Writing

8. Like paintings or essays or photographs, buildings make statements. Write a first-person essay in the voice of the cathedral itself in which you explain the statement made by this cathedral.

**9.** Churches and cathedrals continue to be built today. Write an essay in which you argue for or against the proposition that a replica of Chartres should be constructed in the United States today.

**10.** Imagine that you are a religious leader of the twelfth century charged with instructing the architects of a cathedral. Write a letter explaining what they are to do.

## Cartoon

# "Join, or Die" (1754)

*Questions for Rereading, Discussing, Connecting, and Writing*

### REREADING

**1.** "Join, or Die," the first known American cartoon, appeared in Benjamin Franklin's *Pennsylvania Gazette* in response to the Albany Congress, a conference which advocated the union of the 13 North American colonies. As you read this text, speculate on why Franklin chose these media to make his point.

**2.** Although the drawing and text are very simple, the reader must bring a fair amount of information to make meaning with this cartoon. Enumerate what one needs to know to "read" the cartoon. What, if anything, do you find you still need to know?

**3.** The rattlesnake was frequently used as a symbol by the colonies. In what ways does this seem an especially appropriate symbol?

### DISCUSSING

**4.** Discuss the effect of the title, beginning with the imperative "join." Generate alternative titles for the cartoon and discuss how each would change its meaning slightly.

**5.** Discuss the effectiveness of portraying the colonies as unconnected parts of a snake's body. What metaphorical meanings does this portrayal take on? In what other ways might the same concept be portrayed?

**6.** Considering its purpose—to establish a union among the North American colonies—the Albany Congress was a failure. In a broader sense, however, it can be considered a success because it laid the groundwork for the later union of the colonies. Discuss alternative meanings of "success" and "failure" as exemplified by the Albany Congress.

CONNECTING

**7.** Cartoons are a regular part of political news. Look at a contemporary political cartoon and compare it with this one. What do you notice as you look at the two?

**8.** In using a cartoon, Franklin introduced a new language. The advent of the computer has also introduced a new language. What, in your view, does each of these languages add to contemporary life? How are their contributions similar and different?

**9.** Political statements can take many forms. Compare the political statements made by Sojourner Truth (p. 259) and the Declaration of Independence (p. 251) with the statement made by this cartoon.

WRITING

**10.** This cartoon expresses a strong opinion about the concept of union. Write an essay in which you argue on behalf of the same point.

**11.** After looking at this and several other political cartoons, write an essay in which you explore the language of cartoons. What effects does the combination of pictures and words enable you to achieve? What limitations do the abbreviations of cartoons impose?

### Wolfgang Amadeus Mozart

# 12 Variationen (1772)

## Questions for Rereading, Discussing, Connecting, and Writing

### Rereading

1. Music may be a language you know well or it may be an entirely unfamiliar system. In either event, look closely at the various symbols in this text and try to describe their function. What, for example, is the relationship of the circles on the five-line staff to the lines extending from some of the dots?

2. Whether or not you can read music, consider what an individual would need to know in order to read this text.

### Discussing

3. Mozart has a reputation as an unusual composer. Frequently, he produced finished copies of whole scores at a single sitting. Discuss your composing in writing in light of Mozart's composing in music.

4. Music is often described as an international language. In what ways does this text confirm/disconfirm that statement? (As you probably know, Mozart did not speak English.)

5. Mozart began composing music when he was very young. He wrote his first compositions when he was less than eight years old. Consider the significance of this very early development in composing. Do you know anyone who began written composition at a very early age?

### Connecting

6. This is a copy of what Mozart actually wrote. How is it similar to and different from other musical scores you have seen? If you have never seen a musical score find one to compare with this. What do you notice as you look at the two together? Are all the symbols on the two identical?

7. Even if you have never looked at a musical score before, you have had many experiences with music, and you may know the tune represented by this score—it is commonly known as "Twinkle Twinkle Little Star." Reflect on the similarities and differences between reading this score and your other experiences with music.

8. A musical score is a set of abstract symbols similar to a dance notation (p. 360). How do these two languages compare in terms of the instructions they give the performer?

WRITING

**9.** Most people's experiences with music extend back to early childhood. Think back to your earliest memories of music and then recount in writing what meaning the language of music had for you then.

**10.** Musical scores can be compared to computer programs in that they contain a set of instructions. Write an essay in which you explore the similarities between computer programs and musical scores.

*John Ruskin*

# The Stones of Venice (1853)

## SECOND, OR GOTHIC, PERIOD.

### CHAPTER VI.

### THE NATURE OF GOTHIC.

§ I. If the reader will look back to the division of our subject which was made in the first chapter of the first volume, he will find that we are now about to enter upon the examination of that school of Venetian architecture which forms an intermediate step between the Byzantine and Gothic forms; but which I find may be conveniently considered in its connexion with the latter style. In order that we may discern the tendency of each step of this change, it will be wise in the outset to endeavor to form some general idea of its final result. We know already what the Byzantine architecture is from which the transition was made, but we ought to know something of the Gothic architecture into which it led. I shall endeavor therefore to give the reader in this chapter an idea, at once broad and definite, of the true nature of *Gothic* architecture, properly so called; not of that of Venice only, but of universal Gothic: for it will be one of the most interesting parts of our subsequent inquiry, to find out how far Venetian architecture reached the universal or perfect type of Gothic, and how far it either fell short of it, or assumed foreign and independent forms.

§ II. The principal difficulty in doing this arises from the fact that every building of the Gothic period differs in some important respect from every other; and many include features which, if they occurred in other buildings, would not be considered Gothic at all; so that all we have to reason upon is merely, if I may be allowed so to express it, a greater or less degree of *Gothicness* in each building we examine. And it is this Gothicness,—the character which, according as it is found more or less in a building, makes it more or less Gothic,—of which I want to define the nature; and I feel the same kind of difficulty in doing so which would be encountered by any one who undertook to explain, for instance, the nature of Redness, without any actual red thing to point to, but only orange and purple things. Suppose he had only a piece of heather and a dead oak-leaf to do it with. He might say, the color which is mixed with the yellow in this oak-leaf, and with the blue in this heather, would be red, if you had it separate; but it would be difficult, nevertheless, to make the abstraction perfectly intelligible: and it is so in a far greater degree to make the abstraction of the Gothic character intelligible, because that character itself is made up of many mingled ideas, and can consist only in their union. That is to say, pointed arches do not constitute Gothic, nor vaulted roofs, nor flying buttresses, nor grotesque sculptures; but all or some of these things, and many other things with them, when they come together so as to have life.

§ III. Observe also, that, in the definition proposed, I shall only endeavor to analyze the idea which I suppose already to exist in the reader's mind. We all have some notion, most of us a very determined one, of the meaning of the term Gothic; but I know that many persons have this idea in their minds without being able to define it: that is to say, understanding generally that Westminster Abbey is Gothic, and St. Paul's is not, that Strasburg Cathedral is Gothic, and St. Peter's is not, they have, nevertheless, no clear notion of what it is that they recognize in the one or miss in the other, such as would enable them to say how far the work at Westminster or Strasburg is good and pure of its kind: still less to say of any nondescript building, like St. James's Palace or Windsor Castle, how much right Gothic element there is in it, and how much wanting. And I believe this inquiry to be a pleasant and profitable one; and that there will be found something more than usually interesting in tracing out this grey, shadowy, many-pinnacled image of the Gothic spirit within us; and discerning what fellowship there is between it and our Northern hearts. And if, at any point of the inquiry, I should interfere with any of the reader's previously formed conceptions, and use the term Gothic in any sense which he would not willingly attach to it, I do not ask him to accept, but only to examine and understand, my interpretation, as necessary to the intelligibility of what follows in the rest of the work.

§ IV.  We have, then, the Gothic character submitted to our analysis, just as the rough mineral is submitted to that of the chemist, entangled with many other foreign substances, itself perhaps in no place pure, or ever to be obtained or seen in purity for more than an instant; but nevertheless a thing of definite and separate nature, however inextricable or confused in appearance. Now observe: the chemist defines his mineral by two separate kinds of character; one external, its crystalline form, hardness, lustre, &c.; the other internal, the proportions and nature of its constituent atoms. Exactly in the same manner, we shall find that Gothic architecture has external forms, and internal elements. Its elements are certain mental tendencies of the builders, legibly expressed in it; as fancifulness, love of variety, love of richness; and such others. Its external forms are pointed arches, vaulted roofs, &c. And unless both the elements and the forms are there, we have no right to call the style Gothic. It is not enough that it has the Form, if it have not also the power and life. It is not enough that it has the Power, if it have not the form. We must therefore inquire into each of these characters successively; and determine first, what is the Mental Expression, and secondly, what the Material Form, of Gothic architecture, properly so called.

1st. Mental Power or Expression. What characters, we have to discover, did the Gothic builders love, or instinctively express in their work, as distinguished from all other builders?

§ V.  Let us go back for a moment to our chemistry, and note that, in defining a mineral by its constituent parts, it is not one nor another of them, that can make up the mineral, but the union of all: for instance, it is neither in charcoal, nor in oxygen, nor in lime, that there is the making of chalk, but in the combination of all three in certain measures; they are all found in very different things from chalk, and there is nothing like chalk either in charcoal or in oxygen, but they are nevertheless necessary to its existence.

So in the various mental characters which make up the soul of Gothic. It is not one nor another that produces it; but their union in certain measures. Each one of them is found in many other architectures besides Gothic; but Gothic cannot exist where they are not found, or, at least, where their place is not in some way supplied. Only there is this great difference between the composition of the mineral, and of the architectural style, that if we withdraw one of its elements from the stone, its form is utterly changed, and its existence as such and such a mineral is destroyed; but if we withdraw one of its mental elements from the Gothic style, it is only a little less Gothic than it was before, and the union of two or three of its elements is enough already to bestow a certain Gothicness of character, which gains in intensity as we add the others, and loses as we again withdraw them.

§ VI. I believe, then, that the characteristic or moral elements of Gothic are the following, placed in the order of their importance:

1. Savageness.
2. Changefulness.
3. Naturalism.
4. Grotesqueness.
5. Rigidity.
6. Redundance.

These characters are here expressed as belonging to the building; as belonging to the builder, they would be expressed thus:—1. Savageness, or Rudeness. 2. Love of Change. 3. Love of Nature. 4. Disturbed Imagination. 5. Obstinacy. 6. Generosity. And I repeat, that the withdrawal of any one, or any two, will not at once destroy the Gothic character of a building, but the removal of a majority of them will. I shall proceed to examine them in their order.

*Questions for Rereading, Discussing, Connecting, and Writing*

REREADING

1. This selection is part of a three-volume work in which Ruskin, a British art critic, explores the relationship between architecture and other arts. As you read, speculate on what purposes motivated Ruskin's writing. What purposes does he seem to be trying to achieve here?

2. Ruskin provides a number of cues or directives to readers. He reviews, for example, points made earlier and announces his intention for this section. Consider what these and other directives contribute to your reading of this text.

3. What words or phrases obstruct your making meaning of this text? How can you remove these obstructions?

DISCUSSING

4. Ruskin promises, at the beginning of this selection, to give the reader a broad and definite idea of the true nature of Gothic architecture. Is it possible for writers to give readers both broad and definite ideas?

5. As the conclusion of this selection indicates, Ruskin's strategy for explaining the Gothic is to list and explain its six moral elements. What, in your view, do moral elements have to do with architecture?

6. Listing and explaining characteristics is one way of giving readers a "broad and definite" idea of something. What alternative strategies might a writer employ to help readers understand something as complex as Gothic architecture?

## Connecting

7. Contemporary writers often compose texts about art forms such as painting, music, or architecture. Identify an article you have read, perhaps one about popular music, and compare it with Ruskin's. What do these writers contribute to your understanding of the art they describe?

8. Both Ruskin and Updike (p. 377) focus on the relationship between writing and art. What similarities and differences do you see in their approaches?

9. The nave of Chartres Cathedral (p. 344) is an example of Gothic architecture. What happens when you look at the cathedral in light of Ruskin's work?

## Writing

10. Choose a building with which you are familiar and write an essay in which you explain its architecture in terms of moral elements you think central to it.

11. Ruskin's language reflects its nineteenth-century origins. Write a contemporary "translation" of one section.

12. Consider Ruskin's assertion that it is not one or another quality that identifies Gothic style but the union of all of them. To what extent can you extend this idea of organic unity of qualities to other forms of art? Write an essay in which you explore this concept.

Advertisement

# Hires Rootbeer (1901)

## Questions for Rereading, Discussing, Connecting, and Writing

REREADING

1. Like most advertisements, this one employs both pictures and words. Consider the placement of words in relation to the painting. Why, in your view, are the birds in the two upper corners? What do they add to the whole?

2. Where are your eyes drawn as you look at this advertisement? What relationship do you find between the placement of the product (Hires Rootbeer) and your eye movements?

3. This text captures a single moment in a series of actions. As you look at it, speculate about what happens next and what is on either side of the bench.

DISCUSSING

4. Even if the date of this advertisement were not given, you would probably identify it as not contemporary. Discuss what features enable you to identify it as coming from an earlier period of time.

5. Advertisements usually try to appeal to readers' emotions such as need for acceptance, desire to succeed, sympathy, or uncertainty. Consider the kinds of appeals this advertisement makes. How do pictures and words work together to make these appeals? In what ways might these appeals reflect the time in which the advertisement was produced?

6. Discuss the artist's attitude toward the subject. What features provide you with clues about the artist's attitude?

CONNECTING

7. This advertisement portrays a relationship between a male and female figure. Compare this portrayal of a relationship with the male–female relationship portrayed in Syfers' "I Want A Wife" (p. 330).

8. The painting in this advertisement makes extensive use of lines—the bench, the window, the box around the text at bottom right, and even the body positions of the two people all make extensive use of lines. Compare this use of lines with the lines used in Chartres (p. 344).

9. Both this advertisement and the Steuben ad (p. 365) employ human figures. What similarities and differences do you find in the way these two advertisements use their human figures?

WRITING

**10.** This advertisement makes a persuasive statement on behalf of its product. Write an essay in which you argue that this ad portrays life (even allowing for differences in time periods) and the product inaccurately.

**11.** Imagine that you work for an ad agency charged with updating this advertisement for contemporary audiences. Write a description of the ways you would recommend updating this ad.

**12.** The artist's signature in the lower right-hand corner reminds us of the human being who created this painting. Write an essay from the perspective of this artist, explaining the difficulties and pleasures you encountered in drawing this ad.

# Laban

# Dance Notation (1930)

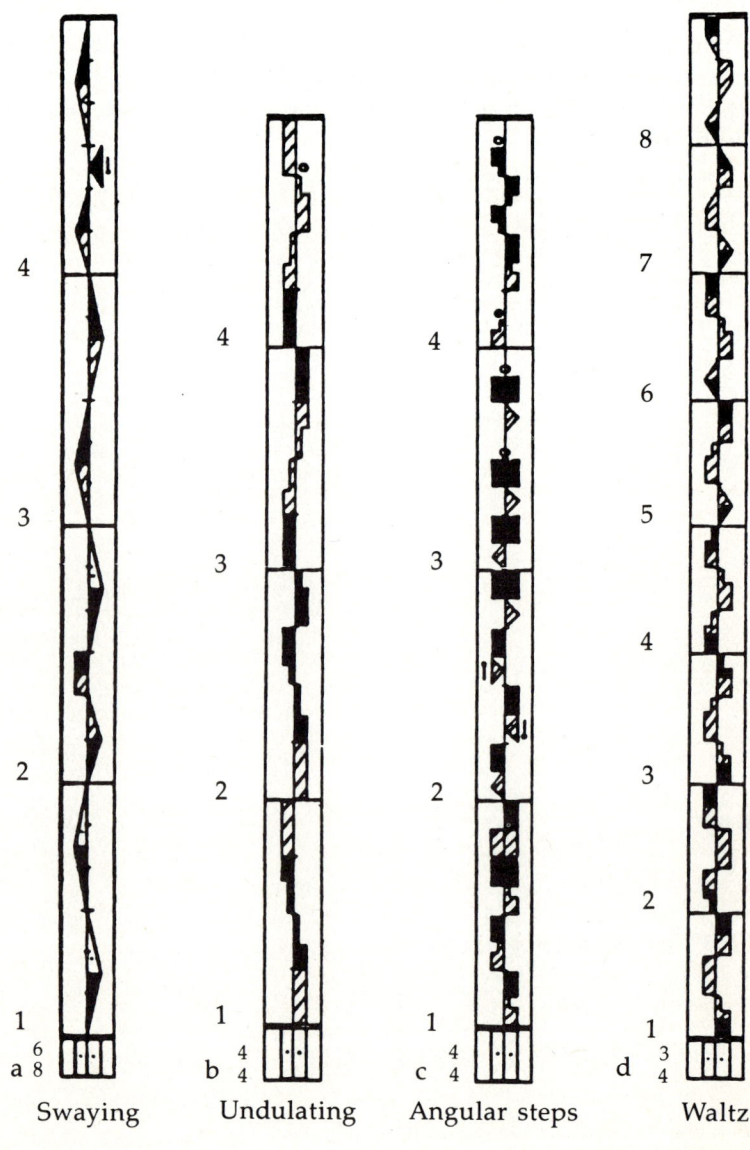

## Questions for Rereading, Discussing, Connecting, and Writing

### REREADING

1. Many forms have been used to represent dance movements. Egyptians are reputed to have used hieroglyphics, and Romans used notations to record gestures of formal greeting. The Laban system was developed early in the twentieth century in response to dance that departed from the classical tradition. What can you learn about movement from looking at these notations, even if you have no precise information about what each figure means?

2. Choreographers who compose dances visualize the movements they want dancers to perform. The Laban system is one of several employed by contemporary choreographers. Speculate on the problems faced by choreographers regardless of which system they use.

3. Determine what you need to know in order to read this text and make meaning with it.

### DISCUSSING

4. Language can be described as a symbol system used in an agreed-upon or conventional way by a certain group. In what ways can the Laban system be designated a language?

5. Several of the choreographers who developed systems of dance notation had interests that extended beyond dance. Speculate on what other areas of human endeavor could benefit from systems like this.

6. If you have learned a foreign language such as Spanish or French, think about what you experienced as you first encountered that language and compare it with your experience with the dance notation.

### CONNECTING

7. You have probably, like most people, faced some situations where it was easier to draw something than to explain it in words. Consider the kinds of drawings you made. Did you ever invent a system for representing something?

8. The element of time or rhythm is common to music and dance. Compare this notation system with the Mozart score (p. 349) and consider the ways each tells you something about time.

## Writing

**9.** You have probably had some experience with dancing, whether folk dancing, dancing lessons, or dancing to popular music. Write about how you perceive movement in dancing.

**10.** Just as people from different countries speak many different languages, so choreographers use a variety of notation systems. Write an essay in which you argue that all should/should not use the same system (choose whichever position you would rather support).

Group

# The Lincoln House Plan (1946)

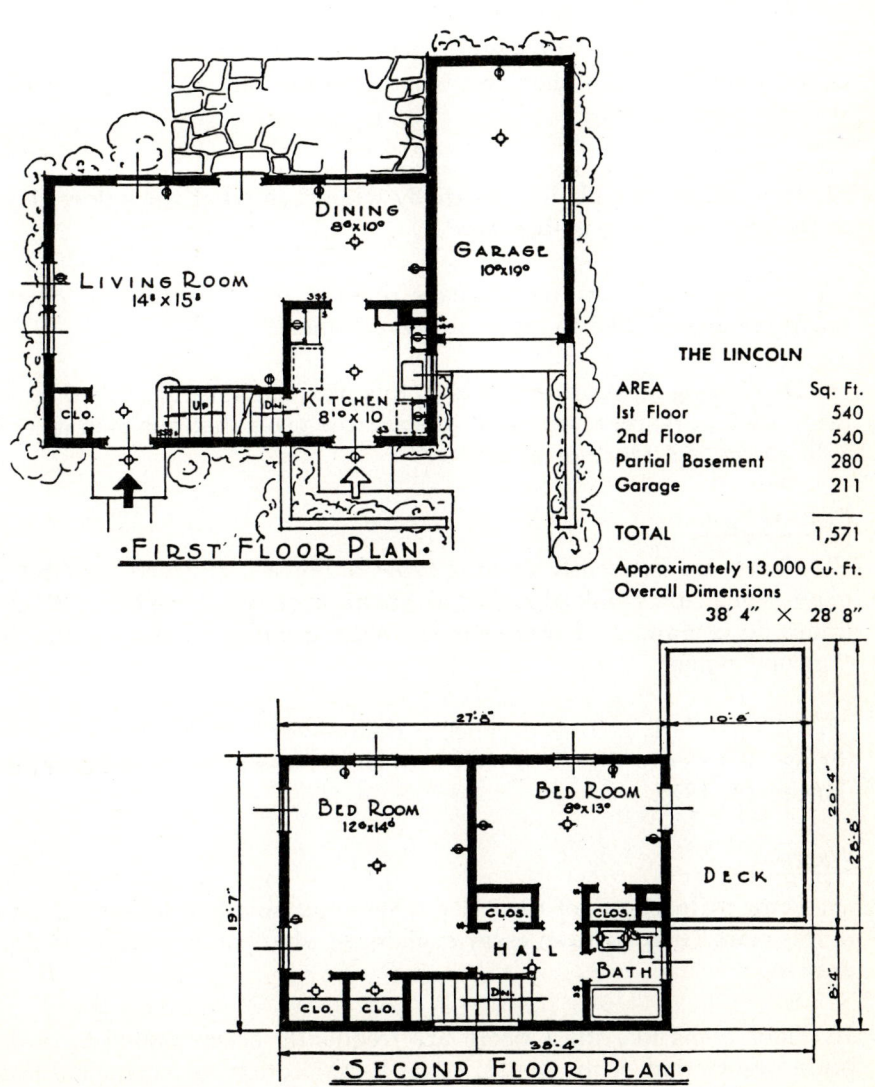

THE LINCOLN

| AREA | Sq. Ft. |
|---|---|
| 1st Floor | 540 |
| 2nd Floor | 540 |
| Partial Basement | 280 |
| Garage | 211 |
| TOTAL | 1,571 |

Approximately 13,000 Cu. Ft.
Overall Dimensions
38' 4" × 28' 8"

## Questions for Rereading, Discussing, Connecting, and Writing

### Rereading

1. As you read, speculate on the audience for which this plan was intended. What clues in this text help you decide?

2. This house plan represents three-dimensional space in two dimensions. What is gained and lost by such representation?

3. Although most features seem clear, there may be some unclear symbols in this plan. What are they and what meaning can you make of them?

### Discussing

4. How might this plan be used? By whom? In what ways does the design of the plan suit its possible uses?

5. Speculate on how the language of floor plans developed. What forces might have combined to aid their development?

6. Depending on your perspective, this plan might be described as an artistic or a scientific representation. Discuss the ways that this plan is written in a language of science or of art.

### Connecting

7. Names are frequently given to types of houses, to streets, to subdivisions, to areas of a city. Think about the names of places you have lived. What significance do you attach to these names? What significance do you attach to the "Lincoln" name?

8. Like painters, architects concern themselves with use of space. Compare the use of space in this floor plan with Degas' use of space in his paintings of dancers (p. 197).

### Writing

9. Draw a floor plan of the place where you now live following the model of this plan. Then write an essay explaining what you learned from doing the drawing.

10. Floor plans like the Lincoln are frequently accompanied by a detailed prose description of the house. Write a description to accompany this plan.

Steuben

# *Advertisement* (1950)

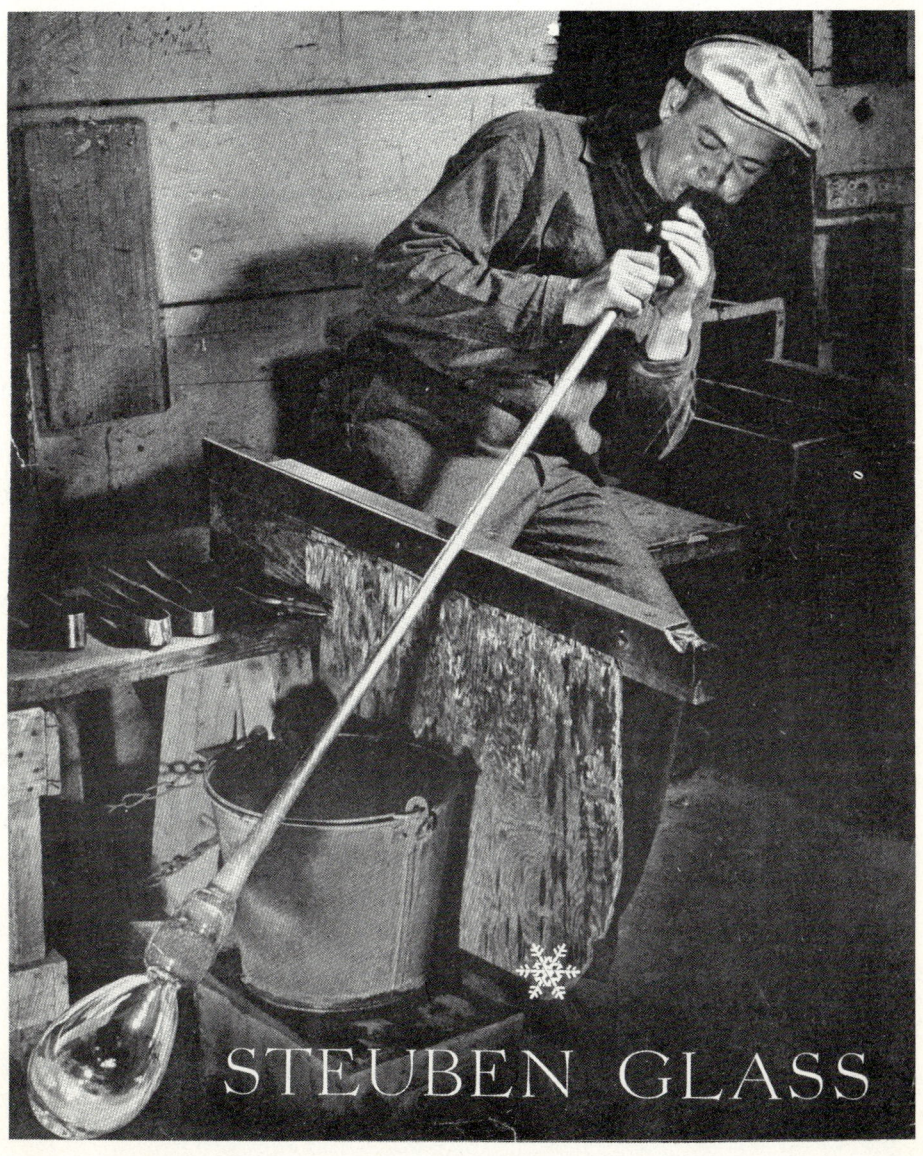

## Questions for Rereading, Discussing, Connecting, and Writing

### Rereading

1. The photograph focuses on a single individual in a glassblower's workshop. As you consider this text, speculate on what surrounds this man and on what he was doing before this photograph was taken.

2. As you look at this advertisement, notice the diagonal line created by the tube and the angle created by the man's body. What do they contribute to the effect of the whole?

3. What does this photograph's use of light and dark contribute to your experience with the ad? How would it change the photograph, for example, if the glassblower's face (rather than his hands) were in full light?

### Discussing

4. Consider how "realistic" this photograph is. What elements convince/fail to convince you that this is a "real" glassblower in a "real" workshop?

5. Discuss the kinds of appeals this advertisement makes. How does the producer of this ad want you to feel about the product?

6. Develop alternative ways of presenting this product. In what other ways might the advertising agency have portrayed the product?

### Connecting

7. Like the Hires advertisement (p. 357), this ad makes extensive use of lines. (In addition to the tube and man's body position, notice the lines created by pieces of wood in the background, the workbench and tools.) Compare these two advertisements in terms of their use of lines.

8. Glassblowing is a kind of work that resembles the shoemaking described in Foxfire (p. 223). What similarities and differences do you find as you consider these two portrayals of work?

9. The Steuben logo appears in this advertisement. How does this logo compare with the Konica logo (p. 374)?

WRITING

**10.** If the logo and product name were removed from this photograph, it might be framed independently. Decide on a title for the photograph and write an essay explaining your choice.

**11.** The Steuben corporation is not currently using this advertisement. Write an essay arguing that this ad should/should not be used today.

**12.** Write a narrative from the perspective of the glassblower pictured here. Explain what you are doing and how and why you are doing it.

# Alfa Romeo

# Wiring Diagram (1973)

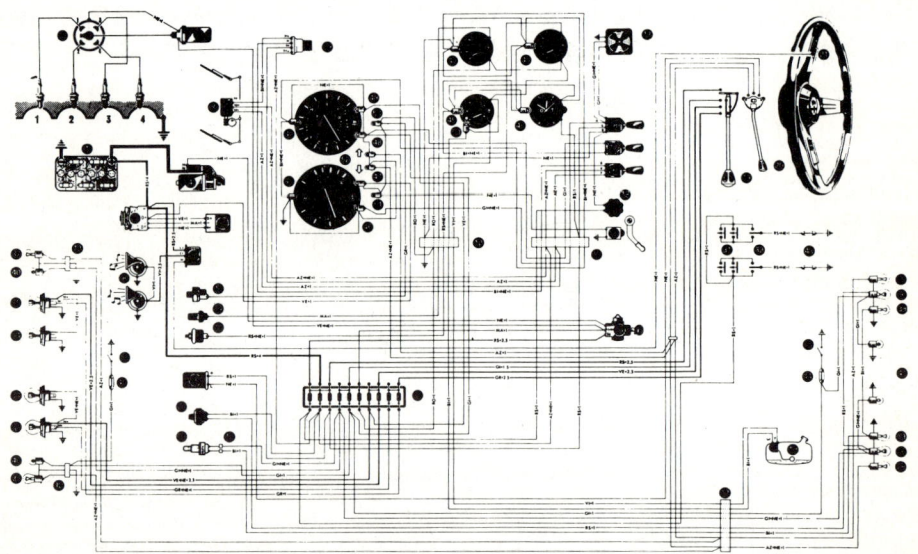

FIG 13:6 Wiring diagram for 1750 Berline (pre 1970)

**Key to Fig 13:6** 1 Battery  2 Coil  3 Distributor  4 Starter  5 Alternator  6 Voltage regulator  7 Windscreen wiper motor  8 Horns  9 Flasher control  10 Fuel gauge transmitter  11 Fuse box  12 Connectors  13 Horn relay  14 Water temperature transmitter  15 Oil pressure transmitter  16 Minimum oil pressure transmitter  17 Two-speed heater:ventilator motor  18 Cigar lighter  19 Side, head and head flash switch  20 Direction indicator switch  21 Horn switch  22 Stop light switch  23 Reverse light switch  24 Ignition and starter switch  25 Choke warning  26 Wiper motor switch  27 Panel lights switch  28 Heater:ventilator motor switch  29 Windscreen washer plunger switch  30 Engine compartment light switch  31 Door pillar light switch  32 Independent interior light switch  33 Boot compartment switch  34 Inner headlamps  35 Outer headlamps  36 Rear parking and stop lights  37 Front direction indicator lamps  38 Rear direction indicator lamps  39 Reverse lights  40 Front parking lights  41 Index plate lights  42 Engine compartment lamp  43 Interior lamps  44 Boot compartment lamp  45 Instrument panel lamps  46 Heater fan warning lamp  47 Alternator charge warning lamp  48 Parking light warning  49 Main head beam warning light  50 Low fuel warning light  51 Choke warning light  52 Flasher repeater lamps  53 Oil pressure warning lamp
**Key to colour code**  **AZ** Blue  **B1** White  **G1** Yellow  **GR** Grey  **MA** Maroon  **NE** Black  **RO** Pink  **RS** Red  **VE** Green  **V1** Violet
The number after the colour code letters indicates the thickness of the cable in sq mm

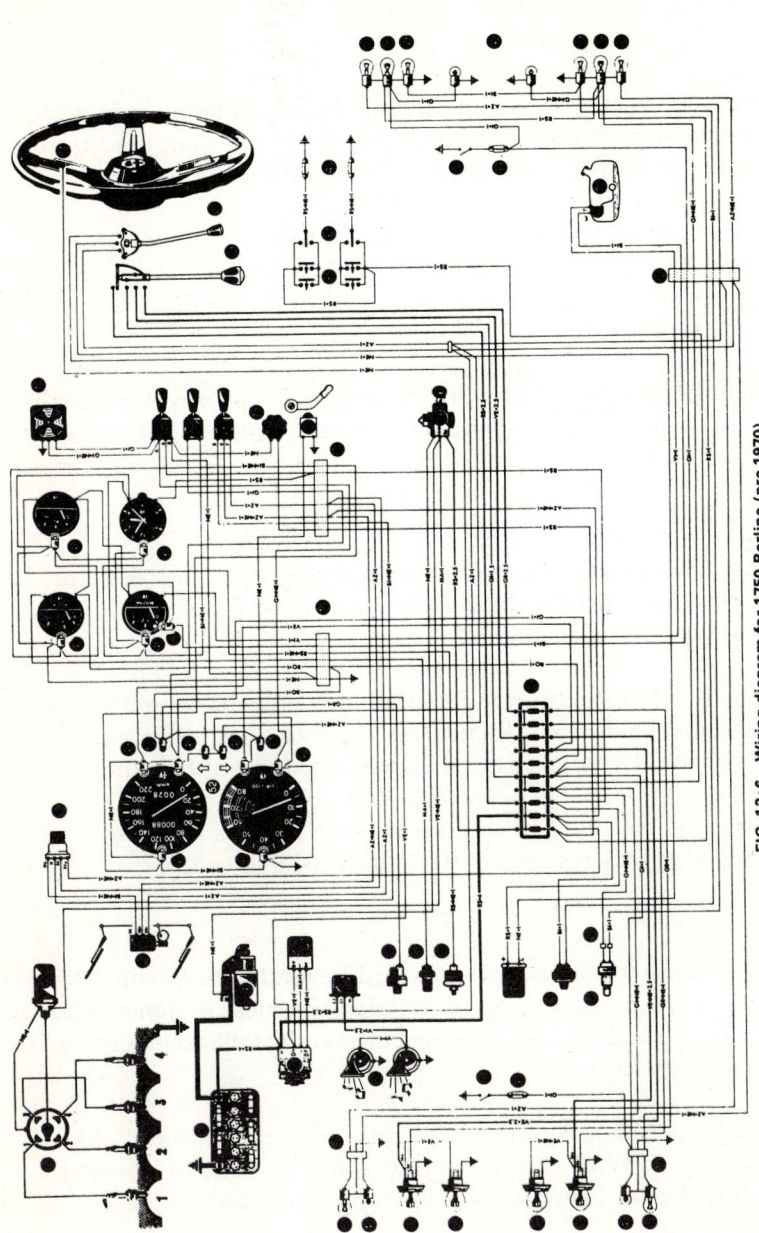

FIG 13:6 Wiring diagram for 1750 Berline (pre 1970)

Key to Fig 13:6  1 Battery  2 Coil  3 Distributor  4 Starter  5 Alternator  6 Voltage regulator  7 Windscreen wiper motor  8 Horns  9 Flasher control
10 Fuel gauge transmitter  11 Fuse box  12 Connectors  13 Horn relay  14 Water temperature transmitter  15 Oil pressure transmitter  16 Minimum oil pressure
transmitter  17 Two-speed heater/ventilator motor  18 Cigar lighter  19 Side, head and head flash switch  20 Direction indicator switch  21 Horn switch
22 Stop light switch  23 Reverse light switch  24 Ignition and starter switch  25 Choke warning  26 Wiper motor switch  27 Panel lights switch  28 Heater:
ventilator motor switch  29 Windscreen washer plunger switch  30 Engine compartment light switch  31 Door pillar light switch  32 Independent interior light switch
33 Boot compartment switch  34 Inner headlamps  35 Outer headlamps  36 Rear parking and stop lights  37 Front direction indicator lamps  38 Rear direction
indicator lamps  39 Reverse lights  40 Front parking lights  41 Index plate lights  42 Engine compartment lamp  43 Interior lamps  44 Boot compartment lamp
45 Instrument panel lamps  46 Heater fan warning light  47 Alternator charge warning lamp  48 Parking light warning  49 Main head beam warning light
50 Low fuel warning light  51 Choke warning light  52 Flasher repeater lamps  53 Oil pressure warning lamp
Key to colour code  AZ Blue  B1 White  G1 Yellow  GR Grey  MA Maroon  NE Black  RO Pink  RS Red  VE Green  V1 Violet
The number after the colour code letters indicates the thickness of the cable in sq mm

# Questions for Rereading, Discussing, Connecting, and Writing

## Rereading

1. The key at the bottom of this wiring diagram for an automobile provides a great deal of information about the figures included in the diagram. As you look at the key and diagram, consider what the key does not tell you.

2. The abbreviations used in the key represent words in Italian, the language of the person who drew the diagram. Unlike the key, the diagram was not translated for speakers of English. Could you describe this writing as written in an international language? Why or why not?

3. The wiring diagram contains many intricate parts, some of which may be confusing. Focus on a particularly difficult part and define what makes it confusing.

## Discussing

4. Find someone who is familiar with wiring diagrams and ask for a "reading" of this diagram. Discuss the difference between that reading and one by someone unfamiliar with such diagrams.

5. You or someone you know has undoubtedly followed a diagram to assemble or repair some household item. Discuss the kinds of difficulties such diagrams impose. How would you describe the source of these difficulties?

6. This diagram represents space in an unusual way. Discuss the effects created by the way this diagram represents three-dimensional space.

## Connecting

7. Your knowledge of electricity may not extend beyond how to flip a light switch or you may have extensive experience with electrical systems. Whatever your level of expertise, draw connections between this diagram and what you know of electrical systems.

8. Like the house plan, this diagram represents three-dimensional objects in two-dimensional space. What differences do you see between the wiring diagram and the house plan in terms of their representation of space?

9. Like the musical score (p. 349) or the dance notation (p. 360), this diagram contains instructions for performers. Consider the conventions observed in the Mozart score, the Laban notation, and this wiring diagram.

WRITING

**10.** Follow a single wire in this diagram and write a narrative account of its function.

**11.** Seen from the perspective of human history, electricity is a relatively recent invention (it has been in common use little more than 100 years). Write an essay in which you explore the ways your life would change if there were no electricity.

**12.** The key lists 53 separate parts of the automobile. Select 10 and write a prose account of how they relate to one another.

## Bob Wallace

# *PC Write* (1986)

```
(NEC, P2/P3 6303, 6306 mods)
@A: 32=20,33=8,34=18,35=20,36=20,37=20,38=20,39=8,40=10
@A: 41=10,42=20,43=20,44=10,45=20,46=10,47=20,48=20,49=20,50=20
@A: 51=20,52=20,53=20,54=20,55=20,56=20,57=20,58=10,59=10,60=16
@A: 61=20,62=16,63=16,64=22,65=20,66=20,67=20,68=20,69=20,70=20
@A: 71=22,72=22,73=22,74=20,75=20,76=20,77=22,78=22,79=20,80=20
@A: 81=20,82=22,83=20,84=20,85=20,86=20,87=20,88=20,89=20,90=20
@A: 91=10,92=20,93=10,94=18,95=22,96=14,97=20,98=20,99=18,100=20
@A: 101=18,102=20,103=22,104=22,105=16,106=16,107=22,108=18,109=22,110=22
@A: 111=20,112=20,113=18,114=20,115=18,116=18,117=22,118=22,119=22,120=20
@A: 121=22,122=18,123=14,124=12,125=14,126=20,127=20,128=20,129=22,130=18
@A: 131=20,132=20,133=20,134=20,135=18,136=18,137=18,138=18,139=14,140=16
@A: 141=16,142=20,143=20,144=20,145=22,146=22,147=20,148=20,149=20,150=22
@A: 151=22,152=22,153=20,154=22,155=18,156=20,157=20,158=20,159=16,160=20
@A: 161=16,162=20,163=22,164=22,165=22,166=20,167=20,168=16,169=20,170=20
@A: 171=20,172=20,173=8,174=18,175=18
@A: 246=20,250=20

#B=02 +27,69-27,70
#C=06 +15-18
#D=16 +14-20$
#E=03 +27,63,51-R
#F=28 +27,63,48-R
#H=24 +27,83,0-27,84
#I=21 +27,45,1-27,45,0
#J=08 +27,114,6-27,114,0
#L=25 +27,83,1-27,84
#M=07 +27,114,2-27,114,0
#O=19 /47
#P=05 +27,63,50-R
#Q=22 +27,63,52-R
#R=30 +27,114,1-27,114,0
#S=01 +27,71-27,72
#U=23 +27,45,1-27,45,0
#V=04 @A240+27,63,54-R
#W=18 +27,45,1-27,45,0/27,83,1,27,45,1,32,27,45,0,27,84
#X=13
#Y=31 +27,114,4-27,114,0
#Z=15
$S02= 27,65,36,27,50
$S03= 27,65,24,27,50
$S04= 27,65,18,27,50
$S05= 27,65,14,27,50
$S06= 27,65,12,27,50
$S07= 27,65,10,27,50
$S08= 27,65,9,27,50
$S09= 27,65,8,27,50
$S12= 27,65,6,27,50
$H20i=27,63,54,27,6,R
$H24i=27,63,54,27,5,R
$H30i=27,63,54,27,4,R
$H40i=27,63,54,27,3,R
$H60i=27,63,54,27,2,R
$H120i=27,63,54,27,1,R
$C
$Q
```

## Questions for Rereading, Discussing, Connecting, and Writing

### Rereading

1. This computer program is from the word processing software known as *PC Write*. It gives instructions to the printer on how to print a document produced on the word processor. As you read this text, note recurring patterns.

2. As you may know, computer programs use combinations of numbers to represent meaning. What information would you need to translate these numerical codes into English?

### Discussing

3. Reading and writing computer programs requires special languages known only to a small percent of our society. What benefits and liabilities do you see in this unequal distribution of knowledge?

4. You have undoubtedly had either direct or indirect (e.g., via reservation clerks, retailers, or information searches) experience with a computer. Identify the kinds of things computers do best and draw relationships between these things and this text.

### Connecting

5. Successful programming depends upon precision in composing. A single wrong number in any of the sequences could cause the program to malfunction. In what areas of your own life is this kind of precision required? What relationships do you see between these areas and computer programming?

6. A computer program resembles a musical score in that it uses a special language to provide instructions for performers. In what ways are the two dissimilar?

### Writing

7. Even if you have never programmed a computer, you know some of the things computer programs can do. Write an essay in which you explore the role of computers in modern life.

8. Computers, because of their capacity to make so many calculations rapidly, can solve problems that humans cannot in a single lifespan compute. Write an essay in which you explore the implications of knowledge (in the form of solutions) generated by computer.

# Konica

## *Advertisement* (1987)

## Questions for Rereading, Discussing, Connecting, and Writing

### Rereading

1. All texts make some kind of appeal to an audience. This appeal may be as general as better understanding of humanity or as specific as proving the truth of a particular statement. One way texts achieve their purposes is through appealing to audience emotions such as sympathy, desire for power, feelings of inferiority, compassion, and so on. As you read this advertisement, consider the kind of appeal it makes to you.

2. Texts of all lengths and types possess a unity that is achieved by internal features that tie the parts together. What, in your view, unites this text? What relationships do you see, for example, among the logo, the written portions, and the photograph?

3. Because it appears on a single page, this advertisement is a compact work in which each element has great importance to the reader. Are there elements in this text that seem to you especially *right*?

### Discussing

4. Try to locate the "voice" of this text. Who, in your view, is speaking and how would you characterize this speaker?

5. Like those of a painting or a poem, the elements of this text are arranged in a specific way. What difference would it make if these elements were rearranged?

6. Consider the kind of information included in this text. What information, in your view, is missing? How would this text change if additional information were added? What, for example, would be the effect of including written explanations about the features of the three machines?

7. Contemporary usage includes the phrase "the language of advertising." Based on your reading of the text, how would you describe the language of this text?

### Connecting

8. A computer program represents the language of a new technology. This text represents language *about* a new technology (copiers like computers have been widely available for less than 30 years). In what ways would your life

change if both copiers and computers were entirely removed from the world? Would one make more difference than the other?

**9.** Copy machines are most often used in offices, and office work could be described as a trade in the same way as carpentry (p. 182) or the steamboat piloting of "The Boy's Ambition" (p. 202). Compare the way these and other texts present trades.

**10.** Consider this text in light of other ads you have seen and explore how you "know" that this is an advertisement and not, say, a recipe or a short story.

## WRITING

**11.** By employing a metaphor that points to features shared by lions and copiers, this text makes a statement about the product. Think of an entirely different metaphor that could highlight features of copiers and write an explanation of advertising copy employing your metaphor.

**12.** This text portrays, among other things, a scene. Imagine that you are communicating with someone who has not seen this advertisement. Write a description of this scene that will enable your audience to "see" it.

**13.** In its combination of lions with copiers, this text could be described as extraordinary. Using whatever form you choose, compose a text that presents copiers in what could be described as "ordinary" terms.

*John Updike*

# The Illustrative Itch (1986)

*T*he itch to make dark marks on white paper is shared by writers and artists. Before the advent of the typewriter and now the word processor, pen and ink were what one drew pictures and word pictures with; James Joyce, who let others do his typing, said he liked to feel the words flow through his wrist.

There is a graphic beauty to old manuscripts, and to the signatures whose flourishes and curlicues were meant to discourage forgery. The manuscripts of Ouida, dashed off with, it seems, an ostrich quill, and the strenuously hatched and interlineated manuscripts of Pope and Boswell are as much pictorial events as a diploma by Steinberg. An old-fashioned gentleman's skills often included the ability to limn a likeness or a landscape, much as middle-class now can all operate a camera; such writers as Pushkin and Goethe startle us with the competence of their sketches.

Thackeray, of course, was a professional illustrator, as were Beerbohm and Evelyn Waugh. Edward Lear was a serious painter and a frivolous writer, and he might be surprised to know that the writing has won him posterity's ticket. On the other hand, Wyndham Lewis now seems to be valued more for his edgy portraits of his fellow-modernists than for his once much-admired prose. Thurber was thought of as a writer who, comically and touchingly (since he was half-blind), could not draw but did anyway, whereas Ludwig Bemelmans is remembered, if he is remembered at all, as an artist who could write; in truth, both men were bold minimalists in an era when cartoons were executed in sometimes suffocating detail. A number of writers began as cartoonists: of S. J. Perelman we might have suspected this, and even of Gabriel García Márquez; but Flannery O'Connor? Yes, when we think back to her vivid outrageousness, the definiteness of her every stroke.

Alphabets begin as pictographs, and, though words are spoken things, to write and read we must see. The line between picture and symbol is a fine one. In the days of mass illiteracy, imagery—hung on cathedral walls, scattered in woodcuts—was the chief non-oral narrative means. Most paintings "tell a story," and even departures from representation carry a literary residue, e.g., the labels and bits of newspaper worked into Cubist collages, and the effect of monumental calligraphy in the canvases of Pollock and Kline. The art of the comic strip exists as if to show how small the bridge need be between the two forms of showing, of telling. Music perhaps the most ancient of the fine arts, is simultaneously more visceral and abstract, and though some musicians become writers (John Barth, Anthony Burgess) the leap is rarer. Music is a world of its own; writing and drawing are relatively parasitic upon the world that is in place.

As those who have both drawn and written know, the problems of definition differ radically. A table or a person becomes in graphic representation a maze of angles, of half-hidden bulges, of second and third and fourth looks adding up to an illusion of thereness. When color is added to line, the decisions and discriminations freighted into each square inch approach the infinite; one's eyes begin to hurt, to water, and the colors on the palette converge toward gray mud. Whereas the writer has only to say "table" to put it there, on the page. Everything in the way of adjectival adjustment doesn't so much add as carve away at the big vague shape the word, all by itself, has conjured up. To make the table convincing, a specified color, wood, or number of legs might be helpful; or it might be too much, an overparticularized clot in the flow of the prose. The reader, encountering the word *table*, has, hastily and hazily, supplied one from his experience, and particularization risks diminishing, rather than adding to, the reality of the table in his mind. Further, the table takes meaning and mass from its context of moral adventure, from what it tells us about the human being who owns it, his or her financial or social or moral condition; otherwise this piece of furniture exists outside the movement of the story and is merely "painterly."

The painter's media are palpable. The more he tells us, the more we know. What he tells us, goes: his strokes are here and not there, this and not that. Although I rarely have cause in my adult life to open the India ink bottle, when I do, and take the feather-light nib and holder again in hand, and begin to trace wet marks over my pencil sketch on the pristine Bristol board, the old excitement returns—the glistening quick precision, the possibility of smudging, the tremor and swoop that impart life to the lines. Drawing, we dip directly *into* physical reality. The child discovers that a few dots and a curved line will do for a face, which smiles back out at him. Something has been generated from nothing. Or the pose of a moment has been set down forever; back in my mother's attic, old sketch pads of mine hold pets long dead, infants now grown to adulthood, grandparents whose voices I will not hear again.

Years before words become pliant and expressive, creative magic can be grasped through pen and ink, brush and paint. The subtleties of form and color, the distinctions of texture, the balances of volume, the principles of perspective and composition—all these are good for a future writer to experience and will help him to visualize his scenes, even to construct his personalities and to shape the invisible contentions and branchings of plot. A novel, like a cartoon, arranges stylized versions of people within a certain space; the graphic artist learns to organize and emphasize, and this knowledge serves the writer. The volumes, cloven by line and patched by color, which confront the outer eye—the most vulnerable of body parts, where our brain interfaces with the world—are imitated by those dramatic spaces the inner eye creates, as theaters for thoughts and fantasies. Unconscious, we dream within vivid spaces; when we read a book, we dream in a slightly different way, again slightly different from the way in which the writer dreamed.

Joseph Conrad, introducing his third novel, the novel that committed him to the writer's vocation, made the visual component central:

> Art itself may be defined as a single-minded attempt to render the highest kind of justice to the visible universe. . . . It is an attempt to find in its forms, in its colors, in its light, in its shadows, in the aspects of matter and in the facts of life, what of each is fundamental, what is enduring and essential. . . . My task which I am trying to achieve is, by the power of the written word, to make you hear, to make you feel—it is, before all, to make you *see*.

"The highest kind of justice to the visible world"—the phrase, expanded to include "psychological" and "social" along with "visible," notably sums up what the writer hopes to render. As training to render such justice, no better school exists than graphic representation, with its striving for vivacity, accuracy, and economy. No wonder writers, so many of them, have drawn and painted; the tools are allied, the impulse is one.

## Questions for Rereading, Discussing, Connecting, and Writing

### Rereading

1. This selection contains references to a number of writers and artists whose names may not be familiar to you. What is the effect of these "gaps" in the text? What meaning do *you* insert to make sense of the whole piece?

2. Updike describes the urge to write or draw as an "itch." Consider alternative terms he might have used and decide what you think about this one.

3. One of Updike's claims is that "to write and read we must see." How do you "see" this selection? In what ways (if any) does your experience of reading this piece confirm Updike's claim?

### Discussing

4. Like the professional writers Updike discusses, many student writers acknowledge an important relationship between drawing and writing. Discuss the ways in which your own experiences affirm (or disconfirm) the assertion that "the tools are allied, the impulse is one." Alternatively, you may want to observe young children writing and discuss what you see.

5. Blind people also write. Consider Updike's claims from the perspective of a blind person, and discuss how the experiences of writing and reading differ for blind people and sighted ones.

6. Updike makes it clear that he has, at least in earlier years, sketched himself. Speculate on the ways that his own experience with drawing shapes his view of the "truth" regarding the relationship between drawing and writing.

### Connecting

7. Updike points to the comic strip as an illustration of the close connection between writing and drawing. Look at your favorite comic strip and consider the relationship between word and picture in it.

8. "Alphabets begin as pictographs," says Updike, and we can see the continuance of the relationship between picture and word in the contemporary logo or advertisement. Examine the logo (p. 374) or the advertisement on page 357 and consider how it manifests a relationship between picture and word.

**9.** Test Updike's claims about drawing by turning to the gold buckle on page 341 and making a sketch of it. How does your perception of the buckle change after drawing it?

Writing

**10.** Pretend that you are an artist who has just read this selection and decides to write a response to it from the perspective of one who draws. Write an essay in which you explore the writing-drawing connection from the artist's viewpoint.

**11.** While insisting on many similarities between drawing and writing, Updike acknowledges that "the problems of definition differ radically." Write an explanation of definition in writing and drawing, including differences between the two.

**12.** Updike asserts that drawing (or graphic representation) is the best possible training for writers. Write an essay in which you argue either for or against this position.

# *Glossary*

ARGUMENT: An effort to persuade an audience to share—or accept—the writer's view of a subject. Where issues of fact (such as the name of the capital of North Dakota) are under consideration, argument has little effect. Rather, argument is useful when considering probabilities.

AUDIENCE: The receiver of, or listener to, any use of language. The audience may be oneself, a partner, a friend, a teacher—and it can extend to hundreds, even millions of listeners. To be sensitive to audience is to understand the identity, expectations, and needs of the receiver.

BRAINSTORMING: A particular process for generating material for the composing act, in which the composer records freely and swiftly—without dismissing—words, phrases, or large segments of writing having to do with the general subject or assignment at hand.

COMPOSING: The act of reading and writing. Composing is the manner in which we intermingle our reading and our writing. We process, comprehend, and interpret symbols through both our reading and writing; the ways in which we combine our reading and writing can be seen as our act of composing.

CONVENTIONS: Accepted rules of language-use—for example, writing in sentences, capitalization, spelling, punctuation, and using quotation marks around directly borrowed material.

DICTION: The level of formality contained in a text depending on word choice; for example, the word "so-so" is a sign of informal diction, while "mediocre" is a sign of a more formal diction.

DISCOVERY: Both the process and the outcome of prewriting activities such as brainstorming and listing. Discovery allows for further, more focused composing.

DRAFTING: Composing a text through use of conventional forms like the sentence and paragraph. Drafts are first attempts at composing texts, and can be messy, tentative, and unfinished because they are trials, just as an artist's sketch is.

Focus: The center of gravity in any text or writing task. The composer, by organization and placement of material, defines in a text what is foreground and background; this foregrounded material can be said to focus the text for both reader and writer.

Image: A representation of an object or objects. To "imagine" or "picture" an object in our minds can be the outcome of vivid use of sensory detail in texts.

Listing: A prewriting activity which, like brainstorming, generates material for further use in a writing task. Listing allows for the composer to disregard any concerns for grammatical structures; also, it can be a way of creating an order for ideas to be included in composing.

Mapping: A prewriting activity that encourages nonlinear play with language, so that the composer can "draw" his or her thoughts in words without regard to formal conventions like left-to-right or top-to-bottom writing on the page.

Prewriting: Gathering information for the drafting or writing phase of the composing process. This gathering can be done through activities like brainstorming and listing and discussing, asking and answering questions, doing research in a library, and through closely observed experience.

Process: The means by which we attain expression through composing. The composing process is a non-linear cluster of activities like prewriting, drafting, revising, and editing—any of which may be primary, but none of which is necessarily "gotten through" and discarded. Each part of the composing process may be called on at any time.

Prose: Language-use that resembles daily or common uses of speakers and writers.

Reading: The act of processing, comprehending, and interpreting texts. Reading can be distinguished from writing most readily for its lack of a visible product; otherwise, its features closely correspond to the act of writing.

Register: The degree of formality employed in diction.

Revising: The act of refining—or "re-seeing"—our language-use to more closely fulfill the intentions and expectations of either the writer or the reader.

Text: A cluster of symbols—either written, visual, or graphic—that the composer encounters and chooses to process, comprehend, and interpret.

TONE: A text's "character," or the reader's response to it in human terms—for example, a "comical" tone may be imparted to a text by the writer, and interpreted as such by the reader.

VOICE: The degree to which the individuality of the writer is imparted to the text by the writer—and "heard" by the reader.

WRITING: The act of processing, comprehending, and interpreting texts in visible language. As we write we process our language, discover meaning, and revise and recast that meaning—text after text.

# Index

Abilities, 98(11)
Achievement:
　positive recognition for, 56(10)
Action (activities), 19(5), 184(8), 343(8)
　complicated set of, 214(10)
　directives, 338
　matched to portrait, 58
Adams, Eddie, 238, 287
Adams, Henry, 81(7), 286(8)
Adams, John, 255(1)
Address:
　direct, in poem, 23(1)
Admiration, 206(12)
Adventure, 99–100
Advertisement:
　appeals, 358(5), 366(5)
　arrangement of text, 375(5)
　attitude toward subject, 358(6)
　as communication, 337
　eye movements, 358(2)
　Hires Rootbeer, 357–359
　human figures in, 358(9)
　identifying time periods, 358(4)
　Konica, 374–376
　language of, 375(7)
　metaphor in, 376(11)
　picture and word, 380(8)
　placement of words, 358(1)
　recognizing, 376(10)
　series of actions, 358(3)
　Steuben, 365–367
　updating, 359(11)
　voice, 375(4)
Aesop, 294–295, 307(8)
Africa:
　Dark Continent, 269(12)
　Europe and (19th cent.), 268(3), 269(10)
　maps, 110(5), 267–269

Age:
　composition at early age (Mozart), 350(5)
　metaphors, 61(3)
　portraying aging, 98(8)
Airplanes, personification of, 46(7)
Albany Congress, 348(6)
Alcohol, 328(5)
Aldrovandus, 190(2)
Alexandria Library, 294, 295
Alfa Romeo, 366(9)
　wiring diagram, 368–370
Alienation, of travelers, 153(4)
Aloneness, feeling of, 153(4)
Alphabet:
　code, 338
　picture and word, 380(8)
Ambition, in childhood, 206(13)
Amman, Jost, 181, 182–184, 206(9), 222(8, 9), 228(8), 236(7)
Amos (prophet): chapters 3–5, 239–243, 261(8), 304(9), 328(7)
Analysis of texts, 162(2)
Anderson, Donald, 340
Anecdotes, 90(2)
Anglo-Saxons, 106, 107(9), 337, 342(1)
Animal(s):
　as human, 307(3)
　stories, 294
Anonymous authors, 256(8)
Antiquary: collector, 61(5)
Antiquity: metaphors, 61(3)
Apollinaire, 31(8), 312–314, 317(9)
Appeal: in advertising, 358(5), 375(1)
Archaeology: views on consideration of objects, 342(5)
Architecture:
　Gothic, 345(2, 7)
　guiding architects, 345(5)

medieval, 337
moral elements, 356(5, 10)
Argument (essay form), 31(12), 304(11), 328(4), 367(11)
    Amos (prophet), 244(5)
    definition, 383
    obfuscation in, 334(3)
Arrangement of words, 317(9)
Art:
    arts and crafts, 183(7)
    and function, 342(4)
    imitates nature, 343(10)
    organic unity of qualities, 356(12)
    and science, 190(3)
    woman's, 83(4)
    writing and, 356(8)
Astronauts, 177
Attitude: writer towards subject, 83(5)
Audience, 4, 23(1), 68(10), 74(3), 228(2), 237, 249(6), 291, 292, 332(1), 364(1), 375(1)
    definition, 383
Augustine, Saint, 255(7), 345(8)
Author (-ship):
    collaboration in, 228(4)
    intentions, 332(3)
    multiple, 255(8)
    the word "author," 255(6)
Autobiographical writing, 73(1), 213(1)
    childhood home as factor in, 213(4)
    role in society, 74(10)
    self and society, 74(3)
    successful, 74(5)

Bacon, Francis, 185–186, 190(2)
Baker, Russell, 7, 49–54
Ballet, 200(9)
Baseball:
    American, 236(4)
    attendance, 236(11)
    box score, 184(9), 235–236
Basketball, 218–222
Battered women, 266(7)
*Battleship Potemkin*, 33(1)
Beauty: definition, 83(8)
Bible: prophetic features, 244(1)
Bird (the word), 316(6)
Black and white, 257(2)

Blindness:
    effect on life; the other senses, 144(4,5)
    handicap, 98
    simulating, 144(8)
    writing and, 380(5)
Borrowing: composing in writing, xi, 21(6)
Bowen, John, 228(4)
Box score, 184(9), 235–236
Bradley, Bill, 181, 200(8), 206(8), 218–221
Brainstorming: definition, 383
British Empire, 153(4)
Brule Sioux Indians, 25–27
Buildings:
    first-person essay, 346(9)
    human scale, 345(6)
    statement, 345(3), 346(9)
Bunyan, Paul, 163(9)
Burma, 153(4)
Butts, Professor, 207

Calculator, 99
Capital punishment, 258(10)
Carpentry, 1, 182–184, 376(9)
Cartoon (-s; -ists):
    allocation of space in, 318(1)
    as art, 335(7)
    attitude towards subject, 335(8)
    caption, 208(1)
    comic effect, 208(2)
    fables and, 295(7)
    graphic and verbal resources, 335(4)
    "Join, or Die," 347–348
    labels influencing, 319(3)
    language of, 348(11)
    personification, 319(5)
    reading, 347(2)
    series of actions, 334(1)
    simple and roundabout, 295(7)
    target of, 208(4)
    titles, 347(4)
    year 1938 and, 319(4)
Cassatt, Mary, 58, 74(6), 82–83, 222(9), 266(9)
Caterpillar, 191(10)
Cause-and-effect analysis, 209(10)

Causes: taken up by non-oppressed persons, 265(5)
Cave painting, 7, 8, 9, 10–12, 28(8), 153(6)
Central image, 24(9)
Change, 304(12)
Chartres Cathedral, 115(6), 344–346, 356(9), 358(8)
Childhood, 213
China: recent events in, 34(8)
Chinese folktales, 163(9)
Choreographers, 361(2)
Cinderella, 163(9)
Cirunuraivar, Kalporu, 8, 21–22, 24(7)
Clarity:
  in arguments, 334(3)
  in description, 144(2)
Clemens, Samuel, 310(9)
Close observation, 98(7)
Codes, 235(2), 236(9, 12), 338
Collaboration in authorship, 228(4), 266(8)
Collecting, 61(4)
Collective pronouns, 90(1)
Collins, Emily, 69–73
Colonies:
  African, 268(6)
  "Join, or Die" (cartoon), 348(5)
Comic strip, 380(7)
Commitment, 234(11)
Commonality:
  appealing, 91(5)
  objects, 317(12)
  power and politics, 238
  situation, 91(4)
Communication:
  language and, 337
  modern forms of, 11
  see also Language; Meaning
Community: Walton, 190(4)
Comparison and contrast, 18(1), 31(9), 46(8), 56(8), 74(6)
Complication: overcoming, 209(11)
Composing:
  creation of meaning, xi
  definition, 383
  describes both writing and reading, xi
  detail in, 58
  exercise in power, 237
  methods, 179
  seeing a form of, 1
  synonym for writing, xi
  vignettes illustrating, 179
  you already know much about c., 2–3
  you do not yet know enough about c., 3–4
  see also Reading; Writing
Computer (-s; -programs):
  language of new technology, 375(8)
  modern life, 373(7)
  musical scores and, 351(10)
  new language, 348(8)
  PC Write, 372–373
  reading and writing, 373(3)
  successful programming, 373(5)
  work and play, 184(9)
Conduct, 103(5)
Connecting: function, 5
Conrad, Pete, 177(8)
Convention(s):
  definition, 383
  language codes, 338
  wiring diagram, 370(9)
  of writing, 255(2)
Coordination, 221(6)
Creation (creativity):
  borrowing from texts read, xi
  material things and, 286(4)
Crime and punishment, 258(6)
Critical judgment, 3–4
  developing capacity, 4
Criticism, negative, 61(1)
Cultures, at war, 153(6)
Current events, 61(7), 255(5)
Custom(s), 19(5, 6), 20(12)
  justification by, 266(12)

Daily tasks, 11, 62(10)
Dance (-ing):
  language, 7
  notation, 350(8), 360–362
  perception of movement, 362(9)
Danger: life and travel, 31(9)
Darwin, Charles, 11, 58, 67(7), 75–80, 91(7), 123(5), 153(6), 288(7)
Death, 67(8), 176(3)

*Declaration of Independence,* 237, 249(8), 251–254, 266(8), 328(7), 348(9)
Definition(s):
  missing elements, 332(4)
  saying what something is not, 19(4)
  in writing and drawing, 381(11)
Degas, Edgar, 83(5), 180, 183(7, 8), 197–199, 216(7), 228(7), 234(8), 317(8), 343(8), 364(8)
Demetrius Phalereus, 294
Depression (the Great), 216(3)
Description (descriptive writing):
  clarity, 144(2)
  combining self-examination with, 152(2)
  detailed, 343(9)
  favorite place, 116(9)
  floor plan, 364(10)
  of space, 115(6)
  vividness, 115(3)
Detail(s), 58, 205(4)
  interior and exterior, 152(2)
  sense-detail, 176(2)
  vivid, 91(3)
Devotion, 67(7)
Dickenson, Fred, 291, 293, 320–324
Diction, 48(3), 337–338
  definition, 383
Dictionary, 98(2)
Differences, suppression of, 144(9)
Directions for doing, 19(8), 228(3), 229(12), 338, 355(2)
Disappointment, 91(10)
Discovery:
  definition, 383
  many meanings, 99
  science writing, 81(7)
Discussing: purpose, 5
Document (the word), 255(7)
Donner Party, 117–122
Drafting: definition, 383
Drawing(s):
  explanation and, 361(7)
  training for writers (Updike), 381(12)
  writing and, 380(4, 6), 381(10)
Dreams (wishes), 48(9)
Drought, 216(5)

Drugs, 328(5)
Dublin, 303(2)

Earle, John, 60
East and West, 153(4)
Education: schooling and relevance to real world, 2–3
*The Egyptians,* (Herodotus), 13–18
Eisenstein, Sergei, 32–33
Elderly people, 98(8)
Electrical systems, 370(7)
Electricity: life without, 371(11)
Elegy, 107(6)
Embalming, 19(8)
Emotion (-s; Feelings):
  advertising appeal to, 358(5)
  feelings about Indians, 30(2)
  feelings about work, 234(7)
  jobless people, 91(6)
  portraying people, 91(7)
  response to poetry, 22(7)
  seafaring men, 106(2)
Employment, 91(12)
Ends and means, 250(11)
Engineering feats, 20
Environment, 80(2)
Epic, 103, 104
Erdoes, Richard, 27
Essay(s):
  model, 152(1)
  progression in, 332(6)
  strategy for opening, 152(3)
Europe: colonies in Africa, 268(3, 8), 269(10)
Events:
  human influence on, 249(7, 10)
  unrelated, 195(5)
Evolution, 80(3)
Executioners, faceless, 258(8)
Exodus (the term), 216(8)
Exotic:
  places, 115(5)
  writing, 144(2)
Expectations, 97(1)
Experience:
  technique, 46(8–11)
  worlds of, 7–56
  writing about, 8

Experimentation, 98(7)
Explanations, 228(3)
Exploration: seafaring men, 107(4)
Eye movement, 199(2)

Fables:
 Aesop, 294
 message, 295(10)
 timelessness of, 295(12)
Face, 258(3, 4)
Failure, 45(4), 46(11), 56(9)
 Albany Congress, 348(6)
Fairy tales, 163(9)
Fame:
 Lotos eaters, 103
 of texts, 67(2)
Fantasy: effecting the fantastic, 144(1)
Farm workers, migrant, 216(6)
Father and son, 214(11)
Fern, Fanny, 292, 308–309
Fernham, 286
Fiction: modern, open ending, 144(3)
First sentence, in essay, 186(2)
Five senses, see Senses
Flies, 190(7), 191(9)
Focus, 57, 59
 definition, 384
Folk tales, 163(9)
Folkways: preserving, 228(5)
Food:
 gathering (ancient people), 11
 and the handicapped, 98(6)
Fool, 28(10), 152(2), 153(9)
Foregrounding, 57
Foreign languages, 361(6)
Formality, degree of, 291, 292
Fortune:
 role in our lives, 249(4)
 violent river (metaphor), 249(4)
 as woman, 249(9)
Foxfire, 206(10), 223–227, 234(7), 366(8)
Franklin, Benjamin, 255(1), 347–348
Freedom:
 controversial issues, 329(11)
 power of the pen, 256(10)
Friendship (the word), 307(5)
Frustration, 56(9)
Fuller, Margaret, 29–30

Gaps, in text, 380(1)
Gendered pronouns, 332(6), 333(12)
Genie (the word), 213(8)
Gettysburg Address, 58, 66, 107(6)
Glassblowing, 366(8)
Glossary, 383–385
Goals, 9, 229(10)
Gods, 103
Gold buckle, 341–343, 381(9)
Goldberg, Rube, 207
Good and evil, 257(2)
Gothic architecture, 345(2, 7)
Governance: Machiavelli, 248(1)
Goya, xiii, xiv, 5, 61(6), 67(8), 74(6), 163(7), 216(7), 238, 255(7), 257–258, 288(8)
Graduates: contest with the world, 319(8, 9)
Graphic representation, xii, 381(12)
Great Depression, 216(3)
Greatest writer, determining, 24(5)
Greatness:
 photograph of Lincoln, 64(1)
 qualities of, 64(6)
Greenland, 110(4)
Grieving, 195(6)
Group writing, 255(1)
Growing up, 55(7), 56(11)
Growth, 98(11)
Guiding spirit, 213(6)
Gumption (the word), 55(2)

Habits, 62(10)
Handicapped people, 98(4–6)
Hate, 153(8), 206(12)
Healing: nature, 30(6)
Heavenly region, 31(10)
Hedgehog (fable), 294, 295(11)
Hemingway, Ernest, 46(6)
Herodotus, 13–18
Hero(es):
 astronauts, 177(4, 7)
 characteristics, 258(7)
 Homer, 100–104
 the word, 107(7)
Hesler, Alexander, 63–65
Hires Rootbeer, 357–359, 366(7)

History:
  categories of, 19(3)
  definition, 19(4)
  many areas of concern in, 19(9)
Home: defining, 145(7)
Homer, 101–102, 107(7), 261(8), 295(9)
Honorings (writings), 107(6)
Horror writing, 144(2)
House plan, 363–364
How-to-do directions, 228(3–7)
Human condition, 8, 48(10)
Human spirit, 67(7)
Humor, xiv, 291–335, 307(8)
  comic voice, 291
  degree of formality, 291
  treat ridiculous topic seriously, 325(11)
  see also Cartoons
Hunger, and the handicapped, 98(6)
Hunting, in prehistoric times, 11–12

Ideas:
  both broad and definite, 355(4), 356(5)
  generative writing, 100
Igbo story, 295(8), 305–306, 319(7), 328(7)
"Ignorant watch," 206(7)
Image:
  definition, 384
  focal points, 257(1)
  reading, 183(2)
Imagination: words affecting, 30(1)
Imitating, 221(6)
Indefiniteness, 176(1)
Indians, American, 25–28, 30(2), 255(7), 261(8), 307(7)
Individuals, 20
Influence:
  power, 237
  variety of contexts, 238
Information:
  efficiency in conveying, 235(1)
  Konica ad, 375(6)
  ways of representing, 268(7)
Injury, fear of, 176(3)
Injustice, 74(9)
Innovators, 200(8)
Inscribing in stone, 340(7)
Insects: Walton on, 190(8)

Interest, 19(5), 30(3), 45(1), 64(2)
  human face, 258(3)
Interviewing, 229(11)
Invention:
  narrative description, 209(12)
  Professor Butts, 208(6)
Ireland, 303(1)
Ironic distance, 56(8, 9)
Irony, 291–335
Isolation, of travelers, 153(4)
Itch (the word), 380(2)

Jefferson, Thomas, 237, 238, 249(8), 251, 261(9), 288(7), 304(9)
Jewelry, 342(7)
Jobless people, 91(6)
"Join, or Die" (cartoon), 347–348
Jones, Karen, 228(4)
Journal:
  Mary Shelley, 195(4, 5)
  representing experience, 233(2)
  writing: work or play? 195(4, 7)
Journalism:
  career, 55(3)
  photography and, 238
Journey:
  astronauts, 177(5)
  Chinese saying, 99
  describe, in letter, 123(7)
  excitement, 107(3)
  imaginary, 163(8)
  must make; first step, 116(10)
  quality of, 162(3)

Keller, Helen, 98(5)
Kingston, Maxine Hong, 100, 154–162, 177(9)
Knowledge, assumed, 228(2)
Konica advertisment, 304(8), 335(6), 374–376
Kubla Khan, 116(7)

Laban system, 361(1,2,4), 370(9)
Labor, physical, 206(9)
Lame Deer (Sioux), 27
Landscapes, in Tamil poetry, 22(6)
Lange, Dorothea, 83(4), 162(7), 181, 183(7, 8), 215, 222(8, 9), 234(7), 286(9)

Language:
  as action, 7
  of advertising, 375(7)
  codes, 338
  conventional, 361(4)
  floor plans, 364(5)
  function, 7
  many purposes, 337
  objects and, 316(4)
  play as function of, 317(10), 333(9)
  precision, 337–338
  telling, 7
Laye, Camara, 180, 210–212
Laziness: time spent on studies, 187(12)
Leadership, approach to, 250(12)
Learning:
  from others, 221(6)
  by writing, 99
Legend, 28(4, 7)
LeSueur, Meridel, 58, 67(7, 8), 74(6), 84–90, 91(7), 162(6), 245(9), 266(9), 286(9)
Letters:
  to the editor, 4
  personal, 30(4, 5), 122(2)
Life:
  bitterness or disappointment in, 91(10)
  control of, 249(4)
  limits and possibilities, 28(8)
  outlook: past, present, future, 62(8)
  possessions and, 62(9)
Lincoln, Abraham:
  Gettysburg Address, 58, 66, 74(6), 107(6)
  photograph of, 57–58, 63–65
Lincoln House Plan, 363
Lines, 358(8), 366(7)
Listing: definition, 384
Locked in/out, 286(5)
Logical thinking, 265(2)
Loss, 194(1)
Lotos eaters, 103, 104
Lottery, 48(6)
Love:
  enduring, 24(10)
  understanding, 22(10)
  ways of writing about, 22(9), 24(6)

Lovers:
  landscapes in Tamil poetry, 22(6)
Lyric poetry, 21

Machiavelli, Niccolo:
  *The Prince* (excerpt), 246–248
Machiavellian (the term's connotation), 248(2)
Machinery: satire, 208(8)
McPhee, John, 179, 183(8), 206(8), 218–221
Magritte, 292, 315, 335(5)
MAL (cartoonist), 295(7), 334–335
Mankind, 80(6)
Map:
  Africa, 110(5), 267–269
  constructing, when reading, 115(2)
  knowledge needed for reading, 266(2)
  learning from, 268(1)
  literary, 110(6)
  Mercator projection, 110(3)
  preparation, 111
  reading, 110
Mapping, definition of, 384
Marginal comments, 4
Markham, Beryl, 7, 35–45, 107(7), 162(6), 266(9)
Marriage, 310(5), 311(10)
Marx, 288(7)
Material comforts, 244(2)
Maturing, 55(5)
Maxims, 55(6)
Meaning:
  communication, 337
  creation of, xi
  cultural context, 332(5)
  dance notation, 361(3)
  determining; Shakespeare's sonnets, 23
  obstructions, 355(3)
  questions and probe of meanings, xv
  reading and making of, xi, 380(1)
  revealing, 28(6)
  unconventional spelling and, 122(1)
Men and women: Mill on relations, 265(1)
Mercator, Gerardus, 31(8), 107(7), 108–110
Mercator map(s), 108–111, 268(9)
Mesolithic Era, 11

Metaphors:
  in advertising, 376(11)
  for age, 61(3)
Middle ages, 337
Migrant workers, 216(6)
Migration:
  American exodus, 216(5)
  exodus (term), 216(8)
Mill, John, 74(6), 83(5), 237, 238,
    244(7), 249(9), 260(7), 262–265,
    286(7), 288(7), 304(9), 335(6)
Mind: curing defects of, 187(9)
Mistletoe, 81(8)
Money-making experiences, 55(4)
Motivation, 345(7), 233(4)
Moveability, of selections, 19(9)
Movies, 33(3), 34(6)
  memorable and effective images,
    34(7)
Mozart, Wolfgang Amadeus, 236(7),
    349–350, 361(8), 370(9)
Museums, 342(4)
Music:
  composition; early age, 350(5)
  earliest memories of, 351(9)
  international language, 350(4)
  language, 7, 350(1)
  popular, 48(4)
  reading, 1, 350(2)
  scores, 350–351
Myth, 27(1), 163(9)
  American Indian history, 28(11)

Names:
  changing, 260(6)
  place, 268(8), 364(7)
  proper, 310(2)
Narrative, 46(9), 343(11), 367(12),
    371(10)
  realistic, 324(6)
Nature:
  art and, 343(10)
  fooling with, 81(9)
  healing powers, 30(6)
  place of wonder, 31(8)
  victim or victor, 153(6)
Navigation: map reading, 110(4)
New York City, 324(4)

*New York Times,* 55(3)
Nigeria, 307(1)
Night: symbolism, 258(5)
Nineteenth century: dangers in, 31(9)
North America, 269(12)
Note taking, 97(2), 115(2)

Objectivity, in writing, 221(4)
Open-endedness, in fiction, 144(3)
Opening:
  indefiniteness in, 176(1)
  strategy; the essay, 152(3)
Oracle at Delphi, 294(3)
Oral:
  language, 227(1), 261(11)
  literature, 162(4,5), 295(6)
  performance, 103(6)
  qualities, 280(1)
  tradition, 261(8)
Orwell, George, 100, 146–152
Outdoor writing, 340(4)
Outer space, 177
Outline, 195(10)

Painting:
  eye movement in looking at, 199(2)
  first look at, 316(1)
  focal points, 257(1)
  simplicity, 83(3)
  subject of, 258(3)
  unity in, 83(1)
Paragraph:
  length of, 205(1)
  topic sentence, 152(1)
Parents:
  ambitions for their children, 206(11)
  Springsteen lyric, 48(10)
Parker, Carol Mont, 162(7), 180, 195(8),
    200(10), 206(8), 222(7), 228(7),
    230–233
Passivity, in reading, 4
Past:
  expectations in reading, 55(1)
  obsession with, 61(7)
PC Write, 372–373
People:
  habits and daily tasks, 62(10)
  profiling and portraying, 57–78

Performances, and rehearsals, 200(6, 11)
Permanence, in technology, 340(5)
Personification:
  in cartoons, 319(5)
  of mechanical object (plane), 46(7)
Photograph:
  of Abraham Lincoln, 57–58, 63–65
  conveying truth, 64(7)
  image of your life, 288(6)
  informality in, 64(3)
  light and dark, 366(3)
  reading third dimension into, 345(1)
  realistic, 366(4)
  still, 33(1)
  subject shown from rear, 216(4)
  taking a memorable, 288(4)
Physical objects, 316(4)
Piano, 234(6)
Picture: worth 1,000 words, 217(11)
Pioneer life, 123
Place:
  best; heavenly region, 31(10)
  exotic, 115(5)
  favorite, 116(9)
  names, 268(8), 364(7)
Planes, *see* Airplanes
Play, *see* Work and play
Pledge of Allegiance, 67(5)
Pliny, 190(2)
Poem (-s; poetry):
  direct address in, 23(1)
  emotional response to, 22(7)
  function and structure, 313(6)
  hardest literature to read, 24(4)
  lyric, 21
  oral presentation, ancient cultures, 106(1)
  questions in, 21
  shape, 313(1)
  translation, 21(5)
  visual appearance on page, 21
  voice, 21
  woodcut and, 184(11)
Point of view, 61(6), 67(3)
Points of focus, 257(1)
Political cartoons, 348(7)
Politicians, 328(2)

Politics, in fables, 294
Polo, Marco, 19(7), 31(8), 100, 107(8), 112–115, 177(9)
Poor:
  injustices to, 244(4)
  plight in today's world, 244(6)
Portraying people, 57–78
Possessions, 62(9)
Pound, Ezra, 58, 313(9)
Poverty, 48(9)
Power, 237–289
  common subject, 238
  influence, 237
  justice and, xiv
  man and nature, 153(6)
  of the pen, 256(10)
Powerlessness, 288(7)
Practices, and games, 200(6)
Pre-writing, purpose of, 8
Precision, in computer programming, 373(5)
Prehistoric mankind, 11–12
Presidential candidates, 64(4)
Presidential portraits, 58
Prewriting, definition of, 384
Printing press, 190(4)
Privacy, right to, 289(11)
Process:
  analysis, 19(2)
  definition, 384
Profiling people, 57–78
  positive/negative, 61(1)
Progress, and subjection of groups, 265(4)
Pronouns, collective, 90(1)
Prophet(s):
  contemporary, 244(8)
  speaking God's word, 244(3)
Prose, definition of, 384
Public events, and public speeches, 68
Pyramid-building, 19(8)

Questions:
  in autobiographical writing, 73(2)
  categories (four), 5
  in poems, 21
  raising, 91(9)
  use of, xv

Quotation:
  in autobiographical writing, 73(2)
  direct and indirect, 221(3), 324(3)
  pithy statements, 186(4)

Rain: shape of poem, 313(1)
Rattlesnake, 347(3)
Reaction, first, 324(1)
Reading:
  active/passive, 4–5
  an act of composing, xi
  Bacon on, 187(11)
  buckle designs, 342(2)
  computer programs, 373(3)
  critical, 3–4
  definition, 384
  information expected from, 183(3)
  maps, 110(1)
  note taking, 115(2)
  sharing experience, 7–8
  starting point, 99
  talking back to texts, 4
  wiring diagram, 370(4)
  writing aided by, xii
  *see also* Texts
Recreation, 190(5), 191(12)
Reed, Virginia, 117–122
Register, definition of, 384
Rehearsals, 200(6, 11)
Relevance: school texts and the real world, 2–3
Replica of Chartres, 346(10)
Rereading, purpose of, 5
Responsibility, 103(5)
Reviewing a text, 80(1)
Revision:
  definition of, 384
  function, 180
Revolution, 258(6)
Riddle, Ernest, 227–229
Right to know, 289(11)
Robots, in space exploration, 177(12)
Room of one's own, 286(12)
Ruskin, John, 352–355

Sacks, Oliver, 58, 81(7), 92–97, 222(8)

Sarcasm, 303(3)
Satire:
  cartoons, 208(8)
  Swift's use of, 304(4)
Schooling, *see* Education
Science:
  and art, 190(3)
  voyages, 80(5)
  writing, 81(7)
Sea voyages: lonely and dangerous, 107(4)
*The Seafarer,* 105–106, 255(8)
Seafaring men: ambivalence, 107(5)
Secret, 162(7)
Seeing, a form of composing, 1
Self and society, 74(3)
Self-examination, 152(2)
Self-help books, 324(8)
Senses:
  detail (Wolfe), 176(2)
  sight given emphasis, 144(4)
Sensitivity, 80(2)
Sentence:
  length, 190(6), 205(2)
Shakespeare, William, 2, 8, 22(8), 24(7), 222(8)
  Sonnet # 116, 23
Shelley, Mary Wollstonecraft, 83(4), 181, 192–196
Shelley, Percy Bysshe, 196(11)
Shoemaking, 228(6)
Simplicity:
  in art, 83(3)
  cartoon, 335(5)
Single women, 265(6)
Sioux Indians, 25–27, 255(7), 261(8), 307(7)
Skill, learning well, 208(7)
Slang, 328(1, 7)
Slavery, 74(6), 260(1,3)
Smith, Dorman (cartoonist), 295(7), 318–319
Smith, Tina, 228(4)
Snake, 213(6)
Social customs, *see* Customs
Social injustice, 74(9)
Social issues: prophetic writing, 245(11)

Song:
  pause in, 47(2)
  reading lyrics of, 47(1)
South America, 110(4)
Southwest, 216(5)
Space:
  descriptions, 115(6)
  exploration: humans or robots, 177(12)
  program: argue for/against, 177(11)
  travel, 177(6)
Speaking, and writing, 227(1)
Speeches, and the media, 65(9)
Spelling, unconventional, 122(1)
Springsteen, Bruce, 8, 28(8), 47
Steamboat piloting, 206, 376(9)
Steuben Glass, 365–367
Stone, inscribing in, 340(7)
Story, and legend, 28(4)
  *see also* Fiction; Myth
Storytelling, 162(5)
Struggle for existence (survival), 11, 80(4,6), 81(8)
Study:
  laziness (Bacon), 187(12)
  purposes, 186(5), 187(10)
  too much, 186(6)
Style: Walton's English, 191(11)
Subjection, and human progress, 265(4)
Subtitle, 80(1)
Success, 46(11), 74(5)
  Albany Congress, 348(6)
  learning a skill well, 208(7)
Suffering, 238
Suffrage, 74(4)
Suppression of differences, 144(9)
Survival:
  Donner Party, 123(5)
  of the fittest, 11
Sutton Hoo Excavation, 190(7), 341–343
Swift, Jonathan, 61(6), 255(7), 291, 292, 296–303, 316(7), 319(6), 328(6), 333(7)
Syfers, Judy, 74(6), 291, 292, 304(7), 310(7), 328(8), 330–332, 358(7)
Symbolism:
  lovers and landscapes, 22(6)
  night, 258(5)

Tale:
  qualities, 27(1), 28(3)
  revealing meaning of, 28(6)
Talking back (in reading), 4
Talking story, 162(4, 5)
Tamil language, 21–22
Task, the word, 195(3)
Technology:
  losses and gains in, 214(12)
  permanence, 340(5)
Tense, shifts in, 45(2), 205(3)
Text(s):
  critical judgment, 4
  definition, 384
  document, 255(7)
  extended meaning of, xii
  graphic images included in, xii
  meaning, xi
  memorization and fame of, 67(2)
  subtitles in, 80(1)
  unity, 375(2)
  variety of, 3
Themes, inherent potential of, xiii
Thesis:
  autobiographical writing, 73(1)
  images illustrating, 73(2)
Time:
  music and dance, 361(8)
  sense of, 67(1)
Timeless/time-specific documents, 256(9)
Title:
  photograph, 216(1)
  poem without title, 24(8)
Tone, definition of, 385
Topic sentence, 152(1), 153(7)
Tortoise, 305–307
Trades, 376(9)
Trajan Inscription, 339–340
Transatlantic flights, 45(1)
Transitions: change in point of view, 67(3)
Translation:
  Anglo-Saxon to English, 107(9)
  from 19th century English, 356(11)
  Shakespearean to modern English, 22(8)
  Tamil poem, 21–22

Trauma, 194(1)
Travel:
  feeling of aloneness, 153(4)
  lessons of, 123(9)
  strange lands, 177(9)
  writing, 31(11)
Trickster tales, 307(1, 4)
Trouble: definition, 123(6)
Truth, in photographs, 64(7)
Truth, Sojourner, 74(6), 83(5), 91(7), 162(6), 238, 244(7), 249(9), 259 (text), 286(7), 333(8), 348(9)
Truthfulness: Marco Polo, 115(4)
Twain, Mark, 115(6), 191(9), 200(9), 202–205, 206, 228(9), 234(7), 310(9)
"Twinkle Twinkle Little Star," 350(7)

Ulysses, 100, 103
Union: "Join, or Die" (cartoon), 348(10)
Unknown, dealing with the, 144(6)
Updike, John, 234(8), 338, 356(8), 377–381

Verb: imperative, 244(1)
Vidal, Gore, xiii, xiv, 4 , 291, 326–329
Vietnam photograph (1968), 67(8), 287
Vietnam War, 288
Viewpoint:
   opposing, 328(4)
   photograph, 289(9)
Villains, 258(7)
Visual artist, 74(7)
Vivid description, 115(3)
Vivid writing, 162(2)
Vocabulary, 97(2)
Voice:
  in advertisement, 375(4)
  change of, 195(2)
  complex, 162(1)
  definition, 385
  in poem, 21(2)
  variety of, 291
  youthful, 48(7)
Voyages, for scientific reasons, 80(5)

Waiting, 177(10)
Wallace, Bob, 372
Walton, Izaak, 81(7), 188–190

War, 67(8), 153(6)
Wardrobes, 3
We (collective term), 90(1)
Weather map, 1–2
Wells, H.G., 124–144, 177(9)
Wife (wives):
  assumption that women are, 265(6)
  of astronauts, 177(7)
  definition, 332(2,5), 333(11)
Wiggington, Eliot, 228(4)
Willis, Sara Payson, 310(1)
Wiring diagram (Alfa Romeo), 368–370
Wives, see Wife
Wolfe, Tom, 164–176
Women:
  binding quality, 162(6)
  fortune as woman, 249(9)
  hair (19th-20th centuries), 83(9)
  inequality, 266(9)
  inferiority, 260(2)
  physical abuse of, 266(7)
  roundtable, 83(6)
  subjection (Mills on), 265(4)
  vulnerability, 266(9)
  woman's art, 83(4)
  work force, 310(4)
Women's Rights:
  Convention, 260(2), 261(10)
  Mill's motivation, 265(3)
  slavery question and, 74(6)
Woodcut:
  exact description, 183(5)
  poem and, 184(11)
  reading, 183
Woodpecker, 81(8)
Woolf, Virginia, 115(6), 249(9), 260(7), 270–285
Words:
  affecting imagining, 30(1)
  determining meanings of, 23(3)
  experience and, 332(2)
  meaning of "gumption," 55(2)
  worm-eaten by time, 61(2)
Work and play, xiv, 179–236
  Bacon on study, 187(8)
  blurred lines between, 181
  definitions, 213(9), 222(7), 234(9)
  fun: work becomes play, 208(5)

# Index

journal writing (Shelley), 195(4)
play as function of language, 317(10)
range of activities included in, 180–181
ritualistic aspect, 180
rituals of preparation, 213(7)
vignettes illustrating, 179

World:
beauties in, 80(2)
of language, xiv
relevance of school texts to, 2–3

World view, 45(3)

Writing:
archaic texts, 255(2), 256(11)
art and, 356(8)
Bacon on, 187(11)
borrowing or responding to texts read, xi
composing as synonym for, xi
current events affecting, 255(5)
definition, 385
drawing and, 380(4, 6), 381(10)
drawing as training for (Updike), 381(12)
gaps in, 33(3)
generative, 100
making common situation universal, 91(4)
many forms of, 5
reading aided by, xii
revision in, 180
sense of time in, 67(1)
sharing experience, 7–8
speaking and, 227(1)
starting point, 99
thematic units, xiii
therapeutic, 194(1)
tool for learning, 99
work of, 310(8)
*see also* Composing

You (the word), 324(2)

**Credits and Permissions**

Guillaume Appollinaire, "It's Raining" from *Selected Poems* by Oliver Bernard. Copyright © by New Directions Publishing Corporation.

Russell Baker, from *Growing Up* by Russell Baker. Copyright © by Russell Baker. Reprinted by permission of Congdon & Weed, Inc.

Kalporu Cirunuraivar, "What She Said" reprinted by permission of A. K. Ramanujan from *The Interior Landscape*, Love Poems from a Classical Tamil Anthology, translated by A. K. Ramanujan (1975; Indiana University Press).

Fred Dickensen, "How to Iron a Telephone Book" from *The New Yorker*, January 17, 1959. Copyright © 1959, 1986 by The New York Magazine, Inc. Reprinted by permission.

Foxfire, "Shoemaking" from *Foxfire 6*, edited by Eliot Wigginton. Copyright © 1975, 1976, 1977, 1978, 1979, 1980 by The Foxfire Fund, Inc. Reprinted by permission of Doubleday, a division of Bantam, Doubleday, Dell Publishing Group, Inc.

Maxine Hong Kingston, from *The Woman Warrior: Memoirs of a Girlhood Among Ghosts* by Maxine Hong Kingston. Copyright © 1975, 1976 by Maxine Hong Kingston. Reprinted by permission of Alfred A. Knopf, Inc.

Camara Laye, excerpted from *The Dark Child* by Camara Laye. Copyright © 1954 by Camara Laye. Copyright renewed 1982 by Camara Laye. Reprinted by permission of Farrar, Straus and Giroux, Inc.

Meridel LeSeuer, "Women on the Breadlines" reprinted with permission of Macmillan Publishing Company from *The American Writer and The Great Depression* by Harvey Swados. Copyright © 1966 by The Bobbs-Merrill Company, Inc.

Beryl Markham, "West With the Night" excerpted from *West With the Night* by Beryl Markham. Copyright © 1942, 1983 by Beryl Markham. Reprinted by permission of North Point Press.

John McPhee, "A Sense of Where You Are: A Portrait of Billy Bradley at Princeton" reprinted by permission of Farrar, Straus & Giroux. Copyright © 1965 by John McPhee.

George Orwell, "Shooting an Elephant from *Shooting an Elephant and Other Essays* by George Orwell. Copyright 1950 by Sonia Brownell Orwell; renewed 1975 by Sonia Pitt-Rivers. Reprinted by permission of Harcourt Brace Jovanovich, Inc., the Estate of the late Sonia Brownell Orwell, and Martin Secker & Warburg, Ltd.

Carol Mont Parker, "The Anatomy of a New York City Debut: A Chronicle" from *Adriane's Thread*, Lyn Lifshin, editor.

Oliver Sacks, "Hands" from *The Man Who Mistook His Wife for a Hat* by Oliver Sacks. Copyright © 1970, 1981, 1983, 1984, 1985 by Oliver Sacks. Reprinted by permission of Summit Books, a division of Simon & Schuster, Inc.

Bruce Springsteen, "Used Cars" from the album *Nebraska*, Columbia Records 1982. Copyright © 1982 by Bruce Springsteen. Reprinted by permission of Jon Landau Management, Inc.

Judy Syfers, "I Want a Wife" from *Ms.*, December, 1972. Copyright © 1971 by Judy Syfers. Reprinted by permission of the author.

John Updike, "The Illustrative Itch" from *The New York Review of Books*, April, 1986. Copyright © 1986 by The New York Times Company. Reprinted by permission.

Gore Vidal, "Drugs" from *Homage to Daniel Shays, Collected Essays 1952-1972*. Reprinted with permission.

Tom Wolfe, from *The Right Stuff* by Tom Wolfe. Copyright © 1979 by Tom Wolfe. Reprinted by permission of Farrar, Straus & Giroux, Inc.

Virginia Woolf, from *A Room of One's Own* by Virginia Woolf. Copyright 1929 by Harcourt Brace Jovanovich, Inc.; renewed 1953 by Leonard Woolf. Reprinted by permission of Harcourt Brace Jovanovich, Inc., and The Hogarth Press.

**Photo Credits**

p. 2, (weather map, Houston Chronicle)
p. 10, Art Resource
pp. 32, 33, from *A History of Narrative Film* by David Cook
p. 63, Louis A. Warren Lincoln Library and Museum, Fort Wayne, Ind.
p. 82, National Gallery of Art
pp. 108-109, Maritime Museum "Prins Hendrik"/Rotterdam
p. 197, Dancers Practicing at the Bar—c. 1876-77, Oil on canvas, 75.6 x 81.3 cm—Lem. 408, Metropolitan Museum of Art, bequest of Mrs. H.O. Havemeyer, 1929, The H.O. Havemeyer Collection 29.100.34.
p. 198, The Rehearsal—c. 1877, Oil on canvas, 23 x 33 in., City Museum and Art Gallery, Glasgow, Burrell Collection.
p. 199, The Dancing Class, 1872—Signed, Oil on wood, 19.7 x 27 cm—Lem. 297, Metropolitan Museum of Art, bequest of Mrs. H.O. Havemeyer, 1929, The H.O. Havemeyer Collection 29.100.184.
p. 207, © Rube Goldberg/King Features Syndicate
p. 215, Oakland Museum
p. 257, Art Resource/Museum del Prado
p. 287, Wide World Syndicate
p. 315, Art Resource
p. 318, © New York American
p. 334, © 1987 Malcolm Hancock. Reprinted by permission of the author
p. 344, H. Roger Viollet
p. 357, from the Saturday Evening Post, 1901
p. 360, from *Labanotation* by Ann Hutchinson
p. 363, from "Book of Small Houses" by Harold E. Group
p. 365, Stueben Glass
pp. 368-369, Alfa Romeo S.P.A.
p. 372, Bob Wallace/Quicksoft
p. 374, Konica, a subsidiary of DuPont